A Guide to
Fairs and
Festivals
in the
United States

A Guide to
Fairs and
Festivals
in the
United States _____

FRANCES SHEMANSKI _____

GREENWOOD PRESS
WESTPORT, CONNECTICUT • LONDON, ENGLAND

Library of Congress Cataloging in Publication Data

Shemanski, Frances.
  A guide to fairs and festivals in the United States.

  Bibliography: p.
  Includes index.
  1. Festivals—Directories. 2. Fairs—Directories.
I. Title.
GT3930.S4   394'.6'025   82-21080
ISBN: 0-313-21437-9 (lib. bdg.)

Library of Congress Catalog Card Number: 82-21080
ISBN: 0-313-21437-9

First published in 1984

Greenwood Press
A division of Congressional Information Service, Inc.
88 Post Road West
Westport, Connecticut 06881

Printed in the United States of America

10 9 8 7 6 5 4 3 2 1

CONTENTS

PREFACE

Festivals have been celebrated down through the ages to mark births, weddings, anniversaries, battles, good harvests and religious events. They also deal with the visual and performing arts, flowers, folkloric customs, seasons of the year and sports. In fact, they are almost endless in theme and purpose. Many celebrations bring enjoyment, help to educate and completely change an area, often making it famous.

Most events and festivals are held annually and attract visitors from other parts of the world. In this way they contribute to local economies by bringing in money and jobs. New buildings are added and localities acquire a sense of well-being and an appreciation of culture where once there was none.

Festivals are often well organized, with many handled by nonprofit associations. Others are aided by government subsidies. Still others thrive with local volunteer help.

This book provides a guide to fairs and festivals in the United States. The book covers all 50 states and territories, including American Samoa, Puerto Rico and the U.S. Virgin Islands. In addition, I am preparing a guide to festivals in the rest of the world, also to be published by Greenwood Press.

The festivals and events in this book are listed alphabetically by state, city and town. All names, with some exceptions, are in English. Dates are by month, since specific dates change. Each event is detailed as to its origin, history, purpose, special features, achievements and future plans, the description of each festival or event varying from one to several paragraphs and also including the month or time of the year that the event occurs.

Special questionnaires were mailed to thousands of festival organizers, state and city tourist bureaus and chambers of commerce. With a background as a newspaper editor and compiler of calendars of events for many top newspapers and magazines, I already had had direct contact with various festivals. The questionnaire was devised to obtain more data in addition to the materials I have collected over the years: when an event started and why; length of the event; awards and/or recognition; founders and features of the event; how it has changed;

when it is held and where; how it has helped its area; how it has been financed; and what age groups are attracted to the event. The various festivals, organizations, state and city tourist bureaus and chambers of commerce were asked to include any pertinent literature. Most did. Thus the information came from the questionnaires, brochures, histories, collected materials, newspaper clippings and souvenir programs. These were often followed up by telephone interviews.

Obviously it was not practical to include all festivals and events in this one volume. Those that appear were selected for many reasons: the age of the festival; the number of people attending; how the event actually changed its area. Not only major events and festivals are included but also many smaller ones, but only if research showed that they have had a strong impact on their communities.

The festivals and events in this book cover cultural programs, sports, religious events, humor, flowers, food, patriotic events, parades and even different New Year's celebrations within the United States.

The appendix lists fairs and festivals according to type for the benefit of those interested in one particular kind of event. Some are listed more than once because they feature more than one type of activity.

The volume also includes a short bibliography and a general events calendar. The calendar lists both the events in the book and those not detailed in the book. All events are indexed by their English titles.

The reader should find this a useful guide to the many fairs and festivals throughout this country.

Frances Shemanski

A Guide to
Fairs and
Festivals
in the
United States _____

Alabama

Birmingham

BIRMINGHAM FESTIVAL OF ARTS

Held annually, March/April
Cultural, economic

The Birmingham Festival of Arts is a ten-day annual spring event honoring a different country each year. It is usually held in late March going into mid-April with all events focusing on the honored country's artistic contributions via films, lectures, art exhibits, crafts, concerts, drama, ballet, modern dance and even an international fair. The country's cuisine is also featured, and a two-day cooking school gives visitors a chance to try their skills at learning those cuisines. The festival attracts world famous conductors, soloists, playwrights and film stars of the honored country. Local city colleges, universities, schools, churches and civic groups also actively participate in the festival. Tickets are sold for most programs, with some free. The festival is officially opened by the ambassador of the honored country at a performance of the Birmingham Symphony Orchestra. Except for opening day, festival events are from sunrise to sundown and include concerts, special foods, a fair, a flea mart, dinners and exhibits. There is also a street dance. Local restaurants feature dishes of the honored country as well as those of the city. The festival began in 1951 as a Festival of Music sponsored by the Women's Committee of Symphony Association. They wanted to incorporate their city's ethnic, economic and cultural events into one big event. The following year, it included the city's visual arts, and by 1953 the Birmingham Festival Association was founded and spearheaded a move for citywide cooperation and imaginative promotion. Various organizations held artistic and social events. Local citizens contributed money prizes for painting, sculpture, photography, drama and literature. Eventually local colleges, libraries and different dance and drama groups joined the festivities. Early festival themes were: Story of Steel, Land of Cotton, Heritage from England, Heritage from France and Spain, a Salute to Italy and America in the New World. By the 1960s, the festival had expanded to schools and ethnic groups. National competitions were held, and soon the festival began to salute the Pan-American countries, Scandinavia, Mexico, the Netherlands, Japan and Greece. An international fair was added as well as parades, park performances, and suddenly the festival received national coverage on television and in magazines and newspapers. Ambassadors, senators and congressmen were attending, and soon the festival was rated among the "Top 20 Tourist Attractions in the USA" by the American Automobile Association. The festival had grown to 27 days but was shortened to 10 because it became too difficult to handle properly. The shortened form was better handled and produced more professionally. The festival took another positive turn during the 1970s with strong civic support and sound financial backing. Businesses joined the academic and cultural institutions in promoting and sponsoring the festival. The most significant development in this decade is the increasing and important role that Black citizens are playing in the festival. The festival is recognizing their cultural achievements as well as their ability to develop the festival further culturally.

Dothan

NATIONAL PEANUT FESTIVAL

Held annually, mid-October
Harvest, economic, agriculture

National Peanut Festival, formerly held the third week of October, has expanded to two full weeks to mark the harvest of the $16-million-a-year peanut industry in the state's Houston County. More than 125,000 people from eight states take part in the Goober Parade, which attracts an additional 350,000 visitors. During the parade, city streets are paved with peanuts by a giant cement mixer that moves along the line of march throwing out a ton of peanuts in its path. Parade watchers scramble for them. While the parade is a festival highlight, it is only one of many events, most of them free. There's the selection of Peanut Farmer of the Year, a peanut cooking contest, craft exhibits, a livestock show, fireworks and a beauty pageant. A fun event that seems to appeal to visitors is a greased pig competition in which 15 porkers are coated with peanut oil and contestants try to catch them. The only admission fee is to the fair at the Farm Center. Exhibits and other events for all ages have been held here since 1959. The festival goes back to 1938, a Depression year. It was held to entertain and give recognition to the peanut, an agricultural product of the Wiregrass Area. It was discontinued during World War II and resumed in 1947 under the sponsorship of the Jaycees and the chamber of commerce. It was held on weekends in October till 1954, when its popularity led to a week-long event. The rapid growth of the festival led in 1952 to the passing of a resolution by the local chamber of commerce to form a nonprofit corporation, the National Peanut Festival Association, with a board of trustees to handle the event. The financing of the festival came a year later with the introduction of a carnival. By 1956 the event was accredited by the Alabama Association of Fairs, entitling it to receive state aid for holding an agricultural fair, livestock shows as well as industrial and commercial exhibits. The Peanut Farmer of the Year feature started in 1959 to honor the man or woman who had the highest average of peanuts produced per acre. The Recipe Contest, another new feature, was to emphasize the nutritious value of the peanut and its by-products. In 1962, a Science Fair was added. The National Peanut Association, Inc., has awarded more than $14,000 in prize and premium money and scholarships alone each year. The growth of the festival is evident by the monies budgeted. In 1948, the chamber of commerce budgeted $7,500, but by 1976, the association's budget exceeded $150,000. All monies earned during the festival go back into the economy of not only Dothan but also the neighboring areas of Florida and Georgia. Dothan is over the state boundary from Plains, Georgia, the home of former President Jimmy Carter, also a peanut farmer. The National Peanut Festival Association, Inc., began full-time operations May 1, 1976. The office is operated on a continuing basis by an executive director and secretary/bookkeeper. The festival, which to date has attracted several million visitors, is supported by area businessmen and hundreds of volunteers.

Mobile

MARDI GRAS CELEBRATION

Held annually two weeks before Ash Wednesday, movable date
Religious, ethnic, historic

The Mardi Gras Celebration in this city is older than the one in New Orleans. This one dates back to 1702 at Fort Louis de la Mobile. It was a one-day event, Boeuf Gras, observed at the Little Fort by the French soldiers. It got added zest when the Spanish occupied Mobile in 1780. They formed a Spanish Mystic Society, whose members paraded annually in grotesque costumes and masks. The paraders carried lighted torches. These parades, however, were on the eve of the Twelfth Night of Christmas. Their last parade was January 5, 1833, but the idea of the society and parade were incorporated into the annual Mardi Gras celebrations. Two years before the last Spanish parade on New Year's Eve, a transplanted Yankee from Bristol, Pennsylvania, Michael Kraft, decided to celebrate by ringing cowbells and by scraping rakes and hoes on the city streets and fences. He also got friends to go from house to house to serenade everyone. They all ended up at the mayor's home, and the mayor invited them in for a New Year's breakfast. The group called themselves the Revellers, later becoming the Cowbellion De Raking Society. They continued their antics and parade to 1840, when a final pageant, "Heathen Gods and Goddesses," was presented. Two years later, a second Mystic Society, Strikers Independent Society, was formed, splitting four years later into a third group until all three groups paraded New Year's Eve in 1861. They offered a tableau and held a dance for members and guests after the parade. Part of the Cowbellions went to New Orleans in the 1850s, formed the Mystic Krewe of Comus and produced the first Mardi Gras parade there in 1857. Today's Mobile Mardi Gras is a two-week event with a riotous climax on Mardi Gras, or Fat Tuesday, the day before Lent begins, Ash Wednesday, a movable observance. Various civic groups stage pageants and parades, many in the evening. Others are held during the day. Groups like the Maids of Mirth, Crewes of Columbus and Infant Mystics are among the many to hold festive marches. One really spectacular parade is the one by Mobile's Black population. It is really the best. Today's Mardi Gras has about 16 parades. Two have floats still drawn by costumed mules as they were in the early days of the event. Mobile's Mardi Gras is more of a civic and "home folks" celebration than the one in New Orleans. All of Mobile is a neighborhood, and the street parades and events are open to all, including the festive evening balls. There are no restrictions on attendance. When Felix, the Mardi Gras emperor, proclaims, "Let revelry be unrestrained and laughter be the language of the day," this means everyone in the city. Plans for each year's festive celebrations take all year. There was no Mardi Gras celebration during the Civil War, but by 1866, a young city market clerk, Joe Cain, had decided it was time that Mobile forget the war years. It was on Shrove Tuesday that Joe, driving an old charcoal wagon and dressed like an Indian chief, "Chief Slackabamirimico from Wragg Swamp," restored the city's Mardi Gras celebrations. Joe repeated his parade each year, adding ex-Confederate soldiers, and finally local citizens joined in, adding something new and festive every year. By 1922, the Crewe of Columbus was established. They selected the Friday night before Mardi Gras for their annual parade and ball. In 1929, the Mystic Crewe of Stripers paraded the night before the Crewe of Columbus. The year 1950 ushered in the Mystics of Time, the Jesters, the Maids of Mirth, the Polka Dots, the Order of Athens and the Daughters of Venus, each adding their own flashy parades. The last four groups are women's societies. Mobile earns millions of dollars from the Mardi Gras celebration, even though it does not enjoy the same fame as the one in New Orleans. The city, however, feels that it has held America's original Mardi

Gras officially since 1830. All events are coordinated through the Mobile Carnival Association, consisting of a board of directors, who in turn are local business and civic leaders. The parades are free. The balls do charge for admission.

Alaska

Anchorage

FUR RENDEZVOUS

Held annually, February
Historic, economic

The Fur Rendezvous is a 10-day winter carnival in mid-February, when temperatures hover around zero and well below zero, attracting more than 10,000 people. The festival dates back to the days when fur trappers after a busy trapping season descended on Anchorage for a round of drinking, carousing and other wild activities. Miners soon joined the trappers, and before long, all of Anchorage was getting into the act. By the mid-1930s, the Rendezvous, known as Rondy, had become more civilized, and a winter carnival became a feature. Today's festival boasts of more than 100 different events. Some are free; some are not. Highlights include a World Championship Sled Dog Race, a 75-mile run with three 25-mile-per-day heats, starting from downtown Anchorage. Prize monies are in the thousands and growing every year. Contestants come from all parts of Alaska and from the lower 48 states and as far east as New Hampshire. Festival "Rondy" events also include a Monte Carlo night for gamblers, the Miners and Trappers Costume Ball, an outdoor parade and a fur auction. There are still some fur trappers around in Alaska. They are dwindling in number since furs are difficult to trap and the current environmental drive to save certain species limits the trapper. An annual melo-drama with barroom performances, a midway and a carnival are other festival features. Special Alaskan foods are sold and include sourdough pancakes. Eskimo blanket tossing is also part of the fun. The festival marked its fortieth year in 1980 and has contributed to Anchorage's economy greatly. It is estimated that $10 million in revenue comes from the 10-day event alone. The success of the event is due to the volunteer work of 2,500 local folks with the help of the Fur Rendezvous office and its board of directors. The Fur Rendezvous is one of Alaska's top winter festivals.

Cordova

ICE WORM FESTIVAL

Held annually, February
Legendary, economic

The Ice Worm Festival is always held the first weekend in February to help the town shake off its winter doldrums by staging an outrageous event based on the legendary ice worm, which some citizens claim is a reality. The three-day event was started in 1961 by Merke K. Smith, former president of Cordova Airlines and the Aviation Hall of Fame, and by State Senator Bob Logan. Each put $500 together to make the town forget about winter and enjoy themselves. A third local resident, Omar Wehr, joined forces with them and after some heated discussions came up with the idea of an Ice Worm Festival. Local legend claims that the ice worm hibernates all winter (winter is long in Alaska) and in early February begins to hatch from the Cordova Glacier. It was decided that the town and ice worm would come alive together in a fun festival. Wehr helped design the festival's symbol or mascot, the ice worm. It turned into a 150-foot-long cloth-covered worm with a dragon's head. The worm wiggled its way down Main Street the first year. It was assisted by 37 pairs of legs wearing tan jeans. The festival began to attract visitors from other nearby towns and eventually from some of the lower 48 states, like Washington, Oregon and California. The ice worm became so well known that it once was invited to parade in Chicago. It disappeared for a while but later mysteriously turned up at the Lions Club in Fairbanks. Cordova recovered it. In 1968, the ice worm fell into the icy waters of Orca Inlet during a violent wind storm. It was rescued and stored in a dockside shack, which burned down. A local resident in his plane took pictures of the blaze. He swears that he saw the ice worm swim away toward the sunset. The ice worm did show up the following February for the festival and has been there ever since. Festival activities were handled by the Cordova Chamber of Commerce, but in 1969, the Visitors' Association joined forces to help the festival grow larger and larger. Festival highlights focus on the annual "hatching moment" when the ice worm emerges from the local glacier ice. There is an Ice Worm Parade, with the ice worm wiggling down Main Street. About 500 local residents follow. There's also a Miss Ice Worm Pageant, a beard-growing contest, a talent show and an Ice Worm King. Dances and parties are hosted by several civic groups. The event attracts thousands of outsiders. Most events are free, except parties and dances. Work is done by volunteers, all local people.

Fairbanks

WORLD ESKIMO INDIAN OLYMPICS

Held annually, July/August
Sports, ethnic

The World Eskimo Indian Olympics are held in late July at the end of the fishing season and before winter hunting begins. The Olympics, based on an annual get-together in various native villages, are games of skill, strength and endurance reflecting Eskimo and Indian tradition and cultural heritage. The three-day event, which is sometimes held in early August, too, includes evening programs and officially starts with the lighting of the Olympic lamps and marching of all contestants. There are also Indian dance team competitions. These dances tell a story as well as entertain. Various events include the knuckle hop contest, which involves getting down on all fours and hopping on one's knuckles. The contestant who goes the furthest on his knuckles wins. A record of 61 feet was set in 1971. The high kick competition calls for kicking as high as possible while still standing on one's feet. The high kick record for one foot is seven feet, eight inches, in 1969. For two feet, the record made in 1969 still stands at seven feet. The Malukatuk event is the popular blanket toss, which originated in ancient days in whaling Eskimo communities on the Arctic Coast. Originally part of the traditional whaling celebration, it enabled hunters to see whales off in a distance. Today it is a game of skill to show that the person tossed has the ability to stay upright on his feet when landing. Both men and women compete, being thrown as high as 28 feet up into the air, which is very usual. The blanket is made of three or four bearded seal skins sewn together with the strings of seal rawhide to make it durable. Widths vary from 10 to 12 feet. Other Olympics events include a seal skinning contest, usually for women only. Using an *oolu* (woman's knife), they try to cut a hair seal down its belly and skin it out as quickly as possible. The sharp-edged *oolu* is crafted by native people. *Muktuk* eating is the swallowing of a whale's blubber as quickly as possible. This skill requires fast hands, tough teeth and a liking for *muktuk*. Another competition is the ear weight contest and ear pulling. In the ear weight event, one-pound lead weights are hung on each ear of the contestant. Weights are added. Up to 17 pounds have been used. The ear pulling event features a cord looped from the ear of one contestant to the ear of another. They both pull until one gives up. While there are many more fearful events, there is actually one charming competition, the native baby contest. Both baby and mother wear traditional tribal dress, which can be Tlingit, Haida, Tsimpshian, Chilkat, Athabascan or Eskimo. Winners of the various events receive awards at a banquet. Most events are held in the Patti Gym at the University of Alaska. The World Eskimo Indian Olympics' insignia is an Arctic polar bear on ice with six interwoven rings on his back, representing the six major Eskimo and Indian tribes of Alaska: Eskimos, Aleuts, Tsimpshians,

Tlingits, Haidas and Athabascans. The rings are symbolic of brotherhood through friendly competition. The Olympics attract more than 10,000 spectators. Since they began in 1961, more than 200,000 have attended. The unified Olympics was started with the support of Wien Airways, which was concerned that the native games might be forgotten. At first, the event was only known as the Eskimo Olympics. The first year, only villagers from Barrow, Unalakleet, Tanan, Fort Yukon and Noorvik competed. It was successful and through the Fairbanks Chamber of Commerce became a major community event. In 1970, the *Tundra Times*, the state's Eskimo, Indian and Aleut newspaper, assumed sponsorship of the event. Native attendance broke all records, and the name of the event was changed to World Eskimo Indian Olympics in 1973. This was because so many Indian athletes were already participating. New events, such as Indian leg wrestling, the Indian rope game and the greased pole walk were added. Today, the Olympics are handled by the World Eskimo Indian Olympics Association, whose ambition through federal aid is to bring in contestants from Greenland, Siberia and Canada for cultural exchange among the athletes.

Arizona

Bisbee

POETRY FESTIVAL

Held annually, August
Cultural

The Poetry Festival is a two-day mid-August cultural event that began in 1979 in this former copper mining town. The town was then being added to the National Register of Historic Ghost Towns when some young artists and artisans moved in. They bought the former miners' homes for back taxes and put their talents to work by restoring the buildings to their 1880 grandeur. Bisbee is located just north of the Mexican border. The first festival featured Lawrence Ferlinghetti and a dozen lesser-known poets, who participated in a three-day marathon poetry reading. The event was launched by Cochise Fine Arts, Inc., a nonprofit group headed by Jon Friedman, originally from New Jersey. That first event attracted only 400 people, some from as far away as Tucson. Today, thousands attend from all over the country. Poetry readings were held in a former church building. Today they are offered at several sites. That first festival also included a cowboy poet, Drummond Hadley, who accented his recitals by firing blanks from a six-shooter, backed by audience yelling. Festival sponsors receive grants from the National Endowment for the Arts plus help from local merchants, who have joined the ranks of promoting the festival, which brings in business. The old Copper Queen Hotel, completely restored to its Victorian gingerbread style, is always booked during the festival. Galleries, cafes, shops and saloons do well, too. The festival, attempting to avoid commercialism, is devoted to the arts, which also includes top-quality crafts. The festival is supported through contributions and the sale of crafts. Work is by volunteers.

Lake Havasu City

LONDON BRIDGE DAYS

Held annually, October
Economic

London Bridge Days, an incongruous event, was started in 1971 to mark the dedication and formal opening of the London Bridge. It was a one-day event. The bridge is the real thing, purchased by the late Robert P. McCulloch, Sr., and C. V. Wood, Jr., of the McCulloch Oil Corporation. The historic bridge was dismantled piece by piece and brought to Arizona in 1968. It was reassembled like a jigsaw puzzle three years later. The one-day dedication expanded into the first two weekends in October, with many events free. Lake Havasu City's location is approximately in the center of a triangle formed by Las Vegas, Phoenix and Palm Springs, attracting in excess of 50,000 visitors. During the event, local residents wear costumes, varying from the Elizabethan to the Victorian era. Lake Havasu City assumes the air of an old English village. Among free events are archery and darts tournaments, a pancake race, a grand parade of bands, drill teams, equestrian units, entertainment and an Anniversary Ball. On some occasions, the lord mayor of London has attended together with state officials. The event continues to grow, supported by the local paper, *Lake Havasu City Herald*. Lee Shoblo, owner of the city's radio station, is also a sponsor. Popular festival features are the parade and Anniversary Ball and entertainment on the promenade beneath the London Bridge. Grand marshals have included movie stars like Peter Marshall and Peter Graves. The event is a communitywide project, with a London Bridge Days Committee handling each year's programs. Committee members include local business, civic and social leaders who work closely with the chamber of commerce. The event is financed by a chamber of commerce budget, allotment by McCulloch Properties, Inc., developers of Lake Havasu City, a Patron's Club membership and individual contributions. The London Bridge, now in Arizona, was originally authorized by English Parliament in 1800 and built by Scots engineer John Rennie. When the bridge opened in 1831, a sumptuous banquet was held on it. A balloon took off from it to mark the official opening. Famous folks like Charles Dickens have walked over it. It was sketched by Gustave Dore, and Rudyard Kipling is said to have leaned across its granite parapets. T. S. Eliot immortalized it in prose and verse, and composer Eric Coates wrote his "London Bridge March" to the sound of footsteps of Londoners walking over it. Field Marshal Montgomery led a mechanized column across the bridge on VE Day in 1945.

Phoenix

HEARD MUSEUM GUILD INDIAN FAIR

Held annually, February
Ethnic, cultural, historic, economic

The Indian Fair is an annual two-day event in late February at the Heard Museum. It is designed to raise money for the continued development of the museum, whose work is to preserve man's heritage, with emphasis on prehistoric man. Top Indian artists and craftsmen demonstrate their skills on the museum's grounds. Potters, rug weavers, silversmiths, wood carvers, kachina carvers, basket makers, sand painters and bead workers not only demonstrate their skills but also explain them to visitors. The items are also for sale. In addition, Indian ceremonial dances are performed by the Hopi, Navajo, Apache, Plains, Pima and Mohave tribes on both days. Visitors also have a chance to taste Hopi piki bread, popovers, parched corn, acorn soup and ash bread. All are prepared and served by the Indians participating in the fair. Young visitors are given an opportunity to participate in special workshops, like Indian hide painting, sandstone and rock painting. The workshops are for children under 12 and are conducted by museum guild members, who are qualified instructors. The fair, which does charge admissions, is open from 10 a.m. to 6 p.m. each day. The fair is more than 25 years old. It continues to attract thousands and is a very popular event in the area. The Heard Museum deals with anthropology and primitive art, and all exhibits are open to visitors during the fair. The museum is well known for the preservation and interpretation of prehistoric cultures. It has more than 50,000 catalogued artifacts, making it among the best of its kind in the country. It originally was held in April but changed in 1983 to February to attract more winter visitors.

Tucson

TUCSON FESTIVAL

Held annually, March/April
Cultural, ethnic, historic, religious

The Tucson Festival is a two-week tribute to the city's Indian, Spanish, Mexican and pioneer heritages and to its contemporary vitality. It is held during the week following Easter Sunday, which enables the Papago and Yaqui Indians to perform their Easter ceremonial dances, a major attraction of the festival. The seven-part festival opens with the evening San Xavier Fiesta, a costumed pageant recalling the founding of San Xavier del Bac Mission, the "White Dove of the Desert," by the Franciscans in the eighteenth century. Bells toll, a hundred mesquite bonfires burn and fireworks explode. The Indians dance. Robed Franciscan friars watch, while mounted conquistadores gallop, shouting, into the mission yard. Other features include a candlelight procession, Indian chants and Spanish hymns. A *castillo*, or large statue of the Virgin of Guadalupe, surrounded by fireworks is ignited on a nearby hill. The mission is conveniently close to Tucson, and admission to the pageant is free. The second festival phase is a two-day pioneer program at Old Fort Lowell. Frontier life is recalled with a Mormon chuckwagon barbecue, Papago and Apache foods, crafts, dances, and old-time entertainment. The famous Fifth Cavalry Memorial Regiment of the 1870s presents a Cavalry Field Day. The third festival feature is a Sunday evening forum centering on a fiesta theme chosen each year. The next event, La Fiesta de los Ninos, is a parade of children throughout downtown Tucson. They wear costumes that reflect the many origins of the local residents. About the same time there is La Fiesta de la Placita, a Mexican fiesta marking Cinco de Mayo (commemoration of the Mexican Battle of Puebla). Refreshments are served, and there is continuous entertainment, presided over by the Fiesta Queen. There follows a three-day combined Festival of Arts and Crafts Fair, featuring the work of artists and craftsmen from Arizona and New Mexico; this is considered one of the best Southwestern fairs. The entire festival ends with a formal Silver and Turquoise Ball, held to raise money for the following year's festival. Exhibits at the Tucson Museum of Art preceding and following the festival extend it from two to three weeks. Works from an annual statewide competition for the best current painting, sculpture, graphics and photography are displayed. A second exhibition centers on art masterpieces borrowed from private collections. The festival attracts more than 100,000 people each year. The Tucson Festival was started in 1951 by a group of community leaders to cultivate and encourage the creative arts and sciences of the Southwest. New features have been added over the years. More than 100 civic and social organizations now collaborate in presenting the festival.

Arkansas

Batesville

WHITE RIVER WATER CARNIVAL

Held annually, August
Economic, sports

The White River Water Carnival is a three-day event in early August and as its name implies involves water activities. The climax is a canoe race, covering

120 miles from Bull Shoals Dam to Batesville. The carnival has a grand parade down Main Street. The parade is complete with floats, bands, military honor guards, horses, antique cars, clowns and contestants hoping to be Queen White River. Nonstop entertainment is held all day long at Riverside Park. There are also crafts shows, musicals, art exhibits, boating and skydiving contests. It ends with a fancy ball. It was started by local businessmen in 1938 during the Depression to put some money in local hands and to call attention to the Ozark region. Amazingly enough the carnival brought in 25,000 people. The following year, local residents built a wharf stadium upstream, and the carnival for the next 32 years was held there. The carnival was discontinued during World War II. In 1976 it was switched to Riverside Park, overlooking White River. About 30,000 people still attend the event every year, contributing greatly to the local economy.

Mountain View

ARKANSAS FOLK FESTIVAL

Held annually, April
Cultural, folkloric, economic

The Arkansas Folk Festival and Craft Show happens the third weekend in April. It focuses on Ozark folk music and dancing as well as local arts and crafts with demonstrations and sales. A special pioneer festival is also part of the annual activities. All events are held at the $3 million Ozark Folk Center, built with a federal FDA grant. The area's traditional folk music is the popular festival feature. There are also concerts in the Court Square. Grand Ole Opry star Jimmy Driftwood, also a folklorist and composer, helped the tiny town organize the Rackensack Folklore Society to provide an organization for local musicians, singers and dancers to revive the area's traditional culture. Driftwood did this at the request of the Ozark Foothills Handicrafts Guild, who wanted not only to sell their work but also to provide entertainment. They wanted top performers. Driftwood convinced them to use local talent. They took his advice, and that led to the folklore society. Today's festival began as a crafts fair in 1962, adding music the following year. In 1977, about 50,000 persons came. It is estimated that more than a million have attended the event since its beginning. The town of Mountain View has only 2,000 residents. The unexpected growth of the festival led to the building of the Ozark Folk Center, which opened in 1973. The festival is financed by state park funds, the Forest Service, admission fees and the sales of arts and crafts.

California

Bishop

MULE DAYS CELEBRATION

Held annually, May
Economic, conservation

Mule Days Celebration coincides with the Memorial Day weekend, with activities getting underway Friday evening and continuing through Monday. The event tries to call attention to the "true value of the mule." Bishop and the surrounding area has a population of some 1,000 mules, many of them used by pack stations to go into the wilderness. The entire region is dependent on the mule to transport people and their gear into the Eastern High Sierra area. The U.S. Forest Service has also used mules. The celebration begins with a Mule Days Dance at the Tri-County Fairgrounds Friday evening, giving everyone a chance to get acquainted. Saturday morning starts with a Mule Days Parade, an all-animal parade with no motorized vehicles allowed. Each year's parade has about 175 entries, including well-groomed pack strings from local pack stations, the U.S. Forest Service, Yosemite National Park and Sequoia–Kings Canyon National Park. Pack load displays show how mules haul machinery, wood and other loads into remote regions. There are also comedy events, such as mules carrying an outhouse and other strange things. Other events include mule-shoeing contests with old-timers doing all four feet in less than 10 minutes. Mule shows, featuring races, mule barrel racing, calf-roping and pole-bending events, are held Saturday and Sunday at the fairgrounds. Packing contests feature veteran packers racing each other to pack a mule for a back country trip. A very popular event is the packer and mule scramble, where packers in bedrolls and mules and horses are loose in the arena. When the whistle blows, packers get up, get packed, catch their mules or horses, pack them, saddle them and ride out of the arena. Excitement mounts when the riders try to get the mules to move. Mules do have a mind of their own. The newest addition is a braying contest, not only for the mules but also for the owners, who attempt to mimic the mule. Other festivities include a barbecue, a pancake breakfast and a mule show to select the World Champion Mule. Monday morning is concerned with a mule sale, topped off by a three-day trail ride by mule, starting at 12 noon through the High Sierra country. Entry fees for the competitions and admission to the fairgrounds help finance this annual event. Campsites are also made available at the Tri-County Fairgrounds for those who prefer to stay near the whole event. The celebration was originated by the U.S. Forest Service, the High Sierra Packers and the local chamber of commerce in 1970, solely for the purpose of calling attention to the mule. It has also helped the local economy by boosting tourism to an all-time high of 80 percent visitors during the celebration. Bishop, a community of 10,000, swells to an extra 30,000 during the event. More than 300,000 have attended since 1970. Grand marshals of the Mule Parade have included President Ronald Reagan, then governor of California, and California Attorney General Evelle Younger. All work and preparation for the annual celebration is by volunteers from Bishop and nearby areas.

Del Mar

JUMPING FROG JAMBOREE

Held annually, last Sunday in April
Legendary

The Jumping Frog Jamboree is based on Mark Twain's famous story, "The Celebrated Jumping Frog of Calaveras County." The event, sponsored by the San Diego (Diequito) Jaycees, starts at 9 a.m. and continues through 4 p.m. at the local fairground. There is a minimal entry fee per person for each frog entered. If a contestant doesn't have a frog, the fee includes one. Part of the fee is refunded at the end of the event if the frog is returned unharmed. Timers give each frog 30 seconds to make the first jump. The distance between the starting point, which is the middle of the launching pad, and where the frog lands on the third jump is measured. The decision of the judges is final. Contestants need not be present, only the frogs that are jumped in their name. Winners receive trophies for first, second and third place in commercial or club, adult and junior categories. Even business groups are permitted to enter. The winning group earns the right to enter the special division of the Preliminary Frog Jump in May at Frogtown, Angels Camp, California. While the event continues, there's entertainment by the Naval Training Center Drum and Bugle Corps and the Six Bayonet Precision Drill Team and a bluegrass concert by local performers. Proceeds from the jamboree are matched by local government and private donations at a rate of 30 to 1. In 1976, $1,000 was collected, matched by a government grant at the rate of 10 to 1, meaning a total donation of $10,000 for cancer studies at Scripps Clinic at La Jolla. The jamboree dates back to 1953, when it was started by local Jaycees. Monies have always gone to charities.

El Cajon

MOTHER GOOSE PARADE

Held annually, November
Economic, traditional

The Mother Goose Parade is a one-day event held in late November, designed to entertain the children of the community. It's the second largest California parade, with the Tournament of Roses in Pasadena the first. Mother Goose and Mother Goose characters and rhymes are depicted in the floats. There are also clowns, bands and marching units plus equestrian units. Each year the parade gets longer and longer, covering four and a half miles of city streets. It takes about 90 minutes. It is held in late November to usher in the traditional holiday season. An average of 500,000 watch the parade. More than 6 million have done so since the first parade in 1947. It was the original idea of a group of local businessmen, who wanted to give a gift to the children of El Cajon and surrounding areas. Movie and TV stars also participate. The event is under the direction of a Mother Goose Parade Association with a board of directors. The group is nonprofit. About 1,000 local volunteers work on the parade details, which takes an entire year to produce. It is financed by an annual fund-raising golf tournament, men's banquet, a Princess competition and various organizations. It is telecast over several television networks to the rest of the country. In 1976, then President Gerald R. Ford personally commended the parade and the work behind it.

Indio

NATIONAL DATE FESTIVAL

Held annually, February
Harvest, economic, agricultural

The National Date Festival marks the end of the date harvest, always in mid-February. The 10-day event is held in the center of the Coachella Valley, the country's date-producing capital and famous desert resort extending from Palm Springs to the Salton Sea. Date palms were brought to this area in 1891 from Arabia as an experiment, since the climate and soil are similar to that of the Middle East. By 1921, enough acreage had been planted to make dates a major crop for this region. The festival is more than a country fair that exhibits dates and citrus fruits. It has an Arabian theme and pageant, an outdoor "Arabian Nights" nightly, with two extra performances on the Saturday of the festival. Queen Scheherazade and Court reign at the pageant, in which 150 local residents participate. The pageant is free and a popular event. Another top event is the National Horse Show and the daily camel and ostrich races. Recently, elephant racing events were added. There is a continuous round of free entertainment as well as an Arabian Street Parade and the Fiesta de Mexico Day on the final Sunday. Annual attendance is about 250,000, well into the millions since the event started in 1921. It was the Indio Civic Club that decided to stage a date festival to mark the success of the crop. It was held at the city park, and local ladies came in colorful Arabian costumes, giving rise to the still popular theme. The festival didn't do well the following year, and it was 16 years later when the third one was held, but its name was changed to the Riverside County Fair and the Coachella Valley Date Fiesta. Again the Indio Civic Club was in charge but under contract with the county board of supervisors. By 1940, the county had bought the present Date Festival site. World War II called a halt to events, but they were resumed in 1947, with the "Arabian Nights" theme being revived and buildings with Arabic motif constructed. Within two years, top features became the pageant, Queen Scheherazade, the National Horse Show and a Gem and Minerals Show. All the local residents came dressed in costume. In 1975, the multipurpose Shalimar Auditorium was completed and to date is home for many other events. The two-story building has an auditorium with stage, exhibit and conference rooms, festival offices and storage areas. It is used year-round for other community events. The festival is the work now of a paid staff of 7 people on a year-round basis and with the help of 1,800 volunteers, who put in about 8,000 hours of work annually. The festival is self-supporting except for funds received from the state for improvements. There are admission fees for some events and to enter the auditorium.

Laguna Beach

FESTIVAL OF ARTS AND PAGEANT OF THE MASTERS

Held annually, July/August
Cultural

The Festival of Arts and Pageant of the Masters is a highly successful annual 45-day event that has attracted more than 10 million people since its start in 1932 during the Depression. It is an art display on six acres of parklike land. Exhibits are by 180 area residents, including graphic artists, jewelers, potters, weavers, wood carvers, sculptors, furniture designers and macrame experts. All displayed items are for sale, and a jury system backs up a guarantee that the items are of top quality. There's a free-for-all art workshop for children and a junior art exhibit of works by about 150 Orange County schoolchildren. Children are entertained by Tony Urbano's marionette show, which the State Department sent on tour to the Soviet Union a few years ago. There are food concession booths, and visitors often see their favorite movie or TV star snacking at one of them. The festival's piece de resistance is the Pageant of the Masters, a recreation of great works of art (paintings and sculpture) posed by live models on stage. Special lighting effects and highly sophisticated technical miracles result in astounding versions of Winslow Homer's "Life Line," Frederic Remington's "Indian Warfare," Salvador Dali's "Madonna of Port Lligat" and even

Leonardo da Vinci's "The Last Supper," all reproduced with accuracy in both form and color. About 500 local residents volunteer for the pageant alone. The pageant is presented nightly at 8:30 p.m. during the overall festival, with tickets costing from $5 to $10 per person. Tickets are sold well in advance of the event. The pageant is staged in Irvine Bowl, an outdoor amphitheater and has been since 1941. The amphitheater seats 2,580, and the distance from the stage to the back row of seats is only 175 feet so that everyone can see the pageant. Other festival highlights include Sunday afternoon entertainment on the grassy area surrounding the artists' display booths. The Ballet Pacifica, Orange County's active dance group, performs for 20 minutes. Festival grounds are open daily from noon to 11:30 p.m., with a low general admission fee, different each season. From 1966 to 1975, the Festival of Arts paid more than $1 million to rent space from the city of Laguna Beach, a percentage of the festival's gross income. The festival has made $500,000 in capital improvements in the grounds and area where festival events are held. After the festival, the grounds revert to the city for its use the rest of the year. The festival has also donated several hundred thousand dollars to various cultural organizations and hundreds of thousands in art scholarships to hundreds of students. The festival, first held in 1932, was the idea of John Hinchman, a local artist. A tiny artist colony in the area was having a hard time making ends meet during the Depression. Hinchman and other artists came up with the idea of exhibiting their work outdoors on El Paso Street. Their works of art hung from the limbs and trunks of eucalyptus trees or were nailed on fences or supported by makeshift easels. There was also spontaneous music and dancing. The art was sold for almost nothing. The first Festival of Arts was publicized by word of mouth. It was such a success that it was repeated the following year. Artists put up booths and charged 10 cents admission. Success continued, and by 1935 the now famous Spirit of the Masters Pageant had been added. The festival was interrupted by World War II from 1942 to 1945. The Festival of Arts of Laguna Beach was established as a nonprofit organization in 1934. Today, it is administered by a nine-member board of directors who serve without pay. Festival membership is 3,600 and includes people from all over the United States. Additionally there are 300 group affiliations with the festival. Since both categories have reached their limits, they are closed. The festival grew to 6 days in 1936 and now is still holding strong at 45 days. In 1983 to mark its fifty-first year, the festival ran for 51 days. The festival's 1933 profit was $475. Today, it's in the hundreds of thousands. Since the festival is nonprofit, the monies go back into the community and for scholarships and also as donations to various cultural groups. Over the years, the festival has built a restaurant, fiberglass seats in Irvine Bowl, an exhibition complex, a festival forum and more. It all reverts to the city and represents an impressive capital improvement. Hundreds of volunteers spend countless hours working on this project. Planning takes all year. One of the earliest volunteers was actress Bette Davis, who painted numbers on the seats.

Lakewood

PAN AMERICAN FESTIVAL WEEK

Held annually, April/May
Ethnic

Pan American Festival Week is a late-April/early May event to foster a "Good Neighbor Policy" with Latin America. Lakewood is on a ranchero grant from the king of Spain, and all of its history is based on Spanish ancestry. The two-day event, formerly a week-long festival, includes the selection of a queen, coronation ball, flag exchange programs, parade, fiesta in the park, cultural displays, games, rides and Latin American entertainment. More recently a soccer game became part of the program, through the recommendation of a Latin American consulate. The event is held in April to coincide with the Pan American Day Proclamation by the president of the United States. It was first held April 14, 1946, and was the inspiration of two active members of the Lions Club. Over the years, it grew to a week-long fiesta. Now it is held for two days in late April. It is estimated that more than 10,000 watch the parade alone. While the total number of visitors is not known, the local economy has prospered enough to ensure a large number of visitors. Each year, the festival salutes a different Latin American country selected from the roster of the Organization of American States.

Long Beach

LONG BEACH INTERNATIONAL SEA AND SPORTS FESTIVAL

Held annually, August
Sports, economic

The Long Beach International Sea and Sports Festival, formerly the California International Sea Festival, runs from 21 to 23 days for most of August, with nine separate water-oriented events. All except two are free. They include a Junior Olympic swimming meet and speed skiing. In 1977, 1,000 swimmers participated. Other events include a fishing rodeo, Hobie Cat 16 Championships, ancient mariner regatta, Sabot regatta, speed ski jamboree and the sand sculpture contest which closes the festival. This event is the most photographed. It is held on the beach at the foot of Junipero Avenue. Contestants have two hours to create their work of art. There's standing room only on the half-mile beach front, noon to 4 p.m. All other events are held along the Long Beach coast. Newer additions to the festival include volleyball tournaments, youth soccer tournaments, tours of U.S. Navy ships, the Catalina Ski Race, lifeguard competitions, basketball tournaments, softball meets, a model sailboat regatta, a 10-kilometer run and water skiing for the physically disabled. The festival was given full impetus in 1966 by two local retired businessmen who wanted to do something for the area economically. The festival was developed from other events held in previous years. The purpose of the current festival is to attract visitors and to use the area's water sports facilities, and the Belmont Pier, which extends a quarter-mile out into the ocean. About 25,000 attend every year. The most popular events continue to be the powerboat and skiing. The festival, according to local officials, has helped local businesses. The city allocates $10,000 for promotion of the event, and some admission fees help finance the rest.

Monterey

MONTEREY JAZZ FESTIVAL

Held annually, third weekend in September
Cultural

The Monterey Jazz Festival is strictly a musical event with performances held the third weekend in September. Five shows headlining top jazz star performers are part of the festival. Original music is often played for the first time. Performances are at the County Fairgrounds, with admission varying according to seat and performance selected. Each performance plays to a full house, about 7,000 persons per show. A small paid staff plus hundreds of volunteers work year-round lining up the performers and programs. The festival started on a small scale back in 1958, originating from a conversation between West Coast jazz disc jockey Jimmy Lyons and composer-critic Ralph J. Gleason in San Francisco. Lyons left the city and selected the Monterey Peninsula as an ideal spot to live and to stage a jazz festival. From the beginning, it was organized as a nonprofit education corporation with Lyons as general manager. The first event was financed with monies that Lyons borrowed from local merchants. A makeshift acoustical shell and stage were built, grass planted and chairs rented, and a sound system capable of carrying high fidelity was erected. Lyons was able to attract such notables as Louis Armstrong, Dizzy Gillespie, Gerry Mulligan, Sonny Rollins, Max Roach, the Modern Jazz Quartet and more, plus an 88-piece orchestra. The following year, each performing artist was given more time to perform, and the event became more unified. There were six different symphonic brass ensembles performing and the premiere of several new works. Jimmy Witherspoon made his first appearance. Critics viewed it as the "American Salzburg." Although $12,000 in the red after the second year, the community wanted to continue the festival. By 1960, it was hosting 5,000 people, and it was on its way. A year later, the festival began to make money and donated

$2,000 of the proceeds to the Music Department of Monterey Peninsula College. Local citizens who had financed the event in the past were also repaid. The hit of the 1963 festival was Thelonious Monk, making his first appearance. The festival is a showcase for American jazz, perpetuating it, featuring original compositions and helping young people through scholarships. It does help the local economy, but the festival is careful to avoid any carnival atmosphere or commercialism.

San Diego

FIESTA DE LA PRIMAVERA

Held annually, May
Ethnic, heritage

Fiesta de la Primavera is celebrated annually in May in the Old Town to recall the area's history and the contributions of early Spanish, Mexican and American cultures. Visitors who attend are encouraged to wear costumes of the era. A free tour of the original buildings of the first California colonists is featured and includes the Casa de Estudillo, the alleged "Ramon's Marriage House," made famous in Helen Hunt Jackson's novel, the Whaley House, the Machado-Stewart House and the Old Adobe Chapel, Casa Bandini and Old Spanish Cemetery. Tours are conducted by the rangers of the State Historic Park and by the Old San Diego Historical Society. The once one-day fiesta now held for three days features a community buffalo barbecue, an old-time banjo and fiddlers' contest, Indian exhibits, sidewalk art and displays of handicrafts and folk art. Strolling mariachis, troubadors and Spanish dances recall the "Days of the Dons" right on the spot where California began in 1769. The fiesta also rolls back prices to include a cup of coffee for 5 cents and a 10-cent pancake breakfast served from 8 to 10 a.m. at Coleman College. The annual event is sponsored by the Kiwanis Club of Old San Diego. It was started in 1969 to mark San Diego's two hundredth birthday and has continued as an annual event, attracting thousands of visitors.

San Francisco

CHERRY BLOSSOM FESTIVAL

Held annually, April
Ethnic

The Cherry Blossom Festival at Japantown, lasting for seven days, covering two weekends in April, is the American adaptation of a similar celebration in Japan. At least 100,000 people attend each year and since 1968 more than a million.

The climax is the grand parade from City Hall to Japan Center at Post and Fillmore streets. More than 1,800 costumed paraders participate, including Japanese singers and dancers. The line of march includes a portable shrine, floats, Akita dogs, Taiko drummer, the current Cherry Blossom Queen and Her Court, bands and others. The three-hour parade ends with the carrying of the traditional Taru Mikoshi, a portable shrine, piled high with sake casks. It takes 100 men to carry it. Daily events are keyed to different ages, ranging from very young children to older folks. There is Japanese dancing, art exhibits, bowling, Japanese obi and kimono demonstrations, floral arrangements, tea ceremony, bonsai exhibit, cultural films of Japan and the selection of the Mother of the Year. The festival originally started to mark the official opening of San Francisco's Japan Center and to redevelop and revitalize Japantown. It also introduces the visitor to a variety of Japanese cultural activities. At the same time it helps the economy of Japantown. All festival work is done by volunteers, consisting of businessmen, housewives, students, lawyers and teachers. It is financed by the advance sale of souvenir programs and by donations. There are admission charges for some evening events.

Colorado

Aspen

ASPEN MUSIC FESTIVAL

Held annually, June/August
Cultural

The Aspen Music Festival is a nine-week program extending from late June through late August. Its purpose is twofold: the Aspen Music School, offering master classes and lecture demonstrations by guest artists and members of the Aspen artist faculty; and weekly concerts with a choice of full-sized orchestras, chamber ensembles and soloists. The festival aims to educate and entertain. Performances are in a 1,600-person-capacity tent, the Aspen Amphitheater and the Wheeler Opera House, a historic Victorian landmark. More than 75 percent of the Aspen Festival Orchestra and almost 90 percent of the Chamber Symphony members are students at the Aspen Music School, offering private instruction also, seminars, ensemble classes, training in theoretical studies, orchestral training and choral and opera programs. The Opera Workshop is also a nine-week program, under the general direction of Richard Pearlman. It trains students in all phases of opera, such as vocal lessons, diction, acting, body movement and dance. Students are given opportunities to sing leading roles as well as to understudy or sing in the ensemble. There is also an Aspen Choral Institute, available from mid-July to mid-August, with Dr. Fiora Contino in charge. Intensive study for choral singers and conductors is offered. In 1977, the institute performed the U.S. premiere of *Utrenja, Part II* and Verdi's *Requiem*, Monteverdi's opera, *L'Incoronazione di Poppea*, cantatas by Bach and three Sunday morning concerts of Renaissance and baroque music at the Wheeler Opera House. Each year, the institute performs equally important works.The Aspen Conference on Contemporary Music annually sponsors the residency of one or more contemporary composers and also offers concerts, seminars, master classes and films. Sometimes the conference will select a theme, while at other times there will be varied musical programs. The Aspen Music Festival also presents the Aspen Jazz-Rock Ensemble performing three concerts under the direction of Gary Gray. More than 45,000 attend performances, not to overlook student enrollments. Since the festival started in 1949, it is estimated that well over a million have attended and participated. The festival got its start in 1949, when the Goethe Bicentennial Convocation and Music Festival was held in Aspen. This event was the idea of Walter P. Paepcke, who felt that Aspen was an ideal setting for "intellectual and physical stimulation." His dream came true with the formation of the Aspen Institute for Humanistic Studies and the Aspen Music Festival. By 1954, the institute and festival had been incorporated separately as the Music Associates of Aspen. Gordon Hady is president and dean, while Jorge Mester is music director. Walter P. Paepcke was chairman of the Container Corporation of America. He and associates of the Aspen Company set out to rebuild and remodel the town of Aspen in 1945, seeing it as a "community in peace . . . with opportunities for man's complete life . . . where he can earn a living, profit by a healthy physical recreation, with facilities at hand for his enjoyment of art, music and education." The current festival schedules regular weekly concerts on weekends, starting Fridays at 6 p.m. with the Aspen Chamber Symphony, a chamber music concert on Saturdays and Mondays at 4 p.m. and the Philharmonia alternating with student concerts on Wednesdays at 4 p.m. In addition, there are many other concerts throughout the summer. A record number of 100 events were held in 1978 alone. Events were so scheduled that one or more musical programs were open daily to the public. This was done to accommodate the growing number of visitors. In 1977, more than 75,000 people from all over the country attended the festival. The festival has had such distinguished performers as Itzhak Perlman, Pinchas Zukerman, Misha Dichter, Emanuel Ax, Zara Nelsova, Carmen Balthrop, Jan DeGaetani, Maureen Forrest and Yo-Yo Ma. The 1977 Van Cliburn winner, Steven DeGrotte, performed in the programs, too. The first annual Aspen Audi-Recording Institute was added in 1978. It was held four times in a two-week session throughout the summer, directed by Harold Boser. Its purpose was to teach basic recording techniques. The festival is supported by student tuitions, private donations and foundation grants. There are admission charges to concerts with prices varying each season. The festival generally attracts those from 16 on up, with the majority being college undergraduates and graduate students. The festival has a full-time and temporary administrative staff. The festival is held only in summer because the climate is better for outdoor performances. Most popular features are the symphonic programs.

Central City

CENTRAL CITY FESTIVAL

Held annually, June/August
Cultural

The Central City Festival is a two-and-a-half-month event devoted entirely to offering famous operas in English. Performances are at the Opera House, built in 1878. June performances are dress rehearsals with tickets available. The entire program is designed to develop the cultural enrichment of the area for local residents and summer tourists. Usually two operas are sung in English by performers from the Metropolitan Opera, the City Opera and other leading American opera companies. There is an apprentice program affiliated with the festival to help outstanding young singers. Free concerts are featured in the adjoining Teller House Hotel (built in 1871) gardens and in the more than 100-year-old stable building. Operas, musical and theatrical offerings are presented in the Opera House. Free square dance exhibitions and other special events are added to the summer program, and the area's historic and art museums are open to the public. The festival is always in summer because the mountain location, 40 miles from a major population center (Denver), is more conducive to visitors. The unheated theater can be too cold in winter, and housing facilities are limited then. Although the operas have been reduced from three to two a season for financial reasons, future plans do call for an expansion. These would include more and varied performances, music-oriented conferences and workshops as well as more activity relative to historic preservation and restoration of the area. The annual event draws more than 20,000 people. It was started in 1932 as the Central City Opera Festival, and the Opera House was selected because it wasn't being used at all. It was started to give Colorado more culture, and one of the founders was Ann Evans, daughter of Colorado's second territorial governor and founder of the University of Denver. Ida Kruse McFarlane, from a pioneer mining family, owned the Opera House. The other founders included Mrs. Delos Chapell, a civic leader, and Robert Edmund Jones, well-known New York stage director. At one time, this festival was the only professional opera company in the state. It is operated by a nonprofit organization with a paid staff plus the help of thousands of volunteers who work most of the year preparing details. It is financed through earned income and 50 percent by contributions. It is both economically and culturally beneficial to the area. The Central City Festival has been honored by the governor of Colorado and the Colorado Council of the Arts and Humanities. It was given the Governor's Award in the Arts in 1976 and honored by the National Music Council as a historic landmark. The Opera House is listed in the National Directory of Historic Places.

Denver

NATIONAL WESTERN STOCK SHOW

Held annually, January
Economic, agricultural

The National Western Stock Show marked its seventy-seventh year in 1983. It is said to be the nation's largest livestock show and also a showcase for agricultural achievements. It also includes a top indoor rodeo. The show, held in the Denver Stock Yards, always begins the third Friday in January and continues for 11 days, 2 more than when it first started. It has attracted more than 375,000 visitors and participants from 47 states and 14 foreign countries. More than 10,000 domestic animals from bulls to rabbits are exhibited over several acres of the Stock Yard exhibition halls in downtown Denver. In 1980, buyers from all over the world attended and spent in excess of $8 million for 10,365 animals. There are also booths where visitors can buy ear tags, cowboy hats, cookware, horse trailers, beer, t-shirts, sheepskin coats, horse blankets, snake skins and Indian oil. The show features a petting area for children, who can watch the piglets, see chicks hatch and pet a variety of animals, ranging from lambs to ponies. There is also the judging of animals with the awarding of blue ribbons and cash prizes. Some impressive animals have been bulls, some weighing more than 2,300 pounds each. The rodeo is a popular event and attracts some very famous contestants, like film star James Caan, who took part in the team-roping competition and was in fifth place after the first round. His partner and double in films was H.P. Everts, also a stuntman. Other celebrities who also breed animals have included film star Robert Redford showing horses, the late John Wayne's Arizona ranch showing cattle, and actress Greer Garson and husband Buddy Fogelson exhibiting cattle, as did the late Winthrop Rockefeller. Besides the famous there are 4-H Club and Future Farmers of America members who raise calves and lambs to be exhibited at this show, considered to be the ''Kentucky Derby'' in its field, according to a January 17, 1980, article in the *New York Times*. Many social events have sprung up in conjunction with the show over the years. Every night some Denver organization stages an Angus Ball, a Hereford dinner or party. All the stores offer ''stock show specials.'' Lounges and nightclubs feature country-western bands. In 1980, the Colorado State Historical Society staged a ''Bob Wahr'' Show—barbed wire, 760 different kinds of barbed wire. The show is financed through admission fees, entry fees, sale of different items and contributions from local industry. The National Western Stock Show has played host to several million people, including participants and visitors. It is a huge economic success and has worldwide appeal.

Durango

NAVAJO TRAILS FIESTA

Held annually, first weekend in August
Ethnic, economic

The Navajo Trails Fiesta is an annual three-day celebration the first weekend in August. There is a real Western-style rodeo plus Indian dances and entertainment. The Indians are from a nearby reservation. The rodeo is a highlight of the fiesta, as are the chuck wagon meals. There is an admission charge. The event attracts more than 15,000 visitors. Several hundred thousand have attended since the first fiesta in 1965. It was based on the early Spanish Trails Fiesta, which combined Spanish and Indian cultures with Western activities. Work on the fiesta is voluntary. The event is held at La Plata County Fairgrounds.

Pueblo

COLORADO STATE FAIR

Held annually, last week in August
Economic

The Colorado State Fair is featured for 10 days, usually the last week in August sometimes through the Labor Day weekend in September. It is more than 100 years old, started in 1872, and is actually older than the state of Colorado. It is primarily a fair to exhibit and sell agricultural products. However, it has become more with a midway and famous name entertainment on the fairgrounds. There is no extra charge, since a general admission fee covers everything. Highlights include an old-fashioned bake sale sponsored by the Colorado Cowbelles and the Colorado Extension Homemakers. Both groups bake a wide variety of cakes and pies at home and also at the fair's completely furnished kitchen on the fairgrounds. Visitors are encouraged to watch the baking and talk with the ladies. This is a very popular event. Most of the home-baked goodies are sold almost as fast as they come out of the oven. Another popular area is the Farmers Market, where fresh fruits and vegetables are sold at less the cost in big city supermarkets. Many fair programs are for the young, like 4-H and FFA (Future Farmers of America). The purpose is to educate and foster an interest in farming among the young. The fair sponsors a Silver Queen Contest, conducted for residents of nursing homes throughout the Rocky Mountain region. Individual nursing homes select a queen candidate, who goes to the fair. The queen is selected at a special luncheon after being interviewed and demonstrating her talent. The Silver Queen reigns for a year until the next fair. She is crowned with a tiara and given a silver cape, a dozen red roses and lots of gifts donated by Colorado merchants. The other contestants also receive gifts. All queen candidates and the winner are given seats of honor at the Colorado State Fair parade, one of the largest in the state. More than 350,000 people attend the fair each year. It is a self-supporting event.

Telluride

INTERNATIONAL FILM FESTIVAL

Held annually, Labor Day weekend, September
Cultural

The International Film Festival is held the Labor Day weekend in September. It is an around-the-clock event. There are two theaters for film showings, indoor and outdoor discussions, parties, picnics and even jeep rides into the mountains. New and old film directors attend and mix freely with visitors. About 500 theater and film professionals and twice that many film fans attend each year. The festival began in 1974, and while small in comparison to other film events, it is more personable. It attracts actors, actresses, distributors, scholars and film buffs. New and current films are screened, and films are international: French, German, Spanish. Very often cartoons, like Walt Disney classics, are shown, as well as the original *King Kong*. The festival operates on a modest scale, but it continues to grow in popularity because of its informality.

Connecticut

Bridgeport

BARNUM FESTIVAL

Held annually, June/July
Economic, legendary

The Barnum Festival has grown from 11 days to 17 days held from late June through the Fourth of July. It pays tribute to Phineas Taylor Barnum, the famous circus man, who also was Bridgeport's mayor in 1875. This city remembers him also for his many community contributions, including new industrial jobs, his fight for the regulation of railroads and the city's many parks. Scheduled events include an antique auto show, ringmaster roadshow, Jenny Lind concert, hobbies and crafts show, circus clowns and other entertainment. The festival also features a visit to the city's Barnum Museum at 804 Main Street, where Barnum's circus and showmanship career is relived through exhibits and a miniature replica of his circus. On the final festival weekend, Friday at 9 p.m., there are fireworks at the Seaside Park. Saturday evening has the Champions on Parade, the largest senior drum corps competition in the Northeast. Sunday is reserved for the annual Barnum Memorial Ceremony at Mountain Grove Cemetery, where he is buried. The festival ends with an 11 a.m. huge parade with bands, floats, marching units, animals and thousands of spectators. It is estimated that 1.5 million came to the Barnum Festival in 1975. The grand total over the years is in the millions. Latest festival additions are speedboat races, parachute jumping demonstrations, a lawn bowling tournament and ethnic programs, such as a German beer festival, Polish polka dancers and Black "soul nights." The festival sometimes goes through July 5, Barnum's birthday. The festival started in 1949 to chase away the postwar recession blues that seemed to hang over this defense plant city. It started as a weekend event with Mayor Jasper McLevy in charge with the help of a local industrialist, Herman Steinkraus, president of the U.S. Chamber of Commerce. Weekend programs featured a parade and clambake. Each year the program expanded until it reached 17 days. There are many preliminary events before the actual opening festival day. These include the selection of Tom Thumb, Jenny Lind and other figures associated with Barnum and the circus. Actually the entire event takes six weeks.

Farmington

CHILDREN SERVICES HORSE SHOW AND COUNTRY FAIR

Held annually, May
Sports, charitable

Children Services Horse Show and Country Fair is an annual fund-raising event that benefits the Children Services of Connecticut, Inc., and the "Village" for emotionally disturbed children. The five-day show is always in mid-May, the start of the competitive season for show horses in the Northeast. It is the second largest outdoor show in the Eastern United States and has been named the Best Show in New England by the United Professional Horsemen's Association. It is also a Gold Star Show and a Connecticut tradition, cited by the governor. The show is accredited by the American Horse Shows Association and attracts more than 600 horse exhibitors from all over the continental United States as well as from Canada, Mexico and Hawaii. The show also includes a country fair. A huge tent displays everything from penny candy to foreign cars. A food tent is open from 6 a.m. to closing. Horses exhibited in the show are worth more than $1 million and show off in ringside parking, hunt course parking and more. Each year about 20,000 spectators come and pay to get in regardless of the weather. Show classes are held for Morgans, three- and five-gaited saddle horses, fine harness, roadster ponies, regular and green working hunters, jumpers, American saddlebred pleasure classes and carriage classes. Winners receive trophies and more than $14,000 in cash prizes. Originally a three-day show, it was first held in May 1951 and was the idea of the late Beth Kilbourn, who loved animals, especially horses. She was very interested in Children Services of Connecticut, Inc., and decided to hold a horse show. With the help of local residents, the prospects of a show were considered, and the first one was held in 1951 on the property of Avon Old Farms School, with only one ring. The show was a hit and led to a second one at Plainville at Tinti's but the bad weather, location and facilities made it a flop. Beth Kilbourn (she was from Simsbury), however, continued the show, and in 1953 the Farmington Polo Grounds were made available for it. Although there still was only one ring, horse exhibitors improved, and more people became interested in the horse show and its purpose. The show marked its twenty-seventh anniversary in 1977 and has attracted TV and radio personalities as well as U.S. and Austrian Olympic equestrian teams. It is financed through entry fees and admission charges, with the bulk of the proceeds going directly to Children Services. The show is still held at the Polo Grounds, now known as the Farmington Valley Recreational Park, Inc. About 700 volunteers work up to 10 months a year preparing for the show.

New London

YALE-HARVARD REGATTA

Held annually, June
Sports

The Yale-Harvard Regatta marked its 118th year in 1983. The one-day event, usually held the first Sunday in June, was formerly held on the Memorial Day weekend. It was changed because the weather was more predictable in June, as was the Thames River. About 18,000 spectators attend together with 150 boats, ranging from yachts to rafts, following the route of the college crew races. Before World War II, more than 60,000 persons lined the banks of the Thames River to view what was claimed to be the country's oldest crew competition. The event begins when the Block Island Ferry, the observation boat for the event, leaves its slip at 3:30 p.m. with a band on board. There is a short cruise before the ferry heads up the Thames to the regatta's finish line, near Gales Ferry. There is a charge for the cruise. The timing of the regatta is set when the tide moves upriver. There is a two-mile freshmen race, usually set to begin at 5:15 p.m., followed by a two-mile combination race, featuring the best rowers from all classes. There is a three-mile junior varsity race, but the major competition is the four-mile varsity race, usually starting about 6:45 p.m. As of 1981, Harvard had won the last 18 regattas, the longest winning streak in the event. The regatta is sometimes preceded the Friday and Saturday prior to regatta Sunday by concerts, dancing and entertainment. The event is economically sound, since hotels and motels are sold out in New London, with the overflow going to other areas, like Niantic. The regatta is aided by the New London Marine Commerce and Development Committee and by ticket sales.

Norwalk

OYSTER FESTIVAL

Held annually, September
Economic, heritage

The Oyster Festival, sponsored by the Norwalk Seaport Association since 1977, is held for three days in early September, the weekend after Labor Day. Its purpose is to remind local residents of the town's nautical heritage, but time has changed it to include more. Festival events are held outdoors under tents that cover an acre of ground at the Veterans Memorial Park at the head of Norwalk Harbor. Friday festivities begin at 5 p.m. with varied types of music concerts. The arts and crafts feature of the festival attracted more than 100,000 people in 1979, and attendance has since doubled. Arts and crafts are demonstrated and sold by more than 100 artisans, who come from as far away as Wisconsin and Texas. However, the theme of the festival is the oyster, and in keeping with this there is an oyster-eating contest and an oyster-shucking competition with prizes for winners. There is also an oyster shell craft contest and Sunday race for hand-propelled boats, such as kayaks, canoes and rowboats, with prizes not only for the winners but also for the most original looking vessel. There is a boat parade and other foods to sample. There is a mock Revolutionary War battle and performances by polka, jazz and folk groups. The festival has a Children's Fun Park, where young visitors can play ring-toss games, watch puppet shows and ride a pony. There's a row of more than 15 food stands serving oysters, hot dogs, knockwurst, chili, clam chowder, fried doughnuts and corn fritters. The event is highly successful due to work done by volunteers and the Norwalk Seaport Association. It is financed by the sale of foods, donations and souvenir sales. There is a general admission fee, too.

Delaware

New Castle

A DAY IN OLD NEW CASTLE

Held annually, the third Saturday in May
Historic

A Day in Old New Castle is held annually the third Saturday in May. Historic private homes, still in residential use, are opened to the public as are other historic buildings not usually open to the public. Buildings are open 10 a.m. to 5 p.m., and private homes 11 a.m. to 5 p.m. An admission ticket is needed for the tour, which also includes entry to two museums. Ticket prices vary each year. The one-day tour covers 41 different buildings and gives visitors an opportunity to learn history firsthand and to see architectural examples of the Dutch, colonial, French, Georgian, federal and empire periods in the town. Most buildings are brick, but some are stone, clapboard and stucco. Visitors to the private homes see mantels, woodwork, paneling, staircases, fireplaces, early flooring, kitchens and exterior woodwork that date back at least 200 years. On Old New Castle Day, silver, pewter, china, glass, jewelry, dolls, quilts, shawls, paintings, furniture, gardens and various important historic records and papers are on display. Among the historic papers is the original deed from Indian Chief Seckatarius to William Penn, as well as one of Penn's grants to John Donaldson in 1699. There is also a letter to George Read from George Washington and a certificate of the Society of Cincinnati, signed by George Washington. Other exhibits feature paintings by Gilbert Stuart, John Hesselius, Benjamin West, Thomas Sully, Charles Wilson Peale, John Inis, Nicholas Hillard and Fred Wright. Visitors also see the Communion silver, a gift from Queen Anne, furniture attributed to William Savery, Chinese export porcelain, and china and silver owned by the revolutionary heroine Lydia Darragh. Among the many buildings toured are the Immanuel Church, founded in 1689 and built in 1703, and the Van Leuvenigh House, built about 1732 and still a private residence. Refreshments and luncheon (for a fee) are available from 10 a.m. on at the Academy. Luncheon is prepared and served by women in colonial costume. The one-day tour program is sponsored annually by Immanuel Church for the purpose of restoration and preservation of the town's historic buildings, including the church. The one-day event attracts thousands every year. New Castle was originally founded as Fort Casimir by the Dutch in 1651, then captured by the Swedes on Trinity Sunday, 1654, and renamed Fort Trefalldigheet, or Fort Trinity. The Dutch retook the town under Peter Stuyvesant September 1, 1655. The name was changed to New Amstel in 1657, only to be captured next by the English under Sir Robert Carr, October 13, 1664. It was then called New Castle. James, Duke of York, conveyed to William Penn August 24, 1682, all land within a radius of 12 miles of New Castle. It was here that William Penn first landed in America, October 28, 1682. On the site of Immanuel Church was enacted the ceremony of "Livery of Seizin," in which Penn received "Turf, Twig, Soyle and Water" as a token of ownership. New Castle was the colonial capital until 1776, the state capital from 1776 to 1777, and the county seat until 1882. Among distinguished visitors to New Castle have been the Marquis de Lafayette, Andrew Jackson, George Washington, David Crockett, Daniel Webster, Sam Houston, Louis Napoleon, John Adams, Stonewall Jackson and Chief Black Hawk.

Florida

Bradenton

DE SOTO CELEBRATION

Held annually, March/April
Historic pageant

The De Soto Celebration relives the history of Manatee County on Florida's West Coast every spring, usually from late March into early April. The eight-day celebration marks the landing of Hernando De Soto and his conquistadores on the southern shore of the Manatee River in 1539. Focal point of the celebration is the landing reenactment at De Soto National Memorial Park, five miles west of Bradenton at the mouth of the Manatee River. Each year one of Manatee County's leading citizens is selected to be De Soto. The candidate is bearded and authentically dressed as the sixteenth-century explorer and is provided with a crew of uniformed conquistadores from the membership of the Hernando De Soto Historical Society. De Soto and his crew rush ashore from a replica of the flagship, *San Cristobal*, as did the original De Soto and crew. Swords swish, cannons boom. They capture the area, which becomes a Spanish fiesta with street dancing, formal balls, humorous captures, sports and a competition of visiting state bands. It is estimated that more than 80,000 watch the state's largest night parade and fireworks display, climaxing the eight-day festival. Other events include a fashion show and the Queen's Court, consisting of 14 contestants with only 7 selected by conquistadores' ballot. In addition to the parade, there is a children's parade, with schools closing in honor of De Soto Day, a state holiday. Miniature floats created by local children are part of the parade, as are bands and a Conquistador Crewe. There are art shows, an orchid exhibit, a beard contest, a children's pet show, concerts, a square dance and sports events. The celebration started in 1939, when Manatee County residents were celebrating the four hundredth anniversary of De Soto's landing in the New World. It's been held every year since, except during World War II. The celebration follows history accurately with regard to all reenactments pertaining to De Soto. Millions have attended the annual event since its start. Among attending personalities have been the governor of Florida, members of the Florida cabinet, U.S. congressmen, representatives of the U.S. Department of Interior and the Spanish ambassador to the United States.

Coral Gables

JUNIOR ORANGE BOWL FESTIVAL

Held annually, December
Sports

The Junior Orange Bowl Festival is an 11-day program that places emphasis on youth sports events similar to Miami's Orange Bowl Festival, both held every December. Events include a festival parade, international junior golf, tennis and soccer tournaments plus a national bowling tournament and local football games. The festival has been expanding because of an increased interest in sports other than football and tennis. It is held in late December to attract participants at year-end holiday recess from school and because the weather is more pleasant.

Future plans call for more sports and competitive events to make the program more interesting. The parade, nationally televised for several years, continues to be the big attraction. It is estimated that some 75,000 watch it. Nearly 1 million have attended the festival since 1949. The festival is financed through business contributions, entry fees and concession charges. The only admission charge is for the football games. Both a paid staff and volunteers work on the event, and as many as 1,000 hours are put into the work behind the festival. Festival events are held at various sports locations throughout the area. It was originally started to provide a youth image for Coral Gables and for economic reasons.

Fort Myers

EDISON PAGEANT OF LIGHT

Held annually, February
Pageantry, commemorative

The Edison Pageant of Light honors Thomas Alva Edison every February, encompassing his birthday, February 11. It is always the second Wednesday through the third Saturday of the month. Edison came to Fort Myers in 1885 and built a house on the Caloosahatchee River. He called it Seminole Lodge. The 11-day festival opens with the King and Queen Ball, a formal affair with music by nationally known bands. The ball is supported by the Lamplighters, an organization of civic and community leaders. They also handle the festival. Events include an Edison Birthday Party program with concerts featuring classical and popular music and a birthday cake. There is also an Edison Pageant of Light Junior Coronation, with a costumed event before the Children's Parade. Trophies are awarded for the best costumes, and the event is open to all children ages four to six. The festival includes exhibits of Edison's various inventions, and sometimes a different invention serves as a festival theme. For example, in 1977, it was the phonograph because of the centenary of its invention. It was the phonograph that made Edison internationally famous. The entire festival features special luncheons, dance groups, ethnic programs, a strolling flower show, sailing regattas, a tennis tournament, an art exhibit, pop concerts and on February 11, a memorial service in memory of Edison at the Thomas Alva Edison Congregational Church. The festival closes with an evening grand parade at Edison Stadium. The Edison Pageant of Light is based on the Sunshine Festival, which was started in 1931 to call attention to the area. By 1938, it had become the Edison Pageant of Light to honor the area's honored resident. The first event lasted three days, February 10–12, 1938, and featured a Coronation Ball, a jalopy derby, a street parade with seven bands, floats and students, a street carnival, a ''cracker'' band contest and the memorial service. The almost immediate success of the event led to the city council contributing $4,250 toward the next pageant. Community and business leaders joined in, and the event went to a week and then 11 days. A permanent pageant committee now handles the event.

Key West

OLD ISLAND DAYS

Held annually, February/March
Cultural, economic

Old Island Days is a seven-week event calling attention to the culture and architecture of the area that was so popular with the late President Harry S. Truman. The event begins in early February and continues through late March. Throughout the event, all old houses in the historic district are especially illuminated from 7:30 to 9:30 p.m., and self-guided tours are offered. There are a variety of guided house tours as well. Other events are a coronation ball, ethnic activities and ethnic foods, sports, a children's fair and a country fair, special luncheons, a pageant, conch shell-blowing contest and the selection of Little Miss Old Island Days. There is also the blessing of fishing fleets and the serving of key lime tarts. Most Key West houses and gardens are open to the public during Old Island Days. Key West is a small island, a mile and a half wide and four miles long, surrounded by reefs. The vegetation is tropical. Old Island Days began in 1961 under the auspices of the Old Island Restoration Foundation to preserve and restore the unusual architecture of the area. Economics was also a reason. Old Island Days is always held at the same time of year, since this is the height of the winter tourist season. Thousands come. Recently night tours were added to accommodate all the visitors coming to the area. The entire community volunteers to work on preparations, each working 100 hours. The event is financed from funding from previous years and admission charges for house tours and food sales.

Sebring

SEBRING 12 HOURS/AUTOMOBILE HALL OF FAME WEEK

Held annually, the third week in March
Sports

Sebring 12 Hours/Automobile Hall of Fame Week is a March event. The race itself is always held the third Friday and Saturday of the month. The Automobile

Hall of Fame Week, a recent addition, is held preceding the big race. The special week includes a parade with floats, Shriner units, cowboys and cowgirls and military marchers. There are also golf and tennis tournaments, boat races, ski exhibitions and the climax, the awards ceremony of the Hall of Fame honoring men and women leaders of the auto industry and auto racing. The governor of Florida always serves as invitations chairman and each year proclaims Automobile Hall of Fame Race Week. The event draws about 55,000 people, who always help the local economy, too. The auto race ranks highly with the Indianapolis and Le Mans races and is considered among one of the three great races in the world. The event goes back to December 31, 1950, and was based on General LeMay's use of airports for races. Local race fans followed in foreign cars. The first race was held in memory of Sam Collier, a Sebring man killed in the Watkins Glen (New York) race. Then the local Firemen's Association organized racing, and eventually it secured local support. Among well-known racers who have participated in the Sebring 12 Hours Race have been Juan Fangio of Argentina, Stirling Moss of England and Mario Andretti. The event is financed through ticket sales, entry fees and the sponsorship of local business leaders.

Tampa

GASPARILLA PIRATE INVASION AND PARADE

Held annually, February
Pageantry, economic

The Gasparilla Pirate Invasion and Parade occurs the second Monday in February. The invasion of Tampa is staged from a fully rigged pirate ship manned by men in pirate costumes. The ship sails down the harbor, and the city is captured. This is followed by a three-and-a-half-hour parade through Tampa streets to celebrate the victory. The event is named for Jose Gaspar, a Spanish pirate of the eighteenth century. He is said to have buried treasures still undiscovered along this Florida coast. In addition to the victory parade, there is usually an illuminated night fiesta parade by the Krewe of Sant'Yago with floats, bands and night lights. Free Spanish bean soup and Cuban bread is distributed to all night parade spectators. There is also a Festival Gasparilla Ball at which King Gasparilla and his Queen are crowned. The ball, however, is open only to members of the various societies, or krewes. Tampa's Latin Quarter, Ybor City, is very festive during the invasion, offering Latin concerts and sidewalk art shows. The annual invasion attracts 600,000 visitors with most from out of town and out of state. Literally millions have attended since the first invasion in 1904. A local social editor, Louise Frances Dodge, and a group of businessmen are credited with the idea, which was designed to give more "spice" to the area's

annual May Day festival. It was changed to February because more tourists come
in winter and the area wanted to compete with other Southern states. There is
no doubt that the invasion is an economic boon for Tampa. Backing comes from
various krewes, or society membership dues and admission charges to the parade
and invasion. Plans for the annual event are made and carried out by three full-
time paid staffers and the various krewes.

Georgia

Atlanta

ARTS FESTIVAL OF ATLANTA

Held annually, May
Cultural

The Arts Festival of Atlanta is an annual May event lasting for nine days. The
arts include painting, performing arts, films, functional arts for children such as
creative dramatics and dance movement classes. There are demonstrations by
visual artists. The festival is held outdoors in the city's Piedmont Park and is
open to all Southern artists, both professional and amateur. Sculpture, photography, drawings, printmaking, graphics, pottery, ceramics, jewelry, weaving,
woodcarving and leather crafts are also offered. Performing groups include the
Atlanta Ballet, Theater Atlanta, Kruger Sinonfietta, Southern Ballet, Youth Symphony of Atlanta, Vagabond Marionetters, Alliance Theater, Atlanta Children's
Theater, Atlanta Symphony Orchestra, Third Army Band and various school
and university groups. A recent addition is the open-air workshop by artists and
craftsmen. Merit prizes in various categories are also awarded, with the money
coming from contributions and proceeds from sales at the festival auction in the
park. The festival also presents scholarships and grants of varying amounts to
promising artists and craftsmen at different times of the year. An auction takes
place two months before the festival itself to raise money for the many festival
programs. More than 4 million people have come to the festival since its beginning in 1954. In 1977, half a million came. The performing arts phase of the
festival is still the most popular. The festival was founded by locally well-known
artists and citizens who wanted to give the city's professional artists a chance
to exhibit their work and to sell it, too. The performing arts group was to give
local folks some entertainment. The festival is administered by the Arts Festival
of Atlanta, Inc., a nonprofit organization. Two paid staff members handle details
with the help of hundreds of volunteers. The executive committee puts in 3,000
hours and the board about 1,000 hours of work per year.

Pine Mountain

MASTERS WATER SKI TOURNAMENT

Held annually, July
Sports

The annual Masters Water Ski Tournament is a two-day competition held in early July at the Callaway Gardens. The tournament features three events: slalom, tricks and jumping, with both a men's and women's division. There are champions in each category of competition as well as an overall man and woman winner. The tournament was shortened from three to two days to heighten the excitement and leave less margin for error for the competitions. It is always held the second weekend of July. About 6,000 spectators watch the tournament every year. It is held at Robin Lake in the Gardens, which helps finance the event. There is no admission to the tournament, only to the Gardens. The tournament began in 1958. It is a combined effort of the American Water Ski Association and Callaway Gardens. The association was looking for a site for a water ski contest. The cooperative venture has led to an important event open to international water skiers.

Savannah

GEORGIA WEEK CELEBRATION

Held annually, February
Historic

Georgia Week Celebration is observed in early February, encompassing February 12, the date of the founding of the thirteenth and last English colony at Savannah in 1733. Originally the founding day was observed only, but it developed into a week-long program as interest increased. Activities are from Sunday to Sunday to include the founding date. Some events are held outdoors and others indoors, all within the city's historic district. Georgia Week is sponsored annually by the Historic Savannah Foundation to commemorate its founding by General James Edward Oglethorpe. Festivities include the reenactment of Oglethorpe and Indian Chief Tomochichi greeting settlers upon their arrival at the new colony. Participants are in costume and lead a parade of local citizens and visiting dignitaries through the city's famous squares, laid out by General Oglethorpe as part of the original city plan. The parade ends at a local hotel for a reception and luncheon. There is also a pageant recalling Oglethorpe's landing in Georgia. It is staged at the original landing site on the Savannah riverfront, where the city's eighteenth-century cotton warehouse has been renovated and now contains boutiques, restaurants and nightspots. The pageant begins with the arrival of the boat carrying Oglethorpe and his colonists to the landing site. They are accompanied by flotillas from Savannah and nearby cities. Other events include exhibits by schoolchildren and displays of colonial and Indian crafts at the Ships of the Sea Museum. Both eighteenth- and nineteenth-century crafts are demonstrated by local artisans. There is a Victorian tea, a musical evening and dinner at the Telfair Academy of Arts and Sciences, a riverside picnic with local entertainment and special bus tours of the historic district. Additionally there are commemorative church services, concerts and a children's day with a patriotic puppet show, paint-in and costume parade. Sales from the preceding year's event and admission charges for some events help finance the annual celebration. Work is done by local volunteers.

Stone Mountain

YELLOW DAISY FESTIVAL

Held annually, second weekend in September
Ecology, economic

The Yellow Daisy Festival is held for three days, usually the second weekend in September, to pay tribute to the rare yellow daisy, *Viguiera porteri*, that grows and blooms on Stone Mountain in weathered granite crevices. It transforms the barren mountain into a golden glow, usually in September. The two-and-a-half-foot-tall daisies germinate in April, grow all summer and toward the end of August show signs of blooming. They are in full bloom at the time of the festival and by October are gone. If picked, the flowers wilt. They only seem to flourish in the stone crevices. The festival, with all events free to the public (except for parking cars), includes tours to view the blooms and to photograph them. Festival events include arts and crafts, the Georgia State Fiddling Championship and bluegrass music competition, a hog-calling contest, buck dancing, district flower show, forestry field events, gymnastics, puppet and magician show, banjo and chorus music and special displays. A Yellow Daisy Princess is selected to reign over the entire event. More than 200 craftsmen exhibit, and there's an art show with prizes in painting, watercolor, drawing and print and photography divisions. The art show is in the area's Coliseum, and craftsmen exhibit in nearby covered facilities. The bright yellow daisies were first discovered in 1846 by the Pennsylvania missionary Thomas Porter, who sent a specimen to Asa Gray, the noted botanist, for identification. At first Gray identified it as in the *Rudbeckia* genus with Gloriosa daisies and Cone flowers but later positively said it was in the *Viguiera* genus with about 60 other species of *Viguiera* growing mostly in Central America and Mexico. The only other place in the United States that the flower grows is in California, but that variety is larger and woody, like a small bush.

The unusual daisies are tended by Harold Cox, Stone Mountain Park horticulturalist. The festival started in 1969 with craftsmen added two years later and the Princess a year after that. In 1977, the festival hosted 100,000 visitors, and the number increases each year. It is financed by the Stone Mountain Memorial Association and by parking and park admission fees. The association works year-round preparing for the festival.

Thomasville

ROSE FESTIVAL

Held annually, April
Floral, economic

The Rose Festival is a week-long event, Monday to Saturday, and always in late April, when the roses in this area are at their peak bloom. Thomasville is the South's "City of Roses." The Rose Show is held in the local gymnasium, which is filled with roses of all types, varieties and colors. The display is held the Friday and Saturday of the festival week. Festival events include a two-hour parade with floats and displays, a three-day antique show and sale, a horse show, concerts, beauty pageant, softball and golf tournaments. As many as 75,000 people come for this festival. It is estimated that since 1922, when the first festival was held, more than 5 million have attended. One of the persons associated with the festival since its start has been Sam Hjort, an expert in rose culture in the South since 1919. His rose nursery was originally owned by his father, dating back to 1898. The festival is a serious event, and the Rose Show, the display case for prize-winning roses. When the event began in 1922, it consisted of rose displays in local stores, gradually spreading to all stores with the full help of the chamber of commerce. By 1948, the greatly enlarged Rose Show had turned into a festival with a parade and daily tours of historic landmarks and plantations. The Rose Show and parade are traditionally held the fourth Friday in April. There is a Rose Queen, and the lucky girl is also the official Georgia Rose Queen. Preparations for the festival are handled by volunteers. It is financed through various fund-raising programs and admission charges to some festival events.

Hawaii

All islands

ALOHA WEEK FESTIVAL

Held annually, September/October
Ethnic

Aloha Week Festival is held at the end of September through mid-October on all the islands with similar programs, but accented by the individual island's flower. There are floral parades, Hawaiian music concerts, arts and crafts exhibits, canoe races and international pageants. All are presided over by their own Aloha Festival Royal Court, honoring Hawaii's monarchy. Members of the Royal Court are formally installed at investiture ceremonies held on each island. For example, on the big island of Hawaii that ceremony is held at the Halemaumau Crater of the very active Kailauea volcano. Hawaiian music features Ho'olaulea and Ho'kie programs at shopping centers, public parks, centers and major resorts. The Ho'olaulea on Oahu is a street party with six stages of continuous entertainment along the main street in Waikiki. Kalalaua Avenue is closed to traffic in the evening. There are concerts, musical tributes to Queen Emma, school glee clubs and commemorative programs. There is usually a series of formal balls and luncheon fashion shows. Most strenuous of all Aloha events is a grueling 38-mile open-sea canoe race from Molokai to Oahu, sponsored by local canoe clubs. The event requires the skill of the most experienced and trained paddlers. The race ends six to eight hours later at Waikiki Beach, where cheering crowds await their arrival. Admission to most Aloha events, except formal balls, luncheons and dinners, is only $2, and instead of a ticket, the buyer gets a yellow Aloha Festival ribbon, appropriately inscribed and attached to a decorative medallion. These have become collectors items over the years. Ribbon sale booths are at all shopping complexes and at various public places on each island. The Aloha Festival is closely related to Hawaii's ancient Makahiki celebration of thanksgiving and tax-paying time with extra features. It was during the Makahiki that the chiefs accepted taxes from the people in the name of the god Lono. After the collections, both the chiefs and commoners celebrated with a festival of thanks to Lono for his bountiful gifts of the land. Aloha Week Festival started in 1946, as a thanksgiving after World War II. The months of September and October also were a slack tourist time. However, since Aloha Week, literally millions have come for the special week. Each island has its own week-long programs, with the big island of Hawaii starting celebrations, followed by Maui, Kauai, Molokai and Oahu. This order changes each year. There is also a different theme for the celebrations, decided upon by Aloha Week Festival, a nonprofit organization that handles all festival details on each island. Fundraising programs and local donations help support the event.

Honolulu (Oahu Island)

CHINESE NARCISSUS FESTIVAL

Held annually, January/February, movable date
Ethnic

The Chinese Narcissus Festival is an annual celebration from early January through early February with dozens of events to usher in the Chinese New Year.

Festivities include a night in Chinatown celebration in downtown Honolulu, cooking demonstrations, a queen competition and pageant, Chinatown tours, a fashion show, ethnic entertainment and cultural displays. The climax, of course, is the Chinese New Year, which varies in date because the Chinese follow the lunar rather than the Gregorian calendar. The New Year runs in recurring cycles of 12, and each year is named for a domestic, wild or mythical creature, for example, horse, dragon, and rooster. New Year festivities are climaxed by a Chinese lion dance through the streets to the accompaniment of gongs, cymbals, drums and fireworks. The lion dances back and forth. The Chinese ceremonial lion is 12 feet long, requiring several men to handle it. The ornately decorated papier-mache and bamboo head of the lion is hollow and large enough to be raised and lowered over one man's head. The head is always in constant motion, with rolling eyes, fluttering eyelashes and moving pom-poms during a performance. The silken fringe under the movable lips is symbolic. White means humility. Red is aggressiveness and ferocity, while black, a young lion or leader. The body and tail consist of strips of colored silk edged with fur and accented by many nailheads. The tail position, though secondary, is also operated by a second person, who must remain in a bent position while flapping his arms in and out. The lion does 30 basic dance routines, with a different one for each occasion. The first Narcissus Festival, sponsored by the Chinese Chamber of Commerce, was in 1950. Narcissus blooms were chosen as a symbol of hope that "things Chinese" might enjoy a renaissance in Hawaii. This festival has been copied by Chinese communities in San Francisco, Vancouver and Manila. Thousands of spectators and residents attend, and to date more than a million have been to the festival. The event is financed through fund-raising programs, admission fees for some events and private donations.

Honolulu (Oahu Island)

CHERRY BLOSSOM FESTIVAL

Held annually, February/April
Ethnic

The Cherry Blossom Festival is an annual event lasting from 42 to 59 days, usually from mid-February to the first week in April. Unlike other cherry blossom festivals, the blossoms do not grow in Hawaii. However, they do appear through the ingenuity of the local Japanese residents. Festival features include the famous Kabuki and a culture and arts show at the Neal S. Blaisdell Center Exhibition Hall late in February. There's bonsai, *bonseki* flower arrangements, vegetable carving, ceramics, *kunihimo* (weaving) and paper doll–making demonstrations. Entertainment includes traditional Japanese dances, martial arts and films featuring Japanese groups from Japan. The Honolulu Symphony performs with guest soloists and a song festival competition. The festival reached its thirty-first year in 1983. It was created by the Honolulu Junior Japanese Chamber of Commerce and the Japanese community "to bridge the cultural gap by sharing with others the essence of the Japanese heritage." The festival promotes Japanese culture and is economically feasible since millions of visitors have attended since 1953. The festival is financed through the sale of souvenir books from previous years and through donations. Although there are some admission charges, most events remain free. Plans for the next year's festival begin almost as soon as the current one ends. All work is on a voluntary basis, with Jaycee members, church organizations and other groups helping out.

Honolulu (Oahu Island)

KING KAMEHAMEHA CELEBRATION

Held annually, June 11
Pageantry, historic

The King Kamehameha Celebration is the only public holiday in the United States that honors royalty. Events are held also on the other islands, June 11, the birthday of Kamehameha the Great, the Polynesian warrior who united all the islands. The main celebration centers in Honolulu and can be a two- or three-day event, centering around June 11. Yards of golden flower leis decorate the king's statue in Honolulu's Civic Center, with a special lei-draping ceremony early in the morning of June 10. The annual floral parade is held the next day, attracting thousands of spectators. A festival Holoku Ball precedes the king's birthday. Attendees wear the Hawaiian formal dress, *holoku* and flower leis. Evening programs include a fashion show of the old and new Hawaiian dress, and there is an elaborate Hawaiian pageant. Tickets are needed for the ball. Other birthday festivities include a concert by visiting bands at the Iolani Palace bandstand the evening of June 11. When the King Kamehameha Celebration parade starts at 9:30 a.m., June 10, at King and Richards streets, there is also a foot race run from Aloha Tower to the Outrigger Canoe Club in Waikiki, a distance of four miles. The high point of the parade is a float with a handsome Hawaiian selected to represent the king. His costume is a replica of the golden amo feather cloak and helmet worn by Kamehameha I. The real cloak is on display at Honolulu's Bishop Museum. The rest of the parade consists of flower-decorated floats, marching bands and horseback riders, including princesses and their attendants, representing the major islands in the Hawaiian chain. Each girl wears a long loose flowing satin riding dress, *pa'u* (*pah'oo*), in the color of her island home with leis of the official flower, shell or vine of her island. Immediately following the parade at around 11 a.m., Na Hana No'eau O Hawaii, an arts and crafts demonstration, is held in Kapiolani Park, Waikiki, plus Hawaiian entertainment. A competition of traditional Hawaiian chants and hulas end the day's and evening's festivities around 12:30 p.m. The final event in the celebration in Honolulu is the Aha'aina Awards Presentation and king-size luau on the second or third day at 2:30 p.m. at Pier 10 of the Aloha Tower. Tickets are sold by the King Kamehameha Celebration Commission. The commission works year-round planning the birthday festivities and finances the event through luau tickets and other admission charges and through contributions.

Idaho

Weiser

NATIONAL OLD-TIME FIDDLERS' CONTEST

Held annually, third full week in June
Cultural, folkloric

The National Old-Time Fiddlers' Contest always comes the third full week in June. The contest is open to fiddlers all over the United States and Canada, and approximately 10,000 visitors come to hear them every year. The event also features a pioneer parade, old-time style show, barbecue, all-you-can-eat breakfast, real old-fashioned melodrama, street dancing and the vigilantes, who are actually master clowns and hijinks pros on the loose, turning up when least expected. Ages 6 to 70 compete on the fiddle. There are also sing-along sessions well into the night and people who make up their own parades at a moment's notice. The purpose of the contest is to perpetuate old-time fiddling and to assure a category for juniors less than 18 years old. Trophies and cash prizes are awarded seniors over 70. There is a ladies division and a grand champion division. More than $2,500 in cash plus trophies are awarded for 16 different categories. There are also special prizes for national categories and a trophy for the Best-Liked Fiddler. The contest is financed through ticket sales, souvenir programs, entry fees and sponsorship by local businesses. All contest events are held in the Weiser High School gym. The contest began in 1914 but was interrupted by World War I. Attempts to revive it failed until Blaine Stubblefield aided by Kenneth Steck and the Weiser Chamber of Commerce brought it back, April 18, 1953, calling the competition the Northwest Mountain Fiddlers' Contest. It continued for 10 years, expanding in all directions and attracting thousands of contestants and tourists. In 1963, the event became the National Old-Time Fiddlers Contest, in conjunction with Idaho's centennial year celebration. The contest not only helps preserve the old-time fiddling of pioneer America but also attempts to develop genuine audience appreciation of old-time fiddling tunes. It is also designed to foster and encourage local, regional and state old-time fiddlers' jam sessions, contests and festivals. This contest is a permanent record and display of the history, relics and momentos of past old-time fiddlers' art. It also recognizes present-day old-time fiddlers as they express themselves traditionally. Visitors and contestants can also visit the Historical Museum and Fiddlers' Hall of Fame, free of charge. The event is supported by private donations and sponsorships.

Illinois

Chicago

CHRISTMAS AROUND THE WORLD

Held annually, November/January
Ethnic, religious, cultural

Christmas Around the World is a combination exhibit and festival of holiday celebrations, decorated trees, foods and carols of many nations held from late November through early January at the Museum of Science and Industry. This event is said to be one of the country's oldest, largest and most popular Christmas activities, attracting so many visitors that it often is extended beyond New Year's Day. It began in 1941, and to date more than 15 million have enjoyed the event. There are giant Christmas trees decorated by various ethnic groups. There are also daily concerts by school and church choral groups, featuring more than 122 performances during the holiday season. In addition there are theater programs keyed to how Christmas is celebrated around the world, with traditional holiday foods to sample. The festival was started as a free community service to bring Americans of different backgrounds together during World War II, and although on a small scale, it grew in popularity. As many as 34 ethnic groups participate annually. Each group decorates its own 18-foot-tall Christmas tree, produces festive pageants and serves meals. Each person comes dressed in his or her own national costume. Even foreign consulate personnel come to hang an ornament, sing a carol or perform a holiday dance. The museum provides the trees, the theater, the public address system and any assistance needed. Events can begin as early as Thanksgiving week, when the artificial trees are assembled and the ethnic groups with hundreds of helpers start the decorations. Actually the museum staff and the ethnic groups work on this event year-round, making and collecting tree decorations, new costumes, songs, dances and plays. The many ethnic meals are served each festival day in the museum's dining room. The meals tie in with the day's theater production. If there is a Polish play, then there's a Polish meal. The museum's chef prepares the food with the help of the different ethnic groups. The museum also prints the recipes on Christmas placemats, which visitors may take home as souvenirs. In 1974, the UNICEF Children's Art Exhibits were added to the holiday festival. They are still a feature. More than 500 works of art by 300 American children and an equal number of foreign children from 50 countries are displayed. The festival attracts as many as 50,000 people a day. Admission to the museum is free, but there are charges for the meals and plays.

Chicago

CHICAGOFEST

Held annually, August
Cultural, economic

Chicagofest is a 12-day event of music, food and fun at the Navy Pier early in August. It is billed as "America's biggest and best music festival with more than 600 acts performing on 12 separate stages." There is a single daily admission price of $6 (as of 1983, always subject to change). Acts in 1983 headlined Willie Nelson, Muddy Waters and more. Programs are continuous from noon to midnight daily. Chicagofest is a combination of a carnival, crafts fair, music festival and foods to sample. The event was started in 1978 as a 10-day program designed to entertain local citizens and to attract tourists. The first year there was a loss of $1 million, but a year later there was a profit of $500,000. The Chicagofest is sponsored by the city and various businesses. The idea was borrowed completely from Milwaukee's Summerfest. The event is handled by Festivals, Inc., a nonprofit organization (which also handles the Milwaukee event). The group approached Chicago's Mayor Bilandic at his invitation to set up a festival for the city. In 1979, 720,000 attended the event, and recently more than a million persons have attended. In 1980, Thomas Drilias, general manager of Festivals, Inc., announced that Chicago netted $1 million out of $5.5 million from ticket sales and revenues from vendors. The organization is paid several hundred thousand dollars plus a percentage of revenues to operate Chicagofest.

Chicago

GOLD COAST ART FAIR

Held annually, August
Cultural, economic

The Gold Coast Art Fair is held for three days in mid-August. More than 600 artists exhibit paintings and sculpture along Rush Street on the city's north side. The fair opens at noon on a Friday and continues through Sunday. It is sponsored by the *Near North News*, a weekly area newspaper, and the Gold Coast Association. There are no admission charges. Ever since the fair started in 1957, approximately 500,000 people have attended, and over a 20-year span more than 1 million. The art fair is not a juried show, but it does attract buyers. The most popular event is the opening night mini-parade, which in 1977 featured the Golden Knights Parachute team. The parade is open to all visitors who want to join it for fun. The fair is financed through donations from exhibitors and is underwritten by both sponsors. Net proceeds from each year's event are donated to local charities and needy groups, including Boy Scout Troop 1151, St. Benedict High School Scholarship Fund, Lower North Center, Mary Bartelme Home, VA Research Hospital, International Visitors Center and the Chicago Heart Association. When the fair began in 1957, it was briefly known as the Gold Coast Art Festival, but later it was changed to a fair.

Chicago

RAVINIA FESTIVAL

Held annually, June/September
Cultural

The Ravinia Festival is an 11-week music, dance and theater program, from June through mid-September, in the city's North Shore. Distinguished conductors lead the Chicago Symphony Orchestra, and they have included such notables as the late Arthur Fiedler, Lawrence Foster and John Green. Soloists are of top quality and in 1977 headlined Metropolitan Opera soprano Martina Arroyo. Music offerings are classical, pop, jazz and folk, with star performers featured. The festival also includes an outdoor sculpture exhibit, and Saturday mornings are reserved for the young with special music and theater programs for them. The festival often premieres new compositions. The Joffrey Ballet, for example, presented an American premiere at the 1977 festival. Special preview programs are available on designated days. These precede the regular symphony concerts and offer two performances for the price of one lawn admission or concert ticket. The Ravinia Festival covers several weeks of theater with works by Bertolt Brecht and Eugene Labich. Programs differ every year. About 380,000 persons attend each year, with tickets always in great demand. The festival is maintained through private contributions, grants and box-office receipts. All festival details are handled by a full-time staff of 15. The festival was started back in 1904 on a 36-acre park by railroad man and banker Albert C. Frosts, who put a baseball diamond, enclosed theater and dance floor in Ravinia Park to attract train travelers. Financial reverses closed down the park, and it was cleared for other projects. In 1911, Ravinia Park was the site of a new 1,420-seat open-air pavilion with first guest Walter Damrosch and a New York orchestra, followed by the Chicago Symphony Orchestra and the Minneapolis Symphony. Between 1919 and 1931, symphonic music moved to the sidelines, making way for the musical stage, a favorite of Louis Eckstein, one of the people involved in shaping Ravinia, making this spot the unofficial summer home of world famous singers like Chaliapin, Schip and Bori. By 1931, deficits had climbed and audiences had no money. Although Eckstein paid off two-thirds of the park's debts, it remained dark for the next four years. In 1936, there was a "Save Ravinia" fund-raising campaign, and the stock market rallied. The Chicago Symphony was hired to play for the summer. Eight years later, the widowed Mrs. Eckstein donated the park to the Ravinia Festival Association. Musicians like Heifitz, Rubinstein and Piatigorsky appeared. The park platform burned down, and the concert hall was in a canvas shelter, replaced in 1949 by a temporary building, which in turn was replaced by another pavilion with 32,000 seats and dressing rooms for the performers and storage for special equipment. In the 1950s, something new was added, namely folk singer-historian Richard Dyer-Bennett, poet-dramatist Archibald MacLeish and the New York Pro Musica. Eventually pop and jazz were added, bringing top performers to the festival. Previews were offered in 1973 by music director James Levine.

Nauvoo

WEDDING OF THE WINE AND CHEESE PAGEANT/GRAPE FESTIVAL

Held annually, Labor Day weekend, September
Folkloric, legendary

The Wedding of the Wine and Cheese/Grape Festival is an annual pageant always held Labor Day weekend in September, planned to coincide with the ripening of the grapes in the local vineyards. The pageant is the story of a shepherd boy in southern France who left his unfinished lunch in a cool limestone cave. He completely forgot about it, and when he returned months later, he found that the bread had molded and spread through the cheese curds, changing it into a blue-veined white cheese. When he tasted it, he discovered that it was edible and tasty. The news spread, and soon the limestone cave was filled with curds infused with the original cheese mold, and Roquefort cheese was born. In the pageant, the shepherd boy appears followed by milkmaids and cheese makers. Grape cutters carry baskets of ripe purple grapes, and the milkmaids their pails of creamy milk. The grapes produce the wine, and the creamy milk the cheese. Wine and cheese are at their best when eaten together, each complementing the other. In the ceremony, the bride carries the wine, which she puts on a wine barrel, and the groom carries the cheese, placing it next to the wine. The marriage contract is read by the chief magistrate, after which the scroll is placed between the wine and cheese. A wooden hoop encircles all three items, symbolizing the wedding ring, and is placed there by the officiating minister, completing the ceremony of the wedding of the wine and cheese. Nauvoo, on the east bank of the Mississippi River, was Illinois's largest city in 1844. It was originally bought by a white settler for 200 sacks of corn from the Fox Indians. The Mormons with Prophet Joseph Smith came in 1839, but Smith and his brother Hyrum were later murdered, forcing the Mormons out. Then came the French and German Icarians bent on establishing a communal colony, but it lasted only a few years. However, it was the Icarians who introduced grape growing and wine making to the area. Several of the original wine cellars are still used for the manufacture not of wine but of blue cheese. Many of the Mormon buildings and homes of the 1840 period have been carefully restored, and free tours are featured. The pageant is held at Nauvoo State Park, with the stage of sod taken directly from a similar festival in Roquefort, France. Held more than 50 years, it is financed through local donations and sponsorship.

Indiana

Fort Wayne

THREE RIVERS FESTIVAL

Held annually, July
Cultural, ethnic

The Three Rivers Festival is a nine-day program in mid-July that attempts to show what various ethnic groups are accomplishing in the area and to bring some activity into the area during summer. Its original intent in 1969 was also to help preserve the area's historical location, the Landing. However, the festival has grown from its original plan to include the entire city's community with citywide celebrations. In 1978, there were more than 140 events, which included music, sports, arts, crafts, parades, a raft and bed race, boat rides, fireworks and a soap box derby. Today there are also tours of an international village, historic Fort Wayne and, for youngsters, a children's zoo and pet parade. Ethnic events feature Latin American, Chinese, Polish, Greek, Jewish, Indian, Scandinavian and Afro-American cultural programs. Approximately 8 million people have come to the festival over the years, adding greatly to the city's economy as well as giving the city an opportunity to help local artists present their work to the public. The festival also attracts celebrities, especially for parades. Among them have been sportscaster Chris Schenkel, U.S. Senators Birch Bayh and Vance Hartke and TV's Donny Most. Hundreds of hours are spent by local citizens on a voluntary basis in preparing for each year's festival. It is maintained by button sales, a beer tent, donations, sponsorships of events and aid from the city government. The great majority of the events are free, with only 10 percent charging admission. The festival takes place at 35 different city locations, such as parks, streets and buildings.

Greenfield

JAMES WHITCOMB RILEY FESTIVAL

Held annually, October
Cultural

The James Whitcomb Riley Festival is an annual three-day program centering around October 7, the poet's birthday. The festival honors James Whitcomb Riley, the poet, and has expanded with other events, all culturally oriented. There's a poetry contest and a fine arts show of more than 400 pictures by 125 local artists. There's the Parade of Flowers for local elementary schoolchildren, arts and crafts plus a two-hour parade on Saturday. More than 10,000 attend the annual festival. Programs are held downtown close to the Riley House and his statue on the courthouse lawn. However, the continued growth of the event makes it difficult to keep everything centrally located. The festival dates back to 1911, when authoress Mrs. Minnie Belle Mitchell introduced a resolution to the Indiana Federation of Women's Clubs to have October 7 recognized by literary clubs and schoolchildren of the state as the annual anniversary celebration of the poet's birthday. It was adopted, and later the same year Samuel M. Ralston, governor of Indiana, issued a proclamation that the poet's birthday be observed statewide as "Riley Day." Greenfield schools invited several of the poet's personal friends to participate in the first program. The following year, Riley himself came to the celebration. Schoolchildren paraded in the streets, and when the poet's car passed by, they threw in bouquets of flowers, covering him. Each year, Riley Day added more events, and eventually it was extended to three days. The festival is financed by rental fees for the artist booths plus a 10 percent commission on everything over $1,000 that is sold. Work on the annual event is voluntary, headed by a specially selected chairman.

Indianapolis

"500" FESTIVAL

Held annually, May
Sports

The "500" Festival is a month-long event climaxed by the famous Indianapolis 500 Mile Race on Memorial Day in late May. For more than 20 years, a variety of programs, such as the "500" Festival Memorial Parade, the selection of a queen, art exhibits, bridge tournaments and special children's activities, have been offered. The festival opens May 1 with the mayor's breakfast and caravan around the Indianapolis Motor Speedway Track. This officially launches the program, including opening day at the track a week later and two weeks later the weekend of qualifications for the big race. More than 300,000 persons attend and view the parade, which is held the day before the race. The parade, seen on national television, features floats, entertaining musical groups and celebrities. The famous race itself originated more than 60 years ago and, of course, is still extremely popular. Working on the "500" Festival is a year-round job involving more than 5,000 volunteers. It is supported by ticket sales and membership in the "500" Festival Associates, Inc.

Indianapolis

ROMANTIC FESTIVAL

Held annually, April
Cultural

The Romantic Festival is held every year the last two weekends in April at Clowes Memorial Hall of Butler University. Its purpose is to revive interest in the forgotten music of the nineteenth century. It was the idea of Frank Cooper, pianist and teacher at the university. Each year, the festival centers on a different composer, such as Henset, Rubinstein, Swendsen, de Beriot, Ernest, Dohnanyi or Joachim. The repertoire is based entirely on neglected romantic composers and works. It features evening concerts, which may be orchestral, choral, cham-

ber music or even ballet. Guest performers are featured. Among notables who
have performed have been pianists Raymond Lewenthal and Gunnar Johansen,
violinist Aaron Rosand, cellist Jascha Silverstein and the Butler Ballet, directed
by George Verdak. The culturally oriented festival attracts more than 10,000
music fans from 40 states. Since the first festival in 1968, more than 100,000
have attended. The festival committee continually strives for a balanced series
of programs. Work is done by a paid director with some local volunteer help.
The festival is financed by Butler University, grants, contributions and admissions to concerts.

Lafayette

FEAST OF THE HUNTERS' MOON

Held annually, October
Ethnic, pageantry

The Feast of the Hunters' Moon recalls through pageantry the traditional eighteenth-century gathering of the early French settlers and Indians at Fort Ouiatenon. The reenactment is as accurate as possible. Ouiatenon was home for
several French families from Canada and for the Ouiatenon Indian tribe, neither
of whom was loyal to either the British or Americans. Though the area was
never considered to be a major strategic point in the American Revolution, it
still had its moments of glory. George Rogers Clark sent detachments headed
by Leonard Helm and Daniel Maurice Godfrey de Linctoto to the post to try for
the loyalty of the Indians. Henry Hamilton, the British lieutenant governor at
Detroit passed through on his way to recapture Vincennes from the rebels. Similar
events are recalled each year after the harvest is in and the leaves change colors.
People from all over Indiana gather. October was the time of the landing of the
voyageurs or traders, to trade goods, gossip and enjoy themselves. Festival events
today include primitive Indian chants, French folk songs, blasts from muzzle-
loading rifles and military cannons. Costumed artisans demonstrate traditional
crafts needed 200 years ago for survival: blacksmithing, spinning, weaving,
candle dipping, gunsmithing, leatherworking, lantern making, rush weaving and
coopering. Foods featured are those cooked over an open fire. Both French and
Indian foods are featured, as well as pork chops, applesauce, corn, fry bread
and herb teas. More than 50,000 attend the event, which began in 1968, when
only 900 people came. It is financed through admission fees and profit sharing.
A paid staff of three plus many local volunteers work on details, continually
researching such items as clothing, foods and events to make the festival even
more authentic.

Mitchell

PERSIMMON FESTIVAL

Held annually, September
Harvest, economic

The Persimmon Festival is celebrated the last full week in September, when the persimmons are ripe and ready to be harvested and enjoyed in puddings and other dishes. Persimmons seem to thrive in this part of the country. Persimmon flowers are yellowish-green and produce a fruit about an inch in diameter. One tree in Posey County is 13.5 feet in circumference and bears more than a ton of fruit. Ripe persimmons are considered nutritious, and the wood of the tree extremely fine-grained and hard. Persimmon trees grow wild in the area around and in Mitchell, and the festival is really a harvest celebration. Events include exhibits, window displays, a queen contest for high school students, a flea market, a parade, a Persimmon Ball, vesper services and a candlelight tour at Spring Mill State Park. Concession stands sell persimmon pudding and ice cream. There is also a persimmon pudding contest, and arts and crafts. The festival attracts more than 25,000 persons annually. The event is financed by fees for commercial tents, flea market and carnival rides. Most events take place on Main Street. It was originated in 1947 by the late George Bishop, then principal of Mitchell High School. He felt that the persimmon was different and deserved to be introduced to the world.

Peru

CIRCUS CITY FESTIVAL

Held annually, July
Economic

The Circus City Festival is held every year the third week in July, Wednesday through Saturday, with a preview the preceding Saturday. There are 10 circus performances with more than 200 youngsters as well as famous names performing. More than 50,000 visitors come to see the performances, the Circus Museum and the melodramas and to enjoy the carnival rides. Also popular is the circus parade, held at 10 a.m. the last day. The 125-unit parade has a herd of six elephants, eight cage wagons with lions, tigers, pumas and leopards, nine marching bands, a variety of floats with a circus theme and two calliopes. Dozens of clowns dance along the parade route. The festival dates back to the days when local merchants marked the first of May, the start of the circus season, with sales and events, calling them Circus Days and Circus Dollar Days. By 1956, former circus performers living in Peru began to take an active interest in reviving Circus Day. In earlier times, Peru was winter headquarters for 10 top circuses. The Circus Historical Society also held its national convention in Peru. A group of local citizens, the Peru Jaycees, sponsored the convention, arranging for a wagon train tour, exhibits and a banquet. The tour included a stop at Ben Wallace's former winter circus quarters, now a big dairy farm that still has the elephant and cat buildings. The idea of a festival came in 1957, but it wasn't until 1958 that the Peru Chamber of Commerce Retail Division promoted the event. The first Circus City Festival was held, drawing 15,000 people. A year later, the festival was incorporated as the Circus City Festival, Inc. It went from a rented tent for circus acts to a concrete arena. It is supported through circus association memberships, ticket sales and donations from businesses.

Iowa

Decorah

NORDIC FEST

Held annually, July
Ethnic

The Nordic Fest comes the last full weekend in July, with events held throughout the city in churches, schools, the college, the business district, parks and homes. It runs from Friday through Sunday and celebrates the area's Norwegian heritage through arts, crafts, food, dances, songs, lectures, concerts, sports and museum visiting. It begins with a Norwegian Festival Parade, the Norse Fire Celebration and folk costume show. There are several concerts, featuring local choral groups, a Grieg program and a folk music presentation. Dances are performed by Decorah's Nordic dancers and guest Scandinavian dancers from other cities and communities. There are also Norse plays for the children. Special Norwegian and English church services commemorate the fest. Bus tours are offered of the city and the fest area, including two outstanding Decorah homes. There is also a walking tour of the Home of the Trolls. Trolls are the Norwegian version of the pixie or elf. There are continuous displays of arts, crafts, food demonstrations, and heirloom quilting and sales by local artists. During the event, both the Norwegian-American Museum complex and the Porter House Museum are open to visitors. As many as 60,000 attend each year's fest. Over 1 million have come since that first fest in 1967. The fest incorporates the ideas of the Luther College Woman's Club, who had sponsored a Scandinavian Festival Day since 1936. The entire community felt it was a good idea and expanded it to three days. The Nordic Fest was an attempt to preserve the Norwegian heritage of the early settlers and their arts, crafts, culture and institutions. The fest is authentic and carefully tries to avoid commercialism. Planning for the fest is a year-round project of the Nordic Fest Committee, consisting of a 12-member board of directors and the entire community. It is maintained through membership in the committee with three kinds of membership and dues, from admission fees, from food sales and from the sale of fest medals. Decorah is near the Wisconsin and Minnesota borders, about 60 miles south of Rochester, Minnesota.

Des Moines

DRAKE RELAYS

Held annually, April
Sports

The Drake Relays are a sports competition for high school and college students. They are an annual event, always held the last full weekend in April. The relays date back to April 1910 and were the idea of John L. Griffith, athletic director at Drake University and later commissioner of the Big Ten Conference. All of today's events are held in Drake Stadium at Drake University. The relays, which actually cover other sports in addition to track, continually expand. The relays were the "front runner" in recognizing women in athletics by including them in the annual event. The event is held in April because it is now part of the "circuit"—Texas Relays, Kansas Relays—and, when the weather warms up, the relays move north. Today, the relays include competitions in sailing, bowling, trap and skeet, golf, tennis and bicycling and a marathon. The Drake Relays continue to expand under the direction of the Des Moines Festival Commission, which has jurisdiction over them. Annual attendance is about 34,000, with the relays still the most popular feature. The original purpose was to showcase the relays, but somehow it caught on and grew into much more. When it began in 1910, there were only 100 spectators for the one-day event. The spectators outnumbered the competitors. Eventually contestants came from schools in Nebraska, Minnesota and Wisconsin between 1912 and 1914, with Purdue and Michigan from the Western Conference coming in 1915. Even World War I didn't stop the relays. By the 1920s, the nation was more sports-minded, and the Drake Relays were national news, taking entries from all over but with continued emphasis on the Midwest and Southwest. By 1922 the one-day relays had gone to two days to accommodate larger audiences and more contestants. A year later, attendance zoomed to 10,000. Entries included schools like Notre Dame, Oregon State, Miami and Texas. Three years later, the relays were moved to a new Drake Stadium, attendance soared to 14,000 and the number of athletes to 1,500. The first Drake Relays Queen chosen to rule over the 1934 relays was

Martha Stull of Northwestern University. Two years later, the audience totaled 20,000. The Drake Relays are often referred to by the media as a showcase for the Olympics. Among the athletes who participated in the relays down through the years was the late Jesse Owens. The roll call of track and field participants reads like a who's who of sports. Preparations for the event are handled by volunteers from the business world. The event has become self-supporting through admission fees.

Des Moines

IOWA STATE FAIR

Held annually, August
Economic

The Iowa State Fair is more than 100 years old and is still going strong. The annual fair is held for 11 days in the second half of August. The fair became known to millions via the Philip Strong novel, *State Fair*, made into a film. Although it is considered to be one of the best agricultural expositions in the country, by 1962 it had more industrial exhibits. More than half a million people go to the fair every year. Visitors entertain themselves at the midway, eat at various booths and restaurants on the fairgrounds as well as watch demonstrations of family living, health contest and future farmers competition. There are also arts and crafts exhibits, fireworks, farm animal teams pulling contests and dozens of other events. A recent addition to the fair's Cattle Barn is the multimedia livestock center, where cattlemen and others interested can sit and watch the record of an animal be viewed and judged. The fair hosts eight national livestock shows with more than $65,000 in premium money offered. Entertainment also gets star billing at the fair. In the past there's been Lawrence Welk, Neil Sedaka and Johnny Cash plus a variety of ethnic folk songs and dances, usually German and Swedish, tracing the state's early pioneer heritage. The fair started as a three-day county event in October 1854 in Fairfield on six acres of land. Today, it is fully recognized and a state-sanctioned fair held on a 394-acre fairgrounds in Des Moines. A livestock exhibit numbered 500 in 1854. By 1975, it was 13,867 head of top livestock. Early fairs drew about 10,000 people. Today it's close to 1 million. The greatest number of events still part of the fair was added between 1880 and 1930. These included special church services, tractor pulls, horse racing, auto races and thrill events like biplanes, high diving horses and auto-to-airplane transfer. In 1927, the fair was visited by both Lindbergh and Chamberlain, soon after their Atlantic triumphs. A great deal of space and time is devoted to youth, Future Farmers of the Midwest. The 4-H Club participation in the fair began in 1916 and has continued to be part of it. Today, the FFA (Future Farmers of America) is also an important part of the fair. The fair is supported through entry fees, rental fees, admission charges, state aid and contributions.

Indianola

U.S. NATIONAL HOT AIR BALLOON RACES

Held annually, July/August
Sports

The U.S. National Hot Air Balloon Races are a 10-day event held in late July/early August at the Simpson College campus. It was started in July 1970 to bring the sport of ballooning into the area of competitive sports. The annual competition is to select a national champion balloonist in ways similar to other sports and following a like pattern. Only 11 participated in the first event, but by 1977 there were 173 competitors. Features of the races are several flights or tasks flown. Each has a different purpose to enable judges to rate a pilot's skill in handling his craft or balloon. The races are always held at approximately the same time of year because the wind is lightest and rainfall the lowest, both important to ballooning. Each year, additional new tasks are part of the competition to determine the better pilot skill. The races also have a great economic impact on Indianola, with 250,000 spectators showing up. More than a million have attended this event since its start. The city has become the ballooning capital of the nation, a direct result of these races. The governor and state senators often attend the opening ceremonies. A volunteer force of 4,000 each donate 10 hours of work for six months prior to the event. In 1978, Indianola was voted by the pilots as the permanent home of the Nationals. It is financed through entry fees, concession fees and donations.

Pella

TULIP TIME

Held annually, May
Ethnic, economic, ecology

Tulip Time is held every year the second Thursday, Friday and Saturday in May, when the tulips are in bloom. It recalls through pageantry the Dutch ancestry of Pella. It is not a commercialized event. There are no stands or sellers. It always opens with a Dutch worship service at the First Reformed Church, 11 a.m. the first day, followed by a recital of Dutch organ music at the Second Reformed Church. Afternoon activities begin at 1 p.m. with Dutch dancers, the Parade of Provinces with floats, coronation of the Tulip Queen, street scrubbers who actually scrub the street and the Volks Parade of bands, unusual floats and creative individual units. The burgemeester and town crier lead the parade through the city's business district and around the park. The Dutch dances feature more than 250 girls, who perform native folk dances of the Netherlands. Clad in authentic costumes, the girls are from local schools. Square dances are held both Friday and Saturday evening. Stage acts are featured every afternoon and evening with an admission fee required. Community tours are led by the Rotary Club with transportation to Tulip Lanes, parks, formal gardens and points of historic interest. Each tour bus has a guide. There is a charge. Displays of artists' arrangements of prize-winning tulips are sponsored by the Pella Garden Club Flower Show. Pella's central business district has stores and shops with old Dutch fronts, creating an Old World atmosphere. Tulip fans can visit without charge both the formal Tulip Gardens at Fair Haven and the Sunken Gardens with a Dutch windmill, a wooden shoe-shaped lagoon and blooming tulip beds. Each festival attracts 100,000 persons. Since its start, more than 2 million have enjoyed the festival, which goes back to 1935, when Pella High School students presented a musical, *Tulip Time in Pella*. In the audience were members of the local chamber of commerce who felt that the operetta was a natural with the community's Dutch heritage and good for business. At that time, Pella's only tulips were in wooden pots made by a local cabinetmaker. The town decided at a meeting to plant tulip bulbs and did so. The following year, they enlisted the aid of a tulip grower and broker from the Netherlands for advice about the planting and care of the tulip. That same year, civic and business leaders revived a long forgotten historical society to handle the festival and preserve Dutch heirlooms. This society has been responsible for the purchase and restoration of several buildings and grounds, now the Pella Historic Museum and Park, one block east of the town square. Within this complex is the boyhood home of Wyatt Earp, Dutch Museum, Van Spanckeren General Store, a log cabin, pottery shop, Beason–Blommers Grist Mill and pond, Sterrenburg Library, Birdsall Delft display, Van Maanen collection, costume display room, blacksmith shop and the wooden shoemaker's shop. All may be visited during the festival. Restaurants offer special Dutch foods during the festival, which became a five-day event. During World War II, with the rationing of gasoline and other restrictions, it became a three-day patriotic pageant, "Defenders of the Flag." Parades were discontinued, but a giant auction in 1946 netted more than $7,000, which was donated for the relief of the people of Holland. This was also the revival of the Tulip Time Festival, and in 1947, Pella marked its centennial year. Most of today's festival program is held at Tulip Torne, a tower with twin pylons more than 65 feet high, erected as a memorial to the early settlers. The tower's stage is used for festival performances. Tulip Time Festival, now known as Tulip Time, was Iowa's official bicentennial event in 1976. Work on the festival is done entirely by all the residents, who work on it year-round. It is supported through tour fees, bleacher seats at performances and admission charges to the Pella Historical Village.

Kansas

Dodge City

DODGE CITY DAYS

Held annually, July
Historic, economic

Dodge City Days conjures up memories of Marshal Dillon, Boot Hill and many other Western ideas in an area that is mid-America. The old days are relived annually in late July for six days of pageantry, melodrama and anything associated with time past. Its purpose is "to celebrate our history and commemorate the Old West." In addition to shootouts between the marshal and the bad guy, there's a rodeo, Old West parades, dances, a horse show, carnival and public picnic. The event started in July 1960 and within the past few years has been attracting record crowds of 50,000, usually tourists looking for something to do. Various events are held in city parks, streets, halls and the arena. It is financed through paid admissions and business donations.

Lawrence

KANSAS RELAYS

Held annually, April
Sports

The Kansas Relays is a top track and field event that dates back to April 21, 1923. Its existence is credited to John Outland, a former Kansas University student who went to medical school at the University of Pennsylvania. He was so influenced by the Pennsylvania Relays that upon returning to Kansas he convinced the athletic director, Dr. Forrest C. Allen, to start a track and field event. With the help of the Kansas track coach, Karl Schlademan, the first meet was set. Dr. John Outland is fondly known as the father of the Kansas Relays. The event went from one to three days and was expanded to include women's events and a marathon. It is an annual event, attracting up to 17,000 spectators at Hershberger Track. There is an admission charge, which varies each season. The Kansas Relays attract world-class track athletes such as Ivory Crockett and Cliff Branch. Work on the event is by volunteer help, which includes business-men, students and teachers at the university. It is financed through gate receipts and the university's Athletic Department.

Lindsborg

SWEDISH HOMAGE FESTIVAL

Held biennially, October, odd-numbered years; next: 1985
Ethnic

Svensk Hyllningsfest, or Swedish Homage Festival, is a biennial event held in
odd-numbered years for three days during the second week in October. It seeks
to honor Swedish pioneer settlers of the area, its Swedish heritage and Smoky
Valley. Local residents dress in Swedish costumes and host a variety of events
for visitors. These include Swedish folk dances, songs, band music, Swedish
art displays, crafts and a tasty smorgasbord. The event begins with a union
church service at Bethany Lutheran Church the first evening. The first full day
features the crowning of the Hyllningsfest Queen, who is always a senior citizen
of Swedish descent. This is followed by Swedish games for children and performances by the Svenskarnas Dag Girls' Choir and the Lindsborg Swedish Folk
Dancers. The smorgasbord is at Bethany College. It is the most popular event,
with tickets sold out well in advance of the entire fest. Usually there's a homecoming concert the second evening at Bethany College and the crowning of the
Homecoming Queen. The final day is highlighted by an American Swedish parade
in the morning, a variety of afternoon activities and folk dancing in the downtown
area at 6 p.m., ending with a concert and dance. The fest is held every other
year because of the work involved preparing for it. Local people devote an entire
year to the preparations. Fest events are citywide and take place at various
locations. The event is self-supporting through smorgasbord tickets and entertainment fees. The event goes back to 1941, when local businesses and the
chamber of commerce decided to do something different for the community
pertaining to the area's heritage and culture. They studied several festivals and
decided on a Swedish one, patterned along the lines of the Holland Festival in
Michigan. The fest was discontinued during World War II, but by 1948 there
was an interest in reviving it. At first it was held every year, but the amount of
work put into it made it difficult to hold annually. It was decided to hold it in
odd-numbered years only. More than 50,000 people attend each event.

Kentucky

Berea

KENTUCKY GUILD OF ARTISTS AND
CRAFTSMEN SPRING FAIR

Held annually, May
Economic

The three-day Kentucky Guild of Artists and Craftsmen Spring Fair is held in
mid-May at the Indian Fort Theater, an outdoor amphitheater, part of the Berea

College Forest, about three miles east of Berea on Kentucky Highway 21. Its purpose is to preserve and develop Kentucky arts and crafts as well as to help guild members sell their work and earn enough to keep the guild going. The fair has more than 100 exhibitors, all sheltered under handmade striped canopies, now a trademark of the annual spring fair. Traditional basketmakers, quilters, blacksmiths, knifemakers, whittlers and even cornshuck doll makers are representative of the state's pioneer craft heritage. In addition to the traditional skills of almost 200 years ago, there are also contemporary craftsmen working in clay, fiber, metal, wood and leather. Recently added are painters, printmakers and sculptors, who work in a variety of styles and media. Also featured are special educational demonstrators who spin, weave, throw pottery, turn the wood lathe, split shingles, grind corn, dip candles and dye with natural materials. Entertainment reflects the sounds of Kentucky: bluegrass and country music concerts. There are daily puppet shows and theater. The fair has been host to an estimated 120,500 since it began in 1967. The last fair reported sales in excess of $75,000. The event supports itself by admission charges and by commissions from the sale of the crafts. The guild, formed in 1961, is a membership nonprofit organization with more than 450 participating artists and craftsmen.

Frankfort

CAPITAL EXPO

Held annually, June
Ethnic, folkloric

Capital Expo is a two-day event held in early June, usually the first weekend. It showcases the talent and folkloric heritage of Kentucky. There are arts, crafts, fireworks, children's games, hot air balloon races, live entertainment, educational exhibits, antiques, regional and ethnic foods, jeep rides and performances by the Louisville Ballet Company and celebrities like country-western singer Charley Rich. Musical performances and concerts offer classical, popular and jazz. There is a special children's area where they learn to do arts and crafts associated with Kentucky folklore, entertainment and even a frog jumping contest. Heritage crafts at the Capitol Plaza Area include sheep shearing, carding, dying, spinning and weaving by the Fleece and Flax Guild. Foods reflect the heritage of the state and include almost everything from pioneer fare to varied ethnic cuisines. There's poke sallet, cheese, breads, corn on the cob, pastries, country ham and biscuits, fresh ground sausages, ice cream and sassafras tea. Expo was started in 1974, patterned after the folklife event in Washington, D.C. Preparations for Expo are handled by volunteers and some paid staff members. It is financed through private donations and state funds. There are also some admission charges for the sports programs. Expo takes place at the Capitol Plaza, Fountain Place, Sports Convention Center, St. Clair Mall and Old State Capitol.

Louisville

KENTUCKY DERBY FESTIVAL

Held annually, April/May
Sports, cultural, economic

The Kentucky Derby Festival is now an annual 15-day event with more than 8 days of art exhibits, drama, sports and other events, leading up to the climax, the Kentucky Derby Horse Race, always held the first Saturday in May. The race, held at historic Churchill Downs, is for thoroughbred race horses, and the competition is keen. The more than century-old race never lasts more than two minutes, sometimes less. Approximately 100,000 fans crowd into Louisville for the big race and to participate in the different festival events prior to the race. The festival, which started with a parade in 1956, has grown each year to include several programs for all ages. Traditionally, it opens the fourth Friday or Saturday in April with a "They're Off" luncheon honoring some outstanding local citizen. That same night, a Derby Ball is held, sponsored by the Fillies, Inc. This is one of the city's top social events, attended by special invitation only. The Great Balloon Race is held the next day, with more than 26 hot air balloons competing in the annual race, which became part of the festival in 1972. Thousands watch this free event. The balloons float over the city. This is also the day that Churchill Downs opens, featuring nine races a day. In addition, there is the Derby Festival Basketball Classic, with high school All-American teams from across the country competing. The last Sunday in April or first in May has four different programs, including the free Derby Festival of Cycling with a hill-and-dale road race with more than 200 top amateurs from North America participating. There is an afternoon horse show at the Rock Creek Riding Club with admission rates varying each season. In the evening there is a dance and cruise aboard the sternwheeler, *Belle of Louisville*, cruising on the Ohio River. Prices vary. Also at the riverfront is a free pop concert and fireworks on the Belvedere, a park. The festival continues the next day with a free mini-marathon, a 13-mile run, sanctioned by the Amateur Athletic Union. Participants, now numbering in the thousands, run the race on city streets, from Iroquois Park to the downtown Belvedere. In the evening, various civic groups hold dinners and entertainment programs. For the next two days there is a traditional preliminary race at Churchill Downs of famous three-year-old thoroughbreds. On Wednesday there is the Great Steamboat Race among the *Belle of Louisville*, the *Delta Queen* from Cincinnati and the *Julia Belle Swain* from Peoria, Illinois. All three compete for the championship of the riverboat world and for the Golden Antlers award. There is also entertainment at Fourth Street and River Wharf while passengers board the sternwheelers for the races. Prices vary each season. However, the evening Festival of Stars entertainment is free, sponsored by Philip Morris. The talent-packed show features big-name stars and attracts more than 20,000 spectators. On Friday there is a Kentucky Colonels Banquet and also a Derby Eve Jam of rock music with famous rock stars. Cost varies, and the events are held at different city locations. The climax comes the first Saturday in May, the big Kentucky Derby Race at Churchill Downs. Excitement runs high, and before spectators know it the race is quickly over. The festival officially ends the next day at the Kentucky Colonels' Barbecue, with special Kentucky foods. The Kentucky Derby Festival is incorporated and is a nonprofit organization. For expenses, it depends upon voluntary contributions from local businesses and individuals. Monies are used to improve festival events and to provide new and imaginative programs. A popular event, in addition to the Derby race, is the Pegasus Parade, the Thursday before the Derby. The mile-and-a-half parade features floats, specialty units, horses and performing bands. It takes place on Broadway in downtown Louisville. Bleacher seat tickets are made available. The festival is a year-long project that involves a paid staff and volunteers who work on as many as 53 committees. Festival events are citywide.

Paintsville

KENTUCKY APPLE FESTIVAL OF JOHNSON COUNTY

Held annually, October
Harvest, economic

The Kentucky Apple Festival of Johnson County is a harvesting event, ranging from one to three days, also designed "to promote and provide a market for the county's apple production." Festival events take place on Main and Court streets, which are closed to traffic. This allows visitors to walk along and browse through the apple displays and listen to band music. The festival has a Miss Apple Day Queen and a four-mile-long parade. Only once, in 1966, the festival was canceled because of a poor apple crop. In 1971, Johnson County produced 60,000 bushels of apples, a record that still stands. Activities include an Apple Baby Contest, the Miss Apple Blossom Pageant, apple art and costume competitions with awards and a festival apple ball. There is an apple auction, country music, square dancing, apple cooking contest with winning recipes printed in the following year's program and more. The apple festival entertains about 100,000 persons annually. The festival is free, with charges for foods and special shows only. The festival recently added an Antique and Special Interest Auto Show, a 10,000-meter Apple Run, a Radio Nostalgia Show and country-western entertainment.

Pineville

KENTUCKY MOUNTAIN LAUREL FESTIVAL

Held annually, May
Floral, heritage

The Kentucky Mountain Laurel Festival is a four-day event that centers around the blooming of both mountain laurel and rhododendron flowers throughout the southern Cumberland Mountains. Originally it was a one-day event in June, with the first one held June 5, 1931. Its original purpose was to preserve the area's mountain heritage. The festival still does and also honors Dr. Thomas Walker, an early explorer and resident of Kentucky. More than 10,000 attend the annual festival. Events are held at the Pine Mountain State Resort Park. There is an annual competition among Kentucky college students for the title of Mountain Laurel Festival Queen. The lucky winner presides over festival grand balls, concerts, gala picnic, a parade and crafts exhibits. The queen's coronation is held amid the mountain laurel blooms surrounding the natural amphitheater in the park. There's also a golf tournament, mountain arts and crafts and sales. The event was changed from June to late May so that colleges and universities could participate. The event is sponsored through ticket admissions, sales of arts and crafts, private donations and state funds.

South Union

SHAKER FESTIVAL

Held annually, July
Heritage

The Shaker Festival takes place the second Thursday in July and continues for 9 days. The entire 10-day event is designed to publicize the Shaker Museum and to tell the world the South Union Shaker story. This is achieved through a nightly outdoor drama, *Shakertown Revisited*, featuring Shaker songs, dances and the history of the South Union Colony from 1807 to 1922. Meals, using Shaker recipes, are served. There are also craftsmen demonstrating Shaker crafts. The first festival was held in July 1962 at Auburn (about three miles away) and was then known as the Auburn Shaker Festival. When the original Shaker site of South Union was acquired, the festival was moved to South Union. It was started by the Shaker Museum, which began operating in 1960. Museum members wanted to do something to call attention to the Shakers. It is estimated that about 2,000 people come to the annual event, more than 32,000 since it began. The event is financed through paid admissions to the play and museum and for meals. It is held on the grounds of the South Union 1824 Centre House.

Louisiana

Breaux Bridge

CRAWFISH FESTIVAL

Held biennially, even-numbered years only; next: May 1984, 1986

The Crawfish Festival is a biennial event held during even-numbered years and always the first weekend in May. Breaux Bridge is a small Cajun village in the bayou country near Lafayette, just off Interstate 10. It is referred to as the Crawfish Capital of the World, a title given it by the Louisiana Legislature in 1959. The event is sponsored by a nonprofit organization, the Breaux Bridge Crawfish Festival Association, to "foster the sale and consumption of the crawfish" by attracting thousands of people to the festivities honoring the crawfish. Local residents say that the devil crawfish is really the lobster that followed the Acadians from their home in Eastern Canada. The two-day event includes crawfish races on a specially constructed circular table with mapped out routes. There is also a carnival street parade and at least 10 tons of crawfish to eat. The little red shellfish are freshly boiled and sold on every street corner. So important is the event that all stores and shops close, and streets are roped off for the crawfish races and other events. In the background is always heard Cajun music, ranging from small bands to piano-accordians, fiddles, guitars and even cowbells. The music is played day and night, from the backs of trucks and on street corners. There's also continuous dancing in the streets. Although the festival association claims that there are no festival highlights, all music and dancing stops when the World Championship Crawfish Peeling Contest is on, with mostly women contestants. Another biggie is the World's Championship Eating Contest held on the Saturday of the festival. About six men dressed in red-and-white-striped vests and hard straw hats set up a table on a huge flatbed truck. The table is the length of the truck. It is surrounded by a dozen straight-backed kitchen chairs. There's always a stack of shiny dishpans and a butcher's scale (the same one used for the peeling competition). Usually the first person to board the truck is the past world champion. The record, which includes shelling, is the consumption of 33 pounds of crawfish in two hours. All the other contestants follow the champion and all line up, each with a dishpan of 5 pounds of crawfish to be eaten. A special signal begins the contest. Each dishpan is refilled and always carefully measured on that scale. Contestants are allowed to ask for liquid refreshments, necessary to keep the crawfish moving. There are often shouts for coffee, water and beer, with beer the most popular. The contest ends two hours later. Often there is more than one winner, sometimes as many as four. The prize is a trophy and some more crawfish to take home. The crawfish races, mentioned before, take place the last day of the festival. The Grand Championship Crawfish Race is held on a circular racing table measuring approximately eight feet across with concentric circles about six inches apart fanning out to the edge. There is a removable barrier in the center to keep the crawfish from jumping the gun. Six bronze-colored crawfish, the size of dinner plates, are dropped in the center. The crawfish fight with each other and often go in the wrong direction—still the Cajuns place bets on these erring crustaceans, a $20-million-a-year industry in the local bayous. The festival's success is evident with the town's 5,000 residents suddenly host to more than 100,000 visitors every other year. Visitors come from all over the United States.

Morgan City

LOUISIANA SHRIMP AND PETROLEUM FESTIVAL

Held annually, Labor Day weekend, September
Economic

The Louisiana Shrimp and Petroleum Festival is now a five-day event that pays tribute to the area's two top industries. The event is held over the Labor Day weekend. Events show clearly that the oil industry and fishing fleets can coexist in harmony. The festival, originally held in July, was changed to September, when the shrimp fishing fleets are in action. It was known as the Shrimp Festival and Blessing of the Fleet and was started in 1937. It is now handled by a nonprofit association chartered in 1948. The festival started out as a revival of an old Italian custom of blessing the fishing fleets before they set out to catch fish—in this case, shrimp, the jumbo size. It was the idea of a local man, Paul Acklen LeBlanc, then vice-president of the Gulf Coast Seafood Producers and Trappers Association, Inc. Previous to this, the association began to mark Labor Day in 1936, with an afternoon parade and evening dance. LeBlanc recommended that they add the fleet blessing. They did, and the ceremony was impressive, taking place in the middle of Berwick Bay with the shrimp boats circling the priest's boat for the blessing. About 143 boats were blessed. The next year, the event was held July 31. In 1939, again in July, the event was enlarged to include aquaplane and motorboat races and a half-ton of boiled shrimp, free to visitors on the wharf. In 1940, more people came, including a special excursion train from New Orleans. A long-distance swimming event was added to the program. The event continued to grow in a community that had always done well, and by 1941, the year of Pearl Harbor, Morgan City was selected as the site of a shipyard to construct floating drydocks. A big city newspaper contained a story about this, pointing out that the annual blessing of the shrimp fleet took place here, increasing the popularity of the event. Now a full-fledged festival, it was held throughout World War II years, and in 1947, the twenty-ninth anniversary of the festival, the world's first commercial offshore oil well out in the Gulf of Mexico, below Morgan City, was drilled. This changed the entire area, making shrimp and oil the two major industries. By 1948, festival officials realized that an organization was needed to handle all the details. A few involved citizens and local legislators applied to the state of Louisiana for funds to pay for the annual festival. A charter was issued to the Louisiana Shrimp Festival and Fair, Inc., with P. A. LeBlanc as president. The event was now held in mid-September. Today, it is always held over the Labor Day weekend. The top attraction still is the blessing of the shrimp fleet, but there are many more activities, focusing on both shrimps and oil. The event begins the Thursday of the weekend. Free mini-servings of shrimp and beer are served on Sunday at the waterfront docks. There is a more substantial noontime meal also Sunday at the Municipal Auditorium, where the local Civitan Club for a fee serves seafood jambalaya. Activities, designed for all ages, include the annual Football Jamboree, featuring teams from four area high schools and a three-day fishing tournament with more than $20,000 in prizes. There are also several square dances with a Children's Day in Lawrence Park on Saturday. There are field day events, which include an afternoon mini-parade with a young royal court (selected the weekend before by lottery) in charge. There is also the coronation of the Festival King and Queen, who participate in their own pageant and parade with floats. The festival includes religious services in addition to the official fleet blessing. There is also a Labor Day Regatta, sponsored by the Morgan City Power Boat Association, held on Lake Palourde. The festival, started during the 1930s Depression, now brings in thousands of tourist dollars to the area. Work on the festival is by volunteers. It is financed through a subscription "Drive for $25," memberships, emblems, souvenirs and paid admission for some festival programs. Morgan City is on an island, and during the festival visitors can go from one end to the other.

New Orleans

MARDI GRAS

Held annually, February or March; movable dates
Cultural, religious, economic

Mardi Gras day and time in New Orleans is known worldwide, and it still occurs the Tuesday before Ash Wednesday, the beginning of Lent. The beginnings of Mardi Gras go back as early as 1838, when there was only an organized street parade with street dancing by the poorer people. Masquerade balls were held by the rich and elite of the city. City annals claim that Mardi Gras celebrations are more than 250 years old and were held as soon as New Orleans was founded by Bienville. The religious significance of Mardi Gras, or "Fat Tuesday," is that it is the last day for frivolity before Lent begins. The carnival, derived from a Latin word, meaning, "Farewell to the Flesh," is a wild festive time with parties, balls and various celebrations before the fasting and penitence of Lent gets underway. The carnival season actually begins on the feast of the Epiphany, January 6, or the Twelfth Night of Christmas. This was the day that the Three Kings visited the Christ Child and paid tribute to him as the Messiah. The carnival season ends on the midnight before Ash Wednesday, when early in the morning lines of carnival goers, now penitents, go to church to receive the cross of ashes on their foreheads. The Mardi Gras theme is traced back to the poet, John Milton. When the Mistick Krewe of Comus, the first carnival society, was founded in New Orleans in 1857, that first night parade was a torchlight procession, based on the theme of the demon actors in Milton's *Paradise Lost*. Today, there are more than 65 societies involved in Mardi Gras parades. Daily parades feature Dixieland bands, magnificent and imaginative floats and dancing in the streets. Watchers reach out to the paraders to try to grab beads, bonbons and metallic Mardi Gras doubloons, considered collector's items. After every parade there is a ball. The men wear masks, and a queen is elected to reign over the evening's events. But when the Mistick Krewe of Comus was formed in 1857, it consisted only of a group of men who gathered in private to entertain friends with a party and please residents with a fancy street parade. Rex, the King of Carnival, whose parade always is held on Mardi Gras morning, came into being in 1872. The Knights of Momus also debuted that year. And eventually more and more krewes were established, each with its own special parade and ball. There are so many organizations today that it now takes two full weeks before Mardi Gras for them to be held. The social calendar grows and grows, so that often the Mardi Gras or carnival season begins earlier than January 6. In addition to the organization parades, 8 to 10 families have also organized a series of smaller parades which follow the great Rex Parade on Mardi Gras day. These include the Elks, the Krewe of Orleanians and the Krewe of Crescent City. They rent their floats, design and make their costumes and contribute to club funds for the favors or "throws" that all parades toss to bystanders. The city of New Orleans and the chamber of commerce are not involved in the expenses of Mardi Gras. The various groups pay their own way. Mardi Gras Day and Rex Parade attract more than a million people. The Rex Parade starts at 9 a.m. and is followed by others throughout the afternoon. The evening parade by Comus attracts just as many spectators. The parades are held on historic St. Charles and Canal streets. Tickets are sold to view the parades, and the prices change each year. They are sold in a set, enabling the buyer to see more than one parade. Work on the various parades is arduous and takes months well in advance of each Mardi Gras celebration. A lot of expense and imagination goes into the design of the floats and themes. The whole celebration of Mardi Gras dates back to pagan times in ancient Rome and Greece and today is a mixture of paganism and Christianity. Today, it is a tongue-in-cheek event, and the identity of the kings of carnival balls is a secret, known only to members of the organizations. Rex is the only one identified. The custom of throwing things to parade watchers probably started in the early days, when marching and riding masked paraders threw candies, oranges and lemons to the crowds. Then it got out of hand, and there was a battle of flour sacks between marchers and watchers. By the time the floats appeared with Comus, the custom of throwing something to the crowds was well established. The floats, originally pulled by mules, were pulled by horse-drawn tractors for the first time in 1850. In past years, violence caused the cancellation of Mardi Gras celebrations. The loss of tourist money to the city changed that, however, and now there is relative calm.

New Orleans

NEW ORLEANS FOOD FESTIVAL

Held annually, July
Economic, gastronomic

The New Orleans Food Festival dates back to 1968, when it was introduced to encourage local residents to patronize restaurants more and to influence tourists to make a stop in the city during the off season, summer. It is a three-day event usually the first weekend in July, although this can change. Festivities open on a Saturday at 11 a.m. at the Rivergate Exhibition Hall on Canal Street. Instead of a ribbon-cutting ceremony by city and festival officials, there is the appropriate breaking of a long large French bread. The first day's programs continue through 7 p.m. and Sunday from 11 a.m. to 6 p.m. Highlights include culinary exhibits by apprentice chefs of Les Chefs des Cuisines de la Louisianne and cooking demonstrations by prize-winning chefs. The public, which pays a small admission fee to the Exhibit Hall, eats picnic style while watching the chefs cook and create. There is an opportunity to sample all kinds of food at low cost, ranging from 50 cents to $1.50. Available for tasting are Creole shrimp, stuffed peppers, gumbo, jambalaya, trout almondine, soft shell crabs, shrimp, crab tempura, artichoke heart soup, fettucine Alfredo, cannelloni, chiles Bellenos, fried catfish, lost bread, bread pudding as well as other regional and international foods. The air-conditioned hall takes on a carnival atmosphere as people eat, talk and laugh. Musical entertainment is featured for the two days at the hall. In 1983, the festival again featured the 400-seat Gourmet Room, offering complete entrees for $5 per plate, obtainable from booths representing the city's top hotels and restaurants. There is also a cooking contest with prizes for winning recipes. While the food festival is held Saturday and Sunday, there is the additional bonus of the Gala Formal Dinner, a genuine gourmet event that traditionally ends the festival on a Monday evening. Each year it is held at a different hotel. In 1983, it was at the Sheraton New Orleans Hotel. This gourmet meal, which 15 years ago cost $35 per person, includes several different courses, complemented by the appropriate wines. The festival attracts more than 40,000 every year, the majority of them tourists. It is economically successful to the local hotel, restaurant and tourist industries. At the same time it has become a showcase for the culinary heritage and talents of the city. Festival details are handled by the New Orleans Food Festival and financed by admissions, charges for the food and gourmet meal plus contributions from local industry.

New Orleans

NEW ORLEANS JAZZ AND HERITAGE FESTIVAL

Held annually, April/May
Cultural, heritage

The New Orleans Jazz and Heritage Festival is a 10-day event in mid-April through early May designed to promote jazz and the city's heritage. Its purpose over the past few years has also been economic, to attract tourists. It hosts more than 150,000 visitors annually, a far cry from the first festival in 1969, which had 300 musicians and only 150 spectators. It started as a civic event thought up by a group of city officials. The festival was originally held at Congo Square, a small area of New Orleans off Rampart Street. In a serious effort to attract more visitors, the festival became more commercial in 1970, when George Wein, the jazz impressario, was brought in to produce and direct the event. The festival moved to the Fairgrounds Race Track, where stages and booths to sell New Orleans food and crafts were set up. Today, the festival features more than 2,000 musicians and more than 32 food booths, offering such goodies as jambalaya and roast pig. The festival highlights such notables as the new Dave Brubeck Quartet, Muddy Waters and B. B. King, plus many local favorites. Ten stages of music operate simultaneously while the food booths sell their wares. An added feature is the evening concert program aboard a Mississippi riverboat, at two hotels and at the Municipal Auditorium. There is a daily admission charge to the Fairgrounds, but it changes each year. There are no charges for the evening concerts, but this may change. Among the 10 stages of continuous and simultaneous music are a gigantic gospel tent, a jazz tent and a special performance tent. There are also four regular outdoor stages and three gazebos. The music includes jazz, rhythm and blues, gospel, Cajun, blues, folk, Latin, country-western and bluegrass, with different music added each year. The event is self-supporting.

New Orleans

ST. JOSEPH'S FEAST DAY

Held annually, March 19
Religious, ethnic

St. Joseph's Feast Day is a gala one-day religious and Italian-oriented festival
with religious services, a parade and St. Joseph altars, weighed down by tons
of Italian breads, fig cakes, vegetables and seafood. More than 150,000 Italian-
Americans celebrate St. Joseph's Day, March 19, with hundreds of thousands
of non-Italians joining in. The parade features real gondolas (on floats) with
lovely ladies in authentic Italian costumes, an ornate Sicilian cart and a St.
Joseph altar, plus marching bands and more than 1,000 Italian-Americans carrying batons decorated with red, green and white flowers. The flowers are given
to spectators in exchange for kisses. St. Joseph is the patron saint of Sicily and
is credited with saving the island from a famine. Ever since, Sicilians and those
of Sicilian descent thank the saint with religious rites and a table of food from
their harvest, sharing the food with the needy. The devotion grew over the years
and was repeated every March 19, St. Joseph's Day. Sicilian immigrants brought
this custom with them to New Orleans and continue to celebrate in the old way,
but with some innovations. The parade is a New Orleans feature with tuxedoed
marchers going through the narrow streets of the French Quarter. They carry a
mobile St. Joseph altar. Usually two days before the actual celebration outdoor
altars begin to spring up everywhere, ranging from the 50-feet-wide, three-tier
altar on the steps of St. Joseph's Church at 1802 Tulane Avenue to table-type
altars in private homes, which are open to the public to share the bounty given.
Outdoor altars are also decorated with dogwood blossoms and azaleas and then
laden with breads shaped like crowns of thorns, lilies, palms and St. Joseph's
staff. There are also fig cakes with symbolic designs, smaller breads and cookies
plus the traditional Sicilian Easter gift, the *pupa-cu-l'uova* (bread with hard-
boiled eggs inside). More than 50 volunteer cooks, 1,500 pounds of flour and
$10,000 are needed to prepare this outdoor altar. The Greater New Orleans
Italian Cultural Society is the prime mover. Home altars involve lots of work
too. One family may bake as many as 8,000 cookies and cook 300 pounds of
spaghetti and other foods to feed visitors. Part of the festivities includes a
procession to each altar by costumed children, dressed to represent various saints
as well as Jesus, Mary and, of course, Joseph. Visitors usually leave donations
at the altars to cover expenses. Most of the displayed food is given to charitable
groups. Visitors to the outdoor altar and organization-sponsored altars are given
blessed bread, a fava (lucky bean) and some *biscotti*, or cookies. Home altar
visitors get to enjoy a spaghetti dinner. The home altars are listed in local
classified ads of newspapers under ''St. Joseph Altars.'' No visitor is ever turned
away.

New Orleans

SPRING FIESTA

Held annually, April, movable date
Cultural, heritage

The 19-day Spring Fiesta consists of a series of walking and bus tours that explore New Orleans inside and out. There are stops at the antebellum Garden District and at plantation houses not open to the public at any other time. The guided tours take all day and include a hot luncheon. Additional afternoon and evening walking tours feature a reception with refreshments, usually punch and cookies. Cost of the tours varies, based on length and when taken. The Spring Fiesta gets underway on the Friday after Easter Sunday with an evening in historic Jackson Square. Here the coronation of the Spring Fiesta Queen takes place. When she is selected, she mounts a float to lead the Night in Old New Orleans coronation parade, covering the French Quarter from Bourbon Street to Chartres Street to Canal Street to Rivergate. The parade features costumes of days gone by. Flower-decorated horses and carriages as well as costumed participants emphasize the culture of Old Louisiana, setting the theme for the fiesta tours. The event attracts almost half a million people, helping the city's economy greatly. The first Spring Fiesta was held in 1937 but not officially governed until the Spring Fiesta Association, a nonprofit group, was formed in 1939 to "organize and promote the event." It is not a commercial event. Its sole purpose is cultural exchange. The event is the work of the association on a voluntary basis. Fees collected for the tours and other events are used to cover necessary expenses for staging the fiesta. It also includes jazz bands that play on every street corner. The Spring Fiesta Association has the cooperation of top civic, cultural, social, patriotic and educational groups in New Orleans and nearby areas in holding the annual event.

New Orleans

SUGAR BOWL CLASSIC

Held annually, New Year's Day, January 1 or January 2 if New Year's
Day is on Sunday
Sports

The Sugar Bowl Classic is a big annual football game that dates back to the Depression. Today, it is one of the top amateur athletic events in American sports. The New Orleans Mid-Winter Sports Association, sponsors of the annual classic, came into existence in late October 1934, when it placed in escrow

$30,000 for the promotion of the "inaugural Sugar Bowl Football Classic." The idea of a New Year's Day football game in New Orleans, however, dates back to 1927, when the idea was presented by Colonel James M. Thomson, publisher of the *New Orleans Item*, and the paper's sports editor, Fred Digby. It was Digby who dubbed it the Sugar Bowl. The association raised money through membership dues. Officers included a president, vice-president, treasurer and secretary. There were 39 original organizers. By 1948, a junior membership was added to the association. The charter was amended in 1954 to admit two regular membership juniors, age 27, with at least one year of service on different committees. The association is not affiliated with any political parties, and any reserve funds are used for "charitable, religious or educational purposes." This was carried out so that a percentage of the TV and radio receipts would be donated to the National Foundation for Infantile Paralysis (March of Dimes) for three years. The first eligible teams to play were selected December 2, 1934, by the association's executive committee. They were Tulane University's Green Wave, unbeaten in the South, and Temple University's Owls, the only unbeaten team in the North. The trophy for the winning team was a real antique silver sugar bowl, donated by the Waldhorn Company, Inc. The bowl was made in London in 1830 during the reign of King George IV. The winning team holds it for one year and then receives a replica to keep. The winning team in the first classic was Tulane, overcoming a 14-point deficit to win 20–14, thereby establishing a sports classic. After the 1936 game, the stadium had to be enlarged to meet the demand for seats. Two years later, the Sugar Bowl outgrew the stadium. By January 13, 1939, there were completed plans to enlarge the stadium and raise $550,000. Forty days later the $550,000 bond issue was completely sold. The project was completed in time for the 1940 kickoff. By 1947, there was another bond issue of $500,000 for a larger stadium. Work began by May. The stadium enlargements and improvements, financed by the Sugar Bowl, constitute an investment of more than $1.5 million. The Sugar Bowlers are credited with the world's largest double-decker steel stadium, on the Tulane University campus. The Sugar Bowl Classic is now the climax of the Sugar Bowl Week, which begins with a Sailing Regatta on Lake Pontchartrain and other events. Today, the game is played in the 18,000-plus-seat Superdome in the downtown New Orleans business district. The event is self-supporting.

Shreveport

HOLIDAY IN DIXIE

Held annually, April
Cultural, economic

Holiday in Dixie is a 10-day event to welcome spring and focus in on the achievements of local citizens. More than 300,000 tourists come to enjoy the festivities, which include sports competitions in tennis, handball, pirogue racing, bowling and checkers. There are arts, crafts, a beauty pageant and a parade with 150 units. Added to the event is the Queen Holiday in Dixie Pageant and the Classic Parade. Events are on a citywide basis. There are also art shows, flower exhibits, crawfish-eating contests, crawfish races, banjo and fiddling contests and concerts. The event is financed and administered annually by a group of local businessmen known as the Ark-La-Tex Ambassadors, Inc., with duly elected officers.

Shreveport

LOUISIANA STATE FAIR

Held annually, October
Economic

The Louisiana State Fair is a 10-day affair in late October attracting several hundred thousand people annually to the 156-acre fairgrounds. Special features include a mile-long midway, "Gladway" with rides, eating places and the Royal American Shows. Large exhibit areas are in buildings such as the Merchants Building, General Exhibits Building, Vacationland Building, Education Building, Family Exhibit Center and College Exhibit Building. The Hirsch Memorial Coliseum, whose roof was once considered the world's largest copper dome, is the site of the championship finals of the Louisiana Rodeo Association, held the last three days of the fair. There are also crab races at the Racetrack Grandstand, where music shows are held, free to fairgoers. There's a Fairgrounds Football Stadium, site of several games, including the annual grudge game during the fair. In addition to all the buildings and stadiums, the fair boasts huge barns, site of the annual All-American Livestock Exhibition, featuring the state's best cattle, horses, poultry, swine and sheep. Owners share in more than $80,000 in prizes and premiums at judging time. There is also a Junior Livestock Auction and sale of feeder calves. The fair dates back to 1906, when it was established to combat the cotton crop failure of 1905. The destructive boll weevil began its work back in 1896, finally succeeding in wiping out cotton in the state. Since the area depended upon cotton and knew almost nothing about the diversification of crops, northern Louisiana almost went bankrupt. As a way to save the area, businessmen and others decided to hold an agricultural exposition or fair as a means of educating local farmers. Next to cotton fields were idle lands where farmers were taught how to make use of the land and grow other crops, raise cattle and start a dairy industry, one of the state's top industries today. The fair has been held ever since. It is financed through paid admissions, entry fees and help from the state.

Maine

Boothbay Harbor

WINDJAMMER DAYS

Held annually, July
Heritage, boating

Windjammer Days is a three-day salute to the days of wooden sailing ships and iron men. The area claims that this is the original gathering of tall ships. They've been at it since 1962. Coastal schooners from Camden and Rockport sail into Boothbay Harbor the first afternoon of the mid-July event. They are met by a flotilla of all kinds of vessels, which include the official boat with a playing band on board. There is an official Miss Windjammer selected the night before to preside over the festivities. The pageant to select Miss Windjammer is complete with entertainment and a special orchestra. Locally, it is a coveted title. Windjammer Days begins with a 10 a.m. boat parade. The boats are decorated with flying flags, and they compete for prizes in various classes. The boats include antique, modern sail and power ones. There is also an arts and crafts show and sale most of the day, held on the lawn of the American Legion Home near the footbridge so that viewers can also see the boat parade and other water-related programs. At 1 p.m. there's a Windjammer Days Street Parade, with armed forces groups marching and original floats of local clubs and businesses. Immediately after the parade come the windjammer schooners under full sail, entering the harbor and met by the official boats. Local restaurants offer shore dinners, and there's a lobster stew supper served (for a fee) at the Boothbay Harbor Methodist Church, followed by a band concert on the lawn of the Greek Revival Library. There are various band concerts and street dances throughout the town. The windjammers leave Boothbay Harbor the last morning of the festivities. Thousands crowd the area to watch them.

Kennebunkport

NATIONAL DUMP WEEK

Held annually, July, Labor Day
Satiric, ecology

National Dump Week comes in early July with the famous trash parade held the Thursday after the Fourth of July holiday and doesn't end until Labor Day in September, the longest week on record. If the Fourth of July occurs on a Thursday, the event begins a week later. Kennebunkport proudly boasts "that it has America's Number One Dump." And the dump marked its bicentennial in 1976 together with the country's bicentennial. Kennebunkport dates back to 1653, but town folk say that residents were too poor to throw anything away for 123 years. Climax of the obvious put-on is the Giant Trash Parade, which goes through the seaport town to the famous dump, reigned over by a Miss Dumpy, selected the previous night. The contest features young women dressed in Clorox bottles, beer cans, empty cottage cheese containers and old newspapers. The most original dump-like contestant has the best chance to win. The parade, which attracts more than 10,000 spectators every year, features more than 30 floats, each based on junk. Each float is also made from junk. Themes are anti-littering. For example, one year there was one float that featured an outhouse at one end and a tame goat and label reading, "Litter Gets Our Goat," on the other end. Another float featured a local resident with top hat and tails riding on top of a horse-drawn, high-wheeled harvester completely covered with milk containers, dog food cans and ketchup bottles. Many visitors are puzzled about National Dump Week and whether or not to take the whole thing seriously, but they enjoy the satirical celebration. All the festivities came about around 1965, when Ed Mayo, an artist, together with a number of other local residents with a sense of humor organized the Kennebunkport Dump Association. The association devotes its time to the marking of more than 200 years of independent dumping. The association and its founders are wary of incinerators. The KDA also presents mock-serious awards every year. For example, there was the Ripoff Award to the oil companies and the KDA Ten Cent Award to the New England Telephone and U.S. Postal Service. The association's stock is more than 275 million worthless shares of bits of elm wood from dead trees found at the dump site. The National Dump Week observance also has a dump art exhibit at the Community House. It strangely resembles New York's avant-garde art. Some visitors buy the stuff, like the styrofoam packing pieces and rusty tailpipes. The KDA issues Dump Trading Stamps, redeemable for trash, and there's a Dump Credit Card, entitling the holder to national dump visiting privileges and to avoid the use of the roadside. The association, however, is serious about antipollution and by the tongue-in-cheek National Dump Week conveys its message clearly. The event is financed through the sale of souvenir buttons, medals, posters and local contributions. It has been featured on national television in the United States and in Japan.

Pittsfield

CENTRAL MAINE EGG FESTIVAL

Held annually, fourth Saturday in July
Economic

This one-day festival is designed to call attention to the area's egg and chicken industry. More than 20,000 visitors spend the day in this town of 4,200 residents.

Preparations begin 6 a.m. the morning of the festival. Eight women volunteer cooks put on the fire the world's largest skillet, teflon-coated, 10 feet in diameter and weighing 300 pounds. The first eggs cracked into this frying pan officially begins the festival, and even at this early hour there are visitors to sample the eggs being fried to order and flipped with four-foot spatulas onto slices of buttered bread, toasting in the middle of the giant frying pan. There are also regular-size skillets for frying eggs, ham and potatoes. There's coffee too. Breakfast is usually over by 8:30 a.m. Festival officials estimate that by then more than 4,000 eggs, 2,000 slices of ham and 1,000 pounds of potatoes have been eaten. The festival continues at Manson Park, where there are rides, games, a stage with entertainment and various booths and stalls selling eggs, souvenirs and drinks. The festival dates back to 1972, started by two former newspapermen, Toby Strong and Donald Brough. They wanted to focus on the area's egg industry, overshadowed by the state's potato crop. The giant skillet was designed and donated by Alcoa. An appropriate-size propane gas burner to heat the huge frying pan was developed by Maingas. The skillet is stored in an airplane hangar after each festival. When it's taken out of storage, it is thoroughly steam-cleaned and made ready for service. Also, one of the original cooks, Betty Shorey, continues to be part of the festival committee and one of 30 women taking turns at the skillet. Festival goers who find the breakfast event too early can catch up at lunch, served 11:30 a.m. to 2 p.m. The big attraction is the 10-inch omelette, prepared by a new shift of cooks. These omelets contain peppers, onions, mushrooms, ham and cheese. These are not prepared in the giant skillet but in normal-size ones. In between breakfast and lunch, there's a parade, a teenage pageant with a pre-selected queen, a window decorating contest, egg-related cartoons, arts and crafts. There is also an agricultural tent with live exhibits of golden eggs, winners in the World's Largest Egg Contest with entries from all over the world. Only chicken eggs may be entered. Imposters are uncovered through special tests. The eggs are put in water and judged by displacement tests at the University of Maine in Orono. The winner is gold-plated after the inside is removed. At noon there is a team of parachutists who jump down to earth, carrying a favorite chicken. These chickens later compete in the chicken flying contest, with roosters allowed. To date the record is 22 feet. By late afternoon there is a chicken barbecue (not the losers in the flying contest), followed in the evening by bandstand entertainment and a fireworks display. The festival is highly successful and economically beneficial to the town. Work is done by volunteers and the festival supported by meals sold and contributions by local business.

Rockland

MAINE SEAFOODS FESTIVAL

Held annually, August
Economic

The Maine Seafoods Festival is a three-day eating event that also includes the crowning of a Maine Sea Goddess, parades and pageantry, entertaining more than 40,000 people, many from out of state. Festivities start with a 5 p.m. pageant on Friday at Fisherman's Memorial Pier. Some 32 Sea Princesses and their escorts participate. Seafood is served at nominal cost and includes a generous portion of lobster, shrimp, clam cakes, steamed cakes, fried clams and fried mussels. This festival has been held in Rockland since 1949. It was moved from nearby Camden, the site of the Maine Lobster Festival, which claimed that you could have all the lobster you could eat for only $1. People took such advantage that the festival went bankrupt. It was moved to Rockland because that city had better-organized civic groups. The name of the festival was changed because too many Maine communities said that they were the Lobster Capital of the World. Other festival events include a Friday morning pancake breakfast from 8 to 10 a.m. on the waterfront, with seafood lunches starting at 11 a.m. and continuing through the evening. King Neptune and his court and the previous year's Sea Goddess show up later in the afternoon to officially open the festivities. The Maine Sea Goddess is crowned later Friday evening. Saturday events also feature special breakfasts at 8 a.m., followed by a 10 a.m. two-mile parade through the city to the festival grounds. Seafood is served starting at 11 a.m. Sunday activities start at noon, with more seafood meals served until all is eaten. At 4 p.m., King Neptune and his court return to the deep, and the festival is over. The idea for this event and the Maine Lobster Festival, parent to the current event, is credited to Carey W. Bok, grandson of the late Cyrus H. K. Curtis, publisher of the *Saturday Evening Post*. He felt that the region needed a summer activity to attract tourists, but because of the greed of visitors in taking more lobsters than they ate, the event failed. It then moved to Rockland the following year. The festival is financed by the seafood meals, donations from the community and business leaders and sponsorships. Work on the event is by volunteers.

Maryland

Annapolis

CHESAPEAKE APPRECIATION DAYS

Held annually, October
Heritage

Chesapeake Appreciation Days are held annually the last weekend in October and involve the state's skipjacks, the country's last working sailboats that dredge for oysters. The special observance includes a race, held to preserve the heritage of these working sailboats as long as possible. They are indeed a vanishing breed. The two-day event also features land programs. It all takes place at Sandy Point State Park by the twin-span Chesapeake Bay Bridge (U.S. Route 50-301) near Annapolis. This site enables spectators to view the entire sailing race from the beach. The skipjacks are the last commercial sailing fleet in the United States. They have been dredging the Bay for oysters since the early nineteenth century. These tall ships follow a dog-leg course between the huge seven-mile bridge and old Sandy Point lighthouse. Among the participating ships have been the oldest, *Ruby G. Ford*, launched in 1891, and the newest, *Lady Katie*, launched in 1956. Most of the captains and crew are senior citizens. Their kind are dwindling since young Marylanders do not want to follow this line of hard work. The skipjack's shallow draft and movable centerboard, substituting for the deep, heavy keel aboard most sailing craft of similar size, enables the ship to navigate in shallow waters. These sailboats are capable of racing close to shore off Sandy Point so that spectators can easily watch them. Chesapeake Appreciation Days, started in 1964, are currently produced by a nonprofit volunteer group, Chesapeake Appreciation, Inc. They also have the support and cooperation of state and local governments as well as the private sector. Land events include exhibits and presentations of regional arts and crafts and more recently an air show, since aviation has had a significant role in Chesapeake's past. The air show is "Ninety-Nines International," an organization of women in aviation and includes a fly-by of classic aircraft, air-sea rescue operations and precision flying. Visitors can go aboard and visit a skipjack and the marine research vessels moored in the park lagoon, where paddleboat and canoe races are also featured. There's also a photo contest focusing on the Chesapeake and an annual "Magic with Oysters" cooking contest. There is a general admission fee each day, and it varies each year. Sandy Point gates are open from 10 a.m. to 5 p.m. each day. The event is host to more than 20,000 visitors on both land and sea, with the number continuing to grow each year.

Baltimore

MARYLAND KITE FESTIVAL

Held annually, April
Sports

The annual Maryland Kite Festival is a one-day event held the last Saturday in April, with a rain date a week later. The festival is a flying competition and also a contest for the most original kite made. The competition, however, is open to kite owners who do not make their own. The first kite event was held April 1, 1967, on the grounds of a local high school. Today, it is held at Fort McHenry. The competition begins at 11 a.m. and continues through 4 p.m., when the awards are made. The festival was inspired by one in Carmel, California, seen by a Baltimore resident, Valerie Govig, and her husband Melvin. For the first two years, it was known as the Liberty Road Kite Festival because it was sponsored by the Liberty Road Recreation Council. Its name was changed to the Maryland Kite Festival, with the competition opened up to the entire state. Judges include city officials and directors of the city zoo and sometimes artists. One of the judges is also an aerodynamicist. During the bicentennial celebration, this festival was expanded to include the First World Kite Competition, but the following year it reverted to its original concept. Approximately 300 entries are received yearly, and more than 1,000 spectators come to watch. The festival has a comprehensive judging division open only to those fliers who make their own kites. Awards are made to the following age classes: primary, through age 7; intermediate, ages 8 through 11; secondary, ages 12 through 16; unlimited; and groups and businesses for kites as advertising. Aspects of judging for 20 points each are for design/ingenuity, craftsmanship, beauty (half on the ground and half in the air), launch, control, retrieval. There are bonus points for duration of flight of 1 point per minute, a minimum of 5 and a maximum of 20 minutes or more. Awards vary but do include cash prizes and trophies. Special kite reels are awarded for the wittiest kite, most ingenious kite breakdown and assembly, largest kite, best flying three-inch or smaller kite and youngest and oldest entrant. The festival also features field events, and this division is open to all kites, whether or not made by their fliers. Events, however, are subject to wind conditions. Participants who arrive early can enter more than one field event. Age classes or restrictions apply only to the Triathalon. Events include altitude, one class for one trophy, lifting power, also one class for one trophy and the Triathalon, a three-in-one event with four age classes for four trophies: climbing speed, kite dash and reel-in. Trophies are presented to overall winners and kites to winners of heats throughout the day. Very often there are special events, such as maneuverability and kite dueling exhibitions by champions. There are also lessons in the art of kite flying. The festival is subsidized by local businesses through the Maryland Kite Society and American Kite Flyers Association. There is no admission fee to the festival or any cost to fly the kites. The festival is open to all ages but with more adults now participating. The aim of the festival is to see it expand and attract wider entries and the world's best kites. The event promotes the art and sport of kiting and continues to maintain a high quality of judging and organization. Preparations are made by the Maryland Kite Society and lots of volunteers.

Baltimore

PREAKNESS FESTIVAL

Held annually, May
Sports, cultural

The Preakness Festival is a nine-day cultural event whose climax is the famous Preakness Horse Race, held the second Saturday in May. It is similar in many ways to the Kentucky Derby Festival. This event is also designed to complement the running of the Preakness Race, referred to as the "middle jewel of racing's triple crown," and to bring more visitors to Baltimore. The race itself is more than 100 years old, with the first one run May 27, 1873. The Preakness Festival dates back to 1969; both are always in May. The city's mayor always officially opens the festival with ceremonies in the Inner Harbor area, thereby launching the first day's events, which include a fashion show, pogo stick jumping contest and Clown Day in War Memorial Plaza. The festival begins either on a Friday or Saturday, with the next day featuring the Great Preakness Balloon Race. This race, with a Gay Nineties theme, takes place at Druid Hill Park and is the highlight of the day's programs, which also include arts and crafts displays around the lake, puppet shows, hayrides, horse and buggy rides, chess and backgammon tournaments, croquet matches and strolling minstrels. The balloon race includes more than a dozen hot air balloons, which lift off from the park as early as 9:30 a.m., wind currents permitting. They race to the eastern shore of Maryland's Chesapeake Bay. The race's progress is continually announced to festival goers via radio station sky patrol planes and helicopters. The festival also includes a parade, which each year has a different theme but includes the usual military bands and marching units and floats. In addition to the parade, there's a sailboat regatta in the Inner Harbor and the annual Federal Hill Celebration. For the rest of the week, there are a variety of events. For example, the Morris Mechanic Theater sponsors a week-long "Preakness Festival of Stars," with TV, movie and country-western talent. The horse race is held either the second or third Saturday in May and begins around 5:40 p.m. at Pimlico Race Course. However, there are a series of events at the infield of the course prior to the big race. The infield opens at 9 a.m., and spectators witness a lacrosse game, continuous live musical entertainment and a chance to buy Baltimore's famed Chesapeake Bay crab cakes and Maryland fried chicken from food booths. The festival officially ends the day after the big race with a model boat race, sports car show in the Inner Harbor and outdoor arts show on the Johns Hopkins University campus. There are more than 400 festival events, and all except the horse race and evening's entertainment at Morris Mechanic Theater are free. Each year, the events multiply and the number of visitors total more than 200,000, with 75,000 just to the big race. When the festival was started in 1969, it consisted of only the race, a four-day Baltimore arts festival, the flower mart and the Fells Point Jazz Festival. The festival is sponsored by the Baltimore Promotion Council and has the backing of the Maryland Jockey Club and Pimlico Race Course. The festival is a year-round job, but intense work begins in January with volunteer help.

Deal Island

LABOR DAY SKIPJACK RACES

Held annually, Labor Day
Sports, heritage

The Labor Day Skipjack Races are an annual event dating back to 1925. Its purpose is to preserve as long as possible the declining number of skipjacks afloat. There are currently less than 25. These skipjacks are North America's only fleet of working sailboats. The skipjack is honored in an October event, too. The Labor Day races, however, are also Mariner, Tanzer 22 and open-class races. There are both land and water events, and Maryland seafood is also served. The day begins at 9 a.m. and continues through 6 p.m. This includes the selection of a Skipjack Princess. Spectators to the races have an opportunity to see these sailboats in action. At the turn of the century there were about 2,000 of them. Motorboats with automatic dredging apparatus are now displacing the skipjacks. The race covers 12 miles and is between the skipjacks and four classes of yachts. It is sponsored by the Deal Island–Chance Lions Club Eastern Shore Sailing Association. Racing begins with the skipjack race, offering three cash prizes and trophies. There are three more races with two Mariner races and one open-class event. In addition to the races, there are swimming and fishing contests. All awards are presented dockside in Deal Island Harbor. Deal Island is on the eastern shore of Maryland in the Chesapeake Bay area. The race is held on Labor Day because the sailboats are hauled, repaired and repainted to begin the oyster season, as required by Maryland law. The race was televised by CBS in 1972 with Charles Kuralt as narrator. The event attracts almost 6,000 people both on land and sea. Many sail in their own boats to watch the races, which take place in Tangier Sound. Other events are held in Deal Island Harbor.

Leonardtown

ST. MARY'S COUNTY MARYLAND OYSTER FESTIVAL

Held annually, October
Economic

The annual St. Mary's County Maryland Oyster Festival is held the second weekend in October. Its purpose is threefold: to attract tourists to the area, one of the oldest settled in the country; to call attention to the more than 300-year-old oyster industry; and to provide funds for a Citizens Scholarship Foundation and other charitable causes. Highlight of the weekend event is the National Oyster Shucking Championship, with a variety of trophies and cash prizes to winners in different categories. The goal is to open as many oysters as quickly and neatly as possible. The winner participates the following year in the Galway Oyster Festival in Ireland in September. In 1975, Maryland resident Cornelius Mackall of Prince Frederick was the first American to win the international contest. This festival focuses in on the tasting of the season's new, fat and reportedly healthy oyster crop. The oysters are eaten raw on the half-shell with sauce, steamed, bathed with sauce, fried to a crispy golden brown, stewed in a broth (based on a 300-year-old recipe). There are also fried oysters on a bun and a fried oyster dinner with all the trimmings. There are other Maryland foods available, like the St. Mary's County stuffed ham sandwich, Maryland fried chicken and crab cakes and home-baked desserts. All the food is prepared and sold by the Women's Club of St. Mary's County. The festival has exhibits on oyster-opening knife collections, worldwide oyster shell collection and the harvesting of the seafood, a $20 million business in this area. There are also films and other exhibitions on the history, geography and culture of southern Maryland and St. Mary's County. The oyster festival is held on Saturday and Sunday, noon to dusk, rain or shine. It is held to coincide with the start of the oyster harvest season in Maryland. To date, more than 100,000 visitors have attended the event, with many participating in the competitions. The festival was started in October 1967 by the local Rotary Club of St. Mary's County with only 50 members. Today, there are several clubs actively participating in the event. There is a general admission fee to cover parking and a program book. All entertainment, including square dancing, and exhibits are free. The festival is held at St. Mary's County Fairgrounds, a 50-acre site.

Thurmont

CATOCTIN COLORFEST

Held annually, October
Economic, environmental, harvest

The Catoctin Colorfest marked its twentieth year in 1983 when a two-day event in early October was held in Frederick County's Catoctin Mountains. Originally a one-day event that featured a nature walk to view the fall foliage colors in Catoctin Mountain National Park, it has grown to two days but still includes the nature walk plus crafts, entertainment and home-cooked, homegrown food. More than 300 craftspeople sell, display and demonstrate their specialties. These include broom making, doll making, leatherwork, jewelry making and basket weaving. Lately, face painting has become a fad among festival goers. Entertainment is by local dance groups, country and folk musicians. Nearby communities sponsor bull roasts and chicken barbecues, and many area churches offer suppers. All food is homegrown and home-cooked. The aroma of food is evident in the area, as is the scent of ripening apples. This is also apple harvest time. Visitors are able to buy apple pies, apple cider, apple tarts and apples fresh from the trees. The process of apple butter boiling is demonstrated. All events are outdoors. The event is financed by sales and contributions from local communities and the Frederick County Tourism Council. Work is by volunteers from Thurmont and nearby towns. Economically the Colorfest is beneficial, attracting thousands of visitors each year. Thurmont is 17 miles north of Frederick.

Massachusetts

Becket

JACOB'S PILLOW DANCE FESTIVAL

Held annually, June/September
Cultural, educational

Jacob's Pillow is probably the oldest dance festival in the United States. It was started in 1932 during the heart of the Depression by the late Ted Shawn. This festival has a dual purpose. First, it is actually a summer school of dance with as many as 100 students. Second, it is a dance festival with eight weeks of varied programs open to the general public. The school sessions and festival performances are both held on a 160-acre farm. There are studios and a country-style theater that fits the landscape. The farmhouse is of eighteenth-century vintage. Students perform in the dance programs after they learn in class. The dance festival programs range from African to East Indian, ballet to modern. Founder Ted Shawn passed away in 1972. Norman Walker is now resident director. Like Shawn, he too is a dancer, teacher and choreographer. He had his own company and was formerly artistic director of the Batsheva Company in Israel. Walker, like Shawn, feels that there is an interconnection between the dance and life, and that is the purpose of the school. Students live, work and think dancing. The festival policy of giving debuts to American and foreign companies is also part of the program as well as the ballet, modern and ethnic dance facets of the event. Among those who have debuted at Jacob's Pillow Dance Festival have been the Ballet Rambert, the Nederlands Dans Theater, the Canadian National Ballet, the Western Theater Ballet, now the Scottish Theater Ballet, and the National Dancers of Ceylon. It was in 1955 that the first group of soloists from the Royal Danish Ballet made their U.S. debut. In 1977, eight soloists from the Royal Danish Ballet opened the season, drawing the largest opening week attendance in the festival's history. Two companies who debuted in 1977 included the Cultural Center of the Philippines Dance Company and the Contemporary Dancers of Winnipeg, Canada. Jacob's Pillow is supported by paid admissions for the dance performances and by tuition at the school, but it does continually have financial problems. The festival and school received $5,000 in 1977 from the Massachusetts Arts Council. Such illustrious names as Alicia Markova have been affiliated with the festival, renting facilities. Thousands come every summer to view the dances, which are said to rank with the best in the country and the world.

Lenox

BERKSHIRE MUSIC FESTIVAL AT TANGLEWOOD

Held annually, July/August
Cultural

The Berkshire Music Festival at Tanglewood is the country's oldest music festival, founded in 1934. Performances are by the Boston Symphony Orchestra during July and August at Tanglewood, a 210-acre estate in the Berkshires. Music director is world famous Seiji Ozawa. However, there are equally famous guest conductors and soloists during the festival season. Actually the festival is part of the Berkshire Music Center, where gifted American and foreign musicians study for nine weeks, during which they give public performances. These are advanced music classes. The school in association with the Boston University School for the Arts also gives concerts, about three per weekend. Such notables as Serge Koussevitzky, Gertrude Robinson Smith and Leonard Bernstein have been involved in the festival's development. Tanglewood is the summer home of the Boston Symphony Orchestra, and more than 350,000 people come to hear them and the Berkshire Music Center Orchestra perform. There are chamber music, choral and vocal concerts, music theater productions and a Composers Forum. There is also a Festival of Contemporary Music, part of the Tanglewood Festival, sponsored by the Berkshire Music Center in cooperation with the Fromm Foundation. This event is in early August and features new works, several of which are specially commissioned for the festival. Ticket prices vary each season. Financial supporters of the festival are Friends of Music at Tanglewood. They receive certain privileges, like advance program notices, ticket ordering forms and admission to more than 40 concerts. The Tanglewood grounds always open two hours prior to a top concert. There is a cafeteria open to ticket holders. Families and others are encouraged to picnic on the lawns. Incidentally, Nathaniel Hawthorne lived at Tanglewood and often wrote about it. Other music events at Tanglewood include jazz programs with well-known soloists and performers. There's Pops-at-Tanglewood with the Boston Pops Orchestra, made so famous by the late Arthur Fiedler. This performance usually benefits the Pension Fund and is a sellout. Another highlight is a mid-August day-long program of concerts, starting at 2 p.m. and ending with a festive evening concert at 8:30 p.m., with three orchestras, the Boston Symphony Orchestra, the Berkshire Music Center Orchestra and the Boston University Young Artist Orchestra. Most concerts are held in the Music Shed, designed by Eliel Saarinen and accommodating 10,000 under cover. The airy shed dates back to 1917. Other concert goers, weather permitting, sit out on the lawn with their picnic baskets.

Marshfield

MARSHFIELD FAIR

Held annually, August
Economic

The Marshfield Fair is more than 100 years old and still very popular. It was started in 1866 as a showcase for the area's agriculture. Today, it is a showcase for both agricultural and horticultural exhibits with premium money provided by the Commonwealth of Massachusetts. It is a 10-day event always held in the latter part of August, the height of the vegetable, fruit and flower season. The fair features a variety of 4-H exhibits also, and there are handicraft competitions. Over the years, additional events have appeared, like daily parimutuel running races, a horseshoe-pitching contest, and horse and pony pulling contests, with only Massachusetts teams competing for prizes. The fair also has a parade the first Sunday with theme floats and several marching bands. Entertainment accents country-western music. Approximately 150,000 persons visit the fair, a far cry from the 9,000 who came to the first one. Two U.S. presidents, Warren G. Harding and Calvin Coolidge, attended in the past. There is a general admission fee, and monies are realized from entry fees and concession rentals. The fairgrounds are at Route 3A in Marshfield.

New Bedford

FESTIVAL OF THE BLESSED SACRAMENT

Held annually, August
Religious, ethnic

The Festival of the Blessed Sacrament is a Portuguese-themed festival that covers four days starting the last Thursday in August. This observance coincides with a similar one on the Portuguese Island of Madeira. The American version, started in 1914, is also by Madeirians—the male descendants of immigrants from that island. It is a religious event of thanksgiving for deliverance of the immigrants from rough seas and stormy weather when they were en route to America. The feast is a continuous thanksgiving by the immigrants through their descendants. The first feast had only 50 participants. Today, it attracts more than 150,000 persons, many visitors. Year-long preparations are done by male descendants from Madeira. Workers like to think of this event as the "largest Portuguese feast in the world." Festivities open on a Thursday evening with official ceremonies, followed by continuous entertainment, a mixture of country-western, rock and Portuguese music, singing and dancing. The entertainment continues for the next three days and often includes name entertainers. Over the years, the festival has added an arcade and midway and a variety of American foods, but Portuguese specialties like *cabra* (goat) and *bacalhau* (codfish) chunks in a sauce of Portuguese spices, garlic, parsley and onions are still very popular. The festival is held at Madeira Field and in a large part of the city, covering Earle, Hathaway and Tinkham streets from Madeira Avenue to Hope Street. Originally it was held in the back of the Immaculate Conception Church on the east side of town. The church was later moved to its present location on Earle Street and Madeira Avenue, and so the festival moved, too. The festival includes a colorful procession to the church on Sunday, and attendance at mass is followed at 2 p.m. by a festive folkloric parade. There is no admission charge to any festival events. It is supported by contributions from various civic and church groups.

Plymouth

FESTIVAL OF THE HOLY GHOST

Held annually, July
Religious, ethnic

The Festival of the Holy Ghost is held for three days on a weekend in mid-July. It is held in thanksgiving by the Portuguese community to the third member of the Roman Catholic Trinity, the Holy Ghost. The event is appropriate in an area where the Pilgrims landed and the first Thanksgiving Day was held. The Portuguese version is centuries-old and was brought by the immigrants to the New World in 1910. More than 10,000 visitors and community residents participate each year, with the number on the increase. The festival begins with religious ceremonies centering on a silver crown, reflecting the devotion of Queen Isabel to the Holy Ghost. There is a 7 p.m. mass at St. Mary's Church and later a candlelight procession to the Holy Ghost Field on Cherry Street in North Plymouth. The next day, Saturday, there is a huge fireworks display, and Sunday another religious procession from Siever's Field to St. Mary's for a 10:30 a.m. mass. Both days feature Portuguese singing, dancing and pageantry and food, including *malacadas, favish, linguica, chorice, tramoce* and *soupas*. The event is financed by donations from businesses and local people and by the sale of foods and souvenirs.

Plymouth

PILGRIM PROGRESS PAGEANT

Held annually, August
Historic, religious, pageant

Pilgrim Progress Pageant is the reenactment of the Pilgrims' procession up Leyden Street to the site of the Fort-Meetinghouse on Burial Hill, now the Church of the Pilgrimage on Main Street. The processions take place every Friday in August and begin when the town clock strikes 5 p.m. Participants, dressed like Pilgrims, include men, women and children. They represent the first Pilgrims who survived that first severe winter more than 300 years ago. The pageant was started by local citizens in 1921 and has been continued ever since. Preparations by volunteers start three weeks prior to the pageant. It is supported by private donations. When the clock strikes five, participants assemble to the beat of a drum. When they reach the site of the fort, they sing psalms, and Bible texts are read, exactly as they were in 1621. The pageant attracts thousands to the area. It is a faithful reenactment.

Plymouth

THANKSGIVING DAY CELEBRATION

Held annually, fourth Thursday in November
Historic, patriotic

Thanksgiving Day Celebration is a nationwide holiday always held the fourth Thursday in November. There are special observances here, too, where the first Thanksgiving was held in 1621. Today, the area's historic homes are open to the public on Thanksgiving. Many owners serve cider and doughnuts to visitors. At Plimoth Plantation, a replica of the original settlement, visitors are taken on a tour of the Pilgrim houses and shops by costumed guides. Local area restaurants serve turkey, cranberries and Indian pudding. In the afternoon, there's a costumed reenactment of the Pilgrims' church procession and service.

South Carver

MASSACHUSETTS CRANBERRY FESTIVAL

Held annually, September/October
Economic, agricultural, harvest

The Massachusetts Cranberry Festival, started in 1949 to promote the use of cranberries, is still held annually for two days the last weekend in September, or early October, marking the cranberry harvest season. About 10,000 people attend, more than 250,000 since the first festival. Highlights include the harvesting of the cranberries, exhibits and a ride on an old-time steam train, the Edaville Railroad, through the cranberry bogs. Other events are a bicycle race, a flea market and auction, a fair with 4-H exhibits, competitions and entertainment, an old-fashioned corn roast, cake sale, cranberry baking contest, crafts show, pie-eating contest and cranberry games. There is also a Cranberry Queen

Contest, open to all girls who live in Plymouth County between the ages of 16 to 22, single and married. There is a festive crowning of the Cranberry Queen and Her Court, held during the Country Music Spectacular, featuring famous country music performers. There is public entertainment through the streets of the town. Five strolling musicians, dressed as seventeenth-century sailors, play old ballads and sing sea chanties, folk, country and bluegrass music. There is a storyteller for children and a local artist who draws free sketches of anyone willing to pose for 20 minutes. The idea for the festival was that of Ellis D. Atwood, founder of the Edaville Railroad, and of Robert Rich, of Ocean Spray Cranberries. Future plans call for the event to be made into an old-fashioned country fair and festival. Preparations are handled by local volunteers, who put hundreds of hours into each festival. Events are citywide, but most are held in parks near the Edaville Railroad. There is an admission fee to the parks.

West Springfield

BIG "E"/EASTERN STATES EXPOSITION

Held annually, September
Economic

The Big "E" or Eastern States Exposition is an annual industrial and agricultural fair of all the New England states: Massachusetts, Maine, New Hampshire, Connecticut, Vermont and Rhode Island. The 12-day fair begins the second Wednesday after Labor Day. Fairgrounds cover 175 acres of land, with 15 of them devoted to midway entertainment with the usual rides, plus a stage for name entertainment. There are exhibits and displays and a pure-bred livestock show, considered to be one of the largest in the East, with more than 3,000 animals entered for $75,000 in cash prizes each year. Competitors vie for the title Eastern States Exposition Grand Champion. The Eastern States All-American Championship Horse Show is one of the top three such shows in the country. Each New England state has its own official building, usually built in the style of the state's capitol building. All the buildings are on the Avenue of States. Each building features its own exhibits. The idea for the fair started in 1912, when a local group of people got together to discuss how to showcase New England's agricultural heritage and industrial development. The movement, headed by Joshua L. Brooks, was designed to delay an agricultural crisis for the New England farmer. Rapid industrialization at the turn of the century and the growth of cities posed a real threat to the farmer. Brooks felt that something that would draw industry and agriculture together would help. So in 1916, the Eastern States Exposition was born. Except for the two world wars, a devastating hurricane in 1938 and a flood two years before, the fair has continued to attract more than 700,000 persons. The exposition is operated by a nonprofit corporation, chartered under the education statutes of Massachusetts. The original exposition was intended to be a means of exchanging knowledge and getting children interested and involved in educational agricultural projects. This basic principle was reinforced in 1974 by the exposition's board of trustees, a 160-member group representing the six New England states. They set up a junior fair board to "institutionalize" input from young people. The exposition has a total of 75 permanent buildings. In addition to the Avenue of States, there is Storrowton Village, a replica of an early nineteenth-century village and gift from the late Helen Osborne Storrow. The village's nine authentic buildings were moved from their original sites and reassembled at the fairgrounds.

Michigan

Alma

HIGHLAND FESTIVAL AND GAMES

Held annually, May
Ethnic

The Highland Festival and Games is strictly an ethnic event, started May 25, 1968, to mirror events similar to those held in Scotland for hundreds of years. The city of Alma has a Scottish tradition. The name is Scottish, and the town was founded by Scots. It has a Presbyterian college, Alma College. The three-day event is always held the last weekend in May because the weather is good and it doesn't conflict with any other event in the area. The Highland Festival includes a large parade, traditional Scottish athletic events, piping, dancing and a pipe band competition. Participants come from all over the United States, Canada and Scotland. The festival also has some modern events, like an art fair, drama, modern dancing and an Alma Queen of Scots. Competitions take place on the Alma College campus and are staged so that visitors can see all of them. About 25,000 attended the first event. By 1976, it was up to 90,000 and growing. The idea for the festival is credited to a local resident, David E. MacKenzie, who attended Scottish games in Boston in 1962. It was thought to be a good idea for Alma, and he brought the games concept to the city. The rest is history. It was an instant success, with competitors coming from Colorado, Florida and New York. The festival attempts "to encourage and preserve the Gaelic arts of Scotland. By providing a place for the finest students of the Scottish arts to compete for prizes, we hope to encourage an ever increasing quality of excellence as well as greater appreciation for our Scottish ancestry." Hundreds of hours are spend each year by local volunteers in preparing for the festival and games. It is supported by gate receipts and donations.

Holland

TULIP TIME FESTIVAL

Held annually, May
Ethnic, floral, economic

The Tulip Time Festival dates back to May 1927, starting with the planting of tulips, as suggested by Miss Lida Rogers, a local high school teacher. She wanted to beautify the city and keep in touch with the area's Dutch heritage. It is now an annual four-day event, held the second week in May, to coincide with the full blooming of the tulips. The festival celebrated its fiftieth year in 1979, and the festival then lasted for eight days. Approximately 200,000 came, and since the beginning, about 5 million people have enjoyed the tulips and Dutch events. Every year, all events are sold out. Among the events are the Tulip Time Market with displays that are for sale, Klompen (wooden shoes) Dancers, the Flower Show at the local Armory, the Volksparade and street scrubbing and dancers. There are musical reviews by the Holland High School band, orchestra and choir. Some events are free. The Flower Show is sponsored by the Holland Garden Club, and the square dance features a nationally known caller. Exhibition square dances are also included. There is a Dutch Heritage Show in which costumed residents recall family life and holidays in all the provinces of the Netherlands. There are also films on the Netherlands. Walking tours of Holland's downtown area are offered, taking visitors through the tulip lanes and displays outside the city. The festival always begins on the Wednesday nearest May 15. It starts with the mayor and City Council inspecting the city streets. They declare them dirty and give the order to scrub. Hundreds of townspeople wearing costumes, using shoulder yokes to carry pails of water and holding willow brooms, scrub the streets. The Volksparade is highlighted by the first performance of the Klompen Dancers, dressed in traditional outfits. The style of dancing is Old Dutch. There is also a children's parade with thousands of Dutch-dressed elementary school-children on foot and on bikes. There is also a parade of barbershop quartets with groups from the nation's top talent. There is a baton-twirling contest and band review with 100 bands. In 1965, a Windmill Island Municipal Park was opened together with a restoration of a 200-year-old windmill, "De Zwaan," the only known authentic Dutch windmill in the United States. It was purchased from the Netherlands. It is 125 feet high and stands on a knoll overlooking Little Netherlands, a miniature Dutch village and the island's Dutch buildings. There is also a *draaimolen*, an imported Dutch merry-go-round for the children. Events are held throughout the city. Daily attractions include art exhibits, the Baker Furniture Museum, a permanent exhibit of antique furniture and period rooms, paintings and a design source material. There's the De Klomp Wooden Shoe and Delft Factory, said to be the largest on the North American continent. Visitors can watch Dutch craftsmen and artists make original wooden shoes. The delftware is in the one and only Delft Factory in this country. Dutch Heritage is another daily attraction that deals with the holidays and family life of Holland. It is presented by the Dutch Heritage Group. There are authentic costumes from the Netherlands on display. Customs, history and traditions are all part of the program. There is an admission fee. The festival is self-supporting, receiving funds from donations and paid admissions.

St. Joseph, Benton Harbor

BLOSSOMTIME FESTIVAL

Held annually, May
Economic, floral

The Blossomtime Festival, started in 1906 as a one-day religious event to bless the fruit tree blooms to ensure a good harvest, has expanded over the years to include other events. It is an economic-oriented, one-week event that clearly attracts tourists to the area. Festival programs are held in both St. Joseph and Benton Harbor, with four counties participating actively in preparations and handling of events. The entire area boasts of more than 52,000 acres of apples, pears, peaches, plums, grapes, strawberries, black and red raspberries, blueberries and eleven other fruit crops. The festival overlooks Lake Michigan and of course can include extra activities like boating, picnics and a visit to the Benton Harbor Wholesale Fruit Market, claiming to be the world's largest noncitrus cash-to-grower market. The festival attracts about 250,000 visitors annually. Festivities include the traditional blessing of the blossoms, with the festival always opening on a Sunday. There is a dance, tours of the flowering orchards with lectures on the different fruits. There is a Key to Cities Tour with the Blossomtime Queen going through communities of southwestern Michigan, a four-day program. There is a fashion show, a youth parade, a three-hour Grand Floral Parade with more than 100 participants, a square dance roundup and a Grand Floral Ball. Work on the festival is performed by local volunteers, who donate thousands of working hours to preparations. The event is financed by contributions, sale of souvenir journals and paid admissions for some events. While the festival originated in 1906 with the bloom blessing on a Sunday in May with excursions through the orchards, it wasn't until 1932 that it finally developed. It was canceled during World War II, but in 1951 it was reestablished permanently with the incorporation of the event as Blossomtime, Inc., a nonprofit organization of 75 members. All activities are carefully supervised by an 18-member board of directors. By 1952, 150,000 visitors had come to the festival and to see the big parade. The event has continued to expand.

Traverse City

NATIONAL CHERRY FESTIVAL

Held annually, July
Harvest, economic

The National Cherry Festival has been an annual event since 1926. Originally only a one-day event, it has grown to seven days packed full of activities and festivities hailing the area's industry, cherries. It is traditionally held the first full week after the fourth of July, the time of the cherry harvest. Approximately 70 percent of the nation's cherries come from Michigan, with the largest amount of trees on the Old Mission Peninsula in Traverse City. The area was once a center of a thriving lumber industry, but that gradually disappeared, causing a depressed economy in the Grand Traverse Bay area. The discovery that the climate and soil were ideal for cherries began a new era. Growers and processors hired hundreds of people and brought new money into the area. So it seemed a good idea in 1924 to hold a ceremony to bless the cherry blossoms to ensure a good crop, an idea of the late Jay Smith, a local newspaperman. This was the start of the future Cherry Festival to mark the harvest. Half a million people now come to the festival annually, bringing in about $5 million to the area. The National Cherry Festival has more than 100 different events, with 75 of them free. The festival was given its national title in 1928 by the Michigan State Legislature in recognition of Traverse City as the cherry capital of the world and an essential part of the state's economy. The festival includes three major parades, national high school band competitions and a mixture of different events to include displays of cherries and cherry products, free tours of the cherry orchards and a weigh-in station for the world's largest cherry. There are cherry-eating contests, cherry pies, cake- and tart-baking competitions and a cherry pie–eating contest. There are sports events, entertainment and arts and crafts, all held at citywide locations. Work on each year's festival is almost a year-round job, with a minimum of 20,000 volunteer hours and a minimum of 5,500 staff hours each year. The festival is administered by a nonprofit association, the National Cherry Festival, Inc. Members are from various area chambers of commerce, hotels, tourist facilities and cherry farmers. Source of income averages from 20 to 25 percent on the midway, 6 percent from the Michigan Association of Cherry Producers, 3 percent from area governmental groups, 25 percent from a sponsor program, 3 percent from festival mini-projects, 20 percent from festival events themselves and 18 percent from miscellaneous sources. The festival association is a member of the International Festivals Association, the Michigan Association of Festivals and Events and the West Michigan Tourist Association. The festival is especially proud that former President Gerald R. Ford, himself from Michigan, officiated at the 1975 event. The festival states its purpose as producing "a top-quality festival of which our area will be proud.

Not to make money but to have adequate funds to operate, to provide for contingencies and to grow in quality.''

Minnesota

Ely

ALL AMERICAN CHAMPIONSHIPS SLED DOG RACES

Held annually, January
Sports

The All American Championships Sled Dog Races are held the third weekend in January, when the snow is the heaviest and deepest and it is cold enough to insure the snow remaining firm for the races. They were started in January 1969, and were originally known as the Minnesota Arrowhead Championship. The town of Ely started the event with help from the North Star Sled Dog Club of St. Paul. Eventually, the Ely Sled Dog Committee was organized to handle the race, and its name was changed in 1971. The races are held to encourage winter recreation for local citizens, but over the years, the races have seen contestants from various parts of Canada, Alaska and as far east as New Hampshire, bringing along spectators. Local residents like to call this the "biggest race in the lower 48 states." Five classes of racing are featured: unlimited class, a 16.5-mile daily; limited 5–7-dog class B, 10 miles daily; limited 3–5-dog class C, 5 miles daily; limited 2–3-dog class D, 3 miles daily; plus a junior class of 2–3 dogs, 3 miles daily (under 14 years old). The races are open to men, women, boys and girls. The races are run against the clock. The fastest time for two days wins. The top five in all classes receive trophies as well as prize money, which now amounts to more than $10,000. Juniors only receive trophies. The two-day sports event has added more racing classes and purse money over the years, attracting more participants. In 1979, race officials added dual starts in the 3–5-dog class. The races attract more than 15,000 visitors each year, which helps the local economy. They are always held on a Saturday and Sunday, but some festivities do begin Friday night with a torchlight parade. Other events include a flea market and bingo games, which help finance the races. There is no admission charge for the races. A special volunteer committee handles details for the races.

Minneapolis

MINNEAPOLIS AQUATENNIAL

Held annually, July
Sports, cultural, economic

The Minneapolis Aquatennial is a 10-day annual festival always held the third week in July, attracting about 3 million visitors to the area. The idea dates back to May 24, 1939. A group of Twin Cities men were in Winnipeg, Canada, to attend a parade honoring King George VI. The event attracted a million people. Suddenly a heavy rainstorm forced the men to hide under the grandstand. The idea came to hold an event like this to attract tourists to Minneapolis. Since Minneapolis is considered to be the gateway to the state's "Land of 10,000 Lakes," it was decided to focus on water and water-related events and sports. July was selected because it's vacation time for many and is the best weather for tourists. The first Aquatennial, a name selected in a special city-run contest offering a cash prize of $50, was a one-day event July 20, 1940. That first festival was financed by the sale of "Skipper" pins, 62,000 of them. The "Skipper" pins are still sold and give purchasers a discount on various items. The festival was an instant hit and was continued. More events and activities were added, and the festival went from 1 to 10 days. Each year, the Aquatennial has a theme. In 1977, it was "Homecoming," and in 1978, "Summer Break." In 1982, it was "The Great American Family Reunion." Each year there is a new theme, which is coordinated with the programming of more than 250 different events held throughout the city and suburbs. The Aquatennial is handled by divisions. There is the hospitality division for hosting dignitaries and coronation events. There is a parade division with three or more parades. There is the special events division of various activities and the sports and lakes division with more than 100 aquatic and sporting events, only part of the grand total. Some 50,000 people work during the Aquatennial, and 3,000 resident volunteers work on preparations for the event. As soon as one Aquatennial is over, work begins immediately on the next one. Popular features include the water and sporting events, Grande Day Parade and Torchlight Parade. The Aquatennial is financed by donations from local businesses, vice-commodore membership, sale of skipper pins and admissions to some events. The festival has entertainment and also attracts famous people, like former Vice-President Walter Mondale and the late Hubert Humphrey, native sons. The Aquatennial brings in up to $18 million annually in new money to the Minneapolis community, and since that first one in 1940, more than $130 million.

Minneapolis

SVENSKARNAS DAG

Held annually, June
Ethnic

Svenskarnas Dag is a one-day midsummer celebration held the fourth Sunday
in June every year. It preserves Swedish heritage and celebrates the longest day
of the year, according to Swedish tradition. Events include an open-air religious
service, a band concert, Swedish folk dancing and choral groups of men, women
and children. There is also square dancing, male and female vocalists, the
coronation of a Midsummer Queen and very often guest speakers of either
national or international prominence. Originally started August 19, 1934, it is
considered to be the largest nationality event in the United States, attracting
more than 100,000 each year, or well over 2 million to date. It has remained a
one-day event. In 1941 it was changed to June so that it would match midsummer
observances in Sweden. Among celebrities who've officiated at the one-day
event have been actress-performer Ann Margaret and Colonel Buzz Aldrin, the
astronaut. It is always held in Minnehaha Park, and local residents handle the
program details. There is no admission charge, but the event is financed through
the sale of both American and Swedish foods, drinks and souvenir program
books.

St. Paul

FESTIVAL OF NATIONS

Held annually, April/May
Cultural, ethnic

The Festival of Nations is a three-day event held the last weekend in April,
sometimes going into early May. Each year there is a theme, the 1983 theme
being "Celebration of Spring." The Festival of Nations is the state's largest
ethnic event, featuring more than 6,000 ethnic participants representing 55 ethnic
groups. The three-day festival is held Friday through Sunday at the St. Paul
Civic Center. There are folk dance performances, music, exhibits, craft demonstrations, special foods and an international bazaar with continuous performances in two cabarets. More than 60,000 persons attend each year, and since
the first festival in 1932, several million. The festival, sponsored by the International Institute of Minnesota, is an outgrowth of the institute's service programs
for new Americans. Part of the three-day festival even today includes a natu-
ralization ceremony for 500 new citizens. Among the international folk arts

demonstrated are kite making and flying, Egyptian hassock making, African hair braiding, American Indian beadwork and Italian pasta making. Various ethnic foods are served at the Cafe International, where 40 different nationalities sell their specialties at the Civic Center Arena. Two formal folk dancing and music programs, "Folk Spectacle," are featured each day in the Civic Center's Old Auditorium with free evening and matinee performances. The cabaret stages offer continuous live entertainment by choirs, dancers and instrumentalists. There are folk dance classes and ethnic clothing from around the world modeled several times each day at the Bazaar Cabaret. The Festival of Nations is financed through admission fees, sale of arts, crafts and foods and contributions.

St. Paul

ST. PAUL WINTER CARNIVAL

Held annually, January/February
Economic

The St. Paul Winter Carnival is a 10-day winter festival held during the last week of January running into the first week of February. It was started in 1886 by a group of St. Paul businessmen who were enraged by an Eastern newspaper story that said St. Paul was "another Siberia, unfit for human habitation." They were so upset by this report that they set out to show the world that ice and snow were assets. The one-day carnival in St. Paul's Central Park was the site of the first Ice Palace, the work of a Montreal contractor. There were six toboggan slides on Cedar Street next to the palace. There were also curling and skating rinks, snowshoe, pushball and a blanket-tossing contest. The highly successful carnival was extended to the entire month of February the following year. The first carnival attracted the city's population, estimated at around 6,000. Nowadays, it attracts in excess of 1.5 million people from many other states, including the East. The history of the festival is rather checkered. There was a period of 20 years when the carnival was completely abandoned. In 1916, railroad baron Louis J. Hill decided it was time to revive the carnival last held in 1896. The big highlight was a giant barbecue in South St. Paul with 17,000 people showing up. The festival still centers around the "Legend of the Winter Carnival," a pageant about Astraios, the god of starlight, and Eos, goddess of the rosy-fingered morn, who married. They had four sons: Titan, Euros, Zephyrus and Notos. Boreas, King of the Winds, gave each brother a permanent power. Titan got the North Wind, Euros the East Wind, Zephrus the West Wind and Notos the South Wind. The brothers wandered over land and sea. Boreas during his travels found a winter paradise, Minnesota. He also discovered seven hills and St. Paul and decided to make it the capital of his empire, designating it as the "winter playground of the realm of Boreas." However, Vulcanus, the god of fire and enemy of Boreas, tried to chase Boreas out of St. Paul. Boreas, however, defied his enemy and declared a carnival celebration. Vulcanus swears that, he, too, will attend. The first day of the carnival, there is a parade headed by Boreas. Festivities in honor of the king include winter sports, games of wit and enter- tainment. Boreas then declares a Grande Coronation to be held in the Great Hall of Jupiter and that he will select a queen to rule with him—the Queen of the Snows. The queen is selected, and festivities reign. The news comes that Vul- canus plans to storm the Ice Palace. Festivities continue, however, with exhibits and displays of ice sculptures. Suddenly the cold night air is shaken by thunder (fireworks and rockets). The King of Fire arrives and appears on a parapet, demanding the surrender of Boreas, who is ready to do battle, but his Queen of the Snows persuades him to give up for the peace and good of his subjects. Boreas and his court leave to spread the gaiety of the carnival to other parts of the country. And so the carnival officially closes for another year. This basically is the way the carnival is still organized, with more than 1,500 committee members and 50,000 workers handling programs in addition to the more than 1.5 million spectators. Carnival highlight is the International 500 Snowmobile Race from Winnipeg, Canada, to St. Paul. The 500-mile race was formerly a three-day event. Now it's done in two days. Other events include ice skating, ice fishing contests, ice sculpturing, trade fairs, ski and sled dog races, softball on ice, square dancing, a Vulcan Victory Party and ice shows. The carnival was discontinued during World War I, and it wasn't until 1928 that the Midway Club sponsored a Winter Carnival through 1930. The Depression took its toll, and the carnival was again discontinued. In 1937, however, a group of local residents decided to revive it to lift the nation's Depression gloom. It was highly successful and was held every year through World War II, but with subdued events. It was from 1939 to 1941 that the parades gained momentum and became carnival traditions. In 1946, the carnival took a victory theme and was sponsored by the Saintpaulites, Inc. Firm and individual memberships were introduced as a means of financing the carnival and are still the main source of income today. The carnival has been attracting celebrities since 1952, when the Dionne quintuplets appeared, bringing worldwide attention to the carnival. The late Ed Sullivan's "Toast of the Town" TV show was seen live in 1954 from the St. Paul Winter Carnival, and in 1956, it was featured in *Life* magazine. Other celebrities who've appeared at the carnival include Gary Moore, Steve Allen, skier Jean Claude Killy, Chet Huntley, David Hartman, the Osmond Brothers and David Frost. The late Hubert Humphrey was grand marshal of the 1965 Grande Parade. He was then vice-president of the United States. Over the years the Ice Palace disappeared, but in 1967, it reappeared as a Snow Palace on a smaller scale. This continued through 1972. In 1975, an authentic Ice Palace reappeared for the 1976 bicentennial. It was a contemporary version of the original 1886 ice palace. Working on the carnival is a year-round job, with thousands of volunteers and a small paid office staff. In addition to memberships, the carnival is financed by paid admissions to events, button sales and sale of programs and souvenirs.

Mississippi

Biloxi

BLESSING OF THE FISHING FLEET AND BILOXI SHRIMP FESTIVAL AND FAIS DO DO

Held annually, June
Traditional, economic

The annual Blessing of the Fishing Fleet and Biloxi Shrimp Festival and Fais Do Do takes place the first weekend in June, together with the start of the fishing season. The religious blessing ceremony, highlight of the weekend's events, "seeks God's favor for the safety of both the fishermen and their families and for a bountiful catch." The actual Blessing of the Fishing Fleet is held Sunday afternoon, with hundreds of boats in parade formation. Each boat passes one by one in front of the official Blessing Boat, containing the pastor of St. Michael's Catholic Church, known as the Church of the Fisherman. Residents and visitors can view the impressive blessing ceremony from the Biloxi Small Craft Harbor and adjacent beach. All the boats are freshly painted and colorfully decorated for the occasion. After the ceremony, trophies and prizes for the best decorated boats are given. Then most of the fishermen take their boats to Deer Island for family picnics. Visitors can arrange to go too for a small fee. Actually the weekend begins on Friday in Biloxi's downtown area. The Vieux Marche with opening ceremonies are at the Golden Fisherman, a gold-covered sculpture dedicated to the angler. After this there are net-throwing and oyster-shucking contests plus mullet and Biloxi bacon to eat. On Saturday, there is the coronation of the new King and Queen of the Shrimp Festival, followed by the Fais Deaux Deaux, or street dances. The coronation and dancing take place at the Biloxi International Plaza, where there is also music and free boiled shrimp for all participants and spectators. The blessing and festival have already received national recognition by being featured on an ABC-TV evening news program. Over the years, new events are added like the Fais Deaux Deaux (Do Do) street dances and the dropping of a memorial wreath from a helicopter. The fleet blessing started in 1924, when the area's fishing fleet was mainly sailing craft. The shrimp festival was added in 1945. The entire event traces its origin to the 300-year-old custom of blessing fishing vessels in countries bordering the Adriatic Sea. The annual event is financed by local contributions. There is a nominal charge to participate in the street dances, but everything else is free. About 20,000 people attend the annual event. Preparations for it are handled on a voluntary basis, with the mayor and priest to the fishermen actively participating.

Natchez

NATCHEZ PILGRIMAGE

Held annually, March/April and October
Economic

The Natchez Pilgrimage is an annual month-long program from early March through early April and again for 15 days in October that consists of a variety of tours to see the mansions, antebellum homes and historic buildings and gardens of the area. Many homes are private residences, which open to the public only at this time. Approximately 70,000 visitors come to see the homes and gardens. So great is the number that the pilgrimage is repeated in the fall, usually the first two weeks of October. The pilgrimage is sponsored by the Pilgrimage Garden, whose members are local residents. Approximately 35 homes and gardens are viewed. There are morning, afternoon and evening candlelight tours. Each tour covers different homes and takes four hours to complete. There is a fee charged for each tour, with the monies going to the club to continue its restoration work of still other properties. Each tour carefully includes five different homes or mansions. The spring tours are held when azaleas, camellias, sweet olive and boxwood hedges are at their best. The fall brings an entirely different set of flowers and foliage. The weather is best in spring and fall for the tours. During the pilgrimage, a Confederate Pageant is featured Friday, Saturday, Monday and Wednesday at 8:30 p.m. in the City Auditorium. There is also a queen and king to reign over the pageant. The entire event is financed through tour charges and paid admissions. The pilgrimage has contributed greatly to the local economy, and the Pilgrimage Garden Club and Tour Association has been responsible for the restoration of many homes and gardens. In addition, the club itself owns some of these properties and is solely responsible for their restoration. The club was formed by the owners of most of the homes and gardens toured. Three of the tour houses are owned outright by the club. These are Stanton Hall, Longwood and King's Tavern. Stanton Hall and Longwood are registered as national historic landmarks. The pilgrimage is also strongly supported by the Natchez Garden Club, owners of Connelly's Tavern and three other houses available during the tour program. Connelly's Tavern is also a national historic landmark. Interestingly enough, some of these landmarks have special restaurants. For example, the Carriage House Restaurant was built in 1946 on the grounds of Stanton Hall. It is open daily, specializing in gourmet meals. Proceeds from the restaurant go toward restoration projects of the Pilgrimage Garden Club. The idea for the entire tour program dates back to 1931 and 1932, when Mrs. J. Balfour Miller, a member of the city's Woman's Club, handled the club's garden department. It seems that a bid came to Natchez to hold the second State Garden Club convention there in spring 1931. The garden division of the Woman's Club withdrew from the club to form the Natchez

Garden Club to handle the convention. Plans called for two garden tours, but the area's gardens were in such poor shape that Mrs. Miller recommended that the antebellum homes be shown. She arranged for cars to take the convention members around, and although the gardens were not well kept, camellias and other flowers were in full bloom. Mrs. Miller asked convention delegates to use their imaginations and think back to how grand these homes and gardens once were. She also mentioned that she hoped one day to see them restored to their original beauty and grandeur. Based on this convention experience, Mrs. Miller, who became next president of the Natchez Garden Club, recommended to the members that they repeat the convention garden tour, opening it up to the public. Plans called for the viewing of 22 homes for an admission fee. The first tour was in 1932, but instead of two days it was for six. Some homeowners did not want to go along with the open house tour idea, but Mrs. Miller convinced them not only to act as hostesses but also to dress up in hoop-skirt costumes. They all liked the idea and cooperated. The first pilgrimage was held March 28 through April 2, 1932. The pilgrimage's slogan, "Come to Natchez, where the Old South still lives and where shaded highways and antebellum homes greet new and old friends," was the work of George Nealy of the *Times-Picayune* of New Orleans. The club paid him $7 for the slogan, since shortened to "Where the Old South still lives." Despite the fact that March 1932 was during the Depression, visitors from 37 states attended that first pilgrimage. To date more than a few million have participated. The Confederate Pageant was added the next year and is still part of the annual event. There is an admission charge, separate from the tour cost.

Philadelphia

CHOCTAW INDIAN FAIR

Held annually, July
Ethnic, Economic

The Choctaw Indian Fair is a four-day showcase for the seven Choctaw communities and their cultural and sports skills and achievements. It is held the second weekend in July, Wednesday through Saturday. It attempts to show both the traditional and contemporary life styles of the Choctaw both to other Indian tribes and to non-Indians. It is a serious attempt to preserve the Native American heritage of the Choctaw nation. All events take place at the football stadium at Choctaw Central High School in the Pearl River Indian Community, headquarters of the tribal government. It's about eight miles west of Philadelphia. Intricate handmade arts and crafts, based on centuries-old skills, are displayed for sale at the Choctaw Exhibit Hall. Sports competitions include the Choctaw's World Series of Stickball, archery, blowguns and the use of ancient hunting weapons. Festivities begin with an all-Indian parade through the streets of Philadelphia near the city's court square. Each of the seven Indian communities vies with tribal organizations and programs for first place. They also compete with each other the first day of the fair by displaying crafts and staging sports events and pageants. Highlight of the first night is the selection of a Choctaw Indian Princess to represent her people at official tribal functions during the next 12 months. All during the fair, there are Indian songs, chants, dances and special foods. A film, *American Indian Influence on the U.S.*, is shown several times in the high school's cafeteria. Together with the ancient Choctaw culture is the contemporary one, taking on the aspects of Indian-style country-western music, a carnival midway for children and an Indian-Gospel sing. However, the traditional Choctaw dances continue to be very popular. The dances, based on the forces of social, war and animal life, manifest the spirit and vigorous feelings of the Choctaws. There is the "It-Ta-Wa-Yah-He-Tha," or wedding dance, a fast war dance and the duck dance. The duck dance is very popular with the Choctaws since the duck gives cooking fat and feathers for arrows. Stickball played by today's Choctaw Indians is authentic and still very warlike in nature. As in ancient times, today's game is accompanied by the rhythmic beat of drums. In olden days, the drums played for days prior to a game. The Indians followed the sound of the drums right to the game. Many celebrities in addition to the state's governor attend the fair. They've included Jay Silverheels, B. J. Thomas, Randolph Mantooth, Danny Davis and the Nashville Brass, Billy Thunderkloud and Chieftones and Kenny Rogers. There are admission charges to the fair, and they vary each year. This fair is also financed by the Choctaw Fair Fund with supplementary funds from both the Mississippi Art Commission and the National Endowment for the Arts. The fair was started in July 1949 and originally was a two-day event. Its popularity, with more than a million visitors to date, extended it to four days. It was held in 1949, when the Mississippi Band of Choctaws met in an open field to pay the first official tribute to their ancestors' ancient and distinct culture. Now all seven of the Choctaw communities participate. Work on the fair is a year-round job with most of the communities involved. The Mississippi Band of Choctaw Indians are direct descendants of the Choctaws who remained in Mississippi during the period of Indian removals in the early nineteenth century. Some tribe members do live in various parts of the state. However, the majority of them reside in the seven rural communities centering around Neshoba County, the traditional Choctaw homeland. They still live as an isolated and rural minority, preserving their ethnic identity. The annual fair calls attention to their heritage, customs and abilities.

Tupelo

GUM TREE FESTIVAL

Held annually, May/June
Cultural

The Gum Tree Festival is held in early May, usually the second weekend. Lately it has shifted to June. Taking its name from the local gum trees, it is strictly an arts and crafts festival, giving area artists and craftspeople a chance to display and sell their work. It is also open to artisans from other states. It is held on the lawn of the Lee County Circuit Courthouse in downtown Tupelo. It is an informal event. Visitors often pull up a chair and sit on the grass and talk to the artists and craftspeople. Sometimes festival goers see artists finishing up their work. There is a Saturday lunch served for a few dollars. This enables artists and visitors to break bread together and learn from each other. The meal is quite substantial and includes large portions of Southern fried chicken and trimmings, served with homemade baked beans, cole slaw and dessert plus iced tea and a piece of watermelon. There is country-western music during lunch, and each year a different group performs. A special dinner is featured Saturday night at Tombigbee State Park and Lake, about a 10-minute drive from Tupelo. Again for a small fee there's cold beer, hot dogs roasted at the fireplace, cole slaw, marshmallows and various juices. Sunday at the festival grounds there are modestly priced box lunches. Each exhibitor pays an entrance fee for a 12-by-4-foot space. Five categories are open: watercolor and mixed media; graphics and drawings; sculpture; crafts; and pottery. Each category is judged and awarded first, second and third prize at varying amounts. Best in the show gets an additional cash prize. There are also purchase prizes, awards of excellence by the judges, meaning more money. These are presented Saturday while other awards are given on Sunday. Cash prizes total in the thousands and do vary each year. The festival draws 12,000 visitors, and since its start in 1972 more than 100,000. It has helped the local economy and at the same time helped to produce an exhibit and festival of top quality, attracting top judges, like H. C. Cassill, head of printmaking, Cleveland Institute of Art. The sole purpose of the festival, started by local residents, is "to expand the cultural and educational objectives of the area and to stimulate interest in the fine arts and crafts and broaden the cultural base of the community." Prior to this, the nearest such show was in Memphis, Tennessee, 100 miles away. Tupelo was once the capital of the Chickasaw nation, and Civil War battles were fought here. In modern times, Elvis Presley was born here. The Gum Tree Festival is organized and handled by the town's residents, which include lawyers, doctors, students, and housewives who work all winter preparing for the event. It is financed by entry fees, private patrons, limited grants from art agencies and limited support from the Community Development Foundation.

Missouri

Branson

KEWPIESTA

Held annually, April
Cultural, art

The Kewpiesta is an annual four-day event the third weekend in April that pays tribute to the memory of Rose O'Neill, Ozark writer, artist, illustrator, sculptor and creator of the famous Kewpie doll, popular in the 1920s and 1930s. The event calls attention to Rose O'Neill's work, the doll, and features a tour to her homestead about 10 miles north of Branson. There are special store window displays and teas at local museums. There is a Saturday night banquet, a scrapbook contest and a Kewpie doll look-a-like contest. The event is held in April for two reasons. First, Rose O'Neill passed away in April 1944, and second, that's the start of the tourist season in the Ozarks. The National Rose O'Neill Club, festival planners, feel that more people will attend at that time. The event is supported by admission fees and club dues. Registration fees and meal and transportation costs also help. Programs are held throughout the Branson–Hollister area, with the main ones held at the School of the Ozarks, Shepherd of the Hills Farm and the Old Shepherd's Book Shop. There is a Trade Corner, where collectors of the Kewpie doll can buy more memories of Rose O'Neill. The Kewpie doll resembles a chubby little girl with tiny wings sprouting from her back. The festival even attracts celebrities. In 1972 it was movie star Sondra Locke, and in 1978, Gavin McLeod. The festival was started as Rose O'Neill Week in 1967, but then changed to Kewpiesta in 1968. More than 10,000 people have attended the event over the years.

Hermann

MAIFEST

Held annually, May
Ethnic

The Maifest is a two-day German May festival offering German folklore, songs, music and food as a welcome to spring. It is always held the third weekend in May, attracting 40,000 visitors. Among the many events are band concerts, musical shows and a Jaycee Entertainment Garden at the City Park, featuring hourly entertainment. A small admission is charged, and black beer, cheese, sausage, crackers and bratwurst are served. There is a house tour covering six historic homes and buildings. Cost is nominal and covers stops at the Stone Hill Winery, now a national registered historic district, South's Butcher Shop from the early 1850s, the Scharnhorst-Eitzen House built in 1850, the Klenk House of 1846, the Reiff House and the Langendoerfer-Haney House of 1861. The area also has a Children's Museum at the German School and a Craft Shop upstairs at the Stone Hill Winery Barn. Festival events include a children's parade, a quilt display, a walking tour and a variety of German foods sold and served throughout the town. The festival is financed by paid admissions, donations and food and souvenirs sold. The present festival dates back to 1952, when a group of local people decided to revive the original Maifest started in Hermann in 1874. It was a children's festival then. Today's event still retains some children's programs but is basically a German ethnic festival for all ages.

Ste. Genevieve

JOUR DE FETE A SAINTE GENEVIEVE DAYS OF CELEBRATION

Held annually, August
Ethnic

Jour de Fete a Sainte Genevieve Days of Celebration is held the second weekend in August. It is a triple-treat ethnic festival: French, German and Spanish. Thousands come every year to take a "walk back into history." The area was settled by the French in 1725. The town prides itself on being a living historic community and not an artificially created tourist attraction. Most of the homes and businesses in Ste. Genevieve are genuine eighteenth- and nineteenth-century buildings still usable. There are a few buildings that have been restored. A house and building tour is one of the festival's many features, as well as local meals that include traditional French dishes like *bouillon*, a hearty chicken and vegetable soup, and *andouille*, a highly seasoned homemade sausage of minced tripe. There is Spanish cuisine to sample, too, like a spicy barbecue (originally *barbacoa*), which the town has translated into peppery pork steaks. German cuisine (dating back to the early nineteenth century) includes a smoked beef sausage, known locally as the Ste. Genevieve sausage. Other German dishes include *leberknaefly*, or liver dumpling. There are also American cured hams, bacon, golden fried chicken and local homemade cakes and jellies. All foods are sold at local restaurants and at special food booths set up during the festival. Ste. Genevieve is the oldest town on the west bank of the Mississippi River. During the festival, seven historic homes going back to 1770 are opened to the public: the Amoureaux House, the Beauvais House, the Bolduc House, the Bolduc-LeMeilleur House, the Green Tree Tavern, the Guibourd-Valle House and the Shaw House–Fur Trading Post. Other points of interest include the City Museum, with its Indian relics and native birds mounted by Audubon, who spent time in this area. Each building may be visited individually or as a group through the purchase of tickets at the Civic Tour Booth on the Town Square. The festival also offers public entertainment at the Town Square. There's an open-air market and International Kitchen serving Spanish, French and German dishes for a fee. Entertainment includes a pageant, songs, music, square dancing and marching bands. Each day there is a special parade, and on Saturday there's a procession of schoolchildren dressed in ethnic costumes. The Sunday parade features floats keyed to the theme, "In Old Ste. Genevieve." There are arts and crafts shows, a flea market, street dancing and modern rock concerts. The festival is financed by the tour costs, sale of antiques, arts, crafts and foods and private donations. Today's visitor can walk on the same ground as Jean Jacques Audubon, the artist-naturalist, Moses Austin, "Founder of Texas," Dr. Louis F. Linn, "Model U.S.

Senator,'' Otto, the first king of Greece, and according to legend, the Marquis de Lafayette and Jesse James. The first festival was held in 1965 and was designed to call attention to the historic value of the town and its ethnic heritage.

Sedalia

MISSOURI STATE FAIR

Held annually, August
Economic

The Missouri State Fair was first held in 1901 and like all state fairs reflected the agricultural crops and achievements of farmers on a statewide basis. It still does and in addition also represents the industrial and cultural achievements of the state. It is an 11-day event held in mid- to late August. The fair features nightly entertainment with famous headliners, like country-western singer Roy Clark and the Osmonds. There is an extra admission charge for the show. However, general admission includes 50 free exhibits and demonstrations of Missouri crafts, skills and wildlife. The demonstrations include wood carving, quilting and fiddle playing. Free entertainment includes ragtime piano and barbershop quartet concerts, on-stage contests and prizes for unusual mustaches, look-alikes, clothing and beards. Among the free exhibits are the Agricultural Building with judging and displays, the archery contest demonstration and tournament, baton twirling, chicken barbecue contest, draft horse pull, Fine Arts Building, 4-H International Show and Highway Gardens. The fair has a midway with rides and concessions. It's called "A Mile-Long Pleasure Trail." The fair also has stock car races and a demolition derby. It is financed through paid admissions, entry fees and rentals.

Montana

Crow Agency

CROW FAIR CELEBRATION AND POWWOW

Held annually, August
Ethnic

The Crow Fair Celebration and Powwow, formerly called the Crow Indian Fair, is an all-Indian event held in mid-August for at least six days. The date changes annually but is always in August. Indian tribes from northwest Canada and the Plains states participate, with more than 10,000 Indians attending and camping out nearby. Visitors are encouraged to attend and witness the various events, such as a daily costume parade. Afternoons are filled with a horse race and rodeo at a local stadium. Ceremonial dances begin late in the evening, and on the last day of the fair, the entire encampment performs a dance. Most events are open to the public, and the friendly Crow Indians, unlike Indians in the Southwest, will allow themselves to be photographed. Part of the fair and powwow is the colorful encampment of tepees set up around the grounds. It looks like a movie set, but it's the real thing. The fair has good food concessions and some Indian craft booths around the camp's dancing area. Though expensive, the crafts are authentic. The Crow craft expertise is in beadwork, especially necklaces and leather accessories. Crow Agency is within the Crow Reservation, which takes in most of the Bighorn Canyon Recreation Area, so visitors to the fair can also enjoy camping, fishing and boating. The Crow Fair was first started in 1904. Especially impressive are the dancers and parade participants, clad in buckskin, bells and feathers.

Red Lodge

FESTIVAL OF NATIONS

Held annually, August
Ethnic

The annual Festival of Nations is a multi-ethnic event dealing with the cultures of nine different nationalities who've settled here over the years. It is meant as a tribute to these groups and to preserve their customs, music, foods, arts and crafts. It is a nine-day event, usually held in early August. The festival features free food, parades, exhibits and evening programs. More than 15,000 visitors come to this area, which was once an early mining town, which explains why it attracted so many different European groups in its heyday. Nightly entertainment is held at the Red Lodge Civic Center. Each nationality presents a tableau of the Old World with songs and dances, usually performed in national costumes. Exhibits include priceless heirlooms, souvenirs and Old World treasures of the early days, carefully preserved. There is a continuous flower show reflecting the tastes of the various ethnic groups and an art exhibit of paintings, sculpture and pottery by both professional and amateur Montana artists. Every afternoon on the city's main street, spinning, weaving, oil painting, china plate painting, wood carving, pottery throwing, quilt making and copper enameling are demonstrated, usually in local store windows. A highlight of the festival is the food. On each designated nationality day, each group prepares its foods in a downtown store. Visitors are able to obtain the recipes and menus and taste the foods. The various ethnic groups send their national flags to be flown during the festival at the Civic Center Auditorium. To date, more than 100 foreign and state flags have been displayed. The nationalities represented and honored during the festival include Yugoslavian, Italian, Finnish, Irish-English, German, Scandinavian (Norwegian, Danish, Swedish) and Scottish. The festival is financed by donations and some paid admissions. It was started in 1951 by a small group of local residents interested in the cultures of the different ethnic groups in the city. It is a communitywide project, with most of the residents contributing time, money and creative ability to the festival.

Nebraska

Minden

NEBRASKA DANISH DAYS/DANISH ETHNIC FESTIVAL

Held annually, May/June
Ethnic

Nebraska Danish Days, or Danish Ethnic Festival, stresses Danish culture and art. The first festival was held June 13, 1973, and was part of a week-long celebration marking the 125th anniversary of Fort Kearny in Nebraska. The event is sponsored by the Danish Brotherhood Lodge 16, and town volunteers each put in 1,500 hours of work preparing for the annual event. Festivities include a parade, complete with a king and queen and floats. There's a Danish smorgasbord and an *aebleskiver* and *sodsupper* dinner, followed by folk dancing. During the special day, the entire town and its buildings and shops are decorated in Danish style with Danish arts and crafts displays. The event is host to more than 4,000 visitors, and over the years, more than 30,000.

Nebraska City

ARBOR DAY CELEBRATION/ARTS FESTIVAL

Held annually, April
Ecology

The Arbor Day Celebration is held for one day every April as close to April 22 or on that day in honor of J. Sterling Morton, who started the observance more than 100 years ago. The day, which sometimes runs for three days during special anniversary celebrations and more recently during the bicentennial, is a conservation-oriented event whose highlight is the planting of trees in the area and throughout Nebraska. It is a state holiday and has been widely copied by other states as a conservation move. It is basically a civic day that includes speeches, a reception, luncheon, a fly-in breakfast at Grundman Airport and the official 1:30 p.m. Arbor Day Parade, followed by Arbor Day ceremonies at the East Portico of the Arbor Lodge Mansion. Inclement weather puts the ceremonies indoors at the Senior High School Auditorium. The ceremonies take about an hour and include the presentation of colors by the American Legion, a 15-minute choral program by the Wesley House Chapel Choir of the University of Nebraska (in Lincoln), an invocation, a welcome to guests and the introduction of special guests, who change each year. There is the presentation of awards, which include the Tree City USA Award and Parade Awards, followed by an Arbor Day speech by a local politician. Trees are planted in honor of someone cited for civic contributions, part of the Arbor Day Foundation Award. The ceremony ends with a benediction, followed by the planting of a tree to honor that special person. Arbor Day became National Arbor Day by proclamation April 24, 1972, by President Richard M. Nixon. Arbor Day was 100 years old in 1972. A special monument was erected that year in Nebraska City to honor the founding father, J. Sterling Morton. The monument's inscription reads: "Other holidays repose upon the past; Arbor Day proposes for the future." That sums up the purpose of the annual observance, the future and replacing of trees, all kinds returned to the earth from which so many have been taken. The idea of planting trees dates back to 1852, when J. Sterling Morton and his bride, Caroline Joy, arrived in Bellevue but then moved near Nebraska City, where they homesteaded. The area was a native prairie, simple, barren and with no sign of any previous white man's settlement. This was shortly after the Nebraska Territory was established. The Mortons chose a site for their home on one of the highest points on the land, with the Missouri River and neighboring Iowa Bluffs in full view. They built their house and also planted flowers, shrubs, vines and orchard trees, shade trees and evergreens. Eventually the barren prairie became a scenic area, and the home, Arbor Lodge, was one of the earliest known attempts at conservation and beautification in Nebraska. Today's Arbor Lodge, part of the original one, has 52 rooms and beautifully landscaped gardens with trees. It is where the Arbor Day ceremonies are held. Arbor Day became a practical movement in 1872, spearheaded by Morton when he delivered a resolution at the State Board of Agriculture meeting, January 4, 1872, calling for the establishment of a statewide Arbor Day observance and the planting of trees. The resolution passed. Reports claim that millions of trees were planted in the state on the first official Arbor Day, and since then, billions. Over the years, Nebraska has become the state with millions of growing trees, the direct result of the Arbor Day planting by J. Sterling Morton in 1872. Today, almost every state in the union has an Arbor Day. Arbor Day became a legal state holiday in Nebraska, April 22, 1885. April 22 was selected because it was Morton's birthday. Thousands come to Nebraska City to Arbor Lodge State Park for the ceremonies. The event is financed by personal and business donations and proceeds from the arts festival, work on the annual observance is by volunteers.

Omaha

AK-SAR-BEN LIVESTOCK EXPOSITION AND RODEO

Held annually, September/October
Economic

Ak-Sar-Ben Livestock Exposition and Rodeo is a nine-day display of Nebraskan youth's interest in agriculture and related agribusiness industries. It claims to be the "World's Largest 4-H Livestock Show." It is held in late September through early October. "Ak-Sar-Ben" is "Nebraska" spelled backward. The exposition's livestock show draws entries from eight states and about 175 Nebraskan counties each year. The event, which dates back to 1928, was started by a group of stockyard owners and operators in Omaha to encourage more of an interest in livestock among the state's young people. It attracts upwards of 50,000 visitors annually, and since its start, several million. There is no doubt that the exposition is an economic boon to the city. Popular features include the World Championship Rodeo and Catch-a-Calf in the stock show. There is also entertainment, which in the past has featured Roy Rogers, Dale Evans and Lynn Anderson. The first stock show opened November 3, 1928, with 450 head of cattle. Today's entries exceed 5,000. For two years, the event continued as a full-scale national breed show, financed by a nonprofit civic group's racing revenue. Parimutuel betting was then banned in Nebraska. The show, however, continues through donations from several Omaha businessmen. The Depression cut into the donations. Livestock events were then restricted to only 4-H competitions. Eliminated were the National Breed and Horse Shows. Actually, this trend was to be the new focus of the show, which did develop into a showcase for 4-H activities. A championship rodeo replaced the breed and horse shows. In fact, the rodeo is far more successful. In the mid-1930s, parimutuel racing when run by nonprofit agricultural organizations, state and county Fair associations, was legalized by the state. Things picked up only to come to a temporary halt during World War II. The Ak-Sar-Ben Field was taken over by the Army and used for a motor transport depot. Today, the exposition is popular because of the thoroughbred racing. Ak-Sar-Ben is able to contribute several hundred thousand dollars annually to agricultural research. There is no admission charge to the livestock show or exhibits, only to the rodeo. The event is financed through the Knights of Ak-Sar-Ben and Purple Ribbon Club (each member contributes $100 or more for the purchase of animals). The event is held at the Ak-Sar-Ben Field.

Wilber

CZECH FESTIVAL

Held annually, August
Ethnic

The Czech Festival is held the first Saturday and Sunday in August in a town
that bills itself as the Czech Capital of Nebraska. It's on the Big Blue River and
is the county seat of Saline County, near Lincoln. It is an authentic ethnic festival
in every sense of the word. Residents wear Czech costumes and dance the *beseda*
in the city streets or do a polka or sing folk songs. Visitors have plenty of
opportunity to sample Czech food, which includes roast duck, sauerkraut, dump-
lings and *kolaches* (sweet buns), all homemade from local Czech kitchens. The
food is inexpensive. There are parades with costumed participants, speeches by
the mayor, the crowning of a Nebraska Czech Queen and a pageant. The festival
attracts 50,000 people every year and since the first event in 1962 has seen well
over a million visitors, who have contributed to the local economy. The festival
includes an art show at the Dvoracek Memorial Library, talent contests, folk
dancing, songs and music. Each year, the festival is keyed to a different theme,
such as youth, the arts or food. There are awards for achievements in promoting
both Nebraska and the Czech culture. Sunday is Awards Day and the day of the
big parade, with more floats and costumed marchers. There are kolache-eating
contests and more entertainment. Folk dance groups come from all over Nebraska
for this event. The local community patterned its festival after the famous Pennsylvania Dutch Festival in Kutztown, Pennsylvania. The sole purpose of this
festival is to foster ethnic culture. It is financed by membership dues in the
various Czech societies, who work on the festival. There is an admission fee to
the festival and a charge for food and sale of handicrafts. The town's residents
and club members work two to three months in advance of the event itself and
on a voluntary basis.

Nevada

Elko

NATIONAL BASQUE FESTIVAL

Held annually, July
Ethnic

The National Basque Festival is an annual meeting of the Basques the first or
second weekend in July. The Basques, originally from the Pyrenees Mountains

of France and Spain, seem to have settled largely in the mountains and deserts of the American Far West. They gather once a year to drink, eat, dance and perform unbelievable feats of strength. While the women serve meals and do some folk dancing and singing, the festival is strictly a male event. There's no women's lib at the festival. More than 10,000 Basques come every year to this small Nevada town, as do thousands of non-Basques to attend a different kind of ethnic event. The Basques speak their ancient language, which still remains a linguistic mystery, since it doesn't seem to resemble any other language. They begin arriving on a Friday, shouting, singing and visiting the local pubs. They are noted for being tough, taciturn, clannish and chauvinist. They are also hard drinkers. The women remain in the campers and motels. The men wear a beret and scarf in addition to their regular clothes. They always end their evening's drinking with the singing of the Basque national anthem, ''Guernica Arboal,'' or ''Trees of Guernica.'' Festival events begin Saturday and continue through Sunday. There is a parade, a big Saturday night dance with a Basque orchestra, a Basque mass, an outdoor barbecue for 5,000 and the strength competitions at Elko's fairgrounds. The Saturday parade has marching bands, floats and local politicians. The parade ends in the fairgrounds, where there is a charge to watch but children watch for free. Although the festival is a gathering of the clans, tourists are encouraged to watch and even participate in some of the events. Inside the fairgrounds there are tubs of ice and beer and quart bottles of brandy, which Basque men drink like soda pop. The strength competitions include the lifting of a two-foot-long, eight-inch-diameter steel cylinder weighing about 250 pounds. It has two depressions for the contestant to put his hand into to lift it. The idea of this lifting event is to raise it onto the shoulder as many times as possible within a two- or three-minute period. In 1975, Jose Arriets established a record of 43 lifts within six minutes. The record still stands. Another mind-boggling event features two small weights, each about the size of a round loaf of bread and each weighing about 104 pounds. The contestant has to carry one in each hand, walking as far as possible before dropping the weights or falling over. Basically the event consists of the competitor picking up the weights to walk or attempt to walk to a marked tree stump 100 feet from the starting point. He must circle the tree stump and return the 100 feet to the original starting point. He then must repeat the feat going to another stump farther away and so on to see how many he can do. One year, a Basque contestant achieved 980 feet. Still another feat of strength involves a sheep, which is let out of a cage into an enclosed ring. The contestant has to hook and tie the sheep as quickly as possible. This takes place in a pen away from the grandstand so that animals who panic and stampede won't harm the crowds. Each contestant is given a hook. He waits in a corner of the ring as the sheep is released from another corner. The contestant watches for the animal's vulnerable knee joint. If there is a quick snapping of the hook into the flesh behind the sheep's knee, there is no pain and the sheep doesn't know what's happened. The sheep is then hustled onto the ground near a stake with its legs tied tight and quickly. Still another

competition is a wood-chopping event but no ordinary one. Six rows of cottonwood tree trunks with seven to a row and with diameters of 55 inches are set
up for chopping right through. It sounds easy but isn't. Competitors have been
known to chop through into their own legs. Saturday night there is a Basque
dance at the local National Guard Armory. Sunday begins with a sung mass in
the City Park with a Basque priest officiating. For those who do not attend the
service, there is a softball contest at the diamond next to the picnic grounds. In
the afternoon, 20 or more tables are set up at the picnic grounds with men in
aprons, ready to serve Basque food. There is a charge of $5 per person. The
portions are more than ample. It is actually an outdoor barbecue, with Basque
chefs taking care of 150 steaks, 300 lamb chops and more. Some 5,000 meals
are served. After the meal, the previous day's winners are announced and given
their prizes. *Bertsolaris*, or troubadours, then entertain with song improvisations.
They are three male singers from Spain, and the songs are stories about Basque
life and culture. Each singer competes with the other by making up verses, all
sung in Basque. This is followed by Basque folk dancing with men, women and
children performing on the tennis court grounds. Costumes are red, green and
white. Men wear berets, sashes, slippers and sabers. The men perform traditional
dances such as the *makil dantza* (stick dance), the *arin-arin* (fast-fast), the
inguritxo (circle dance) and the *porrusalda* (leek soup dance). The festival began
in 1962. Gatherings prior to the formal festival were always held but not organized until the early 1960s. Its purpose is to preserve the Basque culture and
to hold annual reunions. Outsiders are welcome so that they can learn about the
Basque.

Fallon

ALL INDIAN RODEO AND STAMPEDE DAYS

Held annually, July
Ethnic, sports

The All Indian Rodeo and Stampede Days is a three-day program held either
the third or fourth weekend in July. All events are at the Fallon fairgrounds. It
attempts to preserve the heritage and culture of the Nevada Indian and to help
the development of Nevada Indian youth. The highlight is the all-Indian rodeo
at noon each day, with cash prizes for the various events. The rodeo features
saddle bronc, bull riding, bareback, bull doggin', calf roping, team roping, wild
cow milking, senior barrel races, a wild horse race with three per team, wild
horse roping, a junior barrel race for those under 13 and a pony ride for under-
13 contestants weighing less than 120 pounds. There is a top eight saddle bronc
ride-off on Sunday. Indian hand games and dancing are held both Friday and
Saturday with daily craft sales. There is a Miss Indian Nevada Contest and

Pageant Friday evening. The winner competes in the All-American Indian event in Wyoming. There is an Indian parade 10 a.m. Saturday with prizes awarded for the most colorful float or group in costume and for the best dancing costumed group. Indian foods are also sold during the event. Most popular events include the rodeo, powwow and parade because of the cash prizes. In 1977, there was a total of $6,000 in cash prizes. More than 25,000 people come for the stampede, and since the first one in 1967, more than 3 million. Indian competitors all from various tribes come from all over the United States and Canada. The event hopes to build up finances to be used for all Indian youth education activities, like 4-H, vocational and higher education as well as cultural and traditional education. Behind the annual event from its start is the Nevada Rodeo Association, the Fallon Chamber of Commerce and many local residents and businessmen. Even the governor is an active participant. The event is financed by paid gate receipts and by sponsorships.

Reno

NATIONAL CHAMPIONSHIP AIR RACES

Held annually, September
Economic

The National Championship Air Races, once a six-day event, are now held three days in mid-September. The event includes prequalifying heats and races with supporting air shows. The races are widely known and often have international entries. Race officials claim that it is the world's richest air race. The races feature three classes: unlimiteds, AT 6/SNJs and IXL/Midgets. The three classes of planes include two vintage World War II planes and a "home-built" division. They race in the heats. Supporting air show acts, like aerobatic pilots, are interspersed to keep audiences interested and produce a well-rounded event. The races are the same each year with the exception that now only three instead of four classes of planes race. The racing biplane class was eliminated. The races are always held in mid-September because the weather and flying conditions are best. It is estimated that at least 50,000 spectators watch the races, and since the races began in 1963, more than 700,000. Most popular features include the unlimited class, since they are the fastest and seem to appeal to audiences. As for the supporting shows, the Confederate Air Force act and aerobatic pilots like Bob Hoover and Art School are very popular. The annual event is a community effort, with work done on a voluntary basis by residents and community and business leaders. It's a year-round job, but the major thrust comes the month before the races. The races are held at the Reno/Stead Airport. There are admission charges, which vary each year. Originally the races were underwritten by local businesses, but today the event is self-sustaining. All concessions are operated by local service organizations, with proceeds going back into the Reno community. The event is run by an all-volunteer board of trustees comprised of local businesses. The races were started in 1963 by Bill Stead, a Reno industrialist, and other businessmen. They patterned it after the Cleveland, Ohio, Air Races. In 1976, the purse for the races was $100,000. Today it is $300,000.

Tonopah

JIM BUTLER DAYS

Held annually, May
Historic, commemorative

Jim Butler Days cover four days over the Memorial Day weekend in May. It is a memorial to the man who accidentally founded Tonopah, once a rich silver-producing town. The four days are filled with all kinds of activities, such as a street dance, mucking contests and single jack (hammer drill) and double-jack drilling contests. There are Fire Department water fights and a turn-of-the-century costume Grand Ball. It is held in May to attract visitors. About 1,000 come annually. All events take place on Main Street. In addition, tours of the former silver mining town are offered, taking in the sights of this off-beat area. The event was started in 1970, and to date about 10,000 people have attended. Jim Butler was a mining prospector with little success. He was traveling through in 1900. Legend has it that his burro stumbled over a rock. Butler was annoyed at the clumsy animal and picked up the rock to throw it away. Since he was a prospector, he noticed that the rock was a high grade of silver ore. Whether the story is true or not, there was a Jim Butler, and he did discover silver in this area. He was so broke that he couldn't afford an assay of the rock so he appealed to the others with him to chip in on the assay. He not only established his fortune but also that of others, founded Tonopah and put Nevada on its feet. It is estimated that more than $200 million in precious metals, mainly silver, was mined. Nevada was able to send a senator to Washington and later helped rebuild San Francisco after the fire and earthquake of 1906. This also led to a series of mining camp booms for Nevada. Tonopah is located between rugged mountain peaks and today is in the midst of a large ranching area, reached from U.S. Transcontinental Highway 6, Highway 8-A and Highway 95, connecting Reno and Las Vegas. Tonopah is a Shoshone Indian word meaning "little wood, little water," and Jim Butler's wife is credited with selecting the name for the town. Incidentally, the headframe of the famous Mizpah Mine can still be seen. In more recent years, it was the property of the famous and mysterious late Howard Hughes. Work on the special days is by local citizens. There are admission charges for the events, which help to finance the celebration, as does the sale of Jim Butler memorial buttons.

New Hampshire

Newbury

CRAFTSMEN'S FAIR

Held annually, August
Economic

The annual Craftsmen's Fair at Mt. Sunapee State Park is considered to be the longest continuing craft fair, held since 1934. The six-day fair begins the first Tuesday in August and features a juried exhibit, which is open to 3,500 members of the League of New Hampshire Craftsmen. The fair offers sales and crafts demonstrations by about 300 craftsmen, with daily programs. Crafts include pottery, leather, metals, clothing, leaded glass, jewelry, prints, blown glass, blacksmithing, batik, enamel, weaving, wood/metal, lampshades, toys, wood, pewter and even candy. There are both major exhibitors booths and mini-booths. In addition, special crafts are demonstrated daily, giving visitors a chance to learn and ask questions about spoon carving, decoy carving, wood veneering, painting, printmaking, needlecrafts, weaving, spinning and dyeing. The fair also features demonstrations of antique toy replicas, basket making, character dolls, marionettes, embroidering, forging, lace, macrame and pipe making. Occasionally the fair includes performing arts, like theater, songs and country and folk dancing. This varies from year to year. Approximately 30,000 come to the annual fair, and since 1934, well over 1 million. The fair educates the public about the art of crafts and serves as a fund-raising event for the League of New Hampshire Craftsmen. It also helps the local economy because of the influx of extra visitors in August, vacation time. The fair is supported through the sales of exhibited crafts and paid admissions. Work on fair details is a year-round job that involves the league's staff, craftsmen and volunteers.

New Jersey

Flemington

FLEMINGTON FAIR

Held annually, August/September
Economic

The Flemington Fair is more than 120 years old and is held annually for seven days the last days of August right through Labor Day. The fair is thought of as an old-fashioned agricultural event, attracting thousands. Its top events include a state 4-H Lamb Show and Sale. There is a tractor pull with farm and modified tractors, a garden tractor pull and a horse and pony pull. The fair also has a State Dairy Princess contest, Fireman's Day programs and exhibits on agriculture, 4-H, fancywork, nurserymen, flowers and commercial displays. There are various events, which include all types of racing, mini-stocks, modified stocks, midgets and super sprints. There is also a Thrill Show and demolition derby and a horseshoe pitching contest. Special children's events include all 4-H programs and two children's day specials, when they are admitted free to the grounds and to the afternoon show in the grandstand. The fair was started in 1856 by local farmers and industry. It is supported by paid admissions, entry fees and rentals.

Ocean City

BABY PARADE

Held annually, August
Economic, touristic

This Baby Parade is a one-day event always held the second Thursday in August at the resort's boardwalk. More than 300 babies, from infants to 10 years old, participate and compete for prizes. The parade begins at the boardwalk and Sixth Street, going to Twelfth. The judges' reviewing stand is at the Music Pier, at the boardwalk and Moorlyn Terrace. There are four different parade divisions. Division A is for children in fancy decorated go-carts, strollers, kiddie cars, wagons or walking coaches. This division also has three separate sections, based on the age of the parading child. Section 1 is for those up to 2 years old. Section 2 features those from 2 to 6 years old and section three, ages 6 to 10. Division B features children in comic decorated vehicles, as in Division A, and also includes walking. Division C is for floats, consisting of all vehicles with tops or sides built or added measuring more than three by five feet. Division D is also a floats division but for both commercial and noncommercial ones. Special awards, ranging from a $25 savings bond to $50 cash are given to the best entry. All children who enter also receive a sterling silver identification bracelet. The parade which had baseball immortal, Joe DiMaggio as the 1983 grand marshal, serves to help the economy of the resort area while entertaining the area, which is known as a family resort. The parade is watched by 50,000 people every year. The parade is financed by city budget funds and the sale of parade seat tickets and entry fees for each child. Work on the event is by volunteers. The parade dates back to 1901 when it was started by the late Leo Bamberger and perpetuated by Henry Bamberger, son of the founder of Bamberger's Department Store.

Point Pleasant Beach

BENIHANA GRAND PRIX POWER BOAT REGATTA/N.J. OFFSHORE GRAND PRIX

Held annually, July
Sports

The N.J. Offshore Grand Prix, formerly the Benihana Grand Prix Power Boat Regatta, is now a four-day annual race in mid-July. It was started as a challenge to fast offshore speed boats. Today, it is among the largest offshore powerboat races around. The regatta is actually a festival, since it also includes a beauty pageant, band concerts, parties, fireworks. The race always takes place on a Wednesday, starting at 10 a.m. Its course is on the Jersey Coast from Asbury Park to Barnegat. The regatta, expanded over the years, is extremely popular, attracting up to 250,000 spectators on the beaches. About 3,000 power boats watch from offshore. It is financed by entry fees and donations from various businesses. Volunteers from the local area work on each year's details. The regatta dates back to 1964 and originally was the Around Long Island Marathon, covering 265 miles. It was changed to the Jersey shore because there are more open beaches, clear waterways and more spectators. It was originally the Hennessy Grand Prix, sponsored by James Hennessy, who later dropped sponsorship of the event. Odell Lewis was the first winner, and the race was sanctioned by the New Jersey Offshore Powerboat Racing Association, whose president was William Wishnick. Astronaut Gordon Cooper and auto racer Roger Penske have attended the event.

New Mexico

Santa Fe

INDIAN MARKET

Held annually, August
Cultural, economic, ethnic

The two-day Indian Market is held the third weekend in August at the plaza. Its purpose is threefold: to encourage the revival of ancient Indian arts and crafts; to encourage the development of new and contemporary designs in arts and crafts; and to provide a market for the Indians. The event takes place at the Santa Fe Plaza, and the arts and crafts are exhibited in tent booths on the four sides of the plaza. The market devotes itself to displaying both days, but Sunday usually features Indian songs and dances to the accompaniment of drums. The Indian Market is sponsored by the Southwestern Association on Indian Affairs, Inc., a nonprofit organization whose membership includes both Indians and non-Indians. It is mainly concerned with the Indians of the Southwest but will help other minorities. It maintains an educational program, offering financial assistance to Indian students of college age. Both market days are preceded by a day of judging certain entries. Items to be judged are set up in the New Mexico Room of the Capitol Building off the plaza as early as 5:30 a.m. The Friday before the market officially opens to the public, it is not unusual for more than 2,000 items to be entered for judging. These include dolls, baskets, beadwork, sculptures and weaving, exhibited from 10 a.m. to 6 p.m. The official judging begins at 7 a.m. Judges are experts in the field of arts and Indian culture. The number of items to be judged and awarded blue ribbons, certificates and cash prizes is staggering, and competition is keen. In 1976, 1,162 articles were entered for judging, ranging in price from 50 cents to $9,000, and the total valuation of the items was $465,000. When the market opens to the public Saturday morning, all the winning items with their awards are already sold. However, there are thousands of other items displayed for sale. The market features lots of pottery and jewelry but still is low on the graphic arts and sculpture, a situation the sponsoring association is trying to change. The Indian Market, however, is still the best place to buy authentic Indian arts and crafts, and more than 100,000 visitors are there to buy something. More than 400 exhibitors participate in the market, which coincides with one of the big weekends of the Santa Fe Opera Festival, bringing more visitors. Sunday afternoon at the market features a traditional Indian costume competition, and dance groups perform in the patio of the Palace of Governors. There is no admission charge to the market. Among the participating Indian tribes are the Hopi, Navajo and Zuni. All proceeds from the market sales go to the participating artists and craftsmen. The market dates back to September 1922, when the first fair, or exhibit, as it was called, was held in the State Armory, now part of the Museum of New Mexico. It was sponsored by the School of American Research. All the exhibited items were sold, and the market was an instant success. It was originally held in conjunction with the Santa Fe Fiesta, but by 1932 the event was so successful that the school turned it over to the New Mexico Association of Indian Affairs. In 1936 the market moved out of the armory to the open-air plaza and has been there ever since. In 1954, the New Mexico Association of Indian Affairs became the Southwestern Association on Indian Affairs to enlarge the scope and aims of the group. In addition, the Indian Market was held independently of the Santa Fe Fiesta. Both events had grown so large and popular, it was felt by association members that it would be better to hold them separately. So the Indian Market is always the third weekend in August rather than on the Labor Day holiday. The Indian Market is self-sustaining. Exhibitors pay a fee for a booth to the association, whose members pay dues.

Santa Fe

SANTA FE CHAMBER MUSIC FESTIVAL

Held annually, July/August
Cultural

The Santa Fe Chamber Music Festival is a six-week event which starts in July and continues through mid-August. There are five weekday concerts plus one on Sundays. The festival is a major event in the Southwest, attracting thousands. The festival highlights composers and guest performers. For example, in 1977 the festival paid tribute to Aaron Copland, who also participated in the event. The festival goes back to July 1973 and was the idea of concert pianist Alicia Schachter. She continues as artistic director and works closely with Sheldon Rich, festival director. It is always held in summer because the weather is best for outdoor performances. Other celebrities who've performed at the festival include Alfred Brendel, Sylvia Rosenberg and Richard Goode. About 5,000 attend each year. The festival's purpose is to bring culture to Santa Fe and outlying regions, where chamber music is limited. Both volunteers and a paid staff work on festival details. The event is financed by ticket sales, private donations, foundation grants, the New Mexico Arts Commission, State Arts Council and National Endowment for the Arts grants.

Santa Fe

SANTA FE OPERA FESTIVAL

Held annually, July/August
Cultural, music

The Santa Fe Opera Festival is held every July and August, performing to a 95 percent-capacity-filled house. The festival features both traditional and contemporary operas, sometimes well-known performers. Often, the festival serves as premiere vehicle for a brand new opera. The festival, which requires tickets, is only partially financed by sales. The event was started by John Crosby in 1957 and held on his 10-acre San Juan ranch, five miles north of Santa Fe. It was an experiment. Performances were in a theater that seated only 480 persons. The company had 65 members. That experiment is today an annual event of international significance, attracting many European performers and visitors. The theater was destroyed by fire in 1967 and rebuilt to accommodate 1,600 persons. The opera festival is held in a scenic area and in a community that is wealthy and supportive of the annual event. In a *New York Times* interview (August 18, 1976), festival founder Crosby told reporter Peter G. Davis: "The fact that we are a festival operation I think accounts for much of our success with the public. We can afford to take a chance with offbeat items because opera buffs want to see new things now, and we plan our repertory accordingly.'' The festival has been host to 4 world premieres and more than 15 American premieres of various operas. It has also developed an apprentice system, enabling handpicked apprentices to spend summers with the opera company and sing in the chorus or small roles. Many go on to major careers, like Sherill Milnes and Judith Blegen.

New York

Bainbridge

GENERAL CLINTON CANOE REGATTA

Held annually, May
Sports, historic

The General Clinton Canoe Regatta is held for three and a half days over the Memorial Day weekend in May, when the river level is more dependable. The original event was started to give the local chamber of commerce a project to promote the recreational potential of the Susquehanna River and to incorporate the historical trip down that river by General Clinton and his troops during the Revolutionary War with a canoe race over the same course. Today, the event is a 70-mile endurance race on the river from Cooperstown to Bainbridge. When the event started in 1962, it was a one-day affair. The original idea was that of Charles Hinkley, a member of the local chamber of commerce. The race has gained national recognition because of the professional division of the 70-mile race. It is known as the World's Championship Flat Water Endurance Race, the longest one-day race of its kind. There are cash prizes, and the event attracts canoeists from Canada, Michigan, Minnesota and Wisconsin. More than 2,000 enter, and spectators total more than 50,000. The first race in 1962 had 90 canoeists and only a few hundred spectators. The race has three divisions in the 70-mile event, one professional and two for amateurs, based on the type of canoe used. There is a 10-man relay race, covering about a 30-mile distance, which has been extended to women and mixed teams. There is a 1-man race of 20 miles, a 10-mile couples race, a sprint and a youth race of 5 miles for each division. Ashore on the grounds of the 45-acre General Clinton Park, there are activities for the spectators, including a carnival, arts and crafts show, flea market, entertainment, talent show and fashion and dog shows. There is also a youth wrestling tournament, concerts, fireworks and sky diving exhibitions. On the river, there are canoe tilting and handling demonstrations. Monies from race entries made it possible for the local chamber of commerce to finance the purchase of 45 acres of riverfront land, now the General Clinton Park. The event is also financed by paid admissions for land programs and donations.

Cape Vincent

FRENCH FESTIVAL/FRENCH DAY

Held annually, July
Ethnic

The French Festival/French Day is a one-day event that is held the Saturday before Bastille Day, July 14. Cape Vincent, in the Thousand Islands area, has a French background. Not only were early settlers French, but also there was a strong feeling for Napoleon. A cup-and-saucer–style house was built in the area with the thought of helping Napoleon spend his exile in this area. Cape Vincent during the 1800s was a haven for followers of Napoleon like Le Roy De Chaumont, who also was responsible for settling Cape Vincent. The festival dates back to 1968, launched as both an ethnic and cultural event. Early festival planners included the late Mrs. Esther L. Levy of the Thousand Islands Bridge Authority and the local chamber of commerce. An astounding 25,000 visitors poured into tiny Cape Vincent (population around 1,000) for the one-day celebration, with many coming from French Canada. Everything is French—pastry, bread, ice cream, costumes, pageant and home-decorated carts with a French open market. The event takes place on three town streets directly off the main highway. The festival lasts eight hours, starting at 10 a.m. and continuing into early evening, sometimes going on till 9:30 p.m. All carts and exhibits are ready for viewing at 10 a.m., with the official opening an hour later with a parade and the crowning of a French Festival Queen. There are dance performances, popular music concerts and a French mass at St. Vincent de Paul's Church. The evening ends with fireworks at the waterfront. There are no admission charges to the festival, only for arts and crafts sold and for meals. The entire village works on the festival, and it's financed by private contributions and the sale of food and souvenirs.

Franklinville

MAPLE FESTIVAL

Held annually, April
Economic

The Maple Festival, formerly the Western New York Maple Festival, dates back to 1962, when Cattaraugus County decided its maple syrup was just as good as any other state's. Local businesses and civic leaders also felt that a festival was needed to say goodby to winter. The festival attracts more than 10,000 visitors the last weekend in April, sometimes extending to May 1, when the sap is running high, or whatever it does in the local maple trees. Naturally this annual event boosts the local economy. It celebrates the annual rising of the sap in the maple trees, producing a product used since the 1800s and still as tasty as ever, according to local residents. The admission-free festival begins with a parade of floats, bands, drum and bugle corps and a Festival Queen Coronation at 2 p.m. Then it's off to see the sugar-making process at the Sugar Shanty, a small wooden imitation log cabin. The process is demonstrated continually during the festival. Other events center at the local grade school building and grounds on North Main Street, Route 16. Other festival events include industrial exhibits, art, antique steam and gas engines and an antique show and sale (this one requires an admission fee). In addition, there's an exhibit of antique maple syrup tools—many handmade within the last century—at the Miner's Cabin. The festival also sells a choice of three meals: pancakes and sausage with maple syrup, a roast beef dinner and a ham and leek dinner. While the emphasis is on the rising sap in the maple trees and maple syrup demonstrations, many other events have been added to the three-day program, such as a horse show, "Paul Bunyan" competitions and a sports car rally. Maple syrup, of course, is sold as is maple ice cream, as candies and even as sugar maple trees. Work on the festival is done by volunteers, who put in an estimated 4,000 man-hours per year. The event, originally the Franklinville Maple Fest, is financed through the sale of food, renting of exhibit area and donations from local businesses.

Hunter

GERMAN ALPS FESTIVAL

Held annually, July
Ethnic

The German Alps Festival is a summertime version of Germany's Oktoberfest or Beer Festival. It is held at Hunter Mountain Ski Bowl, a year-round resort area. It is an 18-day July event that now also includes a beer fair and display of various beers from Germany. The festival features German foods, beer, wine and entertainment, often from Europe. There are folk songs, dances and handicrafts for display and sale. About 250,000 attend each year. There is an admission charge to the festival grounds. The event was started as a 12-day program in July 1973. The festival is financed by paid admissions, exhibitor fees, donations from businesses and the sale of souvenir journals.

Hunter

INTERNATIONAL POLKA FESTIVAL

Held annually, August
Ethnic, economic

The International Polka Festival, formerly a nine-day event is now held three days, featuring top polka bands and performers from all over the United States, Canada and Europe. It's held in mid-August at Hunter Mountain, a year-round resort area. Band entertainment and polkas are performed in a blue and white tent the size of a football field. More than 60 polka bands compete, and there is a selection and crowning of a Polka Queen. The music is continuous from 11 a.m. to midnight daily. There are polka dance lessons available, as well as craft demonstrations, European puppet shows and ethnic foods. Hunter is on Route 23A in the Catskill Mountain area of the state. The festival features polkas of Polish, Slovenian, Czech, Ukrainian and German groups. There are contests with trophies for the best dancers. The event was started in 1977 as a polka showcase. There is an admission charge to the festival. The event attracts more than 30,000 people every year.

New York City

FEAST OF SAN GENNARO

Held annually, September
Ethnic, religious

The Feast of San Gennaro is New York City's most famous festival, dating back to 1926. Basically a religious event honoring San Gennaro on September 19, it has also become an ethnic and cultural event. The observance still centers around the saint's feast day of September 19 and includes two weekends, always ending on a Sunday. The two-week festival was originally only a four-day event. San Gennaro is said to have led the people out of Naples when Mount Vesuvius erupted in A.D. 431. The saint was a bishop, who was later martyred. During the festival's fiftieth anniversary in 1976, two sacred relic bones of the saint were flown in from Rome to be part of the annual procession and mass at the Church of the Most Precious Blood on Baxter Street. The silver statue of San Gennaro stands on Mulberry Street during the festival, and each year people attach dollar bills to the statue. The money is used for scholarships for children of Italian descent and for community projects. The statue is kept at the San Gennaro Society's headquarters on Mulberry Street the rest of the year. Highlight of the festival is the procession and parade with the statue and marching bands to the church for an afternoon mass. More than 300 stands line Mulberry and adjoining streets. These stands sell all kinds of Neapolitan foods, pastries and drinks. Over the years other ethnic foods have been added, but the annual event that attracts the astounding number of more than 2 million people remains a Neapolitan folklore event with songs, dances and entertainment, not to overlook the biggest drawing card—the food, prepared at the stalls right out on the street. The stands are on Mulberry, Hester, Grand and Broome streets, an area still known as Little Italy, spilling out across Canal Street into Chinatown. Sausages continue to be the number one favorite food. Other tasty dishes include noodles floating in cream, cheesecake, cannoli and pizza covered with mozzarella cheese. There are also wheels of fortune, games of chance and souvenir booths. There are band concerts. Most of the famous restaurants in the area feature special dinners at lower prices during the feast to attract business. Local bakeries, groceries and private butcher shops do a booming business, with many visitors shopping to bring home foods to be prepared from recipes that are given out at the feast. Some food booths serve macaroni pie, homemade manicotti, baked ziti, stuffed peppers and artichokes. The feast has had its share of Italian and Italian-American celebrities, including actress Gina Lollobrigida and Frank Sinatra. The feast continually expands with more booths, music, bandstands and special events. When the feast first began about 100,000 people attended, but within the last 20 years 20 million coming from all over the United States and Canada have attended. All events are popular, but the procession is especially impressive. Work is done by volunteers, with the Tisi family very active. There is no admission charge to the feast, but food and souvenirs must be purchased. The feast is financed through donations, and concessionaires who contribute a percentage of their earnings to the society.

New York City

52ND STREET FESTIVAL

Held annually, September
Economic, fair, touristic

The 52nd Street Festival goes across Manhattan from east to west, attracting as many as 750,000 persons, who come to enjoy a big block party type of event for one day in late September. Events extend from the East River to Ninth Avenue and include antiques, crafts, food vendors, music and dance groups, jazz musicians, puppet shows, magicians and drum and bugle corps performances. It's shoulder-to-shoulder crowds. It is estimated that more than 400 antique dealers and 600 craftsmen show up for the event. They rent street space from the city, and their displays are governed by the 52nd Street Association. Foods are ethnic, ranging from African to Irish, with plenty to eat for only a few dollars. Restaurants along the street benefit greatly from the event, which is held the third Sunday in September. All kinds of junk souvenirs are sold and even t-shirts and comic books. The street fair attracts out-of-town visitors, too. It was started in 1972 as "Americans '72" street fair, sponsored by the city, American Airlines and the former Americana Hotel. The city and the 52nd Street Association, consisting of businesses and apartments on 52nd Street, sponsor it now. The all-day fair begins at 11 a.m. and continues until dusk. All traffic is closed on 52nd Street, which becomes a walking mall. It is financed by private donations, the 52nd Street Association, city funds and the sale of souvenirs and food. It was originally held in mid-June.

New York City

HARBOR FESTIVAL

Held annually, June/July
Patriotic

Harbor Festival owes its origin to a bicentennial celebration on July 4 known as Operation Sail, when 18 tall ships from all over the world sailed into New York harbor in parade formation. The event drew millions to New York, and so the event became an annual festival, stretching out to four days and reaching its climax on July 4. Now it is a combination water, land and air spectacular with all kinds of events and programs that begins in late June. By 1979, sponsors of the event, the Port Authority of New York and New Jersey and the Harbor Festival Foundation, had extended it to a month's celebration, beginning in mid-June. In 1982, it returned to being a one-day event. In 1983, it became an eight-day festival. Events include a Harbor Festival Exhibition at the Customs House in lower Manhattan and the Great Parade of Ships with more than 50 military and commercial vessels sailing on the Hudson River. There are now more than 25 maritime, cultural, ethnic and sporting events. Opening ceremonies start at the Statue of Liberty and at Liberty State Park in Jersey City. There are special events in Brooklyn and Staten Island, too. The festival ends with a Fourth of July Parade and a fireworks display by Macy's Department Store in the harbor around 9 p.m. In 1983, the fireworks moved to the East River. General manager of Harbor Festival is Frank O. Braynard, who created Operation Sail. He is also a founder of the South Street Seaport Museum.

New York City

LINCOLN CENTER OUT-OF-DOORS FESTIVAL

Held annually, August/September
Cultural

The Lincoln Center Out-of-Doors Festival is a three-week free program of more than 65 theater, dance and music events, often with very famous performers.

Events and programs are at Lincoln Center Plaza. It begins in mid-August and sometimes continues through the Labor Day weekend. Concerts and performances, part of the same festival, are also held at Damrosch Park, Fountain Plaza and North Plaza. The festival events are financed by grants from the New York State Council on the Arts, the National Endowment for the Arts and the Exxon Corporation. It includes community theater presentations as well as noontime jazz concerts, quartets, ballet, puppet shows for children, jugglers and clowns. The annual festival attracts more than 100,000 people. It started in 1971 as a community program and a way to interest New Yorkers in the arts during summer. It is a mixture of more than 60 performing arts companies that over the years have included the American Symphony Orchestra, the Chapman Roberts Singers, folk and country-western singer Josh White, Jr., the Richard Morse Mime Theater, the Howard University Childrens Theater and Ballet Hispanico.

New York City

NINTH AVENUE INTERNATIONAL FESTIVAL

Held annually, May
Ethnic, economic

The Ninth Avenue International Festival is a two-day weekend event held either the second or third weekend in May. Started in 1972 by local storekeepers along Ninth Avenue to promote business among the many ethnic-type food stores and restaurants, the event has mushroomed into a highly successful and profitable event. Booths are set up along Ninth Avenue from 37th to 57th streets, and traffic comes to a halt to allow more than half a million people to sample Greek, Turkish, Israeli, Greek and other ethnic foods. Snacks to gourmet meals are possible. Of course, entertainment has also become an integral part of the festival. There are also guided tours of the many irresistible stores and restaurants, where qualified cooks demonstrate the preparation of their specialties. It is still possible to buy old-fashioned two-penny candy and other goodies whose costs are lowered to attract people who usually end up in the good restaurants paying more. The festival is an economic success. Very often the festival attracts celebrities and is always officially opened by the city's mayor. Weather permitting, the festival is in full swing each day from 11 a.m. to 7 p.m. Although the main events are on Ninth Avenue, the popularity and growth of the event has led to many more stalls on side streets off Ninth Avenue. Food samples and tidbits are given out free with the hope that visitors will buy something, and they usually do. The festival is sponsored by the Ninth Avenue Association, which also sells a shopping guidebook complete with recipes from the participating stores and restaurants. The event is often referred to as a movable feast, with visitors eating each course at a different restaurant. In addition to food, there are also street mini-concerts, folk dances and singing and even puppet shows and carnival rides. Participating stores include groceries, butchers, bakeries and tea and coffee shops. Nationalities represented include French, Italian, Greek, Spanish, Bulgarian, Russian, Romanian, Oriental, African and Middle Eastern. The Ninth Avenue Association membership includes about 450 small businesses plus 14 larger food companies. The event is self-supporting.

Palmyra

HILL CUMORAH PAGEANT

Held annually, July
Religious, pageantry

The nine-day Hill Cumorah Pageant is an outdoor drama with music based on the Bible and the Book of Mormon. It is held in an open-air amphitheater at Hill Cumorah about four miles south of Palmyra in the Finger Lakes region of New York State. Approximately 100,000 attend the 9 p.m. performances, which begin the third weekend in July, continuing through the end of the month. There is no admission charge. The event is financed by the members of the Mormon church. More than 500 participate in the pageant at their own expense. The pageant tells the story of a people who lived in ancient America between 600 B.C. and A.D. 421 and of Christ's ministry among them after his death and resurrection in Jerusalem. The theme of the play is that Christ taught his gospels to these ancient Americans. The pageant is presented on 25 hillside stages. Water curtains for the vision scenes are impressive. Each pageant accommodates an audience of 15,000 persons, with additional space for others. There is free parking. There are no food vendors or souvenir stands. The first pageant was held in 1937 and proved such a success that it has been continued ever since. Hill Cumorah is said to be the actual site where Joseph Smith, first prophet and president of the church, was directed in September 1823, by the angel Moroni to find the gold plates containing an account of the former inhabitants of the continent and the Gospel of Christ. The pageant production is entitled "America's Witness for Christ." Adjacent to Hill Cumorah is a Visitors Center, where exhibits, paintings, dioramas and movies about the significance of the hill are featured. Free guided tours are offered daily.

Rhinebeck

DUTCHESS COUNTY FAIR

Held annually, August
Economic

The six-day Dutchess County Fair is an old-fashioned country fair held two weeks before Labor Day. It's been held since 1845. It was originally an agricultural county fair and basically still is but with some modern touches. The fair opens 10 a.m. daily and remains open until midnight, with all events and exhibits held at the Dutchess County fairgrounds. The annual fair attracts as many as 180,000 people, with the number increasing each year. Events include livestock exhibits with a lot of emphasis on sheep, exhibits by 4-H members who live in dormitories on the fairgrounds to be near their live exhibits and projects through-out the fair. There are also exhibits of arts, crafts, field crops, fruits and veg-etables, plus a special horticultural show. Hall of Health commercial exhibits, county exhibits and an antique village are other fair features. There is a midway and carnival plus free grandstand entertainment with guest stars on a daily basis. Admission to the fair changes but is usually only a few dollars, half-price for children under 12 and free admission for those under 5 years old. The fair also has a variety of food booths manned by local organizations. Home-cooked and baked foods are sold at rates far below any restaurant price. Six months of volunteer work goes into the planning of each year's fair and is done by local teachers, housewives and farmers. The fair begins on a Tuesday and continues through a Sunday, ending a week or two prior to the Labor Day weekend in September. The fair is governed and handled by the Dutchess County Agricultural Society and its board of directors. The society goes back to the early 1800s and preceded the fair itself. Many minor fairs were held before the establishment of this one in 1845. The history of the fair is one of ups and downs and financial difficulties, but somehow it has weathered all storms and still is going strong. Despite the fact that it's near an urban area, Dutchess County is still a farm and dairy region, which is stressed at the fair by the farmers of the future through 4-H Club exhibits and programs. The fair has several permanent buildings so that fair goers can enjoy the fair rain or shine. It is supported by paid admissions, exhibit fees and business contributions.

Saratoga Springs

SARATOGA FESTIVAL/SARATOGA PERFORMING ARTS CENTER

Held annually, June/September
Cultural

The Saratoga Festival/Saratoga Performing Arts Center is held mid-June through Labor Day and is a vehicle for ballet, music and theater, with star headliners doing the honors. Its purpose is cultural. It was established in 1966 as a summer home for both the New York City Ballet and Philadelphia Orchestra with maestro Eugene Ormandy. In 1972 the Acting Company, created by actor John House-man, was added. The festival has been the setting for many premieres, such as the world premiere in 1974 of the ballet *Coppelia* and in 1976 the premiere of

Symphony No. 1, the first symphony written by opera composer Gian Carlo Menotti, performed by the Philadelphia Orchestra. During August, the orchestra presents musical variety concerts. The Acting Company, created from the first graduating class of the Drama Division of the Juilliard School, includes both classical and contemporary plays in their repertoire with performances in the 500-seat theater. Each summer, the company introduces a new work, which then becomes part of the following season's tour. The festival contributes both culturally and economically to the area, since it attracts vacationers and often weekend visitors. It is estimated that 413,000 persons have attended various festival performances. And to date, that's more than 4 million. Star performers have included Liberace, Kris Kristofferson, conductor Sarah Caldwell, Robert Shaw and Stanlislaw Skrowaczewski, to name a few. The Performing Arts Center is located on a 1,500-acre site in a state park adjacent to the famous racetrack and near the historic Revolutionary War site of the Battle of Saratoga. Also nearby is Saratoga Lake and facilities for family recreation. Saratoga Springs is a well-known spa, too. The Arts Center is also an educational institution, featuring a four-week program with the New York State Summer School of the Arts. Designated for the most talented high school students, who are selected at statewide auditions, it was established with the help of the New York State Education Department. Students train with members of the New York City Ballet, Philadelphia Orchestra and the Acting Company while the companies are resident in Saratoga Springs. The center has schools of Orchestral Studies, Dance and Theater. The center says its purpose is "to cultivate, promote, foster, sponsor and develop among its members and the community at large the appreciation, understanding, taste and love of the performing arts." Festival performances are in a theater and partially enclosed amphitheater. The event is supported by various grants and by membership in the center. There are different categories for individual, family and corporative memberships. In addition, monies are realized through the sale of individual and season tickets.

Syracuse

I LOVE NEW YORK STATE FAIR/THE GREAT NEW YORK STATE FAIR

Held annually, August/September
Economic

I Love New York State Fair/The Great New York State Fair is held the last week in August, continuing through Labor Day. It is a display of the state's agricultural products, industrial accomplishments, crafts, government and 4-H and other youth-related activities. The 10-day fair is held at the 350-acre New York State Fairgrounds. Children under 12 are admitted free to the grounds, but there is a charge for adults, which changes each year. As with most state fairs, there is big name entertainment with performances at the 15,000-seat covered grandstand. There is a midway with game booths, rides and fast food stands. There is an annual rodeo, demolition derby, stock car race, high school marching band competitions and dancing under the stars. There are 14 permanent fair buildings on the grounds. In 1976, a Youth Promotion Wing of the Farm Machinery Building was added that includes a 30-by-100-foot Haunted House constructed jointly by the fair and the Syracuse Jaycees for activities for the 4-H, Little League, Kiwanis and Baseball Hall of Fame. The fair goes back to 1841 in Syracuse, but from 1842 to 1890 it moved all over New York State. In 1890, Syracuse became the permanent state fair site. In 1982, 714,025 persons attended, establishing a record for the fair.

North Carolina

Linville

SINGING ON THE MOUNTAIN

Held annually, June
Religious, cultural

Singing on the Mountain is a one-day program of gospel singing and preaching that takes place every year on the fourth Sunday in June at Grandfather Mountain. The one-day event attracts more than 25,000 people, and since its start in 1925, well over 1 million. It was started as a family reunion by the late Joe Harley in 1925 and gradually spread to include other families and groups. Preaching has been by such notables as Dr. Billy Graham and Oral Roberts and entertainment by singers like Johnny Cash and Roy Clark. Comedian Bob Hope attended the fiftieth anniversary in 1975. The event is nonprofit, and there are no admission charges. Singing and preaching take place at MacRae Meadows on Grandfather Mountain, alongside U.S. 221 near the Blue Ridge Parkway. The reason given for holding the day-long gospel singing and preaching is that "it's never snowed on the fourth Sunday of June before." It is a community project, and speakers and performers are not paid. While the event was initiated by the late Joe Harley as a family reunion, its roots go back to the days of the camp meetings in the early 1800s. These meetings included gospel preaching two and three times a day and congregational singing. Today's Singing on the Mountain includes many old hymns handed down from generation to generation.

Spivey's Corner

NATIONAL HOLLERIN' CONTEST

Held annually, June
Folkloric

The National Hollerin' Contest is an unusual one-day event that takes place every third Saturday in June. It was started in 1969 by a local man, Ermon Godwin, Jr., to revive the old custom of hollerin'. Hollerin' was an old-time method of communication in this town, not far from Dunn, North Carolina. More than 50 years ago, local folks simply hollered to each other for the purpose of warning, summoning, greetings, calls of distress, directions for visitors. Hollerin' also included calls to bring in the cows, pigs and dogs. And then there was hollerin' for the joy of hollerin'. The contest is also a day of other events, like a pole climb, corn shucking and a greased watermelon carry. But the main emphasis remains on hollerin', with all ages and men, women, boys and girls competing. Winners over the years have been on national television programs with Johnny Carson, "To Tell the Truth" and the "Mike Douglas Show," where they demonstrated their skills. The event draws 5,000 visitors, and since 1969, more than 50,000 have attended the competitions, which are open to anyone who thinks he or she can holler. Even celebrities like Tom T. Hall and Mike Seegar have tried hollerin'. The contest is financed by Spivey's Corner Volunteer Fire Department, and there are no admission fees. The events are held at the Midway High School. New additions include whistlin' and conch shell and fox horn blowin' contests.

Wilmington

NORTH CAROLINA AZALEA FESTIVAL

Held annually, April
Economic, floral

The North Carolina Azalea Festival covers four days in mid-April when the azaleas are in full bloom. The festival features special tours to view the flowering plants, a variety show, the Queen's Coronation and a parade. There are arts and crafts, coin show, sailboat regatta, square dancing, three-day horse show, concerts and a half-hour fireworks display. The event, which started in 1948 to attract more tourists, now has statewide support and recognition. The event is host to 100,000 visitors annually, and since the first festival well over 2 million have viewed the azaleas. The festival is supported by sponsorships of patrons and paid admissions. Events are citywide and both indoors and outdoors.

Winston-Salem

PIEDMONT CRAFTS FAIR

Held annually, November
Economic, arts, crafts

The Piedmont Crafts Fair is held the first full weekend in November and centers around 150 craftsmen, all members of the nonprofit Piedmont Craftsmen, Inc. It is held at the Memorial Coliseum, attracting as many as 22,000 persons. Crafts exhibited are done in a variety of media, including clay, wood, fiber, copper, iron, leather, paper, glass and precious metals. The craftsmen also demonstrate their skills. There are educational exhibits, live music, door prizes and a sidewalk cafe. There is a basic admissions fee. Visitors, however, can leave and reenter all day on a single admission. The fair gives Southeastern craftsmen a market for their wares, and it stimulates a public awareness of top craftsmanship. The fair grosses more than $130,000 in sales, and visitors come from 22 different states. About 100 local residents devote 10 hours each to running the fair. The event is self-supporting. Each exhibiting craftsman is a member of the Piedmont Craftsmen, Inc., and to become a member he or she must have their work accepted by the nine-member PCI Standards Committee. Crafts for sale at the fair are always reviewed by this same committee to maintain continued excellence of craftsmanship and creativity of design. Most booths are manned by the craftsmen, enabling buyers and visitors to discuss the crafts. About 50 different crafts are displayed. The fair goes back to May 1964, when local craftsmen organized to preserve handmade crafts. PCI established the Craft Shop in 1971. The shop is next to Old Salem, the restored community founded by eighteenth-century craftsmen. The shop is open year-round.

North Dakota

Dunseith

INTERNATIONAL FESTIVAL OF THE ARTS

Held annually, June/July
Cultural

The International Festival of the Arts is a six-week program devoted to the arts. Its sole purpose is to provide cultural opportunities for an area that is remote from cultural centers. It is a joint cultural effort with the Canadian province of Manitoba. The programs include dance, old-time fiddling, bands, string groups, drama and country-western and serious music concerts. It is held in June and July because the weather is best then. All programs are held at the International Peace Garden. Some 10,000 people attend, and since the first event in 1969, more than 100,000. In addition to music, dance and drama, the festival offers mime and an art exhibit of professional North Dakota artists. The event is sponsored jointly by the North Dakota Council on the Arts and Humanities, the Turtle Mountain Association, the International Music Camp, the International Peace Garden, the chambers of commerce of Bottineau, Dunseith, Killarney, Rolette, Rolla and Rugby and various business groups. Both American and Canadian performers are featured. The International Peace Garden is also the site of the International Music Camp held each summer and now recognized as one of the top summer schools of fine arts in both the United States and Canada. A staff of 130 artist-teachers, guest conductors and specialists instruct and supervise the camp programs for some 2,500 students from all over the world. These same students together with famous guest performers are featured in the concerts. The festival was originated by Dr. Metron Utgaard, director of the International Music Camp. During the bicentennial it was expanded to 10 weeks. Most popular festival programs continue to be the fiddle contest and military bands. The festival is financed by grants from local chambers of commerce in the area and by gate ticket sales.

Minot

WINTERFEST

Held annually, February
Economic, carnival, sports

The Winterfest is a 7- to 10-day winter carnival type of event designed to help residents survive the monotony of a long winter. It is also open to tourists who don't mind cold temperatures. It goes back to February 1969 but is really a revival of Winter Carnival, discontinued in the late 1930s because of the Depression. It was initiated by the Minot Chamber of Commerce working with city residents, who all volunteer to work on the annual event. Among the many citywide events are a downhill ski race, snowmobile drag races, an international festival of ethnic foods, a snowmobile race between Minot and Regina, Saskatchewan, in Canada, concerts, indoor sports, tournaments, arts, crafts and a cross-country ski race. There's a Winterfest Parade with floats, a Miss Minot Winterfest Pageant and a Snow Dance. Winterfest entertains about 50,000 people every year, with a grand total of more than half a million. The event helps the local economy, too. Popular festival events are the ethnic food festival, the international "250" snowmobile race and the pageant. The event is financed by donations from local businesses, the sale of a souvenir Winterfest button and paid admissions.

West Fargo

PIONEER REVIEW DAYS

Held annually, August
Historical, economic

Pioneer Review Days, Bonanzaville USA, covers two days either the third weekend or the weekend prior to the Labor Day weekend. It is sponsored by the Cass County Historical Society as a means of preserving the area's early history. The event began in 1958 in nearby Davenport but was still sponsored by the same organization. It was first held in mid-September and changed to August because more people attended. The event relives the early Pioneer days. The two-day program is held at Bonanzaville USA, an authentic 10-acre pioneer village on the Red River Valley Fairgrounds in West Fargo. It was this event that led to Bonanzaville in 1967 and the moving of authentic pioneer era–type buildings to the fairgrounds. Buildings include houses, a former town general store, log cabin, movie theater, bar, hotel and church where services are still held. The buildings come from the surrounding communities of Hunter, Arthur and Page. In 1977, a new Indian addition to the Red River and Northern Plains Regional Museum opened, named for Edward A. Milligan by the Cass County Historical Society. It contains Indian culture and artifacts. Pioneer Review Days feature more than 75 live pioneer demonstrations and displays in action, ranging from afghans to wood carving and woodworking. There are special foods, mostly Scandinavian and German. There's entertainment with bands, barbershop quartets, square dancing, musical groups and Indian dancers. A Wheel Parade is held both days at 2 p.m. The parade deals with all forms of wheel transportation and farm equipment. The historical village where many festival events are held is officially known as Bonanzaville USA and is the registered title of the village, which covers the Red River Valley days of the late 1800s and early 1900s. There is also square dancing on the Main Street both Saturday and Sunday afternoons. Both a German and Norwegian service with special music are held Sunday morning at St. John's Lutheran Church on the village grounds. Both days offer continuous music concerts at the church. About 16,000 people attend each of the two day's festivities, and over the years more than 200,000 have gone back in time to the pioneer era of the Red River Valley. The event is supported by paid admissions and the sale of food.

Ohio

Akron

ALL-AMERICAN SOAP BOX DERBY

Held annually, August
Sports

The All-American Soap Box Derby is an annual race with a stormy history. The six-day race is always held in August, since the weather is better then. The derby is a youth community program designed to give children, ages 10 to 15, some experience in industrial arts and sportsmanship. Each contestant is supposed to build his or her own gravity racer. Both boys and girls can participate as well as handicapped youngsters. Making the racer is actually encouraged as a family project. However, in 1973, the derby ended for a while. An uncle of a 14-year-old winner admitted putting an electromagnet in the nose of the car to help at the gate. This incident is alleged to have revealed cheating of all sorts in the derby. The supporters of the derby, the Akron Chamber of Commerce, gave up. However, the event was rescued a year later by the newly formed International Soap Box Derby, Inc., consisting of local businessmen. Now entries must be in Akron two weeks prior to the race. A National Control Board, made up of engineers, spends hundreds of hours going over each car. In 1979, the Derby added a Magnaflux ultrasonic tester to check the axles. That year, 165 racers from 85 cities participated. The Soap Box Derby has two national divisions. The Junior Division-Kit Car is for ages 10 through 12. The Senior Division is for the 12 to 15 year olds. The 12-year-old group may participate in either division. Junior Division entries are required to buy a car kit from the All-American Soap Box Derby and build the car from provided plans and parts. Contestants in the Senior Division design and build a racer with or without using a kit. Local competitions are held in each contestant's city. If they win, they go to Akron for the big derby. Senior Division contestants are also given various publications to use as a guide in building their racers. About 70,000 spectators attend each year's race, and since the first one in 1934, several million. There is an admission charge to the race, which is also financed by private industry contributions. The first race had contestants from 34 cities. The idea for the race came the year before from Myron E. Scott, a Dayton news photographer. And that first race was held in Dayton. In 1935, some Akron businessmen persuaded the race to move to Akron. It had 52 entries, and they raced in the city streets. Up to this time, the derby was little known. An accident in which two radio announcers, Graham McNamee and Tom Manning, were hit by a contestant's car, hospitalizing them, made the front pages of newspapers across the country.

The number of entries doubled in 1936. It was then that the derby went from a street to its own private track, Derby Downs. The first international race was also held in 1936. In 1948, Germans entered the Derby and continued to do so. In 1953, scholarships were awarded to the first five places. The derby marked its silver anniversary in 1962. Among celebrities who've attended the races have been Ronald Reagan, Jimmy Stewart, Dinah Shore, Roy Rogers, Dale Evans and Lorne Greene. By the late 1960s and early 1970s there were more than 250 contestants. Girls entered the races in 1971, making the number of contestants 272. Chevrolet left the program after 1972, ending a 35-year sponsorship. In 1973, the Akron Area Chamber of Commerce obtained the rights from the company and continued the Soap Box Derby. It was this year that dishonesty crept into the contest, and the chamber withdrew its sponsorship. In 1974, a group of local businessmen took it over and administered it under the name of International Soap Box Derby, Inc. That same corporation sponsored the 1975 race, which had its first girl winner in the race's history. Five out of the top nine contestants were girls that year. In 1976, the bicentennial year, the race got a new sponsor, Novar Electronics Corporation, a producer of electronic security equipment. The Junior Division was also started then. In 1977, about 10,000 boys and girls around the world competed to enter the race. Hundreds of volunteers work on race preparations. The event is financed by paid admissions, entry fees and business contributions.

Akron

WONDERFUL WORLD OF OHIO MART

Held annually, October
Economic, cultural

The Wonderful World of Ohio Mart is a four-day event held the first full weekend in October on the grounds of the Stan Hywet Hall and Gardens. It is a combination showcase for the state's arts and crafts as well as Ohio-made food products, such as maple syrup, Swiss cheese, apple products and trail bologna. The mart is sponsored by Akron's Women's Auxiliary Board, with some 1,000 volunteers who work year-round on each mart. Craftsmen work on the grounds and in the gardens on glass etching, leather, metals, weaving, pottery, wood, jewelry, painting and other skills. Home-baked goods and Christmas ornaments are also sold. Tents are set up on the grounds to accommodate the various crafts that are demonstrated for sale. Tours of the Stan Hywet Hall and Gardens, the recreation of a sixteenth-century English Tudor manor built by a twentieth-century industrialist in 1911, are made available. The mart dates back to 1967 and was started by local Akron residents. The mart claims to be the first big craft show in the state. Some 70 craftsmen participate and sell their wares in two tents and the

Manor Auditorium. There is also a ''Country Store'' in a tent and a refreshment pavilion where visitors can buy lunch or snacks. Live entertainment circles the grounds continuously. In addition there's a Stan Hywet Craft Garden Committee, which runs a shop in the Carriage House where handmade gift items are sold. The mart realizes more than $40,000 for the Stan Hywet Hall Foundation every year. The foundation is in charge of restoration work. More than 25,000 people attend the mart, and since its beginning, more than 300,000. There are admission charges.

Circleville

CIRCLEVILLE PUMPKIN SHOW

Held annually, October
Harvest, economic

The Circleville Pumpkin Show is a harvest celebration held for four days starting the third Wednesday in October. It is held on the town's main street, featuring displays of pumpkins in stacks 20 feet high. The pumpkins come in all sizes, with a prize winner weighing in at 329 pounds in 1977. Highlight of the first day's event is the Miss Pumpkin Show parade. Booths line the street. One booth, manned by the Band Boosters, is popular for its pumpkinburgers, a mixture of ground beef and pumpkin, costing less than a dollar. There are other food booths, sans pumpkins. Interestingly enough, many booths are operated year after year by the same families, second and third generation. The harvest show was started in 1903 as a farm exhibit on an unpaved street. It consisted of one large table displaying farmers' pumpkins and corn fodder. There was a band for entertainment, and folks came from other communities to celebrate the harvest. Then, as today, the event was free. Of course, there is a charge for food, carnival rides and souvenirs. Today's harvest show covers most of the town's streets, lined with booths and interlaced with carnival-type rides. However, most booths are staffed by local residents, and the food booths feature homemade dishes. It is not unusual to buy from a booth that's been selling for the last 40 or more years. Among other food delicacies are pumpkin pie topped with whipped cream, pumpkin doughnuts and pumpkin ice cream. The town's old armory is also the center for arts, crafts, preserves and more pumpkins. All exhibitors have to reside within ''tradin' distance of Circleville.'' Over the years, the town has added a Pumpkin Show Building, a former barn, used as a center for display shelves for different foods incorporating pumpkins and other canned goods. The last day of the harvest show, a Saturday, features a hog-calling contest, square dancing and the eating of a 350-pound pumpkin pie, baked by Lindsey's Bakery. More than 300,000 people come every year and from other states and Canada. Since 1903, several million have enjoyed the pumpkins. Work is done by town volunteers, who take their job very seriously. Each year more than 100,000 pounds of pumpkins, gourds and squash are displayed. The event is referred to as the Greatest Free Show on Earth, and economically it is a boon to the town and surrounding areas. It is financed through the sale of foods, arts, crafts and souvenirs.

Crooksville, Roseville

POTTERY FESTIVAL

Held annually, July
Economic, arts, crafts, educational

The Pottery Festival is a three-day event held on the weekend nearest July 20. The festival alternates each year between Crooksville and Roseville, both known for their pottery. The festival was started in July 1966 to promote the pottery industry in the area that began pottery works in the 1800s. It is both an economic and educational venture on the part of both communities. The idea was started by the Crooksville–Roseville Jaycees. Visitors to the festival can take pottery tours, enjoy arts and crafts and see rare and antique pottery in the Ohio Ceramic Center and Cope Art Gallery. Visitors have an opportunity to buy some antique items as well. There is a festival queen and princess competition, a giant parade, entertainment and specially decorated store windows plus food concessions. Festival goers do get a chance to watch pottery making and to buy samples at the end of each tour. There are still many pottery companies in active operation in both towns. From 5,000 to 7,000 people attend the festival, or a grand total close to 100,000 over the years. The event helps the local economy and calls attention to the history of the pottery industry, gaining recognition for today's pottery workers. It is interesting that former Governor James Rhodes, responsible for the Honey Festival in Lebanon, Ohio, also helped this festival. When he visited the festival during his term, he was so impressed with a display of rare antique pottery that he recommended that state funds be made available for the construction and operation of a pottery museum. The Ohio Ceramic Center of the Ohio Historical Society on Route 93 between Crooksville and Roseville was dedicated and opened July 20, 1974, during the ninth annual festival. Volunteers from both towns work on festival details. The event is financed by advertising in a souvenir book, a percentage from concessions, rentals for space leased to antique pottery dealers and paid admissions to the Arts and Crafts Rare Antique Pottery Salesroom.

Lebanon

OHIO HONEY FESTIVAL

Held annually, September
Economic

The Ohio Honey Festival owes its very existence to former Governor James Rhodes, who asked the city and its chamber of commerce to revive a honey festival abandoned by Medina, Ohio, because of a lack of interest. The purpose was to promote and support the Ohio Beekeeping Industry, which prior to the start of this three-day festival in September 1968 did not exist in Lebanon. The industry is now a vital part of the city's economy. Festival events take place in the center of Lebanon's downtown business district—out in the streets. Events include beekeeping demonstrations, cooking classes, crowning of a festival queen and Little Miss Honey Bee and entertainment on a big festival center stage erected at the intersection of the city's main streets. Donald Cook, a local resident, bravely displays his "living bee beard." There are booths, concessions and rides on the side streets. Visitors can buy pure honey, honey by-products and food at any of the booths. There are also educational exhibits throughout the mall area. They are sponsored by local conservation groups, state beekeeper groups and Ohio State University. There are several parades with local bands and floats that compete for cash prizes. Each year the floats have a theme. In 1971 it was "The Wonderful World of Honey." The festival originally attracted local residents and others from nearby towns. Today, it has visitors from more than 37 states and 19 foreign countries. Attendance at each festival day's events number more than 100,000. It now attracts TV personalities, state officials and honey queens from other states. Additional events include an antique car parade and carnival rides, but the festival committee will not allow gambling or games of chance. The Ohio Honey Festival is a member of the Ohio Festival and Events Association, which helped Lebanon to stage the first festival. The event is financed by rental fees, commissions on rides and booth sales.

Lisbon

JOHNNY APPLESEED FESTIVAL

Held annually, September
Economic, folkloric, legendary, harvest

The Johnny Appleseed Festival is a three-day event always held the third weekend in September to coincide with the region's apple harvest season. It focuses on the biggest industry of the area and on the legendary Johnny Appleseed, who went throughout the Midwest planting apple trees. Lisbon is in Columbiana County, the heart of the state's apple country. It was here that the real Johnny Appleseed, John Chapman of Lemonister, Massachusetts, actually planted apple trees in the area in the mid-nineteenth century. These plantings are credited with the start of the area's apple production. Festival events are held in the town's square, Thursday through Saturday. There's a youth parade on the first night and the following days a queen contest and grand parade. Other events include an antique car parade, entertainment and exhibits of apples and apple foods sold at various concessions. Most of the town's store windows feature displays of antiques and items relative to the apple industry. There are arts and crafts demonstrations. Salespeople at all the booths and stands wear old-fashioned clothes from close to the time of Johnny Appleseed. The festival attracts about 50,000 annually, and since its start in 1968, well over half a million. There is no admission charge to the festival. It is financed through booth rentals, concessions and private donations. Details of the event are directed by the Johnny Appleseed Festival, Inc., an incorporated nonprofit association of local people and organizations interested in promoting Lisbon through the festival. It originally was a one-day "Old-Fashioned Day" event in September 1968, handled by local merchants.

Toledo

INTERNATIONAL FESTIVAL

Held annually, May
Ethnic

The International Festival is held the third weekend in May, Friday through Sunday at the Toledo Sports Arena. It honors a different ethnic group and their country each year but also includes foods, arts, crafts, music and dances of the city's 43 ethnic groups. It is sponsored annually by the International Institute and City of Toledo to honor its ethnic heritages. More than 60,000 visitors attend the three-day event, which involves participation by 10,000 additional people. In 1983, the festival marked its twenty-fifth year. Festival sponsors, also including various businesses and organizations, claim that this is the second largest ethnic festival in the country. The first one is Holiday Fair in November in Milwaukee. This festival traces its beginnings back to World War II, when Toledo became home for war refugees from Austria, Germany and Poland. The city had an ad hoc patriotic committee that taught English as a second language to these groups, who in turn produced an "I Am an American" Pageant at a local high school. From this grew several ethnic pageants, sponsored by a prominent Toledo resident. Each small festival evolved into one large festival, eventually handled by the International Institute and the City of Toledo. Each year the different nationalities displayed their costumes, culture, foods and music. Today, there are nine folk shows, featuring folk dances from around the world plus an Old World Beer Garden with polka dancing to the music of well-known bands. There are also many opportunities to sample varied ethnic foods. In 1983, the International Festival honored China and all people of Chinese ancestry via the theme "America, Our Honored Country." It is estimated that almost 2 million have attended the festival and almost a half-million actively participating since it officially began as a festival 25 years ago. It is supported through ticket sales, sale of ethnic foods and souvenirs, contributions and the sponsorship of the city and the institute. Work in preparation for the next event starts almost as soon as one festival ends. Many details are handled by volunteers who represent the ethnic groups as well as the institute's staff. Special awards are presented during the festival to citizens for their civic and cultural contributions to the city each year. This festival has also been copied by other states, with the full cooperation of the International Institute.

Uhrichsville

NATIONAL CLAY WEEK FESTIVAL

Held annually, June
Economic, educational

National Clay Week Festival is held the second full week of June as a salute to the clay industry of Uhrichsville and Dennison. Festival events include tours of the area's clay plants to see how clay sewer pipes and flue liners and chimney tops are made. There are also tours of Union Cemetery, noted for its unusual clay tombstones and markers from the 1880s through 1950. There are also arts and crafts shows, nightly entertainment and a free pet show. The week-long festival also has two queens, Miss Clay Week and Little Miss Clay. In addition, Miss Ohio also attends the event, since in 1951 one of the festival founders was Miss Ohio. The festival has the usual carnival rides, fireworks, an antique car show, parade and square dancing. More than a million have attended the event since it started in August 1951. About 300,000 come annually. There are no admission charges to the festival, which is financed by contributions and carnival profits. Events are held at the Uhrichsville City Park and Claymont High School Stadium. The festival is based on the original clay workers picnic, held from 1907 to 1909. National Clay Week Festival is a member of the Ohio Festivals Association and International Festivals Association. Both groups regulate various festivals.

Oklahoma

Broken Bow

KIAMICHI OWA CHITO FESTIVAL OF THE FOREST

Held annually, June
Ethnic, heritage

The Kiamichi Owa Chito Festival of the Forest is a three-day American Indian event held the last weekend in June. *Owa chito* is Choctaw for "happy hunting party," and essentially that's what this festival is all about. It recalls Choctaw Indian heritage and pays tribute to the culture and industry of this forested part of the state. From 12,000 to 15,000 persons attend the annual event, open to non-Indians. The purpose of the festival is to acquaint the people of Oklahoma, surrounding states and the world with the "beauty, heritage, industry and progress in Kiamichi Country." It is a revival of the popular Forest Festival of the 1950s. This festival began in 1973 and is held at Beavers Bend State Park. Special features include Indian arts and crafts, which are put up for sale. There are displays of traditional Choctaw bows and cane arrows and a tafalla block made of a partially hollow log and used to mash corn and other grains. Choctaw foods are available at the festival. There are sack races for boys and girls, ages 10 to 15, rolling pin throwing for women, 18 and older, old-fashioned horseshoe pitching, tobacco spitting, peanut race and apple dunking. There are also lumberjack competitions and canoe races, plus the Forest Heritage Center Art Show. There is an admission fee to the festival, which is also financed by donations from local industry and state funds.

Lawton

WICHITA MOUNTAINS EASTER SUNRISE SERVICE

Held annually, movable date
Religious

The Wichita Mountains Easter Sunrise Service is held at 2 a.m. every Easter Sunday morning. The life of Christ is retold in more than 50 scenes with hundreds of actors performing against a background of outdoor granite sets in the Holy City in the Wichita Mountains Wildlife Refuge. The performance ends at sunrise. The service or pageant commemorates Christ's resurrection and also tells the story of His birth, ministry and passion. It has been held for more than 50 years.

The living pageant was the idea of the late Reverend A. M. Wallock, who also was instrumental and responsible for the building of the Holy City in the Wichita Mountains. There is also a chapel at the site, a favorite spot for local weddings. A special religious music concert precedes the Easter pageant. Thousands of people come Saturday night and wait until it's time for the service to begin. When the late Reverend Wallock started the first pageant service in 1926, he had a cast of 5 and an audience of 200. Today, the service has a cast of more than 3,000 and an annual attendance of more than 225,000. It is estimated that several million have witnessed the event. The service features 52 tableaux of the Passion, Drama and Prologue. The site is about 22 miles northwest of Lawton and 100 miles southwest of Oklahoma City. The very first service was a pantomime. Today, it has spoken dialogue. The performers are not professional actors but local people from every walk of life. There is no professional director. All the work is done on a voluntary basis. The pageant is now handled by the Wichita Mountains Easter Pageant Association, with a board of directors consisting of local Lawton businessmen. There is an admission fee to the pageant but no charge for parking cars. As at all religious services, a collection is taken up, but attendees are not forced to give. The U.S. government through the secretary of agriculture granted 160 acres in 1933 for the use of the pageant. Later it was increased. The land is within the Wichita National Forest Reserve, which now includes 640 acres. This is the first and last time the U.S. government ever got involved with anything religious.

Muskogee

AZALEA FESTIVAL

Held annually, April
Economic, environmental, floral

The Azalea Festival is a 16-day event held in mid-April, when the azaleas are in bloom. The blooms are predominately in the town's Honor Heights Park. They grow in the shape of a "Wreath of Honor" as a tribute to all war veterans. More than 35,000 azaleas of 625 varieties bloom in this park. Plantings were done by a former park superintendent, Art Johnson, who started in 1957 with roots of plants discarded by local florists and residents. The festival idea came in 1966 from Maurice D. Dighton, president of the Kiwanis and then festival president. It was to beautify the environment and to encourage tourists to come in the spring. The Azalea Festival also offers an Indian art and craft show, an intertribal council and a powwow at the local fairgrounds. There's an azalea parade and fiesta carnival at the Civic Center. There are azalea balls, art exhibits and tours to view the azaleas. As many as 360,000 from 40 states come every year. In 1967, there were only 50,000 visitors. More than 500 bus charter groups come to the area for the festival. The festival is financed by a state tourism grant and by a local hotel-motel tax. There are no admission charges.

Oklahoma City

FESTIVAL OF THE ARTS

Held annually, April
Cultural

The Festival of the Arts is a six-day event held in late April. It offers performing and visual arts plus a street market, flowers, special foods and an educational area for children. All events are held at Civic Center Park. The festival attracts about 200,000 persons, many from surrounding states. Since the event began in March 1967 more than 1 million have participated. More than 200 artists and several hundred performers highlight the six-day festival. A special Art Field is held for schoolchildren to give them a better understanding of the arts. The festival is a project of the Oklahoma City Arts Council. Proceeds from the festival provide almost half of the council's operating budget, while the rest goes toward the support of various cultural and educational groups. Fifty volunteers work five months of each year planning the event. It takes 18,000 people, also volunteers, to keep the festival operating smoothly for the six days. The event is self-supporting through sales of items and private donations.

Oklahoma City

NATIONAL FINALS RODEO

Held annually, December
Sports

The National Finals Rodeo is a nine-day event featuring the top 15 rodeo competitors, both men and women, for more than $500,000 in prize money. It's the world series of the rodeo circuit. It is held in early December, following the end of the regular rodeo season around the country. Competitions include bull riding, saddle bronc riding, steer wrestling, bareback bronc riding, team roping, calf roping and barrel racing. All contestants are members of the Professional Rodeo Cowboys Association or the Girls Rodeo Association. Competitors themselves select the toughest and roughest livestock from more than 30 top rodeo livestock producers in the United States and Canada. The cowboys also get to vote personally on all the announcers, judges, clowns and NFR (National Finals Rodeo) personnel. The event has a Miss Rodeo America Pageant with participants from 45 states and some Canadian provinces. The entire event is cosponsored by the

Oklahoma City Chamber of Commerce and the International Rodeo Management. The event is economically beneficial to Oklahoma City since each year brings in more than 90,000 persons, and since its beginning, well over 1 million. It was started on a small scale in 1959 in Dallas, Texas. All profits from the finals go to the National Cowboy Hall of Fame, which includes the home of the Rodeo Memorial Association and Rodeo Hall of Fame. The first three years, the finals were held in Dallas, Texas, then the next two in Los Angeles and finally in Oklahoma City, where it found a permanent home at the Myriad Convention Center. The finals are financed by donations from local businesses and ticket and program sales. The finals are held at the State Fair Arena.

Oklahoma City

STATE FAIR OF OKLAHOMA

Held annually, September/October
Economic

The State Fair of Oklahoma is a 10-day event held in late September into early October at the State Fairgrounds. A staggering 1.5 million now attend over the entire fair period. The usual livestock and food judging events are still a mainstem of the state fair, as are sophisticated top name entertainers and racing. Today's fair is held at fairgrounds that cover 435 acres of land. There are about 24 permanent air-conditioned buildings, some exhibit halls for agricultural and industrial products, reflecting the change in the state fair. Some buildings include the Modern Living Building, the Hobbies, Arts and Crafts Building, where fashion shows, hobby demonstrations and other events are held, and the International Building, a center for a trade fair with exhibitors from all over the world. The State Fair Park also has a Stockade, a replica of fortlike buildings of pioneer Americans. It has an open-air theater with performances of Indian dances, square dances and fast draw contests. There is also an American Indian village. There is also a Travel and Transportation, Science and Arts and Art Center. The grandstand is for auto and horse racing, ice shows, rodeo and performances by western singers. Youth activities are held at the Future Farmers of America (FAA) Building, which contains an exhibit area, cafeteria and dormitory for the exhibitors. There is also a 4-H Building with similar facilities. The fair, like all state fairs, has a midway with rides and souvenir and snack booths. The fair also has outdoor exhibits and a baseball park. The monorail with three trains carries visitors on a mile-and-a-quarter ride 20 feet above the fairgrounds. There's an outdoor stage with continuous free entertainment. The fair is financed by admission charges, entry fees, concessions and sales of souvenirs. The fair dates back to 1893, when it was known as the Oklahoma Territorial Fair and Exposition. It was sponsored by city merchants and continued until 1907, when it became a formal state fair together with statehood for Oklahoma. It was chartered as a self-supporting, nonprofit corporation. Its aim is still "to serve as a public institution for the people of Oklahoma, to reflect and promote Oklahoma's progress in agriculture, industry, commerce, education, culture and to provide a medium of social exchange." Today by charter the State Fair of Oklahoma must use its funds for improvements on the grounds for public benefit. There is no remuneration for directors.

Sand Springs, Tulsa

GREAT RAFT RACE

Held annually, September
Sports

The Great Raft Race is held on Labor Day. More than 700 entries plus thousands of spectators are part of the event. Contestants race the clock over 9.2 miles of the Arkansas River from River City Park in Sand Springs to the Pedestrian Bridge and Riverside in Tulsa. Although it's a raft race, anything that floats on water is allowed in the race. This includes paddlewheel scows, catamarans, outriggers, rubber rafts, kayaks, rowboats, canoes and even washtubs. Over the years, contestants have begun to decorate their floating craft to add gaiety to the event. All participants must wear Coast Guard–approved life jackets. Entries come from all over Oklahoma and 11 surrounding states. This fun sports competition has been sponsored annually since 1973 by KRMG Radio in Tulsa. Trophies are awarded for the best times in several categories. Each raft or floating object is clocked into the water at Sand Springs and timed out at a pedestrian bridge at Tulsa's 21st Street. There are six division competitions. Many local companies take this opportunity to advertise their wares during the race by sponsored floats, like a plastic foam oil tanker to Daffy Duck. In 1977, the event was rained out. So heavy was the storm that the Arkansas River overflowed and the race had to be canceled. The race is a spectator event. Families, clubs, organizations and singles all crowd the riverbank at every good viewing point to cheer on the racers. Fans picnic, sleep, sing, dance and play ball. The race, started as a promotional stunt by the Tulsa radio station, caught on and gains momentum each year. It is financed through entry fees and donations from local industry. There is no charge to watch.

Oregon

Albany

WORLD CHAMPIONSHIP TIMBER CARNIVAL

Held annually, July
Economic, sports

The World Championship Timber Carnival is a three-day international competition for loggers for trophies in events like tree climbing, tree topping, chopping, sawing, ax throwing and birling (log rolling). There is also a giant fireworks display on the Fourth of July. Loggers come from Canada, Australia, New Zealand and other countries for this competition with U.S. woodsmen, which always centers around Independence Day. Events are held in the outdoor amphitheater at Timber Linn Memorial Park. More than 100,000 spectators watch. The carnival dates back to 1941, when a local man, Dave Bland, was made Fourth of July Celebration Committee chairman. He wanted to publicize the area's timber industry, which then was just coming into its own. In fact, the city's first plywood mill, now the Simpson Timber Company, had just been built. Bland with the help of an executive board launched the first Timber Carnival July 4, 1941. That first carnival featured six competitive events. Log chopping had a $30 first-prize award, high climbing and topping paid $150 for first, bucking paid $50 for first place, log rolling gave $100 to first place and jousting paid $15 to the winner. Local merchants underwrote the event by donating $2,500, which the committee used to buy 10,000 souvenir buttons. All were sold before the then two-day event began. To meet the demand for more buttons, the committee managed to get 300 "Wilkie for President" buttons from the Republican Central Committee. All the buttons were sold. In 1946, the reorganized Albany Junior Chamber of Commerce decided to run the Timber Carnival, and the Jaycees and Wives have been sponsoring the event ever since. More events are added each year, and the prize money increased. In 1941, all contestants except one were local loggers. As the event grew, it attracted entries from all over the United States and other countries. In 1973 there was an entry from Japan, making the Timber Carnival an international competition. There were 120 contestants vying for $15,000 in prize money and trophies that year. The city of Albany is 60 miles south of Portland on Interstate 5 in the center of the Pacific Northwest's timber industry. Contestants dress in their work clothes, namely caulk boots, jeans, plaid wool shirts and red hats. The carnival also has a timber float parade in the city's downtown streets, and there is a coronation of the Timber Carnival Queen. The two most popular competitions are speed climbing for its danger and log rolling because contestants fall in the water and get wet. The Oregon governor competed in double bucking in 1976. The event is financed by local donations and button and ticket sales. Many cash prizes and trophies are donated by local businessmen. The Albany Jaycees and Wives and a board of directors work on each event voluntarily. It takes a whole year to prepare for the annual carnival.

Ashland

OREGON SHAKESPEAREAN FESTIVAL

Held annually, February/October
Cultural

The Oregon Shakespearean Festival runs for eight months, making it one of the longest drama festivals in the country. It has three theaters: Angus Bowmer Theater, Elizabethan Stagehouse and Black Swan. As with all Shakespeare festivals, the drama offerings include contemporary drama as well as Shakespeare in repertory. The Oregon Shakespearean Festival Association, administrator of the event, claims that theirs is the fifth largest not-for-profit theater in America. Since the festival's start in 1935, several million have been in the audience. The stage was dark only during World War II. The performers, designers, directors and technicians come from all over the country and from some foreign countries. In recent years, summer performances and work have been by college students. The festival season originally began as a Fourth of July event. It has grown to be a very important festival. Since the season expanded to eight months, audiences are in the hundred of thousands annually. The event is financed by paid admissions, sale of souvenirs and programs and membership in the Oregon Shakespearean Festival Association. Membership categories include sustaining, contributing, sponsor, donor and benefactor.

Jacksonville

PETER BRITT FESTIVAL

Held annually, August
Cultural

The Peter Britt Festival, formerly the Peter Britt Music and Arts Festival, is a 16-day program of classical music performed by musicians from the West Coast. The performances are given in a wooded outdoor setting on the historic Peter Britt Estate. The festival offers more than 32 varied indoor and outdoor concerts with an orchestra of 60 musicians and 8 or more guest artists and ensembles. There are afternoon and evening concerts plus 4 morning children's concerts and a special Sunday morning program. The festival was founded by conductor

John Trudeau in 1963 to give Oregon a high-caliber music and arts program. Trudeau was graduated cum laude from the New England Conservatory of Music in Boston. He played with the Boston Civic Symphony, the Boston Philharmonic Orchestra and the Boston Symphony. He moved to Oregon in 1951, when he received an offer to serve as principal trombone for the Portland Symphony. His directing and teaching experience led to his founding of the current highly successful festival. Trudeau selected the former site of the Peter Britt home because he found that the hillside had excellent natural acoustics. He also felt that historic Jacksonville had charm. The name Britt was used not as a tribute to the man but because it was an easy name to remember. In the years that Trudeau lived in Oregon, he got to know Jacksonville very well and convinced local people that a high-prestige festival would be an asset. It did prove to be just that. Each festival features top musicians. Intensive morning, afternoon and evening rehearsals are held prior to the festival's opening date in both the Britt Garden Pavilion and the ballroom of the historic landmark U.S. Hotel in town. Rehearsals are open to the public free of charge. The orchestra offers a range of music: classical, baroque, romantic and modern. In 1977, the festival had a first, the appearance of Helen Quach, conductor of the Hong Kong Symphony Orchestra, the first woman guest conductor. The festival is administered by the Peter Britt Gardens Music and Arts Festival Association, a nonprofit group. The festival is financed through membership in the association, donations from individuals and businesses and the sale of tickets. Each year's festival attracts more than 15,000 persons, including children. In addition to classical music, the festival also offers the Silver Cornet Band and its family picnic concerts as well as the German Singing Club and Peter Britt Chorale in concert. Those who attend are encouraged to bring a picnic basket dinner or lunch while they enjoy the outdoor performances.

Portland

PORTLAND ROSE FESTIVAL

Held annually, June
Economic, floral

The Portland Rose Festival is a 10-day event held in early June, the height of the rose blooming season and the closing of state schools. This festival is the state's largest community event, featuring three major parades, stage performances, an international rose show, auto races and a carnival. More than 300,000 attend the annual event. Climax of the festival comes with the Grand Floral Parade toward the end of the event. More than 50 flower-covered floats, bands, marching units and equestrian groups participate. Each year's festival has a theme. During the 1976 bicentennial celebrations, the festival was keyed to ''A

Tale of Two Centuries.'' There are more than 40 different events, which in addition to the Grand Floral Parade include a Queen Selection and Coronation, Junior Parade, Festival of Bands, Milk Carton Boat Race, Bay and Coast Guard Ships Festival, Fun Center and the appearance of celebrities. The Portland Rose Festival has a long history and its beginnings as a rose show in a tent date back to 1889, when local rose fans held a rose exhibit. It became such a popular annual event that in 1902 the Portland Rose Society was organized. This group added a Portland Rose Society Fiesta to the 1904, 1905 and 1906 shows, adding to the popularity of the event. The idea of a festival was presented in a speech by Mayor Harry Lane at the Lewis and Clark Exposition that Portland needed a "festival of roses." Civic leaders agreed, and in 1907, the first Portland Rose Festival was held. Except for 1918 and 1926, the event has been held every year. The slogan, "For You a Rose in Portland Grows," is attributed to Bertha Slater Smith of Portland. That first festival featured 20 illuminated floats on flat cars that rode the rail of the city's electric trolley system and was the main attraction. A Queen Flora ruled over the festivities. In 1908, local businessmen organized the Portland Rose Festival Association, a nonprofit civic group whose purpose was to plan and finance the annual festival. A King Rex Oregonus ruled over the festivals from 1908 through 1913. His identity was kept secret until he removed his huge beard at the festival's annual ball. From 1914 to 1930, it was a Festival Queen, selected from the city's young socialites, who did the honors. Since 1930, the Festival Queen has always been a Portland high school senior, selected from a court of princesses. One princess is chosen by the student body of each high school. The Rose Festival Association was incorporated in 1932. Since then each princess receives a college scholarship contributed by the association. More than half a million dollars have been given in scholarships. The lucky princess who's chosen Festival Queen gets to wear a beautiful robe and carries an impressive scepter. The crown she wears dates back to 1922. Part of the annual festival, but a separate organization, is the Royal Rosarians, who've participated since 1912. The Royal Rosarian Garden and International Rose Test Garden in Washington Park was established by this separate group in 1917. In 1918, youngsters on the city's east side started a junior rose festival, imitating the big one. This turned into a junior parade, and in 1936, it became an official part of the Portland Rose Festival. More than 10,000 children take part in the parade. In 1958, the Festival Center became a festival event. The center is open every day of the festival, and since 1960 it has been held in an expanded area at Holladay Park next to Lloyd Center. But in 10 years, the now Festival Fun Center moved to the west bank of the Willamette River in downtown Portland. There is no admission charge to the center, which is visited by more than 300,000 people. The center offers stage shows, band concerts, commercial exhibits, arts, crafts, hobby displays, ethnic foods, carnival rides and concessions. The highlight and still the most popular festival feature is the Grand Floral Parade, which begins in the Memorial Coliseum to a packed house and then moves out into the city streets, following a four-mile route. All floats are completely decorated with fresh flowers. When the floats finish the parade route, they are taken to an area within the city so that the public can view them during the last festival weekend. The theme for each year's festival is selected via a contest open to all local residents. Prizes include a free vacation or a car. The annual event is financed by the Portland Rose Festival Association, governed by 50 directors. It is a self-supporting group. Most financing comes through associate memberships, with individual memberships costing $25 and up, and business memberships, $50 and up. Professionals and labor organizations are also considered for associate membership. The Portland Rose Festival has one of the only two floral parades in the country. The other is the Pasadena Rose Bowl Parade on New Year's Day. The association has a paid staff of five who work on the festival details year-round. They also have volunteer help. The festival is also financed by ticket sales and the carnival. Events are citywide.

Salem

OREGON STATE FAIR

Held annually, August/September
Economic

The Oregon State Fair runs for 11 days, attracting more than half a million people annually. The fair considers itself the "Showcase of Oregon." It deals with the state's economic and social life, products, industries, commerce, natural resources, history, government, education, science, culture and agriculture. The fairgrounds cover 181.5 acres of land, owned entirely by the state. Originally the fair had 80 acres of land, donated to the state from the estate of a David Presley, on the premise that it always be used for a state fair. The very first Oregon State Fair was held on these grounds in 1862, with 15,000 people attending. Prizes totaling $758 were awarded. Today's fair employs more than a 1,000 persons and works with a budget of several million dollars. The fair is under the direction of a fair commission consisting of five people, men and women, appointed to four-year terms by the governor. They in turn select a manager for the fair. In 1976, new physical plant facilities costing more than $14 million were added to the fairgrounds. This included more than 60 acres for a parking area. Buildings and facilities are continually upgraded. The fair has its exhibits and competitive displays of agricultural products and animals. There's thoroughbred racing, a rodeo, carnival, stage revue and horse show. Competitions cover agriculture, the state's best grains, seed, fruits, vegetables, nuts, bees and honey. The All Oregon Art and Craft Show is another competitive event, with paintings, graphics, sculptures, ceramics, fabrics, glass, jewelry, leather, wood and calligraphy. Students are allowed to compete, too. Another competitive field is floriculture, or landscape gardens, featuring displays, planting, bonsai, specimen blooms and mixed flowers. The 4-H competition is among the more than 5,000 Oregon members who share their skills and knowledge via presentations, contests, exhibits and projects up for judging. The FFA (Future Farmers of America) competition involves those who show livestock and agricultural projects. There's the All-Oregon Hobby Show with crafts and collectibles demonstrated daily. The Home Economics Competition centers on food, clothing and textiles. The All-American Horse Show involves a split show: hunters, junior hunters, junior jumpers, trail horses, Western pleasure horses and stock horses. It also features Morgans and quarter horses, all saddle horses, ponies and roadsters. There are 29 performances with 15 combined with the PRCA Rodeo in the stadium. The fair also has the International Exhibition of Photography, considered to be one of the world's top 10 exhibitions. There are pigeon, poultry and rabbit competitions, too. There is a general admission charge to the fair. It entitles the visitor to many free things. Food, carnival rides and souvenirs are sold. The fair is financed by gate receipts, entry fees and aid from the state.

Pennsylvania

Barnesville

BAVARIAN SUMMER FESTIVAL

Held annually, July
Ethnic, economic

The Bavarian Summer Festival is a July event that lasts for 11 days with a full program of German events each day from 10 a.m. to 10 p.m. The town is right in the heart of the state's anthracite coal region. Most events are held at the 126-acre Lakewood Park. There's German food, beer, daily wine and cheese tastings and two "Bier Halles" to accommodate 5,000 people at one time. There are amusement rides, Maypoles, blue and white Bavarian flags, marionette shows, Alpine horn blowers and more than 40 craftspeople dressed in traditional Bavarian costumes. Entertainment includes performances by the Schuhplattlers and polka dancers. A team of six huge Belgian show horses pulls an old-fashioned beer wagon around the grounds for a Bavarian and Oktoberfest atmosphere. A Fest Show is held in the Main Festival Halle daily at 3:30 and 8:30 p.m. About half a million folks have attended this festival, which started July 1, 1969, when it attracted 96,000 people. The festival has contributed greatly to the local economy. It is supported by paid admissions, the sale of arts, crafts and food and private donations. There is an admission fee to enter the park.

Bethlehem

BACH MUSIC FESTIVAL

Held annually, May
Cultural

The Bach Music Festival is always held in May, with performances in the Packer Memorial Chapel at Lehigh University. Performances are by the Bach Choir of Bethlehem, well-known soloists, ensemble soloists, the Festival Orchestra and the Brass Choir. They are held Fridays at 4 and 8:30 p.m. and Saturdays at 10:30 a.m. and 2:15 and 4:30 p.m. Admission varies each year, and tickets are sold well in advance. The festival traces itself back to 1882, when a 19-year-old resident, J. Fred Wolle, established the Bethlehem Choral Union. Two years later he went to Germany and came back with a doctorate and a great love for Bach. He decided that the area could use a cultural experience, and so in 1898 the Bach Music Festival Choir was formed. The first festival performance was given March 27, 1900. Bach's Mass in B Minor was presented at its first complete American performance. The idea of a choral festival was based on England's Three Choir Festival, one of the oldest in the world. Dr. Wolle took the idea and blended German tradition with English and American traditions and came up with a winner. The festival attracts more than 22,000 people annually. It originally was held only one weekend a year and later was changed to May because the weather was better. It expanded to two weekends to accommodate the growing audience. The festival's only disruption was from 1906 to 1911, when Dr. Wolle took a job with the Music Department of the University of California. He was persuaded to return by Charles M. Schwab and, with the help of friends, reformed the Bach Choir. Rehearsals began for the seventh Bach Festival. Dr. Wolle, of course, has been succeeded by others who furthered the festival. By the thirty-second festival, there was a new conductor, Dr. Ifor Jones, a Welsh-born musician, graduate and fellow of the Royal Academy of Music, former professor at Rutgers University, conductor of the Handel Choir of Westfield, New Jersey, and an organist. Dr. Jones encouraged younger citizens to join the choir, and he introduced Saturday morning performances of instrumental works and recitals with well-known singers and players. This also took care of the increased number of visitors. He is also responsible for repeat performances the second weekend, enabling even more people to attend. The Bach Choir of Bethelehem has traveled and performed all over the United States. The festival is now under the direction of Dr. Alfred Mann. During festival concerts, there is a request for no applause, and neither cameras nor recording equipment are allowed. Festival performances, however, have been broadcast on public service television throughout the country. The choir still consists of volunteer singers, who attend one two-hour rehearsal a week, September to May, right up to the festival itself. All the work is by volunteers. The Bach Choir offices today are located at the former Young Ladies Seminary of 1815, and is a building that dates from 1748, when it was the Brethren's House. Dr. Wolle's father was principal of the seminary.

Biglerville

NATIONAL APPLE HARVEST FESTIVAL

Held annually, October
Harvest, economic

The National Apple Harvest Festival is held the first full two weekends in October, the time to harvest the red and golden apples in Upper Adams County. It is held at the South Mountain Fairgrounds, about ten miles north of Gettysburg on Route 234 west of Arendtsville. The Adams County Fruitgrowers Association originated the idea to attract visitors to the area and to sell apples. This was in the late 1950s, and the event ran for two years but wasn't successful because there weren't enough attractions and help to handle the event. The county, which has more than 17,000 acres of fruit orchards, however, reinstated the festival, and the first fully organized one was held October 10, 1965. Within three years, the festival expanded to two days, and by 1975 to the first two full weekends (four days) in October to accommodate the larger crowds. It is estimated that as many as 50,000 come every year, meaning a grand total of 800,000 to date. Festival events naturally feature apples and apple products, tours of apple orchards, old-fashioned methods of making apple food and products like apple butter, cider and sauce are demonstrated with free samples. Antique equipment like steam engines and old cider presses are used. Apple pancakes made from a special recipe are served with apple syrup. Free competitions are featured in apple bobbing, apple pie eating, apple rolling and apple seed popping. There is a large arts and crafts show and sale, which includes old-time crafts like candle making, broom making and weaving, and there is also musical entertainment. The festival holds a National Apple Queen contest the second weekend. A "Miss Apple Queen, USA" is selected annually from 15 state contestants from California, Maine, Georgia, Ohio, New York, Michigan, Kentucky, Wisconsin and Pennsylvania. Celebrities who've attended the festival have been the late Mamie Eisenhower, actor Eddie Albert and Miss Pennsylvania. The event is financed by the Upper Adams Jaycees and by paid admissions and sales of food and souvenirs.

Devon

DEVON HORSE SHOW AND COUNTRY FAIR

Held annually, May
Economic, competition, fair, sports

The Devon Horse Show and Country Fair has attracted literally millions of spectators ever since the first horse show was held July 2, 1896, and the Country Fair was added in 1919. The horse show is said to be one of the oldest in the United States. It was originally started to promote the breeding of good harness horses. It has developed from a one-day event to a nine-day one to accommodate the growing number of entries in the show. The horse show features a variety of events, including hunters, jumpers, hackneys, saddle horses, pony roadsters and an antique marathon and junior weekend program. More than 1,200 entries are listed each year in the different divisions. The show receives more entry requests than it can accept, meaning that yearly competition is getting tougher. There are also special exhibits and performances by the Budweiser Clydesdales and the Royal Canadian Mounted Police. The Country Fair is really a country fair, with food booths and more than 35 concessions, manned by 3,000 volunteers. The fair was started by a few ladies on Philadelphia's renowned Main Line when they opened a Tea House, featuring lace tablecloths and gleaming silver tea sets to serve refreshments to exhibitors and spectators at the Devon Horse show. It was repeated each year, evolving into the Devon Country Fair. Today, the fair benefits the Bryn Mawr Hospital. Work on both the horse show and fair is done by volunteers, each devoting as much time as possible in preparation for the next event. The event is self-supporting, helped by entry fees for the horse show, general paid admissions and the sale of food and souvenirs. Proceeds from the horse show are used to maintain the grounds and prepare for the next event. Both the horse show and fair are held at the Devon Horse showgrounds on Route 30 in Devon, a suburb of Philadelphia. The show was awarded the United Professional Horsemen's Association Award in 1981.

Doylestown

POLISH FESTIVAL

Held annually, September
Ethnic

The Polish Festival is held on the grounds of the National Shrine of Our Lady of Czestochowa, the Polish-American counterpart of the original shrine in Poland. Although the event started over the Labor Day weekend in 1966, attracting as many as 70,000, to be a fund raiser for the shrine, it soon attracted non-Poles and turned into a showcase for Polish-American culture, religious fervor and achievements. Today the event attracts almost a half-million people. Shrine volunteers who still handle festival details used to hold large picnics for the Labor Day weekend, and soon they added food stands, rides and different events, and the picnic became a five-day event stretched out over two weekends in early September. The festival is a member of the Pennsylvania Festivals Association and has often been featured on PBS-TV. Today's festival features Polish-style family entertainment, games, rides, crafts and cooking demonstrations. Polka bands play nightly, and there are Adam Styka art exhibits. The only admission charge is for parking. The festival is financed through the sale of food, arts, crafts and souvenirs and by private donations.

Kutztown

PENNSYLVANIA DUTCH KUTZTOWN FOLK FESTIVAL

Held annually, July
Ethnic, folkloric

The Pennsylvania Dutch Kutztown Folk Festival was started in 1950 by Dr. Alfred L. Shoemaker and two other professors, Dr. Don Yoder and Dr. J. William Frey, of Franklin and Marshall College in Lancaster, Pennsylvania, to preserve the heritage and customs of the Pennsylvania Dutch people. The festival primarily perpetuates the life and customs of the Pennsylvania Dutch. The festival is sponsored by the Pennsylvania Folklife Society, a nonprofit educational organization. In 1967, Ursinus College became affiliated with the society and is a contributing educational institution that offers credit courses at the festival. All profits go to the college for educational purposes. The festival now runs for nine days during the week of July 4, an expansion of five days over the original event. It has been recognized as the most authentic of ethnic festivals, has been written up in the *National Geographic* three times and has received recognition from the Smithsonian Institute in Washington, D.C. The festival naturally deals with authentic Pennsylvania Dutch crafts, customs, demonstrations, quilting, dances, music and food. The festival is conducted by the "Worldly" Dutch in cooperation with the two sponsoring institutions. Special pageants are staged to show visitors the life of the "Plain" people: Amish, Mennonites and Dunkards. The "Plain" folks do not, of course, participate, since their religion forbids them to do so. Visitors, however, do get to see the Amish pageant and wedding and barn raisings twice daily during the festival. The festival is always held at the same time, since the spring planting has been completed and factory workers in the area take their vacations to help at the festival. Each festival trains younger folks to do the crafts. Craft demonstrations include soap boiling, pewter making, basket weaving, rug making and the preparation of old food recipes. There's a quilt contest, with entries limited to 1,700 to display and present them properly. It is estimated that each year about 110,000 people come to the festival, and since its beginning almost 4 million. This greatly helps the economy of the area and helps to pay each festival worker a small honorarium to supplement their limited farm and factory incomes. Most popular festival events are the pageants, county auction, antique bookstore, food and singer Kenn Brooks. Celebrities are discouraged from participating in the festival, but some politicians manage to come. There is a general admission fee and a charge for parking cars, which help finance the event. Festival events take place on 35 acres of land in the center of Kutztown, behind Main Street. In 1983, a new Folk Arts and Crafts Hall was added, giving the festival three centers.

McClure

McCLURE BEAN SOUP FESTIVAL

Held annually, September
Memorial, food

The McClure Bean Soup Festival is a five-day event started 100 years ago as a reunion of Civil War veterans. It was based on the bean soup made and fed soldiers during the Civil War period. The tradition continues till today with thousands of gallons of bean soup being prepared in 35-gallon iron kettles and stirred with wooden ladles. While this is a five-day event, activities are slated only for two full days and five nights. The town continues the festival in memory not only of the Civil War veterans but also of all war veterans. The story goes that on July 23, 1883, a group of Civil War veterans met on the second floor of the Joseph Peters Blacksmith Shop in Bannerville to organize a Grand Army of the Republic Post. The first meeting was held October 20, 1883, with many reunions and the serving of a special bean soup. In 1891, invitations to sample the soup were extended to the public and billed as a real Civil War bean soup dinner. The chairman of the celebration, Ner B. Middleswarth, had secured from the War Department ''hard tack'' to be served with the soup. The cook for the festival was Henry Kahley, who also was a Civil War cook. As time went by and the Civil War veterans passed away, their sons took over the event, and ever since the festival has been held at the Henry K. Ritter Camp Sons of the Union War Veterans. Added to soup is a ton of beef and a ton of crackers to feed the thousands who attend every year. The soup is still made in large iron kettles over a wood fire battery of furnaces capable of handling 16 large 35-gallon kettles at one time. Each cook stirs two of these kettles during 180-minute shifts. All the cooks are dressed in Civil War uniforms, even the women. Soup is served at 4 p.m. Tuesday through Thursday and at 11 a.m. Friday and Saturday during the festival, which does now include other activities. Other events include political speeches, exhibits, parades, nightly entertainment, amusement rides and concessions. The festival usually is held from a Tuesday through Saturday with Tuesday a Senior Citizens Day, Wednesday All American Day, Thursday Scout Night and Bicycle parade at 6 p.m., Friday Youth Day and Saturday Homecoming Day. Highlight of the festival is the making and serving of the bean soup, based on a recipe from the War of Rebellion. As many as 35,000 people come for the soup. The festival is financed by the sale of the soup, exhibit fees and other events. It is held at Cold Spring Grove, an outdoor setting. The event is a recognized festival and member of the Pennsylvania Festivals Association.

Philadelphia

ELFRETH'S ALLEY FETE DAYS

Held annually, June
Historic, preservation

The Elfreth's Alley Fete Days in early June opens historic homes to visitors and gives them a chance to tour Elfreth's Alley, the oldest continuously occupied residential street in this country. Free tours and lectures are featured daily from noon to 5 p.m. Tours of the homes and gardens whisk people back to 1724. There are colonial crafts, exhibits, historical narrations of individual homes by colonial-dressed guides, musical entertainment and refreshments. Elfreth's Alley is located between Front and Second streets, north of Arch Street in Old Philadelphia. The free lectures and programs are given at the Museum House at 126 Elfreth's Alley. The open house dates back to June 1934, started by Mrs. Dolly Ottey, who also founded the Elfreth's Alley Association, Inc., a nonprofit organization of more than 300 members today. The purpose of the organization and the special days is to preserve and protect both the street and homes. It was also started to expand the cultural life and aspect of the colonial and federal homes. Some houses predate the American Revolution. It started as a one-day event but expanded to two days to accommodate the growing number of visitors, totaling 5,000 annually. More than 200,000 have attended to date. Work on the event is on a voluntary basis and is financed through paid admissions and patrons. The event recently added a bake sale of freshly baked colonial goodies. There are also several musical groups who entertain visitors as they stroll through Elfreth's Alley, which is a registered national historic landmark.

Philadelphia

FAIRMOUNT PARK FALL FESTIVAL

Held annually, September/October
Cultural, sports

The Fairmount Park Fall Festival dates back to September 1974, when it was started to create an interest among local people in their own Fairmount Park through cultural, athletic and environmental programs. It is a 22-day event, always held in the fall because of the flaming foliage of the park trees and because the weather is more conducive to the more than 10,000 visitors who come for this event. More than 70,000 have attended since the first festival. Popular events are the sports, which include a tennis tournament, road races, cricket tournament, junior golf tournament, 24-hour bicycle marathon and rugby tournament, plus a 26-mile marathon. Other festival activities include the Horticultural Society of Pennsylvania's Harvest Show, a sculpture and architecture tour of the Philadelphia Museum of Art and, along the Benjamin Franklin Parkway, a bike drive west, covering 2.12 miles of West River Drive. There's a live wild bird show, a picture-in-the-park photo exhibit, a crafts fair, Centennial Sunday, a recreation of a Victorian Day in the park that recalls that in 1876 Fairmount Park was the site of the Centennial Exposition. There's a guided nature walk and special Fairmount Park tours. There is an admission charge to the festival and some fees for tours and entries in the sporting events. The festival is also financed by the sponsorships of various businesses and by individual donations. Events, continuing into mid-October, are held throughout the park with some indoor programs.

Philadelphia

PHILADELPHIA FLOWER AND GARDEN SHOW

Held annually, March
Economic, floral, horticultural

The Philadelphia Flower and Garden Show has been a part of the Philadelphia scene since 1924, and an estimated 7 million people have viewed the exhibits and displays at the Philadelphia Civic Center. The show grosses more than $600,000 a year. It originally was called the Philadelphia Flower Show, growing out of a series of small shows. The first flower show of value in the United States was held by the Pennsylvania Horticultural Society back in 1829. Today, it is an 8-day event, said to be the largest such show on the East Coast, also rated a high-quality indoor flower show. It covers three acres of gardens, floral and educational exhibits by more than 80 exhibitors, including nurseries, garden clubs, plant societies and floral, educational and government-civic groups. There are also some 95 trade booths selling gardening supplies, equipment and plants. Popular show features are the rose display, designer gardens and 20-foot waterfall. There are now more entries in competitive classes by individuals and less by wealthy estate greenhouse owners. The show was in the public eye in 1976, when a native daughter, the late Princess Grace of Monaco, judged the pressed flower pictures category. No effort, however, is made to attract celebrities as judges. A paid staff plus 1,000 volunteers, many amateur gardeners, works on preparations for the show. It is financed by paid admissions and sponsorship of the Horticultural Society of Pennsylvania.

Philadelphia

SUPER SUNDAY

Held annually, October
Economic, cultural, ethnic, folkloric

Super Sunday is described as a giant block party held on Benjamin Franklin Parkway from the Philadelphia Museum of Art to Logan Circle. It dates back to 1971, when it attracted 75,000 people. Now it easily attracts more than 300,000. It was started as a fund-raising event by the Women's Committee of the Academy of Natural Sciences of Philadelphia. As it developed, the event took on both an ethnic and cultural aspect, exposing the large crowds to cultural and folkloric programs. The one-day event, the second Sunday in October, is held from noon to 5 p.m., and the parkway is closed to traffic so that a variety of events can be held. Participating institutions vary each year but among some of them are the Academy of Natural Sciences, the Philadelphia Museum of Art, the Franklin Institute, the Free Library of Philadelphia, the Academy of Fine Arts (Pennsylvania), the Zoological Society, the Cathedral of SS. Peter and Paul, the Logan Square Neighbors Association, the Philadelphia Convention and Visitors Bureau and Moore College of Art. These various groups also conduct a drive for membership during the one-day festivities and are highly successful. It is also an attempt to reach those who take the city's cultural offerings for granted and make them more aware of them. Some of the day's other activities are a huge flea market, an international bazaar, information booths, carnival rides, chalk-ins, entertainment groups, weather balloon contest, book sales from the library, children's games, artistic sculpture from the Philadelphia Museum of Art and more. In 1977, more than 400 new memberships in the Free Library of Philadelphia were made as a result of Super Sunday. Super Sunday is financed by grants from foundations, contributions and sales of various items.

Pittsburgh

PITTSBURGH FOLK FESTIVAL

Held annually, May
Ethnic, folkloric

The Pittsburgh Folk Festival is more than a quarter of a century old and originally was held the first weekend in June. It was patterned after the Festival of Nations in St. Paul, Minnesota. It is original to Pennsylvania. Its purpose is twofold: to develop ethnic groups in the greater Pittsburgh area and to retain the area's cultural heritage via music, songs, dances, foods and crafts. The three-day event operates from 5 p.m. to midnight each day and is sponsored by the Robert Morris College, a private college. About 3,500 students and local residents actively participate in handling the festival. The event, a nonprofit, noncommercial festival, features two booths for each ethnic group: one for food and the other for the display of crafts, such as woodcarving, books, embroidery, instruments and authentic native costumes. Food booths show how to prepare certain dishes and also sell them, with recipes available to visitors. The festival was held at the Civic Arena but now is at the David L. Lawrence Convention Center to accommodate the more than 30,000 people who come. To date, the grand total is over 750,000. Strolling musicians and spontaneous folk dancing add to the Old World atmosphere. Each evening there is a two-hour stage show based on various themes, such as harvesting or a wedding with live music. The two movers behind the festival were Reverend Father John Schlicht, C.S. Sp., a history professor at Duquesne University, and Richard Crum, linguist and choreographer of Balkan dance. The event is financed through paid admissions and sale of food and crafts. There is a small paid staff who work year-round and are joined by volunteers six months before the festival. Popular festival features include the food kitchens because of the menus and inexpensive costs. Folk dancing runs second in popularity. Among participating ethnic groups are Russian, English, Greek, Lithuanian, Slovakian, Scandinavian, Slovenian, Ukrainian, German, Irish, Indian from India, Croatian, Hungarian, Hispanic, Latvian, Bulgarian, Scottish, Chinese, Serbian, Israeli, Italian, Lebanese, Filipino and Polish. The theme of the folk festival is "Unity in Diversity."

Pittsburgh

THREE RIVERS ARTS FESTIVAL

Held annually, June
Cultural

The Three Rivers Arts Festival is a 17-day cultural event designed to make local residents more culture-minded by taking art out of the museums and presenting it to the people. It serves as a showcase for regional artists and as an experience of visual and performing arts with participation possible through special workshops. The festival deals with art exhibits, some invitational, others juried or screened, and includes paintings, prints, crafts, photography, sculpture and banners, a competition for high school students. The festival's performing arts feature noon, afternoon and evening music, theater and dance performances. There are three stages, a large outdoor main one, a smaller outdoor one and a platform stage in an inflatable structure that also houses visual and performing arts workshops and film exhibits. There is ''Artists in Action,'' a demonstration of arts and crafts daily from noon to 9 p.m. Children's activities include art and dancing. The Three Rivers Arts Festival was started in 1960 and held only over the Memorial Day weekend. It proved so popular that it was extended to 10 days in early June and now to 17 days. About 200,000 attend each year. Most events are held outdoors in the center of the city's Golden Triangle on plazas and grassy areas surrounded by skyscrapers. It is a citywide program with many events free. The festival is sponsored by the Carnegie Institute and financed by contributions from corporations, foundations and individuals and by local, state and federal grants.

Rhode Island

Statewide

HERITAGE MONTH

Held annually, May
Historic, heritage

Heritage Month is a statewide event that commemorates Rhode Island's own Declaration of Independence, May 4, 1776, enacted by the General Assembly, the first colony to do so. Because of this, the entire month of May is devoted to celebrating the state's historic heritage. Originally, the celebration was for only one week and called Heritage Week, but the number of events and visitors grew so that the observance was extended to a full month. Events include May Day breakfasts, concerts, exhibits, tours of historic houses and sites. On May 4, Rhode Island Independence Day, there is a candlelight illumination of University Hall (1770), the original building on the campus of Brown University in Providence. This is the country's seventh oldest college. In 1790, President George Washington visited the university, and to mark the occasion the students lit candles in every window, a tradition still continued. The May Day breakfasts date back to 1867 in the state and are held in churches, grange halls and private clubs. Most are open to the public. The custom originated at the Oaklawn

Community Baptist Church. A Forefathers Service is held at the First Baptist Church in America, established in 1638 by Roger Williams, who also founded Rhode Island in 1636. The present church building dates back to 1775. A Rhode Island Heritage Month Indian Heritage dinner is held at ''Dovecrest'' in Exeter, and a Rhode Island Hall of Fame banquet with induction of new members at Providence. Among historic sites visited on tours are Trinity Church, where Washington worshipped; Old Colony House, where Washington and General Rochambeau, commander of the French forces, met to plan the strategy that led to the victory at Yorktown; and the Hunter House, Revolutionary War headquarters of French Admiral de Ternay, all in Newport. In Providence, there are tours to see the Stephen Hopkins House, home of a signer of the Declaration of Independence and 10 times governor; the Esek Hopkins House, home of the first commander-in-chief of the Continental Navy; and the John Brown House, home of a colonial merchant and a leader of the Gaspee Affair (the sinking of a British ship in the harbor). In Coventry, visitors are able to view the General Nathanael Greene Homestead, home of Washington's second-in-command, who liberated the South from the British. The British revenue schooner, *Gaspee*, was attacked at what is now Gaspee Point in Warwick, June 9, 1772, by 120 Rhode Island men in several boats. After the commanding officer was wounded and the crew taken prisoner, the ship was burned. The month-long event is financed by contributions from each community and civic organizations and proceeds from the May Day breakfasts. There are some admission charges for tours. Work is done by local volunteers.

Bristol

BRISTOL FOURTH OF JULY CELEBRATION

Held annually, June/July
Patriotic

The Bristol Fourth of July Celebration is a well-known 16-day event that claims to be the country's oldest celebration of the country's independence. The very first parade was held July 4, 1785. The 198th annual parade was held in 1983. The parade is the climax of the entire celebration, which starts in late June and includes pageantry, arts, crafts, tours and religious services. The parade goes along the red, white and blue center-striped street in town. Participating in the parade in the past have been the Philadelphia Mummers and Navy Band. The parade has floats and begins 10:30 a.m. July 4, but is preceded by a special patriotic program. The evening ends with a fireworks display. Other events include a ball, Miss Fourth of July Pageant, concerts, drum and bugle corps competition, horse show, tennis tournament, rugby match, Babe Ruth All Star game, slow-pitch softball tournament, custom car show, soccer game, firemen's muster, square dancing and block dance. The event is financed by civic and community donations, and work is done by volunteers.

Cranston, Warwick

GASPEE DAYS

Held annually, May/June
Historic

Gaspee days covers 16 days of programs that reach a climax on the anniversary of the burning of the British revenue schooner, *HMS Gaspee*, on June 9, 1772. It was started in June 1966 by interested citizens who wanted to commemorate the historic event. It was then a 3-day celebration, expanded later to 10 days and in 1977 to 17 days, and now 16 days. Gaspee Days includes a symbolic reenactment of the burning, a parade of colonial-costumed marchers, a colonial fife and drum muster, a clambake, band concert, Pawtuxet Village Arts and Crafts Festival, Miss Gaspee Pageant, children's colonial costume contest, open golf tournament, invitational softball tournament, the David L. Stackhouse Foot-race for men, the Hannah Memorial Footrace for girls, the Abraham Whipple Memorial Footrace for boys, a canoe race, Colonial Ball, Memorial Services and johnnycake breakfasts. The annual event has received lots of national rec-ognition, including the George Washington Honor Medal from the Freedoms Foundation and a Community Award from the Discover America Travel Or-ganization. All events take place in both cities of Cranston and Warwick. All work is handled by local volunteers. The event is financed by funding from both cities and the state and by the selling of tickets to some events.

Newport

CHRISTMAS IN NEWPORT

Held annually, December
Religious, pageantry

Christmas in Newport is a month-long Yuletide celebration on a citywide basis. It features candlelight colonial house tours, a Victorian Christmas celebration at Kingscote, a mansion, and candlelight Christmas music at historic Trinity Church, where George Washington worshiped. There's a dramatic reading of Clement Moore's "Night Before Christmas" and a mass in commemoration of the first Roman Catholic mass celebrated in Newport for the French Army, under the leadership of Count de Rochambeau, which took place in 1780 in the Old Colony House, the nation's second oldest capitol building. There are other concerts, flower shows, art exhibits, historic and religious displays, a Christmas fair, pageants, skating party, Holly Ball, lighting of the Yule log at Washington Square and lighting of the Christmas tree at Rowen's Wharf. Events officially begin December 1 with the firing of the Newport Artillery Company's 1750 cannon. The Artillery Company, chartered in 1741, is the country's oldest active military organization. Throughout the month, children's games and contests are held on Long Wharf. Work on the festivities is by both volunteer and paid help and takes about six months to work out. It is financed through the sale of tickets, contributions and organization funding. Some events are free. Christmas in Newport was started in 1971 by a local resident, Mrs. John C. Myers, who wanted the city to celebrate the religious significance of Christmas, its beauty and simplicity. It subsequently won the support of the Newport Chamber of Commerce, community groups, churches, merchants and local citizens.

Newport

NEWPORT MUSIC FESTIVAL

Held annually, July
Cultural

The Newport Music Festival is a two-week summer event that features chamber music concerts and ballet performances, morning, afternoon and evening, at famous Newport mansions, the "summer cottages" of the gilded age of the rich. Concerts are also held at Fort Adams State Park and at Ochre Court. The festival includes not only the forgotten music of the nineteenth and early twentieth centuries but also works by Bach, Beethoven and Brahms, Ravel and Khachaturian. Past performances have been by the American Symphony Orchestra, conducted by Ulf Bjorlin, Royal Danish Ballet soloists and the Eric Hawkins Dance Company. Performances are held throughout the city but with most in the mansions. The festival began in 1969, an outgrowth of the 1968 Metropolitan Opera Summer Season in Newport. At first it dealt with chamber music, but later it added ballet. It is an internationally known event with many worldwide performers appearing. Notables involved in the founding of the festival include Mrs. Hugh D. Auchincloss, mother of Jackie Kennedy Onassis, Mrs. Harvey S. Firestone, Jr., and Mr. and Mrs. John Nicholas Brown, Jr. Mr. Brown is of a prominent Rhode Island family and a descendant of John Brown, leader of the 1772 Gaspee Affair. Among celebrities who've appeared have been Andrei Gavrilov, Regine Crespin and Peter Frankl. There are admission charges to all concerts, which help to finance the event, also supported by contributions.

Usquepaugh (South Kingstown), Richmond

JONNYCAKE FESTIVAL

Held annually, October
Food

The two-day Jonnycake, or Johnnycake Festival deals with food, the johnnycake, best described as a little pancake-like cornmeal patty favored by the folks in Rhode Island. A great deal of controversy centers around this food, as to its correct spelling, its origin and the correct way to prepare it and the proper ingredients. The johnnycake has been around for 350 years but no one can agree on its original and authentic recipe. Spellings of the tasty tidbit include jonnycake, johnnycake and Shawnee cake. Controversies reign about whether they are made with milk or water and whether they are to be thin, thick or small. For more than 100 years, the Rhode Island Legislature tried to settle this dispute by bringing a stove into the Capitol's rotunda to test several recipes. Instead, a fistfight broke out and nothing was settled. The controversy is still around, but Rhode Islanders continue to eat them in many different ways. Johnnycakes can be for breakfast, served like pancakes topped with butter, syrup or molasses. They can be broken and mixed with milk and sugar, or at dinner they can replace potatoes or pie. Some are served as dessert. Every year, the Johnnycake Festival in October attracts some 12,000 fans who eat the johnnycakes in all shapes, sizes and textures. The festival features tours of Kenyon's 1886 Grist Mill, where cornmeal is ground for the controversial food. There are also Indian ceremonial dances, music and crafts both days. On Sunday, there's an antique car parade at 1 p.m. Events each day are from noon to 5 p.m. and are held at the Richmond and South Kingstown town line.

South Carolina

Charleston

FESTIVAL OF HOUSES

Held annually, March/April
Cultural, economic, preservation

The Festival of Houses is a 26-day program of tours of the city's historic and private houses and gardens, designed to continue ongoing preservation work throughout Charleston. The first event dates back to 1947 and was originated as a fund-raising event, based on the Natchez Pilgrimage in Mississippi. The original name was the Annual Tours of Charleston's Historic Private Houses and Gardens. It was changed to its present name in 1969. It features seven afternoon and candlelight tours. There are also four evenings of galas with music and wine. Most of the houses are of the eighteenth and nineteenth centuries preserved and lived in today. Visits mean an opportunity to view the architecture, furniture and life style of the city. There are also Monday evening candlelight programs at two house museums. Afternoon tours are from 2 to 5 p.m.; the candlelight tours and evening galas from 7 to 10 p.m. Ticket costs vary each year and are limited to the capacity of the houses. Each tour offers visits to three or more buildings. The event is always held in spring when most garden blooms are at their peak and the weather is comfortable for touring. The annual festival brings in 11,000 visitors and puts millions of dollars into the local economy. Work on the event is on a voluntary basis, with almost 1,000 involved. There is also a 20-hour training of guides who each put in 10 hours as guide hostesses during the festival. The event is financed through the sale of tour tickets. More than 100 historic homes and gardens are included in the festival. Tours cover Legare Street, Church Street, Ansonborough, Harborside, Harleston, King Street and Meeting Street. Reservations are required since the demand for tickets is so great.

Charleston

SPOLETO FESTIVAL USA

Held annually, May/June
Cultural

The Spoleto Festival USA is a 17-day event of the most comprehensive arts festival, offering opera, ballet, modern dance, jazz, theater, symphonic, choral and chamber music. It was first held in May and June 1977, founded by famous composer Gian Carlo Menotti as a counterpart to the Spoleto Festival of Two Worlds in Italy, which marked its twentieth anniversary in 1977. Menotti also founded that festival. This event headlines famous performers and conductors and attracts thousands, sometimes more than the area can handle. Spoleto USA was started with the encouragement of the National Endowment for the Arts, originally a supporter of travel by Americans to the Italian Spoleto Festival. They cut back on foreign travel and requested Mr. Menotti to establish an American version, giving him a list of Southern cities to consider. Menotti first visited Charleston and decided it was the place because of its history and architecture. As of 1981, grants totaling more than $250,000 were added to the finances of the American festival. Although it suffered a bad deficit in its third year, it did recover. Its budget of $2 million in 1981 was helped by that grant. The festival is now supported by the city and through grants from corporations like Burger King, Delta Air Lines, McDonalds, Amoco, Mobil and Consolidated Foods. The 1981 festival was highlighted by a new production of Menotti's opera, *The Last Savage*, two world premieres of operas by Stanley Hollingsworth, the presentation of Gluck's opera, *L'Ivorgne corrige*, a recital by pianist Yefim Bronfman and chamber music by the Emerson String Quartet. Also performing was the Los Angeles Philharmonic, conducted by Michael Tilson Thomas and Myung-Whun Chung. Also appearing were Renata Scotto, Ray Charles, the Sydney Dance Company and the Lar Lubovitch Dance Company. Performances are citywide and include the Dock Street Theater, historic churches, parks and the Cistern at the College of Charleston, the Gaillard Municipal Auditorium and Middleton Place, a working rice plantation of the eighteenth century and setting for symphony concerts.

Jamestown

HELL HOLE SWAMP FESTIVAL

Held annually, May
Economic, historic

The Hell Hole Swamp Festival is an eight-day early May event designed for fun and to buy the town whatever it needs. In the past, proceeds from the festival have bought a new rural fire engine and a lighted softball field. While the event was started in 1972 for economic reasons, it has a historic basis, too. Hell Hole Swamp was mentioned in early grants and land sales, and it appeared on Mouzon's map, printed in London in 1775, since there were very productive plantations in the area. Its fame, however, came during the Depression and Prohibition, when bootleggers gave Hell Hole Swamp a bad name. It was the center of illegal moonshining. In those days, anyone looking for Hell Hole Swamp was given misleading directions on purpose. Today, it's easier to find, since it is inside the Francis Marion National Forest, near Highways 41 and 45, south of Jamestown and north of Huger. Part of the swamp drains into the Santee River. No one knows where the name came from, but legend says that General Francis Marion had been in the swamp for some time when he was asked, "Where the hell have you been?" His reply was supposed to have been, "In a helluva hole in the swamp." Festivities today include a parade, band concert, selection of Little Miss and Miss Hell Hole Swamp Pageant, moonshine making with a still borrowed from the revenuers and a concert of spirituals. There are crafts, a Bootleggers and Revenuers Chase, a variety show, square dancing, lancing tournament, bluegrass music, children's games. It attracts almost 15,000 people annually. The event is self-supporting, and there are paid admissions to some events, which are held throughout the town.

Myrtle Beach

SUN FUN FESTIVAL

Held annually, June
Economic, touristic

The Sun Fun Festival covers four days and is designed to attract tourists and
bolster the local economy. It goes back to 1950 and was started by the local
board of directors and community leaders. The more than 50 festival events
include a Miss Sun Fun Pageant, Miss Bikini Wahine contest, Miss Surf competition, beach games, diaper derby, golf tournaments, a band and baton competition, Thunderbird air show and garden tours. It is held the first full weekend
in June and attracts more than 200,000 people, who stay for the entire event,
and of course it helps the economy. Work on the festival is handled by the
chamber of commerce paid staff and some local volunteers. It is sponsored by
the Myrtle Beach Chamber of Commerce and also by paid admissions to the
events.

Salley

CHITLIN' STRUT

Held annually, November
Economic, food

The Chitlin' Strut is a one-day eating and country music event always held in
November, the Saturday or Sunday after Thanksgiving Day. Chitlins are chit-
terlings, or hog intestines, fried to a crispy crunch. At least 8,000 pounds are
consumed annually, but for those who haven't cultivated a taste for them, there's
barbecued pork and chicken. The event goes back to 1966, when the town of
more than 500 residents needed some decorations for the coming Christmas
season. Mayor Jack Able didn't want to raise taxes so he and his councilmen
consulted a local country-western music disc jockey "Friendly" Ben Dekle at
Radio Station WCAY in Cayce, South Carolina, to help raise some money. Ben
told them that he had always dreamed of a Chitlin' Strut but never could find
anyone with nerve enough to do it. So the town of Salley decided to do it.
Salley's first Chitlin' Strut was held November 26, 1966, the Saturday following
Thanksgiving. The first event attracted more than 1,000 people from surrounding
states, and they ate more than 600 pounds of "guts" together with other foods.
Enough profit was made for the town to buy those Christmas decorations. The
Strut was so successful that the mayor and his Town Council made it an annual
event to be held at the same time each year. Today, the annual Chitlin' Strut

attracts more than 25,000 people, many curious about chitlins and others affi-
cionados of the unusual dish. The town has been able to buy needed trash cans,
lawn mowers, signs and a new fire truck without raising local taxes. Events
begin at 10 a.m. and continue through the evening, usually ending with an 8
p.m. outdoor gospel singing session. Day-long activities officially open with a
parade with a local celebrity as grand marshal. Money prizes are awarded to the
best floats and marching units. Eating begins at 11 a.m. and continues throughout
the day. In 1980 alone, more than 8,000 pounds of chitlins were eaten. Proceeds
from that event, a profit of $15,000, went toward renovating the Crescent City
Vocational School to serve as a community center. Cost is $4.50 per plate for
the chitlins, which taste good, but in preparation the odor is not exactly perfume.
The process for preparing them is arduous, but there are enough people in town
to do the job, which includes cleaning the guts, boiling them until tender, then
flouring and frying them to a crunchy crispness. There are also funnel cakes and
cornbread. Country-western music concerts and an evening Chitlin' Strut Country
and Western Music Show add to the day's events. The town of Salley was
founded by Captain Dempsey Hammond Salley in the nineteenth century. The
town was incorporated by a special act of the legislature on December 19, 1887,
and the first railroad train came to Salley from Blackville on December 24, 1887.
Descendants of the town's founder still live in Salley and are active participants
in the Chitlin' Strut. The whole town works year-round preparing for the big
day, and all on a voluntary basis. It's financed by the sale of the chitlins and
other food, souvenirs and baked goods and by donations.

South Dakota

Deadwood

DAYS OF '76

Held annually, August
Historic, legendary

The Days of '76 cover three days in August that turn back the pages of history
to relive the days of 1876. The event is held at this time of year to mark the
anniversaries of the deaths of "Wild Bill" Hickok and "Calamity Jane" Canary.
The rough and tough days of the Black Hills gold rush come back during this
annual event. There are parades, Indian ceremonial dances, a dramatic reenactment of the trial of Jack McCall, the murderer of "Wild Bill" Hickok, and an
action-filled rodeo. More than 20,000 people come every year. Deadwood is
deep in Deadwood Gulch and was settled during the gold rush days of the mid-
1800s. Stories of the West's notorious history actually happened in the gulch,

which comes to life with the Days of '76. The program opens with a historical tour of the area on Friday and Saturday. A midmorning parade goes through more than three miles of the gulch. After the parade, the rodeo is held at the lower end of town. The event started 60 years ago to mark the death of "Wild Bill" Hickok, August 2, 1876, and "Calamity Jane" on the same day but in 1903. The rodeo is a top PRCA event that lures rodeo cowboys from most states to compete for the high prize money. Work on the annual event is done by a 14-man volunteer committee that puts in lots of work hours. The event is financed by a nonprofit corporation and paid admissions to the rodeo. Events take place on Main Street and at the rodeo grounds.

Mitchell

CORN PALACE FESTIVAL

Held annually, September
Harvest, economic

The Corn Palace Festival dates back to September 1892, when it was called the Corn Belt Exposition. It was patterned after the Sioux City Iowa Corn Palace, which went bankrupt in 1891 after five years of operation. The purpose of this event was to encourage settlement of the area by showing farmers that crops could be grown. The four-day festival today is held to display agricultural products of the area, including corn. It is essentially a harvest festival and features top entertainers like Bob Hope, Lawrence Welk, Andy Williams, Red Skelton and Roy Clark. Events are held at the Mitchell Corn Palace, which is redecorated every year. The festival includes displays, entertainment and dancing and, since 1921 a carnival, covering seven blocks of Main Street. The festival draws about 600,000 visitors annually, adding greatly to the local economy. Work on the festival is by students, who are paid a small salary. They usually work 13 weeks before the festival. It is financed by paid admissions. The Corn Palace goes back to 1892. A second building was added in 1906 and built of wood covered entirely by corn. The cost of the building and entertainment was always underwritten by local businessmen. The present building was constructed in 1921 and completely remodeled in 1965. There are a series of panels with pictures made entirely of corn. Some show wild game, hunting and pioneer history. The building's roof has Moorish minarets and towers in bright colors, giving the structure an unusual appearance. It is called the Corn Palace because the entire exterior and some of the interior are covered with corn in red, blue, yellow and white and arranged in geometric designs, outlined with grasses and grains. The building is redecorated each year during Indian summer, costing about $15,000 to do the job and using 3,000 bushels of corn. Individual cobs with the corn on are sawed lengthwise, and the halves are nailed flat side onto the wooden panels, fastened to the building's brick walls. The Corn Palace is used year-round for civic and entertainment programs.

Tennessee

Jonesboro

NATIONAL STORYTELLING FESTIVAL

Held annually, October
Cultural, folkloric, literature

The National Storytelling Festival attracts about 400 storytellers from all over the United States for three days in October. The event is also open to interested visitors. There are workshops and sessions of swapping tales, all sponsored by the National Association for the Preservation and Perpetuation of Storytelling. The highlight is a ghost story session around a bonfire at night in the Old Jonesboro City Cemetery. Storytelling includes the telling of tall tales as well as other yarns. Stories can tell of a slave's revenge or how to kill a hoop snake or about a bird dog who could point ducks by barking softly and ganders by barking loudly. Workshop participants pay a fee, which differs each year. The festival is actually a convention. Aside from swapping stories, there are several professional or celebrity storytellers. Jonesboro is a small town of about 1,700 in the hills of East Tennessee. Andrew Jackson practiced law and even fought a bloodless duel here. It is the oldest town in the state. It was the capital of the state of Franklin (seceding from the state) but rejected by Congress by a single vote in 1780. It was also the center of a territorial tug of war between North Carolina and Tennessee. The festival is sponsored by workshop fees and membership dues.

Knoxville

DOGWOOD ARTS FESTIVAL

Held annually, April
Cultural, economic, floral

The Dogwood Arts Festival is an annual event keyed to the blooming of the area's dogwood trees, usually in early April. The event is not only a floral showcase with marked Dogwood Trails to follow and enjoy but also is a showcase for cultural and sports programs. Today, there are more than 250 events, many free. The festival now lasts for 17 days with arts, crafts, museum tours and historic home tours, bicycle races, rowing regattas and tennis filling the bill. The event lists its official start as of April 12, 1961, but actually it dates back to 1956, when specially marked Dogwood Trails (now six, covering more than 30 miles) began to attract visitors. The blooming dogwood trees and other spring flowers provided a pretty setting so that more people began to come. Within five years, more activities were added. Newer features include a giant river parade, softball tourney, prayer breakfast and a sister city, honoring Kaoshiung, Taiwan. The festival is a tremendous economic asset, with about 150,000 persons attending. Since the event began, the total is well over two million. The most popular festival events are the Dogwood Trails and celebrities, who have included singer Olivia Newton-John, the late Elvis Presley, Bob Hope, Arnold Palmer and Jimmy Connors. Work on the festival is on a year-round basis with 600 volunteers and 2 paid staff members. The festival is supported by contributions, gate receipts and commissions.

Memphis

COTTON CARNIVAL AND MUSICFEST

Held annually, May/June
Cultural, economic

The Cotton Carnival is a 16-day traditional salute to "King Cotton," climaxed by a 10-day outdoor music festival or MusicFest, offering variety entertainment and well-known performers. Today's carnival is an outgrowth of the original Memphis Cotton Carnival, which goes back to March 1931. It was started to cheer up folks during the Depression years and to influence people around the country to wear more cotton apparel. The carnival idea in turn came from the old Memphis Mardi Gras celebrations of 1872 to 1881, when Ole King Cotton and his royal troupe entered Memphis triumphantly. Even though 40,000 people attended, it was discontinued because of the Depression. Part of the Mardi Gras included a Cotton Carnival. The first carnival, though a success, was changed to the second week in May, when the weather was more pleasant, and attracted thousands. The carnival was publicized in magazines and newspapers, and by 1952, its budget exceeded $100,000. It was not held during World War II but was resumed soon after. In 1983, the developers of the carnival, the Memphis Cotton Carnival Association, decided that from now on future Cotton Carnivals would always start the third Saturday in May and end the first Sunday in June. The River Pageant is held the first day of the carnival and the major parade the following Saturday. The carnival's climax is the 10-day outdoor music festival, "MusicFest," which headlines musical attractions and variety shows. For less than $10, a visitor can choose to hear country music, rock and roll, jazz, big bands and "golden oldies," all performing simultaneously on seven stages and concert areas located throughout the Mid-South Fairgrounds in the center of the city. Famous performers have included Ray Charles, Jerry Lee Lewis, Aretha Franklin, Rick Nelson, Dick Clark, the Charlie Daniels Band, Merle Haggard, Waylon Jennings, Eddie Rabbit and Henny Youngman. There are also a variety of magicians, clowns, brass bands and puppet shows, part of the more than 250 different acts performing continuously from noon to midnight daily. The Carnival has a giant midway with an assortment of chilling rides, a large arts and craft fair plus sports. Carnival highlights include the arrival of the Royal Barge, bringing the King and Queen of Carnival with their Royal Court to open the festivities. There is also the Maid of Cotton, the Cotton Maker's Jubilee Parade and the Grand Krewe Parade with colorful floats. Other carnival features include a masked ball, blues festival, river pageant with a flotilla of decorated boats, aerobatics, shoreside events, such as crayfish boils, fireworks, street dances, fashion shows and spur-of-the-moment picnics. Many carnival goers come in outlandish costumes and do impromptu zany stunts. There is also a special area for children and a dance hall with recorded music, electronic games and pinball machines. There is a marketplace offering crafts and souvenirs. It is estimated that the festival now is host to more than a million people each year, and over the years several million. Work on the Memphis Cotton Carnival is by a paid staff with volunteer help. It is financed through ticket sales, booth concession commissions and contributions from business firms.

Memphis

MEMPHIS IN MAY INTERNATIONAL FESTIVAL

Held annually, May
Cultural, economic, ethnic

The Memphis in May International Festival is a month-long event that celebrates the city's cultural heritage and at the same time salutes a different foreign nation each year. In 1983, Israel was the honored nation, and there was a wide variety of Israeli art exhibits, films and multimedia productions. The month-long festival centers around six top weekend events, all free. The festival always begins the first weekend in May, sometimes on April 30 to encompass May 1 and 2. This kicks off with an International Day salute to nations honored in past festivals. For example, in 1983, entertainment featured folk singers from Canada, belly dancers from Egypt, a German puppet theater and a jazz group from the Netherlands. The day also includes an international marketplace offering merchandise from around the world. The second day is devoted to the honored country. In 1983 it was Israel Day, focusing on that country's art, music and culture, with concerts and performances by Israeli stars and troupes and exhibits by Israeli artists. The second festival weekend is usually a fiddlers convention or competition among fiddlers and pickers competing for prize money at the Mud Island Amphitheater. This weekend also has other competitions and demonstrations, which vary. In 1983 it was a flying disc competition and a K-9 demonstration with dogs. The third festival weekend is always the International Barbecue Contest, covering two days. Barbecue competitors from all over the country compete. In 1982 there were more than 200 barbecue teams in competition. The event seeks the best in pork barbecue, with the contest beginning at 2 p.m. on Friday and continuing until the winners are announced late Saturday afternoon. As the chefs compete, spectators snitch samples, and it turns into a merry all-night tasting party. As the competition continues on Saturday, there's live entertainment. In 1983 it was rocker Keith Sykes and the Hog Calling and Ms. Piggy Look-Alike contests. While there is an entry fee for the cooking contest, it is annually supported by a grant from Union Planters National Bank of Memphis. Cash prizes vary. The next weekend is the popular Beale Street Music Festival, which attracts many international musicians. Beale Street is considered to be the birthplace of the blues. There is continuous entertainment on four separate stages. The music begins 5 p.m. Friday and 2 p.m. on Saturday, going late into the night. There is also a Fine Arts Festival, featuring performances by the Metropolitan Opera, visual and performing arts and music. Another popular festival event is the Sunset Symphony, a pops concert by the Memphis Symphony Orchestra. More than 150,000 attend this concert alone. In 1983 world famous Israeli pianist David Barr-Illan was the featured artist. Bass-baritone James Hyter again sang "Ole' Man River." This concert traditionally ends with Tchaikovsky's *1812* Overture complete with live cannon blasts and an impressive fireworks show. This also ends the month-long festival. The festival attracts in excess of a half-million visitors and a few million over the years. The Fiddlers Convention and Beale Street Music Festival are partially funded by grants from the Tennessee Arts Commission. The mall concerts are partially funded by a grant from the National Endowment for the Arts. The Memphis in May International Festival was originally a regional event which grew in popularity. Part of the festival was the Cotton Carnival, which also grew so large that it became a separate event, held in late May into early June. Festival details are handled by the Memphis in May International Festival, Inc., organized in 1978. They planned and staged the first Mid-Winter Festival in January 1979, honoring the Federal Republic of Germany. It was a fund-raising event for the festival itself. Almost $5,000 was raised. In May 1979, the Finance Committee held a cabaret, raising more money for Memphis in May. Among countries honored by the festival have been Japan, Venezuela, West Germany and Canada. The festival is a definite economic boon to the city of Memphis. Work is a year-round job for a paid staff, joined by hundreds of volunteers. The festival is financed through grants and donations from major industries in the city and state.

Nashville

INTERNATIONAL COUNTRY MUSIC FAN FAIR

Held annually, June
Cultural, economic

The International Country Music Fan Fair is for country music fans. The seven-day June event (formerly the Music City Fanfare) dates back to June 1972. It was started with the help of Grand Ole Opry and CMA (Country Music Association), which still serve as cosponsors of the event that plays to 150,000 fans. There is a registration fee per person covering most events and programs except the Grand Ole Opry performances. Programs are held at Nashville's Municipal Auditorium and include more than 25 hours of live entertainment: top country music artists, a bluegrass concert, an old-time fiddlin' contest and picture taking and autograph sessions with the stars. There's also a record label exhibition and Country Music Hall of Fame ceremonies, plus three lunches. For several years, the fair opened with a Fan Fair slow-pitch softball tournament at the city's Two Rivers Park, off Briley Parkway near Opryland. It's still held and is free to the public. The fair is also a vehicle for competitions for the country music organizations around the country. Work on the fair is by a paid staff. It is financed through ticket sales, registration fees and donations. Other concerts and events are held at Grand Ole Opry in Opryland.

Paris

WORLD'S BIGGEST FISH FRY

Held annually, April
Economic

The World's Biggest Fish Fry originally started out in 1938 as Mule Day with a fish fry on the first Monday in April. It was the day that farmers came into Paris to trade mules and other farm products. They would shop, visit friends and exchange conversation. By early 1950, there were less mules to trade. The area's Kentucky Lake was becoming a tourist attraction, and the local Chamber of Commerce decided to give something different to the farmers and tourists. In January 1954, the Paris Chamber of Commerce made plans for the first World's Biggest Fish Fry. That first event was three days long. By 1956 it had grown, and the Queen of Tennessee Valley Pageant was added plus a Fish Fry Parade covering two miles. In the early days, community clubs fried the fish right on the court square. As the event attracted more people, frying the fish became a big job, assumed by the Jaycees and Travis Lax, who handled the whole event.

Now the fish is fried at the city parking lot. As much as 5,000 pounds of Kentucky Lake catfish is fried and served. By 1961, the Jaycees assumed the entire responsibility for the Fish Fry as their annual club project. They continued to handle the event and added more activities, including a carnival on four streets next to the court square, later moving it to the old hitchlot, where the original Mule Day celebration was held. Other additions included a hog calling and bowling contest and entertainment. It is now a week-long event, usually the last full week in April. It is financed through food sales, contributions and the sale of a souvenir journal. It attracts as many as 75,000 people annually. Work is done by Jaycee members and volunteers.

Shelbyville

TENNESSEE WALKING HORSE NATIONAL CELEBRATION

Held annually, August
Sports, competition

The Tennessee Walking Horse National Celebration is a 10-day horse show featuring more than 1,800 entries in more than 60 classes. It is the world series and super bowl event of horse shows. It goes back to September 1939, when the very first show was held. Its purpose then and now is to honor and promote the Tennessee walking horse and spread its popularity. The event attracts as many as 150,000 annually, with a grand total now of several million. This is rather remarkable since the town of Shelbyville has a total population of 15,000. There are other events, like pageants, special programs and activities that have received national recognition in the press and national television. There is a 28-minute film on the celebration narrated by Tennessee Ernie Ford and shown to visitors. The show is financed by business donations, entry fees and paid admissions. Show events are held at Celebration Grounds, 100 acres of land in the middle of the town.

Smithville

OLD TIME FIDDLERS JAMBOREE AND CRAFTS FESTIVAL

Held annually, July
Cultural, economic

The Old Time Fiddlers Jamboree and Crafts Festival is held every Fourth of July weekend, attracting 50,000 people and competitors to this tiny town, located off Interstate 40 and 65 miles east of Nashville. The jamboree is internationally known and was the subject of an hour-long documentary on national television. Music played is the native sound of the southern hills and the area that went to the city and became bluegrass. The competitions are in the traditional form, the pickin' and fiddlin' contests, with events held on an outdoor stage in front of the DeKalb County Courthouse. The formal jamboree covers contests in 21 different categories, from fiddle, banjo, mandolin, guitar, dulcimer and harmonica to gospel singing, folk singing, string bands, bluegrass bands, buck dancing and clogging. Prize money varies from $35 to $100, with lesser amounts for second- and third-place winners. In addition to the competitions, there are music performances everywhere, under the trees on the courthouse lawn by a fiddler or wandering banjo player with other strolling musicians joining in for an impromptu concert. More than 200 working artists and craftsmen also display their crafts and demonstrate their talent. Each year's jamboree opens at noon on the Friday of the weekend with a warm-up session and preliminary competition in 11 of the total 21 categories, including a novelty performance by musical saws, spoons, autoharps and any other inventive instrument. The Saturday competition begins at 9 a.m. with the dobro guitar contest and ends with the Junior and Senior Fiddlers' Show, a down-head-to-head contest between the best of the fiddlers. The winner receives $100 in cash, the Berry C. Williams Memorial Trophy, named for the founder of the jamboree, and the right to claim the title of Smithville Jamboree Champion Fiddler the following year. All other music during the jamboree is continuous and extemporaneous. There is an entry fee for the competition. Work is done by volunteers, and the event is also financed by contributions from businesses and organizations.

Texas

Athens

BLACK-EYED PEA JAMBOREE

Held annually, July
Economic, culinary

The Black-Eyed Pea Jamboree is a three-day fun event that honors a local product, the black-eyed pea, and attracts visitors to a town about 73 miles southeast of Dallas. It has been an annual event for the last 13 years and continues to grow in popularity with both Texans and non-Texans. The jamboree includes an arts and crafts show, carnival, square dancing, races, beauty pageant and the big event, the Black-Eyed Pea Cook-off, with modest cash prizes of $1,800, but the honor seems to be worth it all. Hundreds compete with original recipes, which must use the black-eyed pea. Judging is keen and is by a noted food expert. Twenty top recipes are selected. The cook-off is open to town residents, all of Texas and outside Texas. The only requirement is that each contestant use his or her own original "reci-pea" focusing on the black-eyed pea. Past winners have come up with quiches, New Year's Day Pea-Tiser, Lickity-Split Sweet and Sour Salads and more. All this happens on the grounds of the Henderson County Junior College in Athens. Other fun events include pea shellin', pea poppin' contests. There's a Miss Black-Eyed Pea competition and pageant, parade, pet show and terrapin races. On Sunday, all visitors are given a chance to sample for free all 20 of the prize-winning recipes at a special taste-in. The jamboree also features entertainment by famous country-western singers and performers. There is an admission charge for the shows and an entry fee to enter the cook-off. Most other events are free. The event is financed by ticket sales, entry fees and contributions from local industry. Work is done by town volunteers.

Dallas

STATE FAIR OF TEXAS

Held annually, October
Economic

The State Fair of Texas attracts more than 3 million people to the 250-acre park, only minutes from downtown Dallas. The fair has become a festival dealing with culture, commerce, music, folklore and travel. Each year's fair has a theme. For example, in 1980 it was "Around the World in '80," and back in 1977 it was "The Great Food Round-Up." The state fair dates back to 1885, when it was the showcase for products, crops and cattle. The fair is in keeping with Texas bigness. It runs for 17 days and has enough activity to keep the millions who flock there every October busy. There are livestock displays and competitions, exhibits of products and crops, football in the Cotton Bowl, a rodeo, creative arts and Broadway shows with famous stars at the fair's own Music Hall. There is a midway with all kinds of rides, food booths, ethnic entertainment and concerts. Most events require an admission fee. However, there is free entertainment in the Cotton Bowl, which includes the Parade of Champions, an all-day competition among top high school musicians. There are fireworks, fashion shows and more. Special programs are held at the six civic museums located within the State Fair Park. The fair is financed by paid admissions, entry fees, rental fees from concessions and contributions.

El Paso

SUN BOWL CARNIVAL

Held annually, November/January
Sports, economic, pageantry

The Sun Bowl Carnival is probably one of the longest running annual events around. In 1982, the event marked its forty-eighth year. And it has gone from a month-long salute to the sun to over three months of events. The event was known as the Southwestern Sun Carnival until 1979. It offers sports events, pageantry and parades that center on the entire Southwest. Although it didn't start out that way, the event began in 1934, when a sun carnival was staged to raise money to build a press box for the football stadium of El Paso High School. A local resident, Dr. Brice W. Schuller, promoted a prep all-star contest to obtain money for the press box facility atop R. R. Jones Stadium at El Paso High School. On January 1, 1935, Schuller, Dr. C. M. Hendricks and members of the El Paso Kiwanis Club launched an all-star game with a coronation feature. The all-star game included top players from the city's three high schools, who defeated powerful Ranger (Texas) High, and the midwinter celebration was underway. A year later the game was called the Sun Bowl and played on New Year's Day, sponsored by El Paso civic clubs and the Kiwanis Club. The Downtown Kiwanis Club of El Paso still handles the Sun Bowl football game. The first official Sun Bowl game was with New Mexico State University, a tied game. The first Queen of the Sun Carnival was crowned, selected from six El Paso girls. Today, the queen is selected from 18 El Paso princesses, and 23 are duchesses at an annual Coronation Ball at the El Paso Civic Center. In 1935, the Downtown Lions Club of El Paso organized the first Sun Carnival Parade in conjunction with the football game and queen's coronation. More than one parade is now held in addition to the New Year's Day one, which includes more than 110 different units, out-of-town bands from all across the country. The parade and football are televised. In 1950, the carnival added a college basketball tournament that continued for four years and then was dropped. But in 1961, the two-night four-team tourney was back on the program. It has since grown into the national cage scene with teams like Indiana, Houston, Southern Illinois, Southern California and Memphis State competing in El Paso. The Sun Bowl football game was held in Kidd Field until 1963, when the El Paso County passed a $1.75 million bond to build a new 30,000-seat stadium called the Sun Bowl. In 1969, the Sun Bowl became a national item as a result of a television contract from CBS-TV, still going strong and reaching more than 40 million people every year. One Sun Bowl game even had a halfback from Florida State in 1955. He's now actor-director Burt Reynolds. The Southwestern Sun Carnival not only included all of El Paso County, Texas, but was extended to New Mexico and several other Southwestern states. This later changed back to Texas only.

Other festive events are a bicycle race, bowling tournament, pro–am golf tournament, art exhibit, twirling contest, interscholastic tennis tournament, sky diving, rodeo events, band jamboree and concerts by the El Paso Symphony Orchestra, which becomes the Sun Carnival Symphony Orchestra during the carnival. The carnival is often attended by sports, music and film celebrities. The carnival work is handled by thousands of volunteers and some paid workers. The year-round administration is handled by the Sun Bowl Association with a president, executive vice-president, secretary and treasurer. There is an executive director and six vice-presidents, with each one responsible for some phase of the carnival. Since its beginning, the carnival has hosted several million visitors. It is financed by donations from business and civic groups, paid admissions and the sale of souvenirs.

Huntsville

TEXAS PRISON RODEO

Held annually, October
Sports, rehabilitation

The Texas Prison Rodeo is held inside prison walls every Sunday in October and is billed as the "wildest rodeo behind bars." Participants are prisoners, many of them lifers who take chances just for the thrill of it. Each Sunday's performance attracts more than 25,000 visitors, who pay to get in. The participating inmates vie for prizes, sometimes cash money. Rodeo performances are from 2 to 4 p.m. but there are other events beginning as early as 8:30 a.m. These include bands on the midway, booths selling prisoner-made handcrafts and paintings and cutting horse demonstrations. There's even a booth where a visitor can have a mug shot on a wanted poster taken. Rodeo events are far from tame. For example, one event features a tobacco pouch of money tied between the horns of a wild bull. The trick is to be brave enough to run up to the snorting, charging bull, rip the pouch loose, and hang on to it. The winner gets to keep the pouch and money, which can be as much as $350. The rodeo is extremely popular, and one year a French television team from Paris filmed it. Tickets are bought a year in advance by folks from other states and some foreign countries. The rodeo opens with a grand parade of a drill team, barrel racers, officials and clowns. When they leave, the chutes are opened immediately, and prisoners in striped suits try bareback riding on wild horses, bronc riding. The one who manages to stay on top for eight seconds is the winner, and the one with the best form also wins. All performers must be in excellent physical shape, brave and intelligent. There are the all-important clowns, too, the bullfighter and the barrelman, either of whom serves to distract the bull and perhaps save a performer's life. These clowns also see that the animals leave the arena when and where they should. Other convicts work the chutes, sell programs, rent cushions, play in the band and handle the booths. All are paid for their services. The performers compete for cash prizes and the coveted championship silver and gold belt buckle. This rodeo also includes women prisoners, who participate in two events. One is to try on foot to throw a rope around a wild calf and lead, drag, push and pull it on to the judges. The other event is to attempt to push a greased pig into a sack. During intermission, there is entertainment by famous performers like Jimmy Dean, Tennessee Ernie Ford and Johnny Cash. Many spectators buy rodeo tickets just to hear and see their favorite performer. Every inmate with a good record gets to see one show. Most entertainers refuse payment for their appearances and turn over their checks, adding something extra to a fund used for the medical, religious and educational services for the 20,500 inmates in 15 units. The fund also provides for Thanksgiving and Christmas meals for the prisoners. During the rodeo, armed guards are on duty, just in case there's a break for freedom. The Prison Rodeo was started more than 51 years ago by Colonel Lee Simmons, general manager of the Texas Prison System, when he came to Huntsville. As a rancher and politician, he saw a need for recreational programs for the prisoners and employees. He came up with a rodeo, with prisoners participating. His friends in ranching loaned him stock. An area was fenced off from the ballfield. Employees and some people from town were invited to come to the rodeo. Only a handful of prisoners participated. The next year, it was recommended that the rodeo be held again but that there be an admission charge. Admission was a quarter, and the proceeds were used to buy books. Up until this time, there had been no rehabilitation program at the prison. The following year, the rodeo drew a larger crowd, and it was decided to make it an annual event with some other activities. It was expanded from one to four Sundays in October.

Kerrville

TEXAS STATE ARTS AND CRAFTS FAIR

Held annually, May/June
Economic, cultural

The Texas State Arts and Crafts Fair is always held over the Memorial Day weekend, followed by an extra weekend in early June. It is held on the tree-shaded campus of Schreiner College. It is a mixture of arts, crafts, entertainment and food. About 240 carefully selected artists and craftspeople exhibit their best work under large colorful tents. They also offer educational demonstrations and lectures, explaining special art methods. In 1982, three young Texas artists, winners of the Texas Arts and Crafts Education Foundation's Young Artists Competition, were featured at the fair. One received a $500 scholarship, and all had booth space, lodging and meals as they exhibited at the official state arts event. The fair was first held in 1972, patterned after a West Virginia fair. Its purpose is still to educate the public about the fine arts and crafts in Texas and to provide an opportunity for family activity in the atmosphere of an old-fashioned country fair. There is also an attempt to bring to the fair those artists and craftspeople who can demonstrate the pioneer arts and crafts of Texas. There are now more than 200 of them. When the fair first began it lasted only three days. Now it is held over two weekends, or four days, to accommodate the growing number of visitors. The fair is recognized by the state of Texas as the official state art fair. The fair does include historic arts and crafts. Fair planners continually search for more pioneer arts and crafts and for more sales opportunities for their craftspeople and artists. More than 150,000 people attend each year. It is financed by sales made at the fair and by paid admissions. Other fair events include entertainment on two shaded stages that features country and western, bluegrass and mariachi music concerts. In 1982, there were special performances by the Dallas Black Dance Theater and Houston's Theater on Wheels. The children's area was newly defined in 1982 with magician Jules Caplan, a storyteller and special crafts instruction featured.

Round Top

INTERNATIONAL FESTIVAL-INSTITUTE

Held annually, June/July
Cultural, educational

The International Festival-Institute at Round Top marked its twelfth year in 1982. It has gained an international reputation. Distinguished musicians, critics and talented students come every year to Festival Hill, one of the smallest incorporated communities in Texas. The six-week session, consisting of concerts and classes, always begins in early June. The festival-institute, founded by concert pianist James Dick, is an educational program for young musicians. Its scope covers solo instruments, orchestral and chamber music studies. Piano soloists, string groups and entire symphony orchestras perform for the public on the stage of the Mary Moody Northern Pavilion on Festival Hill. In 1976, a new orchestra, the Texas Festival Orchestra, debuted at the Round Top festival, with 50 young talented musicians performing. James Dick, founded the International Festival-Institute in 1971 at a place that is rich in pioneer heritage. It was his idea to establish a center where dedicated music students and beginning professional artists could make a smooth transition from student life to a professional career. In 1971, only 10 pianists studied with James Dick in a 10-day workshop, presenting a concert at the close of the session. The students then lived and performed at various locations in Round Top, but by 1976, a permanent home had been established on the 30-odd acres of Festival Hill on Texas 237 north of the town square. By then, more students had been added, and the Texas Festival Orchestra was formed. Over the years, guest conductors have led the orchestra. In 1976, two worked with the orchestra, Leon Fleisher, from the Peabody Conservatory in Baltimore, and John Giordano, music director and conductor of the Fort Worth

Symphony and Youth Orchestra. Today's concerts place emphasis on pianists, but there's also chamber music, a guest symphony orchestra, and in 1981, the Houston Symphony Orchestra and performances by the resident orchestra. There is also a free children's day concert now. Those who attend the concerts are encouraged to bring folding chairs and blankets and even a picnic meal. For the first time in 1981, gourmet picnic boxes for lunch and dinner were sold at Festival Hill. Admission prices to the grounds and concerts vary each season. James Dick, founder of the International Festival-Institute, is himself an accomplished pianist, having won international fame in 1965 when within an eight-month period he won top prizes in three international competitions. He made his Carnegie Hall debut in New York in 1975 and was acclaimed by Harold Schonberg, then senior music critic for the *New York Times*, who wrote, "This is modern piano playing at its best." Dick usually begins the session with a solo piano concert. The Festival-Institute began on Festival Hill in a small converted school building. Today it includes a restoration, the William Lockhart Clayton House, used for teaching and seminars and as a faculty residence. The festival attracts hundreds of students and thousands to the concerts. The event and institute are supported through donations by those who become Friends of the Festival-Institute. About 1,000 each contribute $125 or more to support it. It is also financed by tuition fees and paid admissions.

San Antonio

FIESTA SAN ANTONIO

Held annually, April
Cultural, folkloric, patriotic

The Fiesta San Antonio marked its eighty-seventh year in 1982. It was started in April 1855 for patriotic reasons to recall the anniversary of the Battle of San Jacinto on April 21. It is still patriotic, honoring all those who died winning independence for Texas. It encourages Pan-American friendship and culture by offering fun, food and friendship. There are more than 80 different events, many free. The event draws millions of visitors annually. In 1976, the bicentennial year, exactly 2.5 million attended. That year, the fiesta brought more than $1 million a day into the economy of San Antonio. The fiesta continues to draw record crowds who spend record amounts of money. The fiesta officially opens with the arrival of King Antonio, Monarch of Merriment, as he enters San Antonio at the head of a procession of illuminated floats, part of the Fiesta River Parade on the San Antonio River. He proclaims fun for all and sets the tempo for the next 10 days. King Antonio is dressed in a fitting uniform, has a sword and five stars on his collar and wears a plumed hat. He is selected from the ranks of the Texas Cavaliers and is crowned during torchlight ceremonies in front of the Alamo on the opening Saturday of the fiesta at 7:30 p.m. He takes over and the festivities begin. There are six major parades, a carnival, a Mexican rodeo, Mexican folklore and food. There is a solemn procession through the city streets on Monday and a pilgrimage to the Alamo. Participants leave flowers and tributes at the Alamo chapel in honor of the men who died there. Fiesta events include art exhibits, sports events, band concerts, fireworks, fashion and flower shows, a mariachi festival on the San Antonio River, the coronation of the Queen of the Order of the Alamo, arts, crafts and a fair. Events are citywide with many centering in the downtown area around the San Antonio River. Other highlights include river parades, a night in Old San Antonio, and the Battle of Flowers parade. Actually the fiesta started out as a Battle of Flowers on Alamo Plaza. A group of local ladies were looking for a way to celebrate the visit of President Benjamin Harrison to their city. They decided to hold an event similar to the flower festivals of Europe's Mediterranean coast. They gathered blossoms from their own gardens and decorated a dozen carriages and surreys with them. The rest of the flowers were used in a real battle of flowers. This gave way to the Battle of Flowers Association, which sponsored this one event annually, honoring the heroes of Texas independence. More events were added through the 1940s. By 1960, events and sponsoring organizations were so numerous that the Fiesta San Antonio Commission, Inc., was formed to coordinate the huge celebration. Today, more than 60 organizations sponsor and more than 80 scheduled events are held. For Fiesta 1976, also the bicentennial, special post-fiesta events were added with the San Antonio Symphony, a participating member organization of the fiesta, in concert. That is continued today. Each year's fiesta attracts several million, now putting about $12 million back into the city's economy. Work on the fiesta is a year-round job, done by volunteers. The event is financed through membership dues and subscriptions collected by the Fiesta San Antonio Commission with the help of Fiesta Men, the commission's official membership solicitation agency. It is also financed by concession payments, including the carnival and street chair permits issued by the Fiesta Commission to charitable, civic, patriotic and other groups. It is additionally supported by interest on bank deposits of the commission and income from special events that charge admission.

San Antonio

TEXAS FOLKLIFE FESTIVAL

Held annually, August
Ethnic, folkloric

The Texas Folklife Festival is a four-day ethnic event held in San Antonio on the HemisFair grounds of the Institute of Texan Cultures. It attracts more than 100,000 visitors every year with about 6,000 participating in all activities. Its purpose is to perpetuate and honor the state's ethnic cultures (as many as 36 different ethnic groups) and pioneer skills. Those who actively participate in demonstrating the crafts, work skills, costumes, foods, customs and folkways of all the ethnic groups come from 130 towns and cities in Texas. The highlight continues to be all the exotic ethnic foods that are authentically prepared for sale. The recipes are available in special souvenir cookbooks sold at the event. Food preparation and preservation techniques are demonstrated throughout the festival grounds. For example, German Texans from New Braunfels show how to make sausage stuffing. Italian Texans demonstrate the proper way to pickle olives. Swiss Texans show how to make the perfect fondue. The list goes on and on. Craftsmen teach visitors how to make a wooden puzzle, cowhide chairs, etchings, kites, sandcastings and pottery. Visitors can even learn how a herbalist works. There is also music, dancing and other entertainment reflecting the ethnic and pioneer heritage of the state. Festival events cover 15 acres of land belonging to the institute. Events begin on a Thursday at 5 p.m. Entertainment competes for audiences on nine stages. Cloggers and square dancers perform on a wooden platform in one area, while Ukrainian folk dancers do their thing on another stage. There are Mexican folk dancers and flamboyant flamenco dancers on another stage, not to overlook Lebanese belly dancers, Indian tribal performers and Polish royalty dances in still other areas. Music features traditional bluegrass, German oompah bands, Czech accordionists and Dutch singers. There are Italian lawn bowling games, *bocci*, and another group betting on a favorite chicken to win a flying contest. Storytellers spin yarns under shade trees, weavers demonstrate the art of clothmaking and a Swiss yodeler gives lessons. The festival attracts the famous, too. In 1974, Soviet cosmonaut Aleksey Arkhipovich Leonov came. He was taking a breather from training for the joint U.S.–USSR space project. Today, the festival is sponsored and staged by the Institute of Texan Cultures, a learning and communications center that year-round presents history and folk culture. Visitors to the festival can tour the institute's football-field-size exhibit floor. The festival is often described as the largest Texas block party in the state. There is an admission fee, which varies each year. A hand stamp allows visitors to enter and leave the festival grounds as often as they wish during a single day. The festival is open from 5 to 11 p.m. on Thursday and from noon to 11 p.m. Friday, Saturday and Sunday. The Texas Folklife Festival was born in 1972, developed by O.T. Baker, then the institute's exhibits manager and over the years an animal sculptor and rancher. In 1968, he was asked to go to Washington, D.C., to assist the Smithsonian with their second American Folklife Festival. He applied his expertise to developing a folklife event for Texas, since his own state has a rich ethnic and pioneer heritage. Baker stressed that the Texas Folklife Festival has more people involvement than any other world festival. The festival is supported by paid admissions and grants from different foundations and donations from local business. In 1974 alone, there were grants from the Ewing Halsell Foundation of San Antonio, Houston Endowment, Inc. of Houston, Moody Foundation of Galveston, Sid Richardson Foundation of Fort Worth and Strake Foundation of Houston. The very first festival in 1972 was financed by $35,000 in grants from the Ewing Halsell Foundation, Moody

Foundation and Houston Endowment. Admission to the institute itself is free, and guided tours are available by appointment for both small and large groups.

Utah

Logan

FESTIVAL OF THE AMERICAN WEST

Held annually, July/August
Cultural, economic, legendary, heritage

The nine-day Festival of the American West is held on the campus of Utah State University in Logan. It is a fairly new event, dating back to 1972, but already it has attracted more than 1 million people. It focuses attention on America's Western heritage, both the pioneer and Indian cultures of the 1890 period, by featuring drama, dance, song, arts, crafts, Western American exhibits, agriculture, a parade of animal-drawn vehicles and pioneer cooking. In 1973, the year-old festival received the George Washington Honor Medal from the Freedoms Foundation at Valley Forge, Pennsylvania, citing it as "an outstanding achievement in bringing about a better understanding of the American way of life." Epic legends and Old West lore are relived every summer at the USU campus. The festival was developed by USU's president, Glen L. Taggart. The event includes a multimedia historical pageant, exhibit of Western art, photographs and engravings, an Old West parade of horse-drawn antique wagons and noisy entertainment. There is a replica of a frontier town street and a display of vintage steam tractors and other equipment of the era at the Ronald V. Jensen Living Historical Farm. There is also an antique quilt show, an antique gun exhibit, a Western cookout, a posse meet and river float trips. The original festival was helped by seven famous people, including actor Chill Wills, singer Peter Toubus, who performed in *Jesus Christ, Superstar*, Monte Montana, Jr., of Wild West Shows and rope trick artist, actor Peter Strauss, actor James Drury, Ben Murphy alias Smith and Jones and singin' Sam Agins, a folk singer. There are about a dozen different events, the newest addition being the Great Western Fair. Future plans call for ethnic events and programs to show their influence on the area's development. The festival contributes to both the culture and the economy of Logan and Utah. Money from the festival over the years has made possible a new center for the Outlaw-Lawman History Association at Utah State University, the establishment of the Western Writers' Conference and two editions of Western magazines. It fills up local motels during the festival. Additional motels have been built here since the festival began. Celebrities participate, too, like actors Robert Redford and James Stewart, who also does the taped narration every year. Work on the festival is done by both volunteers and a paid staff, each putting in three to four months of labor. The event is financed by state grants, donations, gate receipts and extra paid admissions to the pageant, fair, farm and cookout. Events are held on the campus of Utah State University and in surrounding areas.

Ouray, Randlett, Whiterocks

UTE BEAR DANCE

Held annually, April
Ethnic, cultural, legendary

The Ute Bear Dance is a traditional rite of the Ute Indians to welcome spring. It ranges from three to five days, with the actual dates decided by a special Bear Dance Committee, who are influenced by weather conditions and other community activities. Each Ute community stages its own bear dance. The dance has been performed from time immemorial, possibly thousands of years—no one really knows. It was done to perpetuate the cultural tradition of the Ute Indian people. The dance is a Ute Indian version of the arrival of spring as told by the bear. It is always the same, never changing because it is the Ute tradition, belief and culture. About 1,000 attend the annual event with hundreds more participating. According to the Ute Indian, the Bear Dance originated from the first thunder in spring. This thunder awakens the bear, who has been hibernating all winter. The bear leaves his den and begins to move around. He usually runs back and forth to a tree and scratches on the tree's bark. Spring has arrived, and the bear is happy because the grass will grow and there will be plenty to eat. The Ute Bear Dance interprets all this, following the actions of the bear. The Utes gather in spring and imitate the bear's scratching by the drawing of a notched stick over a surface, giving out a deep scratching-rumbling sound. The Indians sing in harmony, making up the songs heralding the new season. When the Bear Dance Committee, which includes the Bear Dance chiefs, dancers and singers, decides the exact time for the dance, posters are printed and distributed. Singing practice and rehearsals are held a month in advance. The chiefs and their committees decide when to hold the Bear Dance Feast and who should prepare the food. The business committee budgets funds, covering poster printing costs and the food plus roundtrip transportation to the dance grounds from the various reservations. Each Ute community has its own Bear Dance ground. Prior to the event, a huge bear's head is elevated on a pole within an enclosure of boughs and willows, interlaced to form a large circle. All ages, from small children to elderly men and women, dance. Women wear shawls, which they flip in the face of the men, an invitation to dance. The men line up on one side, and the women opposite them, about three feet apart. The lines move back and forth in unison to the rhythm of the beating drum. In addition to the Bear Dance, there's lots of intercommunity socializing and gambling, a favorite extra. The gambling usually takes place between the afternoon and evening dances. Gambling games include the stick-and-hand game, two-card monte and poker. The object of the stick-and-hand game, played by teams, is for a person on one team to hide a marked and unmarked set of bones from the opposing team by using sleight-of-hand tricks. The opposing team tries to guess which hand or hands hold the bones. If they miss, they lose a stick. When 10 sticks are lost by one team, or when a team has all the sticks, the game ends. The Ute Bear Dance is open to the public, but advance reservations are required.

Salt Lake City

UTAH ARTS FESTIVAL

Held annually, June
Cultural

The Utah Arts Festival is a five-day cultural event in downtown Salt Lake City, now held in June. It originally started as an event in September 1976 to mark the country's bicentennial. The festival is both a performing and visual arts event with full programs each day from 11 a.m. to 11 p.m. Concerts, drama, art exhibits, a film festival, banner project, demonstrating craftsmen, food, a poetry alley and a children's art yard are all part of the festival. It attracts thousands of visitors and almost as many participants. It claims to be the first state-sponsored arts festival in the country. It attempts to encourage more residents to be culturally conscious of the state's artistic facilities and artistically talented residents. The city has seven major professional performing companies: the world famous Mormon Tabernacle Choir, Utah Opera Company, Utah Symphony Orchestra, Ballet West, Pioneer Memorial Theater Company, Repertory Dance Theater and Ririe-Woodbury Dance Company. Guest performers are also part of the event. Performances are on a citywide basis in the city's downtown area on West Temple in front of the Salt Lake City Art Center, Symphony Hall, Salt Palace and in the Bicentennial Arts Complex. There are special concert series every year with performances at both the Symphony Hall and the Capitol Theater. There are more than 100 performing arts groups from all over Utah. They appear at the Main Stage and Bistro Stage on the festival site. These free performances include classical, bluegrass, jazz, folk music, theater, opera and dance. Approximately 70 booths deal with the visual arts and are located throughout the festival grounds. The children's Art Yard enables children to watch the wheel-thrown pottery, loom weaving, community sculpture, storytelling and even an African Village with mask and musical instrument demonstrations. In 1983, the festival added "Dial a Play" literary project. Telephone booths were set up throughout the festival area. Visitors were able to dial and listen to a variety of westerns, dramas, comedies and mystery plays, all written by local writers. About 20 prerecorded selections, ranging from 15 seconds to two minutes were made available. Also new in 1983 was a billboard project designed to give recognition to participating visual artists. Three billboard designs were selected by a jury and placed in 63 citywide sites. Each design was reproduced on approximately 20 poster boards and one handpainted bulletin board. The designs were chosen for their visual impact and ability to use a billboard as an artistic medium. The festival, which was called the Salt Lake Festival of the Arts in 1977, has added sidewalk cafes and decorative booths and carts all serving traditional and ethnic foods, which featured Navajo tacos, crepes, quiche, empanadas, oysters, clams on the half shell and egg foo young. The festival is supported by state funds, donations from business and ticket sales.

Salt Lake City

UTAH STATE FAIR

Held annually, September
Economic

The Utah State Fair is held every September and runs for 11 days. It is an agricultural and industrial fair with livestock judging, other competitive events, a midway, special youth fairs and entertainment with famous performers. Although the fairgrounds only cover 63 acres (less than any other state fairground), attendance is as high as half a million annually. Each year the fair has a theme. In 1976, it was "Horizons of Progress." The fair dates back to 1856, when it was organized and sponsored by the Deseret Agricultural and Manufacturing Society "with a view of promoting the arts of domestic industry and to encourage the production of articles from the native elements in this Territory." The society's officials worked without pay to promote industry in communities removed from manufacturing sources. This profited every agricultural town in Deseret. One of the society's earliest projects was Deseret Gardens at the mouth of Emigration Canyon. This was the first experimental farm west of the Mississippi River. Early winners of exhibits in the fair's early days included Brigham Young, who received $25 for the best stallion and first prize for the best celery exhibited in the fair. There was no carnival atmosphere or horse races, although sideshows and rides usually associated with fairs did come later. During lean years, the fair was not held at all, but in 1902 it moved to its present location on land that the state purchased especially for the fairgrounds. Prior to that, the fair was held in different locations such as old social halls, various Mormon wards and the site of today's Trolley Square. There is a general admission fee to the fair. Once inside, many things are free, but there is an additional charge for the entertainment programs. The fair always opens with the state's governor officiating at a parade. Grandstand entertainment has included such famous people as folk singer Donna Fargo, Bill Anderson, TV star Jim Nabors and ethnic programs.

Vermont

Enosburg Falls

VERMONT DAIRY FESTIVAL

Held annually, June
Economic

The Vermont Dairy Festival is a two-day event that honors the state's dairy industry. It officially begins 10 a.m. the first day with the introduction of visiting dignitaries, which often includes the Vermont governor, both state and federal senators and representatives as well as dairy, agricultural and creamery officials from all over the state and neighboring states. These same dignitaries then join a big dairy parade by riding in special convertibles. A dozen school bands from Vermont and Canada march with dairy motif floats (they vie for prizes), farm machinery, horses and antique cars. At noon, there's a big chicken barbecue hosted by local firemen, who serve it at the town's athletic field, where there are also booths selling homemade foods, farm products, ice cream, cotton candy and the usual snacks and, of course, milk. The State Dairy Princess is selected the first day, too. She is chosen from several county dairy princesses also selected in May at other state events. There's a coronation ceremony, and prizes are four-year college scholarships. There is also a drawing for "Maple Mabel," a valuable milking cow and for "Jack the Steak," a steer good for lots of steaks in the freezer. Both animals are carefully chosen, and thousands of tickets are sold as chances for them. The winner can elect either to keep the cow or steer or sell the animal. There is always a local dairyman willing to buy either animal. The afternoon offers colorful drills by visiting Canadian bands, and there are competitions for small cash prizes in milking stool heave, three-legged races and sack and egg races. Entertainment for children includes rides on live ponies, a merry-go-round and a ferris wheel. The evening is for a talent show, which might include old-time fiddlers, singers or instrumentalists. There used to be dancing on Main Street. The second festival day is devoted to horse-drawing or horse-pulling competitions like the kind seen at state fairs. Each festival hosts more than 15,000 visitors, and since it began in 1956 as a one-day event, more than 500,000. The festival was the idea of Ruth Wright of Wright's Dairy. She and her husband, Donald, together with County Agent Walter Rockwood, staged the very first festival to celebrate Dairy Day and June is Dairy Month. It was

held June 1, 1956, in the town's Lincoln Park. The big event was a milking
contest, featuring four cows from Wright's Dairy. Milk was served to everyone.
A year later the Enosburg Lions Club took over the event and launched it as the
Franklin County Dairy Festival, with more events and a parade. In 1970, Governor Deane Davis proclaimed the event the Vermont Dairy Festival, making it
a state event, and it has remained one. It is held in June because June is Dairy
Month. The event also now includes arts, crafts, painting exhibits and more.
Work on the festival is by Lions Club members and volunteers. It is supported
by proceeds from the previous year's event. All events are held on Main Street
or at the Athletic Field.

Manchester

FESTIVAL OF THE ARTS

Held annually, June/October
Cultural, educational

The Festival of the Arts reached its fifty-third year in 1982. It takes place from
early June through mid-October at the Southern Vermont Art Center. Though
the center is a year-round operation, the festival is not. The festival includes
study programs in the visual and performing arts for all ages, charging a fee to
cover expenses. More than 1,400 artists and lay people participate in the annual
event, which has expanded into related fields of art classes and film festivals.
Both the center and festival began in 1929, when a small group of dedicated
artists living in the Dorset–Manchester area got together to hold a public exhibit
and sale of their works in August. It attracted so much attention that another
exhibit was held the next year at the Equinox Hotel Pavilion in Manchester. The
show was such a great success that the group decided to organize on a formal
basis "for the primary purpose of holding an annual exhibition." In 1933, the
group was incorporated as the Southern Vermont Artists of Manchester, Vermont, under the laws of Vermont. The annual summer exhibit continued to grow
in importance over the years, and the strong support of local residents, visitors
and vacationers led to acquiring a permanent gallery and the start of seasonal
exhibitions by SVA and guest artists. It wasn't until 1950 that the SVA purchased
Yester House, a colonial mansion on 375 acres of land on a wooded slope of
Mt. Equinox for $25,000. Eleven of the mansion's 28 rooms were made into
galleries, and the house became the Southern Vermont Art Center. It is open to
the public, June to mid-October. There are exhibits of sculpture, paintings, prints
and other visual arts such as photographs. Other activities at the center include
study programs, art classes, concerts and film festivals. Additionally there is a
Botany Trail, the conservation project of the Garden Club of Manchester at the
Art Center. Trees, ferns and wildflowers are all identified by permanent markers,

and the pool and waterfall were developed by the club. There is a more than 200-year-old sugar maple tree in the Sculpture Garden. Half-hour walks are featured as well as woodland trails on all of the center's property. Southern Vermont Artists, Inc., a nonprofit educational institution supported solely by private contributions, administers the center and all of its programs. There is a president, two vice-presidents, treasurer, secretary, board of trustees, honorary trustees and executive board, as well as various committees in charge of finances, membership and publicity. The center is financed through private donations, membership dues, admission fees, concerts, exhibit charges and tuition fees and through a Beaux Arts Ball held in mid-June every year. The ball not only helps financially but also helps to promote interest and membership in the center. There are also regular artist memberships and associate artist memberships available, which entitle members to attend and vote at SVA meetings, submit works of art for the annual art show and more. The SVA also receives the support of individuals, foundations and corporations and, through the Art Center's Bartlett and Louise Arkell Endowment Fund, through lifetime gifts and bequests.

St. Albans

VERMONT MAPLE FESTIVAL

Held annually, April
Economic

The fifteenth annual Vermont Maple Festival in 1982 attracted thousands who had never seen a sugar maple tree tapped for maple syrup. The three-day April event is held when the sap is running. Each year the festival receives the governor's proclamation, and festivities begin. The sugar maple is Vermont's official state tree. The festival gives visitors a first-hand view of how the huge evaporators turn out quantities of maple syrup. It is even possible to sample it while it's hot, but visitors are always told to be sure to wear warm clothing and waterproof boots. Events include guided bus tours to the sugar maple houses, square dances, ice shows, a gymnast show, fiddler's contest, barbecues, supper and pancake breakfasts. There are arts and crafts, old and new maple syrup–making equipment displays, a maple store and Vermont cheese booths. There is a parade and Maple Sap Run, a foot race. Popular are the Vermont breakfasts of hot pancakes, maple syrup, sausages and hot coffee at nominal costs. The event is supported through charges for meals and tours, the sale of different items and local donations. The festival promotes the maple industry and educates folks about sugaring.

Stowe

STOWE WINTER CARNIVAL

Held annually, January
Economic, sports

The Stowe Winter Carnival is a nine-day mid- to late January event designed to attract tourists at a slow period and to encourage more winter events. The carnival includes a variety of winter sports events and competitions, entertainment, snow sculpture, the selection of a Snow Queen and coronation ball. The carnival has attracted 100,000 people since it was started in 1975. Local resort owners and businessmen launched the event. Carnival highlights feature the Equitable Family Skiing Challenges, Celanese Sled Dog Races, a snowgolf tournament, a Ski America Fiddlers' Contest, Tyrolean night, a Coca-Cola Snow Sculpture Competition, the Yankee Cross-Country Race and a photo contest sponsored by Kodak. Opening Friday night ceremonies include the crowning of a king and queen plus the governor's dinner. The following days are devoted to skating races, square dancing, sled dog racing, a Las Vegas night and more, ending with a Winter Carnival Queen's Ball and sculpture awards. The various receptions, dances and meals are held at the different ski lodges and resorts in Stowe. The event is handled by the Stowe Winter Carnival organization and financed through paid admission and sponsorship of the different programs.

Tunbridge

VERMONT'S WORLD'S FAIR

Held annually, September
Economic

The Vermont's World's Fair reached its 121st year in 1982 and shows signs of continuing full force. It is held for four days in mid-September on a long weekend, Thursday through Sunday. It is not really a world's fair as its name seems to indicate but a real and very popular country fair. More than 40,000 come every year to enjoy such events as sulky races, horse and oxen pulls, daredevil car drivers, jugglers, acrobats, old-time fiddlers contest, brass band concerts, displays of agricultural crops and food judging contests of freshly baked breads, cookies and pies. There's a midway, arts and crafts and the traditional livestock and 4-H Club judgings with blue ribbons and prizes for the best. There is an admission charge, but season and single-entry tickets are sold. There is an extra charge for the auto racing and grandstand performances. The Tunbridge fair began in 1861 as a one-day event in a cow pasture in North Tunbridge. Four years later it was called the Little World's Fair and 10 years later moved to its present location. The fair went to three days, and the grandstand and exhibit halls were built with more added throughout the years. A valuable collection of farm and home antiques was acquired in 1929. Today, the fair runs for four days and is still a showcase for competing exhibitors and other old-fashioned events. The fair is administered by 100 shareholders of the Union Agricultural Society, who meet annually at a special banquet to elect officers for the following year. Shares in the society originally sold for $5 each. They are not for sale to anyone other than members of the society. The shares are worth a lot of money today and are status symbols for the members. The society's directors handle parking, cattle stalls, racing, midway attractions and maintenance of buildings. The fair is also supported by paid admissions, exhibit fees, gambling and private donations.

Virginia

Statewide

HISTORIC GARDEN WEEK

Held annually, April
Educational, horticultural, preservation

Historic Garden Week is a statewide nine-day program of tours of gardens and homes that date back to colonial times. The first garden week was held April 29 through May 10, 1929, and since then several million people have toured the state's gardens and historic homes. It was in 1928 that a member of the Garden Club of Virginia suggested that the group organize a pilgrimage and charge a small admission to give the public a chance to visit some of the state's homes and gardens. The funds were to be used to restore historic gardens. The first Historic Garden Week included a tour of the grounds and gardens at Kenmore, home of Colonel Fielding Lewis and his wife Betty, sister of George Washington. As a result the grounds and gardens were restored, and the established Kenmore Association raised funds to restore the house. The statewide program begins the last full week in April, Saturday through the following Sunday or Monday. The event has been cited by many historic groups and has received the Outstanding Award from the Virginia Travel Council for the beautification of the state for 43 years. The event celebrated its fifty-third year in 1982. During Historic Garden Week, tours are offered to 34 areas of the state, with private homes and gardens opened by owners as a courtesy to the special observance. All proceeds go toward the restoration of the gardens and grounds of Virginia's historic shrines. Every year, more than 200 homes and gardens open to the public for this week only. The event was discontinued from 1942 to 1946 as a war measure. To date, the grounds and gardens of more than 23 historic shrines have been restored. In addition, the week adds to the economy of all areas where tours are conducted. Members of the Garden Club of Virginia and volunteers (45 clubs) work year-round on preparations for the annual event. They usually line up the homes first, do publicity and obtain hostesses for the tours and homes. The event is financed by tour charges and the sale of guidebooks. All-day tours now include box lunches sold at reasonable rates. Tour costs vary, but block tickets for several tours make it more feasible for visitors.

Alexandria

GEORGE WASHINGTON BIRTHDAY CELEBRATION

Held annually, February
Historic, economic, commemorative, patriotic

The month-long George Washington Birthday Celebration in February has been held since 1977, but Washington's Birthday (now a movable date) has always been celebrated since 1719 in Alexandria, considered to be the first president's hometown. The very first parade honoring Washington was held in this city in 1798, when the Revolutionary War Dragoons brought him from Mt. Vernon to review the troops in front of Gadsby's Tavern. Now every February that same parade is recreated, featuring specially selected George and Martha in colonial costume. They arrive in an antique carriage and stop at Gadsby's to review the parade. More than 20,000 spectators line the streets to watch the parade and pageantry. Washington was one of the city's original surveyors, and he owned a home in town, worshipped at Christ Church, socialized at the Tavern (now completely restored) and did business with local merchants. He visited the city often from his home in Mt. Vernon. The annual parade takes place in Old Town Alexandria, beginning at Wilkes and St. Asaph streets, covering 13 city blocks. It is said to be the largest parade to honor the first U.S. president. The parade includes horse-drawn carriages, high school marching bands in colonial costume, antique cars, bagpipe bands, colonial regiments, clowns and fife and drum corps, totaling more than 90 marching units. Other events are a "New" Homes Tour of the city (houses built in the federal and colonial styles), followed by an Old Homes Tour of restored and preserved eighteenth- and nineteenth-century homes. There is a traditional colonial costume George Washington Birthnight Ball and Buffet held in the restored Gadsby's Tavern. Colonial military units reenact a day in the life of a Revolutionary War camp at Fort Ward Park, and there are special exhibits, plays, a visit by a naval ship to one of the city's piers and strolling minstrels singing in the Old Town restaurants. The event is very popular, and work on it is handled by historic organizations and volunteers. It is financed by paid admissions for tours, the ball and other events.

Chincoteague

CHINCOTEAGUE PONY ROUND-UP AND PENNING

Held annually, July
Conservation, economic

The Chincoteague Pony Round-Up and Penning, has become an internationally known event that always comes in late July, lasting three days. It dates back to 1925, when it was devised by the local volunteer fire department to add something special to their annual carnival. The pony roundup was and still is a way of raising money for the small fishing village's fire department and of helping the Chincoteague National Wildlife Refuge keep nearby Assateague Island's pony population down to a manageable size. The pony penning or roundup attracts more than 50,000 visitors, who bid on the ponies at an auction. The ponies, made famous in Marguerite Henry's book, *Misty*, are smaller than horses but larger than Shetlands. They are rounded up (about 100 of them) from the nearby island, swimming across the narrow channel to Chincoteague. The ponies are usually bought as pets for children. Those not auctioned off swim back to their island home. The ponies' presence can be traced back to the sixteenth century. Two legends try to account for their existence on the tiny Delmarva island. One is that they were cargo on a Spanish ship wrecked off the coast and that the ponies swam ashore to the island. The other story claims that the ponies belonged to pirates who used the island as a hideout and were forced to leave in a hurry without the ponies. In 1973, 174 ponies made the swim, but only 54 colts were sold. Average price per pony was $102.50, with the highest $160 and the lowest, $55. Proceeds benefit the local fire department.

Fredericksburg

FREDERICKSBURG DOG MART

Held annually, October
Historic, economic

The Fredericksburg Dog Mart is without a doubt the nation's oldest dog show, begun in 1698 as a peaceful trade between the Indians and settlers. Today's dog show and competition are held on the outskirts of the city, attracting thousands of people. The event is sponsored by the Fredericksburg-Rappahannock chapter of the Izaak Walton League of America, Inc., to perpetuate the historic dog mart. Today's mart opens with a 9 a.m. parade. The one-day event includes the registration of all animals for the dog show judging. The parade includes dogs and people, followed by a dance of the Pamunkey Indians and Order of the Arrow–BSA. There's an old fiddler's contest, turkey calling, fox horn blowing, harmonica contest, a folk guitar competition and hog calling. After a lunch break, there's a dog auction of all unwanted dogs, then the dog show and competition, followed by exhibits, rides and other programs. The day's activities end at dusk. Area Indians sell painted gourds, beads, rubber-tipped spears and muskrat bones. Others tell stories about the time when the Indian was the only resident in the woods along the Rappahannock River. The event is financed by dog show entry fees, exhibit fees and donations from local industry.

Norfolk

HARBORFEST NORFOLK

Held annually, June
Heritage, economic

Harborfest Norfolk is a water-related event now held annually since the country's bicentennial celebration in 1976. It attracts thousands of visitors and at least 1,000 visiting vessels. Harborfest began as the result of Operation Sail, the 1976 bicentennial spectacular in New York City with a parade of tall-masted ships from all over the world. Some of those ships visited Norfolk in the summer of 1976 and gave birth to the first Harborfest. It is the celebration of the sea, highlighted by visiting tall-masted sailing ships, military ships and working boats of the Chesapeake Bay. Oystermen, yachtsmen, crabbers and sailors plus fishermen and pleasure boaters all meet in Norfolk for the four-day celebration. There are waterfront rock concerts, a water ski show, sky-diving demonstrations, fireworks and a parade of ships. There is a pirate regatta and a water balloon and cannon battle by boat and land. Registration for the regatta is by purchasing an official 16-by-21-inch Harborfest pirate flag to be flown from the highest yardarm. The Cousteau Society, headquartered in Norfolk, exhibits equipment used in the famous undersea explorations of Captain Jacques-Yves Cousteau. The society also sponsors an Ocean Science Day program. The event also features a variety of seafood and ethnic meals sold at moderate prices. Most events are free, except the Pirates Ball. The event is sponsored by donations from local businesses and groups. Work on the event is by paid staff and volunteer help.

Norfolk

INTERNATIONAL AZALEA FESTIVAL

Held annually, April
Economic, cultural, political

The International Azalea Festival marked its twenty-ninth year in 1982, drawing a record crowd of nearly 500,000 visitors. The festival salutes spring with the blooming of azaleas and the allied forces of all nations. The festival was started in 1952, one year after NATO established its Supreme Allied Command Atlantic (SACLANT) in Norfolk. The really big event, however, was launched in 1954 and has continued to this day. Each year, Norfolk's mayor and chamber of commerce invite one of the 15 NATO countries to be the festival's honored nation, represented by a queen, usually the daughter of a very high-ranking government official of the honored country. Princesses from the other 14 NATO countries and attendants from local high schools and colleges make up the court. Usually the ambassador of the honored nation officiates at the crowning of his country's honorary queen in the festival coronation ceremonies. In past years, several U.S. presidents—Johnson, Nixon and Ford—have crowned their own daughters. Festival events, all open to the public, include sports, sailing regattas, parades, concerts, square dancing, the Azalea Ball, Naval Air Show, sightseeing tours, fashion shows and the coronation ceremony amid the azaleas in the Norfolk Gardens-by-the-Sea. The festival originally was for five days, but the growing number of visitors and events extended it to eight days. More recently it is held for three days. Several million have attended the spring event since its start. The increased number of events has contributed to the growth of cultural groups like the Norfolk Symphony Orchestra. It also helps international relations. The festival attracts not only international and politically famous people but also those in the entertainment world. Work on the festival is done by hundreds of volunteers. It is supported by some paid admissions and charges for luncheons and by contributions from city, the Retail Merchants Association and corporate underwriting of selected events.

Williamsburg

PRELUDE TO INDEPENDENCE

Held annually, May/July
Patriotic, historic, educational

Prelude to Independence commemorates the period in Williamsburg between May 15 and July 4, 1776, when important legislative activity paved the way for

the founding of the United States. It begins with an opening ceremony at the
Capitol in Colonial Williamsburg at 5:30 p.m. with military fife and drums. The
authentic observance dates back to May 15, 1951, when the Colonial Williamsburg Foundation decided to celebrate the period that led to the founding of this
country. Today's observance is designed to call attention to the contributions of
Virginia patriots, meeting in Williamsburg, to the American Revolution, the
independence movement and the U.S. constitution. It also reflects the adoption
in Williamsburg of the Virginia Resolution for Independence (May 15, 1776),
the Virginia Declaration of Rights (June 12, 1776) and the Virginia Constitution
(June 29, 1776). Today's event has been honored twice with the George Washington Honor Medal from the Freedoms Foundation of Valley Forge, Pennsylvania, in 1953 and 1956. Prelude to Independence events extend over the entire
period and include a parade of costumed militia fife and drum corps to the
Capitol. There is the changing of the flag from the British Great Union to the
American Continental. There is a reading of excerpts or full text of either the
Virginia Resolution for Independence or the Virginia Declaration of Rights.
There are always welcoming remarks and observations of Colonial Williamsburg
by the chairman of the board, president or some famous person. In 1951, the
first year's event, guest speaker was Samuel Eliot Morrison. The event attracts
5,000 visitors, and since 1951, about 105,000. It is financed by the Colonial
Williamsburg Foundation, with work on the event handled by Colonial Williamsburg staffers.

Winchester

SHENANDOAH APPLE BLOSSOM FESTIVAL

Held annually, May
Economic

The Shenandoah Apple Blossom Festival marked its fify-fifth anniversary in
1982, although it actually began in 1924. It was not held for three years during
World War II. It was started to call attention to the area's apple production and
historical significance. More than 250,000 people come every year, and since
the festival began, a few million. More than 2 million pink and white apple
blossoms are in full bloom for the festival, always held the first full weekend
in May. Highlights are the festive coronation of Queen Shenandoah, who in the
past have included Luci Baines Johnson, younger daughter of the late President
Lyndon Johnson, and the daughters of foreign ambassadors. Local girls, too,
have been crowned. The crowning is done by a celebrity like actor Howard Keel
or the governor. Former President Gerald Ford has also officiated. Festival events
(some require paid admissions) include concerts, an apple pie baking contest, a
midway, sponsored luncheons, fireworks and a sports breakfast with sports ce-

lebrities. There is also the knighting of the grand marshal of the parade by Queen Shenandoah, followed by The New Virginians, 35 talented young performers from Blacksburg, Virginia, with a ten-piece orchestra. Additional events include the mayor's lunch, the Battle of the Bands and a country music dance. The last day, usually a Sunday, is devoted to arts, crafts and square and folk dancing in the park. About 2,000 volunteers work on festival plans starting nine months prior to the event itself. It is supported by paid admissions, membership dues in the festival organization and donations from industry and various associations.

Washington

District of Columbia

CHERRY BLOSSOM FESTIVAL

Held annually, March/April
Floral, economic

The Cherry Blossom Festival celebrated its fiftieth anniversary in 1982 but had its very beginnings farther back than that to 1909. The wife of President William Howard Taft told a friend that she liked cherry trees and would like to plant some in the capital city's Potomac Park. Dr. Jokichi Takamine, a Japanese chemist famed for the discovery of adrenaline, was visiting the city at the time and learned of Mrs. Taft's wish. Through him, a gift of cherry trees was presented in 1912 to Washington, D.C., as a "gesture of friendship." It was on March 27, 1912, that Mrs. Taft in a simple ceremony planted the first cherry tree and Viscountess Chinda, wife of the Japanese ambassador, planted the second one on the northern bank of the Tidal Basin, about 125 feet south of today's Independence Avenue. Workmen finished planting the trees around the Tidal Basin and in east Potomac Park. The festival has no set dates since it is dependent on weather conditions, but the cherry blossoms usually flower in late March or the first week in April. It wasn't until 1927 that the original 1912 planting was recalled in a pageant by schoolchildren. By 1934, it grew into a three-day event, sponsored by the District of Columbia commissioners. The following year, several civic groups joined to launch the Cherry Blossom Festival, interrupted only by World War II. In 1940, the festival pageant became part of the festivities, and by 1948 the festival was reinstated and Cherry Blossom Princesses were chosen from every state and the territories. From these, a Cherry Blossom Queen was selected to reign during the festival. Every year's festival now officially opens with the lighting of an ancient ceremonial Japanese lantern, a gift to the nation's capital in 1954 from the governor of Tokyo to mark the centennial of Commodore Perry's historic visit to Japan. The giant lantern is over eight feet high, weighs 6,000 pounds and is more than 300 years old. On the west side of the Tidal Basin is a Japanese pagoda made of rough stone and presented to the city by the mayor of Yokohama to "symbolize the spirit of friendship between the United States of America and Japan manifested on the Treaty of Peace, Amity and Commerce signed at Yokohama on March 31, 1854." It was dedicated April 18, 1958. During the war years, cherry trees in Japan deteriorated from lack of care. It was these trees on the bank of the Arakawa River that had been given to Washington in 1912. In 1952, the Japanese government requested cuttings from the U.S. trees to restore their own plantings in the Adachi Ward. The U.S. National Park Service helped out. In 1965, the Japanese government gave another gift of 3,800 Yoshino trees, with 700 planted on the Washington Monument grounds and the rest throughout the Mall. In 1974, the festival added the selection of the College Girl of the Year, with scholarships for the top winner and lesser prizes for all 51 girls. Festival events include the cherry blossom sailboat regatta on the Tidal Basin and the parade at 11 a.m. on Constitution Avenue, N.W., between 7th and 13th streets. This is handled by the Downtown Jaycees and is the capital's largest parade. There is a charge for grandstand seats. Official opening ceremonies begin at 2:30 p.m. The rest of the week is filled with theater, concerts, art exhibits and festival dances. Several million people have attended the festival over the years. It is financed by some paid admissions and contributions.

Washington, D.C.

FRISBEE FESTIVAL

Held annually, September
Sports

The Frisbee or Frisbee Disc Festival is a one-day event, usually held the first Sunday in September, the day before Labor Day. The free festival, sponsored by the National Air and Space Museum, is said to be the world's largest non-competitive frisbee disc event. It was started in 1976 as a bicentennial event by the Smithsonian Institution. It has continued ever since, attracting as many as 10,000 entries each year. It was held earlier in the year, but changed to September because the weather was better. The event is held from noon to 5 p.m. on the National Mall with a rain date, usually Labor Day. The 1983 festival featured Judy Horowitz of Forest Hills, New York. She was named women's overall U.S. Open Frisbee Disc Champion, while Jens and Erwin Velasquez of South Plainsfield, New Jersey, were the world freestyle champions. Local resident Jendi Holmes performed with McTabish, a five-year-old border Collie, the 1983

East Coast regional dog disc-catching champion. The festival usually includes afternoon workshops for beginning, intermediate and advanced levels of disc throwing. The hearing impaired are helped with sign language interpretation.

Washington, D.C.

PAGEANT OF PEACE

Held annually, December/January
Religious

The Pageant of Peace, cosponsored by the Department of the Interior's National Park Service and the Pageant of Peace, Inc., is a Christmas holiday tradition in the nation's capital. It begins around mid-December (December 15) with the U.S. president's Christmas message and the lighting of the national Christmas tree, which usually happens at 5 p.m. This is followed by Christmas carols and music concerts performed by various groups from all over the United States. The Christmas tree is a gift to the nation by a different state each year. The tree is from 65 to 70 feet tall and is decorated with more than 6,000 sparkling Christmas lights. There is an illuminated Nativity scene near the tree, visited by thousands. Children are treated to ''Santa's Eight Reindeer,'' live from the National Zoo and parked at the Ellipse, where the tree stands. There is a Yule log, the trunk of last year's tree, which burns continuously. The musical programs and Christmas caroling continue to New Year's Day, when the tree lights are turned off and the Pageant of Peace ends. The national Christmas tree has been a holiday tradition since Christmas Eve 1923, when President Coolidge lit a giant fir on the Ellipse south of the White House. The tree was a gift to him from Middlebury College in his own home state of Vermont. It was then lighted by an electric storage battery. People were so pleased by the tree, which the President shared with the nation, that the following year a live Norway spruce was planted in Sherman Plaza, southeast of the Executive Mansion, to be the national Christmas tree. Tree-lighting ceremonies continued at Sherman Plaza for the next 10 years, with the first broadcast nationwide in 1929. In 1932, loudspeakers, hidden in the branches of the first ''singing tree,'' sent Christmas carols to the whole country. In 1937, chimes sounded as the tree was lit. The chimes told the exact moment for the president to push the button to turn on the tree lights. It was also the signal to light all community Christmas trees across the nation. Ceremonies were moved to Lafayette Park, north of the White House, remaining there until 1939. Two live Fraser firs were planted to the east and west of the statue of Andrew Jackson in the park. The idea was to use the trees on alternate years. The use of live trees was discontinued in the early 1950s because the decorations and lights harmed the trees, making them look too bare the rest of the year. Ever since, cut trees have been used and their branches recycled in January as mulch for the capital's parks and tulip beds. Within the next 15 years, the tree lighting site was moved to the Ellipse and then to the south grounds of the White House. In 1954, the site was permanently set on the Ellipse, and the Pageant of Peace, Inc., a nonprofit citizens committee, was formed to work with the National Park Services to handle the holiday event and program. As many as 10,000 people attend the lighting ceremonies, and over the years, a few million.

Washington

Puyallup, Tacoma, Sumner, Orting, Fife

PUYALLUP VALLEY DAFFODIL FESTIVAL

Held annually, March/April
Economic

The Puyallup Valley Daffodil Festival covers five cities and coincides with the exact blooming of the daffodils, depending upon the weather, which can be in late March or early April. The nine-day festival salutes the valley's industry, daffodils, with a Grand Floral Parade, a musical extravaganza, the queen's coronation, a three-day daffodil show, a four-day all-Arabian horse show plus 100 special events keyed to the flowers. More than 1,000 acres of daffodils are in bloom over the valley floor in the shadow of Mount Rainier. The valley's soil conditions and mild winter climate are good for these flowers. Valley farmers turned to daffodil growing around 1923, after Prohibition prevented them from growing their usual crop of hops. The daffodil-growing industry caught on and is still highly successful. With the coming of air cargo, cut daffodil blossoms were sold to Eastern cities, and the market thrived. In 1976 alone, more than 15 million daffodil buds and 23 million blooming daffodils were harvested. In the early 1930s, local valley residents launched a spring daffodil festival, with the first one in 1934. Today, the festival's floral parade is rated as the third largest in North America. The three-city parade (Tacoma, Puyallup, Sumner) includes bands, marching and mounted units and more than 40 daffodil-decorated floats. A half-million fresh-cut flowers are displayed against the backdrop of the bay and mountains. The forty-ninth festival was held in 1982 and themed to "country-western." The festival calls attention to the daffodil and Puyallup Valley and helps to bolster the local economy. The now famous Grand Daffodil Parade was the idea of Tacoma photographer Lee Merrill, who suggested that the daffodils be used for decorations. It began with decorated bicycles, then cars and finally floats. The parade attracts more than a half-million people and several million on TV, since the event is always televised on the West Coast. Parade marshals have included the state governor and other officials, and the musical show has featured well-known performers. The festival is handled by a nonprofit corporation, the Puyallup Valley Daffodil Festival, and funding is by donations from individuals, civic groups, organizations and business. There is an admission charge for the grandstand parade seats, the queen's coronation and the flower and horse shows.

Seattle

PACIFIC NORTHWEST FESTIVAL

Held annually, July/August
Cultural

The Pacific Northwest Festival devotes itself to presenting Wagner's *Der Ring des Nibelungen* by the Seattle Opera the last week in July, and the first week in August. Richard Wagner's work is performed in its entirety, with a choice of either German or English versions of all four operas. It was in July 1975 that Seattle Opera, guided by General Director Glynn Ross, presented the first summer Wagner Festival in the Western Hemisphere. The Wagner Festival is the Pacific Northwest Festival. The opera also features leading international Wagnerian artists. Among them have been Ute Vinzing, Herbert Becker, Margaret Kingsley and Paul Crook. The festival marked its eighth consecutive year in 1982. Complete performances of *Der Ring des Nibelungen* (The Ring of the Nibelung) are performed back to back in German the first week and in English the second week. The Seattle Opera performs the uncut "Ring" with an augmented orchestra. Seattle Opera Music Director Henry Holt leads the "Ring" each summer. At the first festival, he became the second American conductor in history to lead a complete production of the "Ring," and he has as of 1982 conducted 14 complete "Ring" performances as well as more than 1,000 performances of the Seattle Opera. Complete cycle tickets to all four operas in German and English are sold at varying costs. The festival is always 20 percent sold in advance with orders from all over the world. The Seattle Opera itself was founded in 1964 and has enjoyed a tremendous growth, contributing greatly to the city's cultural scene. It originally produced two performances of two operas. Now it operates on an annual budget of several million dollars and plays to an audience of 130,000. Operas are performed at the Seattle Center. In 1966, it became the first company in the country to offer a regular series of performances in English but using the same sets and costumes as any international company. The Seattle Opera dabbles in experimental works, even a rock opera, and in 1975 launched the Pacific Northwest Festival to fill a void. There was no major music festival within a 1,000-mile radius of Seattle. A large grant from the Fisher Foundation of Marshalltown, Iowa, for the physical production helped the first event. So prior to 1975, the grant enabled the Seattle Opera to feature a series of productions of the operas from Wagner's "Ring," presented individually each season since 1973. In 1974, the Washington State Legislature appropriated $100,000 to the Seattle Opera, giving it the responsibility of using the money to develop a music festival. In 1975, it became a reality.

Seattle

SEAFAIR

Held annually, July/August
Economic, touristic

Seafair is an annual summer festival designed to entertain the residents of the Greater Puget Sound region and to attract tourists. It dates back to 1950. It claims to be one of the largest festivals in the country, and as its name indicates, many events are water-related. Seafair is devoted to the theme of "A festival of people—people participation" and is today handled by a highly organized nonprofit corporation that promotes not only the annual Seafair programs but also year-round events for local residents. Programs deal with education, culture and sports. Memberships are possible in the Seafair corporation at nominal cost, entitling joiners to discounts to many events and sites. Summer festival events cover 16 days and begin with the Seafair Pirates Landing at Alki Beach in West Seattle around 7 p.m. That officially launches the celebration with events that include music concerts, Bon Odori Japanese event, bike championships, tug-of-wars, coronation of the Seafair Queen, clowns, parade, sports tournaments, torchlight parade, ethnic programs, water shows, a fair, salmon barbecue, flower show and unlimited hydroplane race. Local businessmen are honored by being named commodores, and there are scholarships for the Sea Princesses and Queen. This event, since its inception, has attracted the staggering number of 54 million visitors. Famous folk, like the late Bing Crosby, Phil Harris and Lawrence Welk, have officiated. Work on Seafair involves almost a half-million man-hours year-round. The event is financed by donations from individuals and from business leaders. Events are citywide.

West Virginia

Davis

ALPINE WINTER FESTIVAL

Held annually, January
Economic, sports

The Alpine Winter Festival is a six-day event designed to chase away the winter blues and to promote all of Tucker County as a winter destination. Winter sports events plus arts, crafts, ski films, cross-country skiing, German fest and Alpine dances are held at Blackwater Falls State Park Lodge, the Canaan Valley State Park and Thomas. The festival is held the first full weekend in January. A highlight is the West Virginia State Governor's Cup Ski Race on the last festival day. The event was started in 1959 by local politicans and chamber of commerce. It attracts 10,000 people annually, and since 1959, a total of 230,000. It is financed by the Tucker County Arts Council and West Virginia Arts and Humanities Council and by some paid admissions. Work is by local volunteers.

Elkins

MOUNTAIN STATE FOREST FESTIVAL

Held annually, October
Conservation, economic

The Mountain State Forest Festival is now a five-day event held in October to call attention to the area's natural resources and to promote conservation. The first festival was for three days, October 30 through November 1, 1930, but it caught on and has been continuing ever since. Originally it was a homecoming event, started by local lumberman George H. Dornblazer. Over the years, it changed to eight days but then settled down at five. It is held the first full weekend in October, Wednesday to Sunday. Events include tours to view the changing fall foliage, forest exhibits, parades, pageantry, sports, competitions, dancing, Grand Ole Opry shows, a Royal Coronation Ball, special foods and arts and crafts. The coronation of Queen Silvia is by the governor at the Davis and Elkins College Amphitheater. The festival attracts many famous folks, some of whom participate in the festival activities. In the past there have been Grand Ole Opry performers, Presidents Roosevelt, Truman, Nixon and Ford, Joe Garagiola, actress Nanette Fabray, Don Meredith and Ed McMahon. Work on the festival is performed by local volunteers; the festival's executive secretary is the only paid person. About 200,000 persons attend each year's festival and at least a few million since 1930. The event also features conservation displays and exhibits to help educate visitors and locals about the need for preserving natural resources. The event is supported by some paid admissions, and one-fourth of the cost of the festival is covered by the state.

Sisterville

WEST VIRGINIA OIL AND GAS FESTIVAL

Held annually, September
Economic

The West Virginia Oil and Gas Festival is now a four-day mid-September salute to the area's historic one-time industries of oil and gas. It was started in August

1968 as a project of the year by the U.S. Jaycees at their national convention for towns with small populations. As the name indicates, events and exhibits are keyed to oil and gas. Other events include a West Virginia regional antique auto show, gas engine show, oil and gas exhibit, Grand Oil and Gas Parade, queen's pageant, arts, crafts, firemen's parade, banjo and fiddle contest and a Gib Morgan contest for all ages. Gib Morgan was a folk hero from the oil fields. Some 30,000 people come for the event, which also includes a wrestling championship, riverboard exhibits, flea market, food booths and a silent auction. The festival is administered by special festival directors and is financed by paid admissions and local and state appropriations. Festival events are held in the City Park, which requires a general admission fee.

Wisconsin

Cable

BIRKEBEINER CROSS-COUNTRY SKI RACES

Held annually, February
Sports

The Birkebeiner Cross-Country Ski Races cover one day, the last Saturday in February. Based on the Norwegian Birkebeiner, it has been held annually since 1932. While it is a top sports event, it is also Norwegian and ethnic in nature. It has received worldwide coverage in the newspapers, magazines and on television. The 55-kilometer cross-country ski race goes from Mt. Telemark in Cable to Hayward, Wisconsin. It attracts annually 8,000 entries and thousands of spectators. It is said to be the largest cross-country ski race in the United States. It is always held in February because snow conditions and temperatures are the best for the race. It is designed to promote the sport of cross-country skiing. It is a boon economically to the area and since its inception has attracted millions of competitors and spectators. Members of the national Olympic cross-country ski teams have also participated. The race is financed by entry fees and subsidized by Mt. Telemark. There is no admission fee to watch the race.

Fish Creek

PENINSULA MUSIC FESTIVAL

Held annually, August
Cultural

The Peninsula Music Festival dates back to August 6, 1953, when the very first concert was held, thereby launching the festival, the work of the late Dr. Thor Johnson, an American conductor who had a home in Fish Creek in Door County. This summer vacation area for people in the Midwest needed a summer event, and vacationers urged Dr. Johnson to help set up a summer musical event, which he did in 1953. His dream of more than 20 years was to create a music festival around a chamber-sized symphony orchestra. It took 18 months of work and planning before that first concert was given. About nine concerts are now offered during two and a half weeks in August. Dr. Johnson was conductor for the Cincinnati Symphony and Nashville Symphony and a director of the Interlochen Arts Academy. He was active in the summer music festival until his death in 1975. The festival has been continually sponsored by the Peninsula Arts Association, in existence since 1937. The concerts feature famous artists, and performances are given in the Gibraltar Auditorium in Fish Creek. The festival has featured works by Beethoven, Schumann, Haydn and Dvorak and arias from famous operas as well as chorus performances. The event has its own Festival Orchestra. The festival has expanded to include a master class with a major performer. The purpose of the festival is to use good taste and introduce young artists and composers as well as offer standard classical repertoire. The event is a cultural achievement since it brings live symphony music to an area not able to enjoy it otherwise. About 700 persons can be seated at one concert, and season tickets are sold as well as individual tickets. It is estimated that since the first 1953 concert the event has attracted more than 200,000 persons. The Festival Orchestra consists of professional musicians from different symphonies and music schools around the country. Some once played for Dr. Johnson and have been part of the Festival Orchestra for many years. No local talent is used because there isn't any. The festival is financed by ticket sales and donations.

Hayward

LUMBERJACK WORLD CHAMPIONSHIPS

Held annually, July
Sports, economic

The Lumberjack World Championships cover three days of all kinds of competitions in chopping, sawing and logging, recalling the logging days of northern

Wisconsin. Hayward was once a wild logging town. The championships attract international competitors from as far away as Australia. Events are held at Lumberjack Bowl at Historyland on a quiet inlet on Lake Hayward surrounded by bleachers right near the water's edge. The bowl seats 5,000. Overlooking the bowl are two 100-feet-high cedar poles, where world champions defend their tree-topping title. In the speed climbing, daredevil lumberjacks attempt to better the 25 split-second world record. Cash prizes total several thousand dollars. The competition in Hayward dates back to 1960, when it was incorporated with the National Logrolling Championships. The very first ever tournament was held in Omaha, Nebraska, in 1898. Today's competitions are chopping, standing and horizontal cut, power saw bucking, lumberjack relay race and more. There are both men and women log rolling competitions as well as trick and fancy log rolling. This event has received both national and international news coverage and has been featured on ABC's "Wide World of Sports." The event was started by two local men who wanted to bring something to Hayward and relive some of its logging history. The event attracts about 15,000 visitors, and since 1960 well over 1 million. The event is financed by paid admissions, entry fees and sponsorships.

Milwaukee

HOLIDAY FOLK FAIR

Held annually, November
Ethnic

The Holiday Folk Fair pays tribute to the city's more than 50 ethnic groups through their customs, songs, dances, arts, crafts and foods. The groups themselves prepare the food for sale at their own booths at the fair and also sell ethnic gift items. Evening programs feature a variety of folk dancing. The name Holiday Folk Fair is a copyrighted trademark and is reported to be the largest and oldest annual folk festival in this country. The event dates back to December 10, 1944, when an ethnic fair was held, sponsored as it still is by the International Institute of Milwaukee County. An institute representative had been to the St. Paul Festival in Minnesota and came back with the idea for a similar event. A local resident, Mrs. Vlasta Vojta, chair of the first fair, knew of a "Captive Nations" event in Chicago and thought that it would be good to incorporate several nationalities in the fair. This first fair offered a meal with different courses prepared by the different ethnic groups, a parade of people in costume and some exhibit booths. About 3,500 people came. It grew in popularity, with more ethnic groups being added. Attendance increased, and soon the one-day fair became a three-day affair. By 1966 the fair would salute a different special nationality each year. This is still continued, with the honored group featured in the Folk Spectacle (ethnic dance performances) and the script keyed to their customs and old country heritage. Among the honored have been Croatian, Japanese, American Indian, Slovak, Italian, Danish, German, Serbian, Filipino, Polish and Ukrainian. The show is different each year. About 70,000 people attend annually, and since that first fair, almost 2 million. Food is the most popular feature, and to date there are more than 50 ethnic food booths. The staggering number of 6,000 volunteers work year-round to prepare for this event. It is financed through ticket sales, food and craft sales and sponsorship by the institute. The fair is self-sustaining. All events are held at the Convention Center complex in downtown Milwaukee.

Milwaukee

LAKEFRONT FESTIVAL OF ARTS

Held annually, June
Cultural, economic

The Lakefront Festival of Arts is recognized as one of the finest outdoor art events in the Midwest. It is held along the Lake Michigan shoreline in downtown Milwaukee. It was originally started as a showcase for local artists when the first event was held in June 1962. It grew in popularity and scope and was taken over by the Friends of Art of the Milwaukee Art Center. The festival deals with about 185 tightly juried national exhibiting artists. There are demonstrations in various art techniques and family participation projects. There are special art/visual projects of national and international fame and the performing arts as well. The festival has attracted more than 2 million people since it began, with about 200,000 every year. The event in the past was sponsored by the Jos. Schlitz Brewing Company. Today it is sponsored by various businesses.

Milwaukee

SUMMERFEST

Held annually, June/July
Cultural, economic

Summerfest is billed as the World's Greatest Music Festival, with events held on permanent Summerfest grounds along the city's waterfront on Lake Michigan. There are separate stages for jazz, country, ethnic and other music performances. There is a daily feature show on the main stage and children's events. There's a midway, craft marketplace and sports demonstrations. The festival was started by Milwaukee Mayor Henry W. Maier. It was meant to be a display of the city's cultural and ethnic heritage and a response to the civil unrest during the racial turmoil of 1967. Over the years, this event has been cited by Goodwill Industries for the absence of architectural barriers to the handicapped. It was also recognized as the third largest civic festival in the United States by the International Festival Association. Originally a 10-day event, it's now an 11-day festival and always held at the same time of year to include the Fourth of July holiday, to bring out more people. The very first Summerfest was held July 12–21, 1968. It was changed when Milwaukee's July 4th Schlitz Circus Parade was discontinued after 1973. Summerfest encompasses Fourth of July celebrations. Almost 33 percent of festival goers are from outside Milwaukee, with 14 percent from Chicago. Each Summerfest hosts about 700,000 people, and since the beginning, about 5 million. The most popular part of Summerfest continues to be the top name music performers and groups, jazz, country and ethnic music concerts. Summerfest has changed from cultural exhibits to music. Summerfest has featured over the years such talent as the London Philharmonic, Sammy Davis, Jr., Bob Hope, Joan Baez, Johnny Cash, Arlo Guthrie, Van Cliburn, Dionne Warwick, the Beach Boys and Duke Ellington. Work on the Summerfest is done by 5 full-time paid professionals, 300 part-time paid workers and, during the festival, 800 volunteers. Summerfest is financed by an annual city grant of $85,000, corporate contributions, ticket sales and food and beverage sales.

Oshkosh

EAA FLY-IN

Held annually, July/August
Aviation

The EAA Fly-In is considered to be the largest aviation event in the world. Experimental Aircraft Association (EAA) members and visitors see daily air shows over Wittman Field. There is also a chance to see acres of aircraft, including home-built, antique and war planes. The fly-in attracts as many as 750,000 visitors, who come from all over the world. Association members fly in their own homemade planes. There are more than 400 homemade planes on exhibit, and it is not unusual for some 4,000 plane movements to take place each day. The event has attracted many who were pioneers in aviation and flying. For example, Blanche Noyes of Washington, who is called the dean of women pilots. She made her first solo flight in 1928 and in January 1930 took 90-year-old John D. Rockefeller, Sr., on his first and only plane ride. The fly-in also had Clifford Henderson, who managed the National Air Race from 1928 to 1939, during which time Charles A. Lindbergh was a participant. Another was E. R. Woods, who flew one of the planes in the film *Hell's Angels*, produced by Howard R. Hughes. The fly-in is actually the EAA's convention. In 1979, 12,000 planes flew in, including 1,492 built by association members. The EAA now has 75,000 members who live all over the world. The EAA was founded in 1953 by Paul Poberezny, after his return from duty as a fighter pilot in Korea. He started to build his own plane, "The Little Popdeck," and attracted the attention of some local fliers. This led to the EAA. The annual meeting is open to the public, who pay a fee to watch the show or shows. Every afternoon there's a barnstorming and aerobatic display by expert pilots, such as the Red Devils. The event is financed by membership dues and local business contributions. Members pay their own way to the convention.

Wyoming

Cheyenne

CHEYENNE FRONTIER DAYS

Held annually, July
Sports

Cheyenne Frontier Days are often called the Daddy of 'em All and reportedly the world's biggest and oldest outdoor rodeo celebration. It features 10 days of events, four free Western parades, top country-western entertainment, the U.S. Championship Chuck Wagon Races, free pancake breakfasts, Indians, a carnival and a midway. The rodeo marked its eighty-sixth annual year in 1982 and is also the oldest rodeo in North America. Cheyenne was a "cowtown" in the 1890s, and the whole state was cattle country. Cattle roamed over miles and miles of unfenced grasslands. Many strayed far from their owner's land. So each year they had to be rounded up so that the young calves could be roped and branded. Fat cattle had to be cut out of the herd to be sold and shipped to market. During these roundups, the cowboys lived outdoors for weeks at a time, eating from the chuck wagon and sleeping on the ground. Cowboys from other outfits often met to participate in the roundups, and there was a great deal of competition among them. They tried to outdo each other in the speed with which they could rope, "hogtie" and brand a calf. They also exhibited their skill in riding bucking broncs and raced their little cow ponies against each other. It was from that spare time fun and roundup contest that the Cheyenne Frontier Days rodeo was born. The idea for an annual "Old West Show," according to Warren Richardson, first chairman of the original Frontier Day Committee, was originated on a train between Greeley, Colorado, and Cheyenne, Wyoming, in the summer of 1897. Returning from the annual Potato Day celebration in Greeley, a Mr. Slack, editor of the *Cheyenne Daily Sun Leader*, and Richardson, one of Wyoming's top citizens, talked about holding a similar celebration in Cheyenne. It was Colonel Slack who suggested the name, ''Cheyenne Frontier Days,'' that would be an old-timers' get-together, with cow punchers and wild horses. The colonel presented the idea in the next issue of his paper. There is still some controversy, however, as to who named the event Frontier Days. However, in late August 1897, a group of local businessmen met to make plans for the first Frontier Days, to be held September 23, 1898. Today, the event has grown from one to 10 days and is a world famous rodeo with all the top stars of the rodeo circuit competing for purses worth more than $500,000. About 1,000 professional cowboys compete each year. The rodeo attracts 150,000 visitors each year, totaling a few million over the years. Most popular rodeo events continue to be the bull riding and wild horse races. The rodeo attracts famous TV stars for the night shows. The rodeo is financed by paid admissions, entry fees and donations from local business. It is a self-supporting event.

Pinedale

GREEN RIVER RENDEZVOUS

Held annually, July
Historic

The Green River Rendezvous commemorates the meetings of the trappers, Indians and traders, forerunners of the westward movement by so many people that eventually led to settlement of the West. The rendezvous was first recreated July 26, 1936, to mark the hundredth year since Narcissa Whitman and Eliza Spaulding attended the 1836 rendezvous held near Pinedale. The ladies were early pioneers in the area. It was Mary Hurlburt Scott, author of *The Oregon Trail* and president of the Sublette County Historical Society, who formed a pageant committee to recreate the rendezvous in 1936. It was (and still is) staged on U.S. 187, the shortest scenic route from Interstate 80 to Yellowstone and Grand Teton National parks. The historical society was the recipient of the National Award 1964 and certificate of commendation from the American Association for State and Local History. The rendezvous was continued the second Sunday in July. It authentically recalls the first meeting with trappers, pony dancers, Indians, wagon teams and drivers. Today's participants are all in costume. The day-long program features a prelude to history, opening ceremonies, the antelope soldiers, Fort Bonneville and the arrival of the fur trappers. There are the mountain men, the Shoshones, followed by Indian dances and games. Father Pierre Jean De Smet appears, as do the American Fur Company and the Rocky Mountain Fur Company. There is a pony dance, Protestant missionaries and finally History on Parade. The day ends with a barbecue. More than 2,000 people attend every year, with a grand total over the years estimated at 92,000. Work on the pageant is by local volunteers, who work about six months in advance. The event is financed by ticket sales, the barbecue and donations. The rendezvous is staged in a separate larger area near the Pinedale Rodeo Grounds and Race Track.

Thermopolis

GIFT OF THE WATERS PAGEANT

Held annually, August
Historic pageantry

The Gift of the Waters Pageant is now a three-day reenactment of the deeding of the world's largest mineral hot springs to the people of Wyoming from the Shoshone and Arapahoe Indians. It is held the first weekend in August. The pageant is held at Hot Springs State Park and is based on the words of Washakie, chief of the Shoshones: "I have given you the springs, my heart feels good," spoken April 21, 1886. Washakie, elders of both the Shoshone and Arapahoe tribes, some civilians and military officials met in a primitive storeroom at the Wind River Indian Reservation headquarters at Fort Washakie. There was a signed treaty, selling a tract of the reservation almost 10 miles square to the United States. In return, the Indians were to receive $60,000 worth of cattle and food supplies. Within the boundaries of the land were several hot mineral springs noted for their healing powers. Congress, however, turned down the deal, and it was only through the efforts of Wyoming's representative, Frank Mondell, that the treaty was ratified and a square mile around the springs ceded to the state. In 1889, the Wyoming State Legislature established the site as a park and said that one-quarter of the water from the main spring be set aside for free use by the public. There has been a free bathhouse there since 1902. In 1925, the Wyoming State Federation of Women's Clubs was to hold its convention in Thermopolis. The program featured a pageant about Chief Washakie written by Marie Montabe, who spent an entire summer on the reservation researching. The first pageant was given October 1, 1925. It wasn't until 1950 that the pageant became an annual event. In the first pageant, Dick Washakie played his father, and in later pageants Chief Washakie was played by Charles, another son. Later on, the chief was portrayed by his great-grandson, Chief Felix Perry. The water given long ago is today's Big Spring, the largest mineral hot spring in the world. Out of it flows 18.6 million gallons of water every 24 hours at a temperature of 135° F. Thousands come every year for the pageant. However, there is no real record of the total number. Work on the pageant is by volunteers. The event is financed by donations and by the local chamber of commerce.

American Samoa

Pago Pago

FLAG DAY

Held annually, April
Patriotic

Flag Day is a one-day islandwide celebration marking the raising of the first U.S. flag in Samoa over Tutuila and the establishment of the local constitutional government. It is a public holiday. The flag was raised April 17, 1900, and Samoans have been celebrating it every year on April 17, except during World War II. Events change each year. Sometimes it is a one-day event, and at other times it stretches out to three days. Events include patriotic ceremonies, sports, games, regattas, copra-cutting competitions, local arts, crafts, folkloric programs and speeches.

Puerto Rico

Barranquitas

CRAFTS FAIR

Held annually, July
Cultural, economic

The Crafts Fair was started in 1961 to comply with a government policy of preserving and promoting traditional crafts. This fair is timed to coincide with the anniversary celebration of the birth of Puerto Rican political and literary figure, Luis Munoz Rivera, who was born in Barranquitas. There is no particular connection between Munoz and the crafts except that it is held in his birthplace and his birthday is an official public holiday. The idea of the fair received the support and backing of Ricardo Alegria, then director of the Institute of Puerto Rican Culture. The three-day fair is held on the main plaza of the town. There are booths exhibiting arts and crafts. Contemporary crafts are discouraged since the aim of the fair is to feature crafts that stem from the island's past. That would include articles made from coconuts, seeds and wood carvings and hand-made *cuatros*, guitarlike instruments. The fair helps to keep old skills and crafts alive, passing them down to the youth, who continue the process. It also makes crafts economically viable by generating sales and promoting an awareness of the artisanry. The fair attracts as many as 40,000 a year, and to date, a grand total of almost 240,000, many tourists. The fair also features local entertainers, folk and contemporary. Work on the fair is by volunteers and is almost a year-round project. The event is financed by a special budget provided annually by the Institute of Puerto Rican Culture with additional funds coming from the legislature. There are no admission charges to the fair.

Jayuya

JAYUYA FESTIVAL OF INDIAN LORE/JAYUYA INDIAN FESTIVAL

Held annually, November
Ethnic, heritage

The Jayuya Festival of Indian Lore/Jayuya Indian Festival is held in mid-November together with the anniversary of the discovery of Puerto Rico by Columbus on November 19, 1493. The town of Jayuya was the center of the Taino Indian tribe's activities. The area has numerous Taino stone carvings, and within an hour's drive is Caguana Ceremonial Park, one of the most important pre-Columbian archeological sites in the Greater Antilles. The festival, however, only goes back to November 1969, and was started when new traces of the Taino Indian culture in and around Jayuya were discovered. Credit for originating the festival goes to Mrs. Aura Pierluisi de Rodriguez, who at the time was president of the Jayuya Cultural Center. The festival features Indian ceremonies and dances as well as concerts, using conch shells (*fotutos*) as instruments. There is a soccerlike ceremonial ball game played by Taino Indians and the coronation of a festival queen. Awards are presented to those who've done scholarly work on Puerto Rico's pre-Columbian cultures. Other festival features include a village (*yukayeque*) of thatched-roofed huts, representative of the Indian community. There are exhibits, demonstrations and sale of Indian arts and crafts. There are displays of typical garments worn by Indian princesses. Kiosks serve foods typical of the island's indigenous population. There are lectures on the Indian language, customs and related subjects. Tours are conducted to nearby caves that contain Indian drawings. The festival successfully helps to educate others about the Taino Indian cultures and encourages more research about them. Since the festival attracts 10,000 visitors annually and to date more than 150,000, the local economy benefits, too. Work on the festival is by volunteers, mostly students and educators, who work year-round preparing for the event. It is financed by local contributions, the sale of posters and help from the Institute of Puerto Rican Culture. There is no admission fee at all. However, goods and handicrafts are sold. Events take place in the Town Plaza, schools and countryside caves.

San Juan

CASALS FESTIVAL/FESTIVAL CASALS

Held annually, June
Cultural

The Casals Festival dates back to the late 1950s, when Pablo Casals took up residence in Puerto Rico. He helped organize the festival, designed to give Puerto Ricans who studied music abroad a home showcase for their talents. Casals was also responsible for setting up a Music Conservatory at the University of Puerto Rico. The festival consists of a series of concerts featuring Puerto Rican and worldwide artists. The Festival Casals Organization, which still administers the festival, was established in April 1956, and the first Casals Festival held April 22 through May 8, 1957. Others involved in organizing the festival were violinist Alexander Schneider, also founder of the Budapest Quartet and assistant musical director, and Carlos M. Passalcaqua, chairman of the board of directors. The festival features a total of 11 concerts covering 16 days and held in two halls in San Juan. The series feature vocal and instrumental soloists and guest conductors. The concerts are taped for rebroadcast for the Voice of America. Local television and radio stations carry the programs. The Casals Festival Orchestra is composed of top musicians from major orchestras, mainly from the mainland United States, and more recently the Puerto Rican Symphony Orchestra has performed at the first two concerts. More and more Puerto Rican compositions are being featured in the annual festival. The festival was originally held in late April but conflicted with the Prades Festival (also founded by Casals) in France. So it was changed to late May into early June and finally to June only. The festival not only attracted lots of tourist dollars but it also brought Puerto Rico into the world's musical mainstream and made it a part of the world's cultural and social scene. About 16,000 attend the annual performances, and to date, that's a grand total of 400,000. Work on the event is done by a full-time festival staff that functions year-round administering the festival, the conservatory and local symphony orchestra. Actor Jose Ferrer has served as a board member. The festival is financed by grants from the government and by paid admissions. In San Juan, the concerts are at the University of Puerto Rico Theater on the main campus.

U.S. Virgin Islands

St. John

ST. JOHN FOURTH OF JULY CELEBRATION

Held annually, June/July
Patriotic, cultural

The St. John Fourth of July Celebration reaches its climax on July 4 but actually begins a week earlier with all kinds of family-oriented events and programs.

The roots of the festival go as far back as 1900, when the Moravian church in the area encouraged family gatherings as a way to preach the Gospel and educate the local people. These gatherings featured recreation and refreshments and were for all age groups. They were originally held in Coral Bay on Easter Monday and later extended to Cruz Bay on Whitmonday. In 1923, the local government took over the events, and the family picnics and games were combined with a yacht regatta and held on July 1. In 1949, a Fourth of July celebration was added. It attracted so many people that a riot broke out on the ferry dock on the St. Thomas end (Red Hook), because the ferries couldn't accommodate the large crowds that wanted to cross. After this, the event fizzled out. It wasn't until 1959 that it was decided to revive the celebration. Today, the week-long festivities again include family picnics and games, like a greased pole climb, greased pig chases and three-legged and sack races. Steel bands, calypso singers and dance groups perform free of charge. Since 1974, a week-long Festival Village is staged, preceded by a queen selection competition and coronation ball. The festival parade on July 4 is the climactic end to the event. Every year, it grows larger and larger. The festival attracts thousands of visitors and encourages islanders to research more history to come up with different costumes and floats for the parade. Work on the festival is by local volunteers. It is financed by government grants, the sale of food at the festival, entrance fees to the queen talent show competitions and the coronation ball. Most events remain free. Festivities take place in Cruz Bay Park and the entire business section of town.

St. Thomas (Charlotte Amalie)

VIRGIN ISLANDS CARNIVAL

Held annually, April
Economic, cultural

The Virgin Islands Carnival is held the last two weeks in April and has nothing to do with Lent or any religious observance. The first week is concerned with a calypso competition, while the second week is devoted to a community free-for-all, ending with some major festive parades. The carnival starts with a Calypso Tent, which is not really a tent but a week-long calypso song competition in Charlotte Amalie's Roberts Stadium. No one knows why it is called a tent, but it has continued and means parade of original calypso songs. The best talent is chosen as Calypso King or Queen of the World on the final night. The carnival tent folds, and the Carnival Village and Children's Village open in the municipal parking lots and in the Market Square. Food booths sell conch, salt fish cakes, pates, stewed mutton and fresh fish. Others sell drinks, including West Indian favorites like gin and coconut water. The Market Fair operates at the same time in the old Market Square, where homemade stewed tamarinds and sugar cakes are sold. The Children's Village offers rides of all kinds, and there is often a ferris wheel and merry-go-round, while there is nightly entertainment at the Carnival Village with local entertainers and steel band concerts. On a Thursday of the second week, the "J'ouvert," an early morning tramp through downtown streets, begins at 4 or 4:30 a.m. on the waterfront with a massive "jump-up" through town to the accompaniment of steel bands and fireworks exploding over the harbor. The tramps or dancing marches are spontaneous in and around the Carnival Village all week. There is a Children's Parade on a Friday from 10 a.m. to 2 p.m. The Adult's Parade is usually on Saturday, also starting at 10 a.m. and continuing for six hours. It is a mixture of lilting music, exotic costumes, songs and dances. Each carnival has a theme, and all costumes are keyed to it. Although this spring carnival dates back to 1912, it wasn't really organized until 1952. A local radio personality, Ron de Lugo, known as Mango Jones and a delegate to the Congress, was the moving force behind this organization together with some local people. Hundreds of thousands have participated and attended the annual carnival, which has been very beneficial to the local economy. Work on the carnival starts more than eight months in advance, with hundreds of volunteers working on it. The carnival is financed by a government grant, sale of souvenir booklets, some paid admissions, donations from individuals and businesses and rents from the different booths.

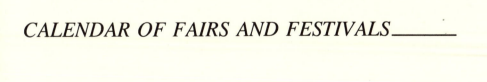

CALENDAR OF FAIRS AND FESTIVALS

Unless otherwise noted, events are held annually.

Alabama

February/March
  Mardi Gras celebration, Mobile, movable date
March
  Azalea Trail and Festival, Mobile, through May
  Festival of Arts, Birmingham, late March through early April
  Indian Dance Festival and Pioneer Fair, Childersburg
  Southeastern Livestock Exposition Rodeo, Montgomery
April
  Alabama History and Heritage Festival, Montgomery, through May
  Azalea Spectacular, Montgomery
  Spring Craft Show and Sale, Mobile
May
  Alabama Jubilee Hot Air Balloon Classic, Decatur
  All Arabian Horse Show, Montgomery
  International Folk Festival, Montgomery
  May Flower Show, Birmingham
June
  America's Junior Miss Pageant, Mobile
  Blueberry Festival, Brewton
  The Miracle Worker performances and Helen Keller Festival at Ivy Green,
    Tuscumbia, through July
July
  Alabama Shakespeare Festival, Anniston, through mid-August
  Birmingham Summerfest, Birmingham, through August
  Seafood Festival, Bayou La Batre

Spirit of America Festival, Decatur, July 4
August
   Dixie Cup Regatta Boat Races, Guntersville
   United States Space Camp, Huntsville, through early September
   W.C. Handy Music Festival, Florence
September
   All-Bluegrass Festival, Childersburg
   Northeast Alabama State Fair, Huntsville
   Oktoberfest, Birmingham
   Outdoor Arts and Crafts Fair, Mobile
October
   Indian Summer Arts and Crafts Festival, Eufaula
   National Peanut Festival, Dothan
   Tennessee Valley Old Time Fiddlers Convention, Athens
November
   Creek Indian Thanksgiving Day Homecoming and Pow Wow, Poarch
   Festival of Sacred Music, Birmingham
   Southern Championship Charity Horse Show, Montgomery
December
   Blue-Gray All Star Football Classic, Montgomery
   Christmas on the River, Demopolis
   Festival of Trees, Birmingham
   Hall of Fame Bowl Game (football), Birmingham

Alaska

January
   Kuskokwin 300: Sled Dog Race, Bethel to Aniak and return
February
   Fur Rendezvous, Anchorage
   Ice Worm Festival, Cordova
   Tent City Winter Festival, Wrangell
March
   Eaglecrest Winter Carnival, Juneau
   Iditarod Trail Race, Anchorage to Nome
   Winter Carnival, Aniak
   Winter Carnival, Fairbanks
April
   Alaskan Crab Festival, Whittier
May
   Crab Festival, Kodiak
   King Salmon Derby, Wrangell
   Little Norway Festival, Petersburg

Salmon Derby, Ketchikan, through mid-June

June

Alaska Arts Southeast Folk Dance/Folklore Festival, Sitka

All Alaska Logging Championships, Sitka

Summer Music Festival, Sitka

July

Alaska Arts Southeast Fine Arts Camp, Sitka

Golden Days Celebration, Fairbanks

Mount Marathon Race, Seward, July 4

World Eskimo Indian Olympics, Fairbanks, through early August

August

Alaska State Fair and Midsummer Festival, Palmer

Golden North Salmon Derby, Juneau

Kenai Peninsula State Fair, Kenai

Southeast Alaska State Fair, Haines

Tanana Valley State Fair, Fairbanks

September

Alaska Music Festival, Anchorage

October

Alaska Day, Sitka and state holiday, October 17

Arizona

January

Lost Dutchman Days, Apache Junction

Mineral and Gem Show, Yuma

February

Gold Rush Days and Rodeo, Wickenburg

Heard Museum Guild Indian Fair, Phoenix

O'Odham Tash: Indian Days, Casa Grande

Parada del Sol Rodeo, Scottsdale

March

Arizona Highland Games, Phoenix

Tucson Festival, Tucson, through mid-April, moveable date

Windsurfer Mid-Winter Races, Lake Havasu City

April

All Police Rodeo, Prescott

Copper Dust Stampede, Globe

Old Town Festival of the Arts, Tempe

Sunflower Trail Ride, Fountain Hills

May

Arts and Crafts Festival, Payson

Tour of Unique Old Homes: Paseo de Casas, Jerome

Wyatt Earp Days, Tombstone
June
    Festival of the Arts, Flagstaff
    Frontier Days Rodeo, Prescott
    Old Time Country Music and Bluegrass Festival, Payson
July
    Gospel Music Festival, Payson
    Navajo Indian Show, Flagstaff
    World Championship Inner Tube Races, Yuma
August
    Poetry Festival, Bisbee
    Smoki Ceremonials and Snake Dance, Prescott
    World's Oldest Continuous Rodeo, Payson
September
    Navajo Indian Fair, Window Rock
    State Fiddler's Championship, Payson
    Wild Bunch Rendezvous of Gunfights-Wild West Days and Parade,
        Tombstone
October
    Halloween Carnival, Tempe
    Helldorado Days, Tombstone
    London Bridge Days, Lake Havasu City
    October Art Fest, Payson
November
    Christmas Parade, Winslow
    Fall Festival of Arts and Crafts, Cave Creek
    Junior Parade and Rodeo, Florence
December
    Fiesta del Sol Rodeo, Apache Junction

Arkansas

March
    Jonquil Festival, Old Washington Historic State Park
    Pioneer Crafts Festival, Rison
April
    Arkansas Folk Festival, Mountain View
    Dogwood Arts and Crafts Fair, Siloam Springs
    Spring Tour of Historic Homes, Eureka Springs
May
    Arkansas-Oklahoma Rodeo, Fort Smith, through early June
    Back-in-the-Hills Antique Show and Folklife Fair, War Eagle Miles Farm
    Quapaw Quarter Spring Tour, Little Rock

Riverfest, Little Rock
June
    Arkansas Fun Festival, Hot Springs
    Pink Tomato Festival, Warren
July
    Libertyfest-Fourth of July Celebration, Petit Jean Mountain
    Riverboat Days and State Catfish Cooking Contest, Jacksonport State Park
    Rodeo of the Ozarks, Springdale
August
    Arkansas Prison Rodeo, Grady
    Water Festival, Greers Ferry Lake
    White River Water Carnival, Batesville
September
    Arkansas State Fair and Livestock Show, Little Rock
    Clothesline Arts and Crafts Fair, Prairie Grove Battlefield State Park
    Old-Time Fiddlers Association State Championship, Mountain View
October
    Arkansas Rice Festival, Weiner
    Family Harvest Festival, Mountain View
    Four States Fair and Rodeo, Texarkana
    Ozark Frontier Trail Festival and Crafts Show, Heber Springs
November
    Original Ozark Folk Festival and Craft Show, Eureka Springs
    Wings Over the Prairie: World's Championship Duck Calling Contest,
        Stuttgart
December
    Christmas on the Mountain, Queen Wilhelmina State Park, Mena
    Christmas Showcase of the Ozark Foothills Handicraft Guild, Little Rock

California

January
    Bob Hope Desert Classic: Golf, Palm Springs
    Mounted Police Rodeo and Parade, Palm Springs
    Rose Bowl Parade and Football Game, Pasadena, January 1
    Sled Dog Races, Long Valley
February
    Chinese New Year Celebration and Parade, San Francisco, movable date
    National Date Festival, Indio
    Winter Carnival, Mt. Shasta
March
    Camellia Festival, Sacramento
    Fiesta de la Golindrinas or Return of the Swallows, San Juan Capistrano

Grand Prix International Formula I Race, Long Beach
Whale Festival, Fort Bragg, Mendocino
April
   Apple Blossom Festival, Sebastopol
   Arts Festival, Santa Barbara, through early May
   Cherry Blossom Festival, San Francisco
   Jumping Frog Jamboree, Del Mar
   Pan American Festival Week, Lakewood, through early May
May
   Dixieland Jazz Festival, Sacramento
   Fiesta de la Primavera, San Diego
   Jumping Frog Jubilee, Angels Camp
   Mule Days Celebration, Bishop
   Wine Festival, Healdsburg
June
   Music Festival, Ojai
   Napa Summer Music Festival, Oakville
   Russian River Rodeo and Stumptown Days Parade, Guerneville
   Summer Arts Festival, Grass Valley
   Summer Festival, San Francisco
July
   Festival of Arts and Pageant of the Masters, Laguna Beach, through August
   Garlic Festival, Gilroy
   National Horse and Flower Show, Santa Barbara
August
   Long Beach International Sea and Sports Festival, Long Beach
   Mozart Festival, San Luis Obispo
   Old Spanish Days, Santa Barbara
   Redwood Empire Fair, Ukiah
September
   Artichoke Festival, Castroville
   Danish Days, Solvang
   Los Angeles County Fair, Pomona
   Monterey Jazz Festival, Monterey
   Sonoma Valley Vintage Festival, Sonoma
October
   Cheese and Wine Exposition, Riverbank
   Grand National Rodeo, Horse Show and Livestock Exposition, San Francisco
   Italian American Cultural Festival, San Jose
November
   California Wine Festival, Monterey
   Mother Goose Parade, El Cajon
   St. Nicholas Christmas Fair and Music Festival, Grass Valley
   Thanksgiving Festival, Mendocino

December
     Channel Islands Harbor Parade of Lights and Decorated Boats, Channel
          Islands Harbor
     Las Posadas: Traditional Mexican Christmas Processions, Los Angeles

Colorado

January
     National Western Stock Show, Denver
     Snowdown Winter Carnival, Durango
     Winter Carnival, Winter Park
February
     Crystal Carnival, Leadville
     Winter Carnival, Steamboat Springs
March
     Hidden Valley Spring Snow Festival, Estes Park
     Masters Ski Series, Leadville
April
     Fine Arts Festival, Durango
     Otero Arts Festival, La Junta
May
     "Trip Into Yesterday" via Narrow Gauge Railroad, Durango to Silverton,
          through mid-October
June
     Arkansas River Boat Races, Salida to Cotopaxi
     Aspen Music Festival, Aspen, through mid-August
     Bluegrass, Chamber Music and Jazz, Telluride
     Central City Festival, Central City, through August
     Colorado Opera Festival, Colorado Springs
July
     Pikes Peak Hill Climb, Colorado Springs, July 4
     Shakespeare Festival, Boulder, through late August
August
     Colorado State Fair, Pueblo
     Navajo Trails Fiesta, Durango
     Pikes Peak Marathon, Colorado Springs
September
     International Film Festival, Telluride
     Long's Peak Scottish Highland Festival, Estes Park
     Oktoberfest, Manitou Springs

Connecticut

January
  Old Fashioned Ice Harvest, New Preston
February
  National Autorama, Hartford
  New England Ski Jumping Championships, Salisbury
  Norwalk Armory Antiques Show, Norwalk
March
  Antiques Show, Cheshire
  Small Craft Winter Display, Mystic
April
  Belltown Antique Gas and Steam Engine Meet and Flea Market, East
    Hampton
  Greater New Haven Home Show and Energy Expo, New Haven
May
  Arts and Crafts Fair, Salisbury
  Children Services Horse Show and Country Fair, Farmington
  Dogwood Festival, Fairfield
  Dory Races, Mystic
June
  Barnum Festival, Bridgeport, through July 4
  Crafts Festival, Middlefield
  Laurel Festival, Winsted
  National Trolley Festival, East Haven
  Sea Music Festival, Mystic
  Yale-Harvard Regatta, New London
July
  Lobster Festival, Niantic
  Muster Fife and Drum Corps, Deep River
  Sail Festival, New London
August
  Bluefish Festival, Clinton
  Long Island Sound America Festival, Milford
  Lyman Orchards Country Antiques Festival, Middlefield
September
  Chrysanthemum Festival, Bristol, through early October
  Flotsam-Jetsam Raft Races, New London
  Four Town Fair, Somers
  Oyster Festival, Norwalk
October
  Apple Harvest Festival, Southington
  Chowder Celebration, Mystic
  North Atlantic Road Racing Championships, Lime Rock

November
Festival of Light, Hartford, through early January

Delaware

March
Caesar Rodney Half Marathon, Wilmington
April
Winterthur in Spring Tour of Winterthur Museum and Gardens, Winterthur,
through early June
May
A Day in Old New Castle, New Castle
Old Dover Days, Dover
July
Delaware State Fair, Harrington
August
Boardwalk Arts Fest, Bethany
Marlin Tournament, Lewes
Sandcastle Contest, Rehoboth
September
Country Fair, Winterthur
October
Fall Harvest Fest, Dover
Surf Fishing Tournament, Bethany
November
"Yuletide at Winterthur" Tours at Winterthur Museum and Gardens, Win-
terthur, through end of December

Florida

January
Epiphany Celebration, Tarpon Springs, January 6
Orange Bowl Football Classic, Miami, January 1
Rodeo, Homestead
February
Asolo State Theater Season, Sarasota, through Labor Day
Bach Festival, Winter Park
Edison Pageant of Light, Fort Myers
Gasparilla Pirate Invasion and Parade, Tampa
International Folk Festival, St. Petersburg
Old Island Days, Key West, through early March

Seminole Tribal Fair, Hollywood

March

De Soto Celebration, Bradenton, through early April

Festival of States, St. Petersburg, through early April

Fun 'n Sun Festival, Clearwater

King Neptune's Frolic, Sarasota

Sebring 12 Hours/Automobile Hall of Fame Week, Sebring

April

Indian River Festival, Titusville

Music Festival, Daytona Beach, through early May

May

Fiesta of Five Flags, Pensacola

Florida Folk Festival, White Springs

International Sandcastle Building Contest, Sarasota

Isle of Eight Flags Shrimp Festival, Fernandina Beach

June

Billy Bowlegs Festival, Fort Walton Beach

New College Music Festival, Sarasota

Shark Rodeo, Pensacola

Spanish Night Watch, St. Augustine

July

Celebration of the Launch of Apollo II, Cape Canaveral

Silver Spurs Rodeo, Kissimmee

Tampa Bay Bluegrass Festival, Riverview

August

Captain's Billfishing Tournament, Panama City Beach

Days in Spain Fiesta, St. Augustine

September

Belleview Junction Western Round-Up, Pensacola

Blue Crab Festival, Panacea

Great American Raft Race, Port St. Lucie

Open Spearfishing Tournament, Panama City

October

Mayport and All That Jazz, Jacksonville

Pioneer Days Folk Festival, Orlando

Rattlesnake Festival/International Gopher Race, San Antonio

Seafood Festival, Panama City Beach

Swamp Buggy Races, Naples

Venetian Sun Fiesta, Venice

World's Chicken Pluckin' Championship, Spring Hill

November

Great Gulf Coast Arts Festival, Pensacola

Market Days, Tallahassee

Space Coast Art Festival, Cocoa Beach

December
    Junior Orange Bowl Festival, Coral Gables
    Misccosukee Tribe's Annual Indian Art Festival, Miami
    Orange Bowl Festival, Miami, through mid-January
    Winterfest and Christmas Boat Parade, Fort Lauderdale

Georgia

January
    Winter Arts Festival, Macon, through early February
February
    Arts 'n Crafts Fair, Macon
    Georgia Week Celebration, Savannah
March
    Cherry Blossom Festival, Macon
    Dogwood Celebration, Fitzgerald
April
    Arts Festival, Albany
    Arts Festival, Savannah
    Dogwood Festival, Atlanta
    Rose Festival, Thomasville
May
    Arts Festival of Atlanta, Atlanta
    Deep South Arts and Crafts Festival, Thomasville
    Scottish Games, Savannah
June
    Arts and Crafts Festival, Stone Mountain
    Marigold Festival, Winterville
    Oconee River Raft Race, Dublin
July
    Arts and Crafts Fair, Jekyll Island
    Indian Awareness Day, Cartersville
    Masters Water Ski Tournament, Pine Mountain
August
    Festival of Painted Rocks, Roswell
    Georgia Mountain Fair, Hiawassee
    Summer's End Festival, Winder
September
    Deep South Fair, Thomasville
    Pecan Festival, Albany
    Powers' Crossroads Festival, Newnan
    Yellow Daisy Festival, Stone Mountain
October

Georgia State Fair, Macon
Gold Rush Days, Dahlonega
Indian Trade Days Festival, Kingston
Oktoberfest, Savannah
November
Arts and Crafts Festival, Waycross
South Georgia Fair, Valdosta
December
Colonial Christmas in Georgia, Savannah

Hawaii

January
Chinese Narcissus Festival, Honolulu, movable date, can occur in February
Hula Bowl Game, Honolulu
February
Cherry Blossom Festival, Honolulu, through April
Hawaiian Open International Golf Tournament, Honolulu
March
Hawaiian Song Festival and Song Composing Contest, Waikiki
Kona Stampede, Kailua-Kona, Big Island of Hawaii
Prince Kuhio Festival, Lihue, Kauai
April
Hawaiian Festival of Music, Honolulu
Merrie Monarch Festival, Hilo, movable date
May
50th State Fair, Honolulu, through mid-June
Lei Day, Honolulu, May 1
Sea Spree, Haleiwa
June
King Kamehameha Celebration, Honolulu
Mission Houses Museum Fancy Fair, Honolulu
July
International Festival of the Pacific, Hilo
Japan Festival in Hawaii, Honolulu
Parker Ranch Rodeo, Waimea
August
Hawaiian International Billfish Tournament, Kailua-Kona
Hula Festival, Waikiki
Macadamian Nut Harvest Festival, Honokaa
September
Aloha Week Festival, all islands, through mid-October
Hawaii County Fair, Hilo

October
  Bishop Museum Festival, Honolulu
  Championship Jackpot Fishing Tournament, Lahaina
  Kona Coffee Festival, Kailua-Kona
November
  Christmas Fair, Honolulu
  International Film Festival, Honolulu
December
  Festival of Trees, Honolulu
  Rainbow Classic: Basketball, Honolulu

Idaho

January
  Winter Ski Carnival, Schweitzer/Sandpoint
February
  Busterback Stampede: Cross-Country Ski Race, Stanley
  101-Cross-County Snowmobile Race, Island Park
  Winter Carnival, Spirit Lake
March
  Sawtooth Derby: Cross-Country Ski Races, Stanley
  Sled Dog Races, Island Park
April
  Spring Art Show, Idaho Falls
May
  Air Show, Sandpoint
  Apple Blossom Festival and Boomerang Days, Payette
  Folk Life Festival, Cottonwood
  Spring Festival and Flotilla, Priest Lake
June
  Clearwater Valley Rodeo Celebration, Kamiah
  National Old-Time Fiddlers' Contest, Weiser
  Shakespeare Festival, Boise, through mid-August
July
  Chief Joseph Memorial: Four Nation Pow Wow, Lapwai
  Folk Festival, McCall
  Idaho State Square and Round Dance Festival, Moscow
August
  All Girls Rodeo, Mackay
  Art on the Green: Festival of Arts, Coeur d'Alene
  Buckaroo Rodeo, Rigby
September
  Art in the Park: Arts and Crafts Festival, Boise

Harvest Hoedown, Weiser
North Idaho Fair and Rodeo, Coeur d'Alene
October
Fiddlers Jamboree, Riggins
Octoberfest: German Beer Fete, Sandpoint
November
Basque Carnival and Bazaar, Boise
Winterfest Art Show, Coeur d'Alene
December
Christmas Craft Fair, Sandpoint

Illinois

January
Central Illinois Jazz Festival, Decatur
Winter Carnival, Crystal Lake
February
Maple Syrup Time Festival, Springfield
Rock Cut Winter Carnival, Caledonia
March
Spring Flower Show, Chicago
April
Folk Art Festival, Lockport
Old Settler Days, Sumner
May
Dogwood Festival, Quincy
Lilac Festival, Lombard
Old Capitol Art Fair, Springfield
June
Fort de Chartres Rendezvous, Prairie du Rocher
Old English Faire, Brimfield
Ravinia Festival, Chicago
July
Bluegrass Festival, Peoria
Lincolnfest, Springfield
Shakespeare Festival, Bloomington
Taste of Chicago, Chicago
August
Chicagofest, Chicago
Gold Coast Art Fair, Chicago
Illinois State Fair, Springfield
National Sweet Corn Festival, Mendota
September

Abraham Lincoln National Railsplitting Contest and Crafts Festival, Lincoln
Southern Illinois Folk Festival, DuQuoin
Venetian Night: Parade of Illuminated Yachts, Chicago
Wedding of the Wine and Cheese Pageant/Grape Festival, Nauvoo

October
Fine Art Fair, Peoria
Halloween Festival, Carbondale
Heritage Fair, Downers Grove
Indian Summer Festival, Springfield

November
Christmas Around the World, Chicago, through early January
Julmarknad or Christmas Market, Bishop Hill

December
Lucia Nights or Festival of Light, Bishop Hill
New Year's Open Figure Skating Competition, Evanston

Indiana

January
Winter Carnival, Indianapolis
Winterfest, Hobart
Winter Festival, New Carlisle

February
Parke County Maple Fair, Rockville, through early March

March
Indiana Flower and Patio Show, Indianapolis

April
Ohio River Arts Festival/Jazz Festival, Evansville
Romantic Festival, Indianapolis
Sassafras Tea Festival, Vernon

May
"500" Festival, Indianapolis
May Wine Fest, Indianapolis

June
Freedom Festival, Evansville
Indiana Rose Festival, Indianapolis
Mint Festival, North Judson
Rose Festival, Richmond

July
Circus City Festival, Peru
Round Barn Festival, Chesterton
Three Rivers Festival, Fort Wayne

August

Indiana State Fair, Indianapolis
Old Settlers Fun and Sports Festival, Indianapolis
Wine Festival, Vevay
September
Little Italy Festival, Clinton
Oktoberfest, Terre Haute
Persimmon Festival, Mitchell
October
Feast of the Hunters' Moon, Lafayette
James Whitcomb Riley Festival, Greenfield
Parke County Covered Bridge Festival, Rockville
November
Acorn Festival, Frankfort
Harvest Fest, Indianapolis
December
Festival of the Trees, Columbus
Spring Mill State Park Pioneer Winter Festival, Mitchell
Victorian Christmas Festival, New Albany

Iowa

February
Winter Sports Festival, Estherville
March
St. Patrick's Day Celebration, Emmetsburg
April
Drake Relays, Des Moines
May
Cherokee Memorial Weekend Rodeo, Cherokee
DubuqueFest/All Arts Festival, Dubuque
Houby Days, Cedar Rapids
North Iowan Band Festival, Mason City
Tulip Time, Pella
Tulip Festival, Orange City
June
Art on the Square, Oskaloosa
Folk Arts in the Forest, Osceola
"Golden Age" Radio Reunion Festival, Atlantic
Grant Wood Art Festival, Stone City
International Folk Festival, Bettendorf
Scandinavian Dager Celebration, Eagle Grove
Steamboat Days, Burlington
July

Bix Biederbecke Memorial Jazz Festival, Davenport
Czech Folk Fest, Traer
Nordic Fest, Decorah
Railroad Heritage Days, Creston
Riverboat Days, Clinton
U.S. National Hot Air Balloon Races, Indianola
Van Buren County Summer Arts Festival, Keosauque

August
Ag Fest, Cresco
Great River Days, Muscatine
Iowa Championship Rodeo, Sidney
Iowa State Fair, Des Moines
Mesquakie Indian Pow Wow, Tama
National Hobo Convention, Britt
National Sprint Car Championships, Knoxville

September
Civil War Muster and Mechantile Exposition, Davenport
Creston-Southwest Iowa Professional Hot Air Balloon Races, Creston
Czech Village Festival, Cedar Rapids
Midwest Old Settlers and Threshers Reunion, Mt. Pleasant
Pioneer Crafts Festival, Oskaloosa
Rural Music Reunion, Hopeville
Tri-State Rodeo, Fort Madison

October
Covered Bridge Festival, Winterset

Kansas

January
Kansas Day Observance, Bird City

February/March
International Pancake Race, Liberal, movable date, always the day before
Ash Wednesday

April
Jazz Festival, Wichita
Kansas Relays, Lawrence
Messiah Festival, Lindsborg

May
Old Fort Days, Fort Scott
Wichitennial River Festival, Wichita

June
Old Shawnee Days, Shawnee
Smoky Hill River Festival, Salina

July
  Dodge City Days, Dodge City
  Mid-America Inter-Tribal Pow Wow and Arts and Crafts Fair, Wichita
August
  Indian Peace Treaty Pageant, Medicine Lodge
September
  Kansas State Fair, Hutchinson
October
  Swedish Homage Festival, Lindsborg, biennially, odd-numbered years
November
  Thanksgiving Feast, Wichita

Kentucky

February
  National Farm Machinery Show and Tractor Pull Championships, Louisville
April
  Dogwood Trail Celebration, Paducah
  Kentucky Derby Festival, Louisville, through early May
May
  Kentucky Guild of Artists and Craftsmen Spring Fair, Berea
  Kentucky Mountain Laurel Festival, Pineville
June
  Capital Expo, Frankfort
  Heritage Weekend Celebrations, Louisville, also July, September
  Kentucky Folksong Festival, Grayson
  National Flea Market Jamboree, Bowling Green
July
  Bluegrass Festival, Renfro Valley
  Shaker Festival, South Union
  Summer Festival, Paducah
August
  Great Ohio River Flatboat Race, Owensboro
  Kentucky Lake Fall Fishing Derby, Benton
  Kentucky State Fair, Louisville
  Strassenfest: German Festival, Louisville
September
  Corn Island Storytelling Festival, Louisville
  Golden Armor Festival: Gospel Music, Radcliffe
  Harvest Festival, Washington
  Kentucky Arabian Horse Show, Lexington
October
  Butchertown Octoberfest, Louisville

Kentucky Apple Festival of Johnson County, Paintsville
Kentucky Dam Bluegrass Festival, Gilbertsville
Lincoln Days Celebration, Hodgenville

Louisiana

January
   Louisiana Fur and Wildlife Festival, Cameron
   Sugar Bowl Classic, New Orleans, January 1
February
   LSU Livestock Shows and Rodeo, Baton Rouge
   Mardi Gras, New Orleans, or in early March, movable date
March
   Audubon Pilgrimage, St. Francisville
   East Feliciana Arts and Crafts Festival, Clinton
   Louisiana Festival of Arts, Monroe
   Louisiana Redbud Festival, Vivian
   Oyster Day, Amite
   St. Joseph's Feast Day, New Orleans, March 19
April
   French Acadian Music Festival, Abbeville
   Holiday in Dixie, Shreveport
   New Orleans Jazz and Heritage Festival, New Orleans, through early May
   Spring Fiesta, New Orleans
May
   Arts and Crafts Festival, Bossier City
   Cajun Country Outdoor Opry and Fais Do-Do, Houma
   Crawfish Festival, Breaux Bridge, held biennially, even-numbered years
   Louisiana Balloon Festival and Air Show, Hammond
June
   Arts and Crafts Festival at Melrose Plantation, Natchitoches
   Catfish Festival, Pearl River
   Crab Festival, Lacombe
   Jambalaya Festival, Gonzales
   Pirogue (canoe) Races, Slidell
   World Championship Pirogue (canoe) Races, Lafitte
July
   Bastille Day, Kaplan, July 14
   Creole Summer Festival, French Settlement
   Louisiana Legend Heritage Festival, Monroe
   New Orleans Food Festival, New Orleans
   South Lafourche Seafood Festival, Galliano
August

Festival in the Forest at Hodges Gardens, Many
Fine Arts Festival, Lafayette
Seafood Festival, Lafitte
Shrimp Festival, Delcambre
September
Ameri can Indian Pow Wow, Baton Rouge
Louisiana Shrimp and Petroleum Festival, Morgan City, always Labor Day
   weekend
Louisiana Sugar Cane Festival, New Iberia
North Louisiana Cotton Festival and Fair, Bastrop
Original Red Beans and Rice Festival, Metairie
October
Festa D'Italia, New Orleans
Gumbo Festival, Bridge City
International Acadian Festival, Plaquemine
International Alligator Festival, Franklin
Louisiana Art and Folk Festival, Columbia
Louisiana Gulf Coast Oil Exposition, Lafayette
Louisiana State Fair, Shreveport
Prison Rodeo, Angola
November
Arts and Crafts Fiesta, Lafayette
Cajun Sailing Regatta, Houma
Pecan Festival, Colfax
December
Bonfires on the Levee-River Road, Baton Rouge to New Orleans, Dec
   ember 24
Christmas Festival, Natchitoches
Louisiana Crafts Council's Christmas Crafts Fair, New Orleans

Maine

January
Maine Sno Pro-Snowmobile Competition, Scarborough Downs
Ski Focus Week at Sugarloaf/USA, Kingfield
February
Rangeley "100" Snowmobile Race, Rangeley
Winter Festival, Bethel
Wild Mountain Time Weekend, Rangeley Village, through March
March
Fishermen's Festival, Boothbay Harbor
Rangeley Lakes Sled Dog Races, Rangeley
Winter Carnival at Squaw Mountain, Greenville

April
  Home and Garden Show, Augusta
  Professional Maine Craftsmen Craft Show, Portland
May
  Maine Coast Artists Open Art Show, Rockport, through mid-June
  Memorial Day Weekend Fly-In, Owls Head
  Rocky Coast Road Race, Boothbay Harbor
June
  Heritage Days, Bath, through early July
  North Atlantic Festival of Storytelling, Rockport
  Old Port Festival, Portland
  Sail and Wind Surfer Regatta, Ogunquit
  Shakespeare Festival, Camden, through Labor Day
July
  Acadian Scottish Festival, Trenton
  Bean Hole Bean Festival, Oxford
  Central Maine Egg Festival, Pittsfield
  Clam Festival, Yarmouth
  National Dump Week, Kennebunkport, through Labor Day
  Potato Blossom Festival, Fort Fairfield
  Tuna Tournament and Fisherman's Derby, Bailey Island
  Windjammer Days, Boothbay Harbor
August
  Blueberry Festival, Rangeley
  Downeast Jazz Festival, Camden
  Maine Festival of the Arts, Brunswick
  Maine Seafoods Festival, Rockland
  United Craftsman's Fair, Cumberland
September
  Blue Grass Festival, Brunswick
  Common Ground Country Fair, Windsor
  Kite Flying Contest, Ogunquit
October
  Fair, Fryeburg
  Fall Fly-In, Owls Head
  Fall Foliage Weekend Festival and Fair, Boothbay Harbor
November
  United Maine Craftsmans Fair, Brewer

Maryland

January
  Heritage Antiques Show, Annapolis

February
    Antique Valentines at Surratt House, Clinton
    Black History Month, Baltimore
    Craft Fair, Baltimore
March
    Bethesda Chase Road Race, Bethesda to Kensington
    Festival of Nations, Churchville
    Maple Syrup Demonstrations, Thurmont
    Science Fair, Baltimore
    Spring Arts and Crafts Show, Gaithersburg
April
    Maryland House and Garden Pilgrimage, statewide, late April through early
       May
    Maryland Kite Festival, Baltimore, last Saturday in April
    Mason-Dixon All-Breed Dog Show, Hagerstown
    Spring Arts Festival, Hagerstown
    Trolley Car Spectacular, Wheaton
    World Championship Wildfowl Carving Competition, Ocean City
May
    May Day Festival, Ellicott City, May 1
    Preakness Festival, Baltimore
    Sugarloaf Spring Crafts Festival, Timonium
    Tea Party Festival, Chestertown
    U.S. Naval Academy Commissioning Week, Annapolis
    Water Festival, Snow Hill
June
    Arts Festival, Annapolis
    Great Strawberry Wine Festival, Mt. Airy
    Open Air Crafts Fair, Bethesda
    St. Anthony's Festival, Baltimore
    Victorian Wedding Reception, Clinton
July
    Bastille Day, Annapolis, July 14
    Chesapeake Turtle Derby, Baltimore
    Greater Cumberland Fair, Cumberland
    Lotus Blossom Festival, Buckeystown
    Summer Festival Theatre, Baltimore, through August
August
    C&O Canal Boat Festival, Cumberland
    Maryland State Fair, Timonium, through early September
    Old St. Joseph's Jousting Tournament, Cordova
    Seafood Festival, Havre de Grace
    Western Maryland Tennis Championships, Mountain Lake Park
September

   Festival for the Arts, Bel Air
   Labor Day Skipjack Races, Deal Island, always Labor Day
   Maryland Renaissance Festival, Columbia
   National Hard Crab Derby and Fair, Crisfield
October
   Catoctin Colorfest, Thurmont
   Chesapeake Appreciation Days, Annapolis
   Fell's Point Fun Festival, Baltimore
   Indian Summer Festival, Germantown
   National Craft Fair, Gaithersburg
   Southern Maryland Farm Festival and Craft Fair, Brandywine
   St. Mary's County Maryland Oyster Festival, Leonardtown
November
   Sugarloaf Autumn Crafts Festival, Gaithersburg
   Waterfowl Festival, Easton
December
   Child's Colonial Christmas, Edgewater
   Christmas in Annapolis, Annapolis
   Colonial Christmas at Mount Claire, Baltimore

Massachusetts

January
   International World of Wheels, Boston
February
   Yankee Doodle Drummer Antique Show, Boston
March
   Maple Sugaring, Milton
   Spring Flower Show, Worcester
   St. Patrick's Day Festival, Boston, March 17
April
   Boston Marathon, Boston, third Monday
   Daffodil Festival, Nantucket
   Patriot's Day, Lexington, Monday closest to April 19
May
   Boston Early Music Festival, Boston
   Cambridge River Festival, Cambridge, through early August
   Martha's Vineyard Road Race
June
   Back Bay Street Fair, Boston
   Battle of Bunker Hill Celebration, Charleston, always June 17
   Blessing of the Fleet or St. Peter's Fiesta, Gloucester, last full weekend
   Jacob's Pillow Dance Festival, Becket, through early September

St. Anthony Festival, Boston
July
   Berkshire Music Festival at Tanglewood, Lenox
   Festival of the Holy Ghost, Plymouth
   Harborfest, Boston
   Yankee Homecoming Festival, Newburyport, last Saturday and Sunday
August
   Celtic Irish Festival, Holyoke
   Festival of the Blessed Sacrament, New Bedford
   Heritage Days, Salem
   Marshfield Fair, Marshfield
   Pilgrim Progress Pageant, Plymouth
September
   Big "E"/Eastern States Exposition, West Springfield
   Colonial Fair and Fife and Drum Muster, Sudbury
   Kielbasa Festival, Chicopee
   Massachusetts Cranberry Festival, South Carver, through early October
   New England Renaissance Festival, Carver, weekends only
October
   Haunted Happenings, Salem, October 31
   Head of the Charles Regatta, Boston
November
   Peach Basket Festival and Tip-Off Classic, Springfield
   Thanksgiving Day Celebration, Plymouth, fourth Thursday
December
   "First Night" Celebration: New Year's Eve Arts, Boston
   Re-enactment of the Boston Tea Party, Boston

Michigan

March
   Lumberjack/Spring Carnival Days, Bessemer
   Maple Syrup Festival, Bloomfield Hills
   Spring Carnival, Cedar
April
   Fine Foods Festival, Detroit
   Maple Syrup Festival, Shepherd
   Polka Fest, Wyandotte
   Spring Art Fair, Ann Arbor
May
   Blossomtime Festival, St. Joseph, Benton Harbor
   Fort Michilimackinac Pageant, Mackinaw City
   Highland Festival and Games, Alma

National Mushroom Hunting Championships, Boyne City
Tulip Time Festival, Holland

June
Around the World Festival, Detroit
Bavarian Festival, Frankenmuth
Cereal City Festival, Battle Creek
International Freedom Festival, Detroit/Windsor
National Asparagus Festival, Hart, Shelby
Rose Festival, Jackson
Seaway Festival, Muskegon
Storytellers Festival, Flint

July
Blue Water Festival, Port Huron
Colonial Music and Military Muster, Dearborn
Dancing Hippopotamus Arts and Crafts Fest, Huron Beach
National Cherry Festival, Traverse City
Pickle Festival, Linwood

August
Danish Festival, Greenville
Michigan State Fair, Detroit
Renaissance Festival, Clarkston
Summer Polka-Fest, Frankenmuth
U.S. Coast Guard Festival, Grand Haven
Upper Peninsula State Fair, Escanaba
Yesteryear Heritage Festival, Ypsilanti

September
Carry Nation Festival, Holly
Folk Life Festival, Hastings
Indian Summer Festival, Saugatuck
Montreux-Detroit Kool Jazz Festival, Detroit
Old Car Festival at Greenfield Village, Dearborn
Wine and Harvest Festival, Paw Paw/Kalamazoo

Minnesota

January
All American Championships Sled Dog Races, Ely
Paul Bunyan Sled Dog Races, Bemidji
St. Paul Winter Carnival, St. Paul, sometimes through early February
Winter Carnival Polka and Music Festival, Moundsview

February
International Peanut Butter and Milk Festival, Litchfield
Winterfest, Pine City

World Series of Snowmobile Drag Racing, Alexandria

March

Minnesota Finlandia Ski Marathon, Bemidji

Northern Lights Juried Art Show, White Bear Lake

Spirit Mountain's "Spring Has Sprung" Festival, Duluth

April

Festival of Nations, St. Paul, through early May

May

Eclipse People's Fair, Mankato

Rivertown Arts Festival, Stillwater

World Festival, Rochester

June

Art Fair, Minneapolis

Craft Americana, Shakopee

Fiesta Days, Montevideo

International Polka Festival, Hill City

Lower Town Art and Music Festival, St. Paul

Minnesota State Pack Horse Championship, Dorset

Straight River Days Canoe Derby, Medford

Svenskarnas Dag, Minneapolis

July

International Marble Tournament, Mankato

Minneapolis Aquatennial, Minneapolis

Mississippi River Revival Festival, St. Cloud

Riverboat Days, Aitkin

Sinclair Lewis Days, Sauk Centre

Trans Superior Race and Regatta, Duluth

Victorian Craft Festival, St. Paul

Wheels, Wings and Water Festival, St. Cloud

Wild Rice Festival, Kelliher-Waskish

August

Berne Swissfest, West Concord

International Folk Festival, Duluth

Minnesota Ethnic Days, Chisholm

Minnesota State Fair, St. Paul, through early September

September

Great Balloon Race, Rochester

Harvest Festival, Underwood

International Muskie Tournament, Walker

International Northern Pike Fishing Tournament, Brainerd

Minnesota Jam to Preserve the Arts, Minneapolis

Threshing Bee, Faribault

October

Halloween Celebration, Anoka

Oktoberfest, New Ulm
Pumpkin Festival, Owatonna
Twin Cities Marathon, Minneapolis, St. Paul
November
Art Show and Sale, Fergus Falls
Snow World, Minneapolis
December
Auto Races on Ice, Cross Lake
Christmas Festival, Wadena
Cross Country Ski Race, Duluth
Lake Enduro Snowmobile Racing, Cass Lake

Mississippi

January
National Tractor Pull, Jackson
February
Dixie National Livestock Show, Jackson
Mardi Gras Parade, Biloxi, movable date, can be early March
March
Natchez Pilgrimage, Natchez, through early April, also October
April
Catfish Festival, Belzoni
Railroad Festival, Amory
Spring Pilgrimage: Tour of Homes, Columbus
May
Gum Tree Festival, Tupelo, through June
Heritage Festival, Biloxi
Mississippi Broiler Festival, Forest
June
Atwood Bluegrass Festival, Monticello
Blessing of the Fishing Fleet and Biloxi Shrimp Festival and Fais Do Do,
    Biloxi
Hot Air Balloonfest, Greenville
Jimmie Rodgers Memorial Festival, Meridian
Music Festival, Natchez
July
Choctaw Indian Fair, Philadelphia
Mississippi Deep Sea Fishing Rodeo, Gulfport
Neshoba County Fair, Philadelphia
August
Gulf Coast Square Dance Festival, Biloxi
Lake Lowndes Folklife Festival, Columbus

Newton County Fair and State Dairy Show, Newton
September
Delta Blues Festival, Greenville
October
Gumbo Festival of the Universe, White Cypress-Necaise Crossing
Great River Road Craft Fair, Natchez
Mississippi State Fair, Jackson
Natchez Pilgrimage, Natchez, also March through early April
November
Mistletown Marketplace, Jackson
December
Chimneyville Crafts Festival, Jackson
Christmas at the Old Capitol, Jackson
Trees of Christmas at Merrehope, Meridian

Missouri

February
NAIA National Track and Field Competition, Kansas City
March
St. Pat's Celebration, Rolla
Women's Jazz Festival, Kansas City
April
Kewpiesta, Branson
Lake of the Ozarks Dogwood Festival, Camdenton
Spring National Crafts Festival, Silver Dollar City (Branson), through late
   May
May
Family Bluegrass Music Weekend, Hermitage
International Festival, St. Louis
Maifest, Hermann
Story Telling Festival, St. Louis
Valley of Flowers Festival, Florissant
June
Great Meramec River Raft Float and Festival, St. Louis
Jubilee Days, Warsaw
National Ragtime and Traditional Jazz Festival, St. Louis
National Tom Sawyer Days, Hannibal, late June through July 4
Riverfest, Cape Girardeau
July
Family Bluegrass Festival, Patterson
Ozark Empire Fair, Springfield, late July through early August
Stassenfest, St. Louis

Veiled Prophet Fair, St. Louis
August
Fete des Petites Cotes, St. Charles
Frontier Folklife Festival, St. Louis
Jour de Fete a Sainte Genevieve Days of Celebration, Ste. Genevieve
Missouri State Fair, Sedalia
Pershing Balloon Derby, Laclede
September
Cotton Carnival, Sikeston
Forest Park Balloon Rally, St. Louis
National Crafts Festival, Silver Dollar City (Branson), through mid-October
October
American Royal Rodeo, Livestock and Horse Show, Kansas City, late
October through mid-November
Prairie View Festival, St. Joseph

Montana

January
Cabin Fever Days, Columbia Falls
February
Native American Games, Billings
Wine and Food Festival, Great Falls
Winter Carnival, Whitefish
Winter Carnival, Red Lodge
March
Charlie Russell Art Auction, Great Falls
April
Art Festival, Glendive
Flea Market, Helena
Home and Garden Show, Missoula
May
All American Car Show and Swap Meet, Great Falls
Square and Round Dance Fest, Missoula
Sun River Valley Rodeo, Vaughn
Whitewater Races, Bigfork
June
Adult Chamber Music Festival, Bozeman
Arts and Crafts Show, Seeley Lake
Music Festival, Red Lodge
Outdoor Festival, Billings
Whoop-Up Days Rodeo, Conrad
July

Ethnic Food Festival, Anaconda
Home of Champions Rodeo, Red Lodge
Lewis and Clark Festival, Cut Bank
Montana State Fiddlers, Polson
Northeast Montana Fair, Glasgow
August
Crow Fair Celebration and Powwow, Crow Agency
Ethnic Festival, Butte
Festival of Nations, Red Lodge
Montana State Fair, Great Falls
Summer Art Festival, Missoula
September
Festival Days, Havre
Harvest Festival, Glasgow
Old Timers Rodeo, Great Falls
Western Days and Art Show, Ennis
October
Fall Festival, Great Falls
Halloween Parade and Midnight Madness, Eureka
Octoberfest, Scobey
November
Craft Festival, Libby
Renaissance Art Fair, Missoula
Winter Art Fair, Kalispell
December
Christmas Bazaar, Red Lodge
Holiday Extravaganza, Kalispell

Nebraska

April
April Festival of Arts, Fairbury
Arbor Day Celebration/Arts Festival, Nebraska City
Craft Fair, Broken Bow
May
Balloon Festival, McCook
Country Music Festival, Fremont
Nebraska Danish Days/Danish Ethnic Festival, Minden, through early June
Spring Arts and Crafts Festival, Fremont
June
Countryside Village Fair, Omaha
Days of '56 Celebration and Rodeo, Ponca
Ethnic Festival, Omaha

Nebraska State County Music Championship Contest, Springfield
NEBRASKAland Days, North Platte
Summer Arts Festival, Omaha
July
    La Fiesta Italiana, Omaha
    Prairie Pioneer Days, Arapahoe
    Rough Riders Rodeo, North Platte, through early September
    Swedish Festival, Oakland
August
    Cobblestone Festival, Falls City
    Czech Festival, Wilber
    German Harvest Fest, Wisner
    Omaha Pow Wow, Macy
September
    AK-SAR-BEN Livestock Exposition and Rodeo, Omaha, through early
      October
    Country Music Festival, Fremont
    Nebraska State Fair, Lincoln
    Square Dance Festival, Sidney
October
    Oktoberfest, Sidney
    Olde Towne Harvest, Bellevue
    Nebraska State Cornhusking Contest, Lincoln
    Northeast Nebraska Craft Show, Norfolk
November
    Christmas Pageant, Gothenburg
    Ne-Mo-Ka Craft Fair, Falls City
December
    Christmas Pageant: "The Light of the World," Minden

Nevada

January
    Bowling Tournament, Elko
    Winter Carnival, South Lake Tahoe
February
    Chariot Races, Elko
    Snowmobile Races, Elko
March
    Jazz Band Festival, Reno
    Soaring Glider Meet, Minden
April
    Military Appreciation Days, North Las Vegas

Mrs. America Pageant, Las Vegas
May
   Helldorado Days, Las Vegas
   Jim Butler Days, Tonopah
   Pioneer Arts and Crafts Festival, Elko
June
   Rodeo, Reno
   Spring Festival of the Arts, Elko
July
   All Indian Rodeo and Stampede, Fallon
   National Basque Festival, Elko
   Pageant in the Pines, South Lake Tahoe
August
   Arts Alliance Festival, Carson City
   Nevada Fair of Industry, Ely
September
   Camel Races, Virginia City
   Fall Festival of Arts, Elko
   Hydroplane Boat Races, Sparks
   National Championship Air Races, Reno
   Nevada State Fair, Reno
October
   Art Festival, Boulder City
   Great North American Indian Pow Wow, Las Vegas
   Nevada Day Celebration, Carson City
   Regional Square Dance Festival, Jackpot
November
   Judo Championship, Las Vegas

New Hampshire

January
   Chowder Party and Sleigh Ride, Greenfield
February
   Dartmouth Winter Carnival, Hanover
   Winter Carnival, Concord
May
   Lilac Time in Lisbon Celebration, Lisbon
   May Fair, Hampton
   New Hampshire State Open Bass Tournament, Milton Mills
June
   Antique Auto and Classic Car Show, Greenfield
   International Children's Festival, Somersworth

Market Square Day, Portsmouth
July
Monadnock Music Festival, Peterborough, through Labor Day
New Hampshire Music Festival, Lakes Region Area, Plymouth, through
    mid-August
Strawbery Banke Chamber Music Festival, Portsmouth, through early
    September
Summer Festival, Exeter
August
Craftsmen's Fair, Newbury
Lobster Festival, East Kingston
New Hampshire Folk Festival, Concord
New Hampshire Gem and Mineral Festival, Newbury
Plymouth State Fair, Plymouth
Summer Festival, Dover
September
Deerfield Fair, Deerfield
Fine Arts and Crafts Festival, Meredith
Riverfest, Manchester
October
Fall Foliage Festival, Warner
Guild of Strawbery Banke Antiques Festival, New Castle
Waterfront Festival, Exeter
November
Christmas Craft Fair, Portsmouth
Monadnock Music Christmas Fair, Peterborough
December
Craftworkers Guild Christmas Fair, Bedford Center

New Jersey

January
Mid-Winter Antique Show and Sale, Millville
February
Antique Auto Show, Atlantic City
March
Boat Show, Atlantic City
April
Cherry Blossom Festival, Belleville
Tulip Festival, Cape May
May
Iris Gardens Festival, Upper Montclair, through June
Teen Arts Festival, North Branch

June
  Strawberry Festival, Bergenfield
  Victorian Fair at Physick Estate, Cape May
July
  Benihana Grand Prix Power Boat Regatta/N.J. Offshore Grand Prix, Point
    Pleasant Beach
  Boardwalk Mile Foot Race, Ventnor
  Country Farm Fair, New Egypt
  North American Blueberry Festival, Ocean City
  Raritan River Festival, New Brunswick
  Surfing Contest, Atlantic City
August
  Baby Parade, Ocean City
  Flemington Fair, Flemington, through Labor Day
  Folk Festival, Sandy Hook
  International Street Fair, Lakewood
September
  Country Fair, Tinton Falls
  Harvest Days Festival, Cape May
  International Food Festival, Red Bank
  Miss America Pageant, Atlantic City
  New Jersey State Ethnic Festival, Jersey City
October
  Oktoberfest and Crafts Faire, Smithville
November
  Grand Christmas Exhibition at Wheaton Village, Millville, through December
December
  Candlelight Walk on the Mall, Cape May
  Winter Holiday Arts Show, Atlantic City

New Mexico

January
  Gymnastics Invitational, Albuquerque
  Three Kings Day Celebration and Installation of Pueblo Governors and
    Council Members, most Pueblos, January 6
February
  Bach Festival, Santa Fe
March
  Rock Hound Round-Up, Deming
April
  Film Festival, Santa Fe
  Spring Festival, Santa Fe

May
    San Felipe Feast Day Dances, San Felipe Pueblo, May 1
    White Water Races, Pilar
June
    Arts and Crafts Fair, Albuquerque
    June Music Festival, Albuquerque
    School of Music Summer Series, Taos
    Summer Festival, Ruidoso
July
    Rodeo and Pow Wow, Dulce
    Santa Fe Chamber Music Festival, Santa Fe, through mid-August
    Santa Fe Opera Festival, Santa Fe, through August
    Spanish Market, Santa Fe
August
    Feria Artesana: Hispanic Heritage Arts and Crafts, Albuquerque
    Indian Market, Santa Fe
    Intertribal Ceremonial, Gallup
    Old Lincoln Days, Lincoln
September
    Fiesta de Santa Fe, Santa Fe
    New Mexico State Fair, Albuquerque
    San Augustin Feast Day, Isleta Pueblo
    Whole Enchilada Fiesta, Las Cruces, late September through early October
October
    Balloon Fiesta, Albuquerque
    Festival of the Arts, Santa Fe
    Harvest Festival, Santa Fe
November
    Indian National Finals Rodeo, Albuquerque
    Southwest Arts and Crafts Festival, Albuquerque
December
    Luminaria Tours, Albuquerque, December 24.
    Our Lady of Guadalupe Feast Day, Jemez Pueblo, December 12

New York

January
    National Boat Show, New York City
    Twelfth Night Celebration at Fort Crailo, Rensselaer, January 6
    Winter Antique Show, New York City
    Winter Carnival, Livingston Manor
    Winter Carnival, Saranac Lake
February

Westminster Kennel Club Dog Show, New York City
Winter Carnival, Bridgeville
March
St. Patrick's Day Parade on Fifth Avenue, New York City
Spring Flower Show at Macy's, New York City, through early April
April
Arts and Crafts Fair, Watertown
Contemporary American Crafts Festival, New York City, late April through
early May
Ethnic Heritage Festival, Buffalo
Maple Festival, Franklinville
Mohawk Valley Craftsmen Show and Sale, Albany
Renaissance Faire, Stone Ridge
Spring Arts Festival, Plattsburgh
May
Adirondack Folksinging and Storytelling Festival, Raquette Lake
Apple Blossom Festival, Plattsburgh
Arts in the Park, Elmira
Bard College Annual Antique Fair, Rhinebeck
Catskills Irish Festival, East Durham
Festival of Bands, Cazenovia
General Clinton Canoe Regatta, Bainbridge
International Indian Pow-Wow, Niagara Falls
Ninth Avenue International Festival, New York City
Tulip Festival, Albany
June
Antique Car Meet, Monticello
Arts and Crafts Festival, Troy
Craft Festival with 100 American Craftsmen, Lockport
Festival of St. Anthony, New York City
Harbor Festival, New York City, late June through July 4
Kool Jazz Festival, New York City, late June through early July
Saratoga Festival/Saratoga Performing Arts Center, Saratoga Springs,
through September
Steuben County Dairy Festival, Bath
White Water Canoe and Kayak Races, Phoenicia
July
Baseball Hall of Fame Induction Ceremonies, Cooperstown
Caramoor Music Festival, Katonah, through August
French Festival, Cape Vincent
German Alps Festival, Hunter
Hill Cumorah Pageant, Palmyra
Mostly Mozart Festival, New York City, mid-July through August
Pepsico Summerfare, Purchase, through early August

Stone House Day, Hurley

Sullivan Festival: Arts, Loch Sheldrake, through mid-August

August

Country Music Festival, Hunter

Dutchess County Fair, Rhinebeck

Festival of Nations, New Rochelle

Greenwich Village Jazz Festival, New York City

I Love New York State Fair/The Great New York State Fair, Syracuse, through Labor Day

Indian Pow-wow, Barryville

International Polka Festival, Hunter

Lincoln Center Out-of-Doors Festival, New York City, through Labor Day weekend

Little World's Fair, Grahamsville

Polish Town Street Fair Festival, Riverhead

U.S. Open Tennis Championships, Flushing Meadows, Queens, late August through mid-September

September

Arts and Crafts Festival, Lake George

Feast of San Gennaro, New York City

52nd Street Festival, New York City

Harvest Festival and Crafts Fair, Old Chatham

International Food Festival, Kingston

Mt. Eagle Native American Indian Festival, Hunter

New York Film Festival, New York City, through early October

Wine-Water-Wilderness Festival, Watkins Glen

October

Fall Foliage Festival, Chocton

Full Moon Bass Tournament, Montauk

Harvest Festival, Ballston Spa

Oktoberfest, Lake Placid

Pumpkin Jubilee Festival, Watertown

Stone Fort Days, Schoharie

November

Festival of Nations, Syracuse

Herkimer County Arts and Crafts Fair, Herkimer

Macy's Thanksgiving Day Parade, New York City

North Atlantic Figure Skating Championships, Lake Placid

December

Holiday Basketball Festival, New York City

North Carolina

January

Old Christmas Observance, Swansboro, January 6

February
  Camellia Show, Charlotte
  Mid-Atlantic Boat Show, Charlotte
  St. Thomas Celebration of the Arts, Wilmington
  Winterfest Art and Craft Show, Asheville
March
  Antiques Fair, Southern Pines
  Folk Festival, Louisburg
  Outdoors North Carolina Expo, Raleigh
  Spring Frolic, Maggie Valley
April
  American Indian Dance Festival, Wilmington
  Artsplosure: Raleigh Arts Festival, Raleigh
  Carolina Craftsmen's Spring Classic, Greensboro
  Carolina Dogwood Festival, Statesville
  North Carolina Azalea Festival, Wilmington
  Old North State Clogging Championships, Apex
  Spring Arts Festival, Washington
  Wild Foods Festival, Gastonia
May
  Hang Gliding Spectacular, Nags Head
  Mayfest International, Winston-Salem
  Spring Wildflower Pilgrimage, Asheville
  Strawberry Festival, Chadbourn
  Ole Time Fiddler's and Bluegrass Festival, Union Grove
  Water Festival, White Lake
June
  American Dance Festival, Durham, through late July
  Great Smoky Mountain Heritage Festival, Robbinsville
  National Hollerin' Contest, Spivey's Corner
  North Carolina Rhododendron Festival, Bakersville
  Singing on the Mountain, Linville
July
  Black Cultural Arts Festival, Southern Pines
  Blue Ridge Mountain Fair, Sparta
  Brevard Music Center and Festival, Brevard, through mid-August
  North Carolina Shakespeare Festival, High Point, through early September
August
  Mountain Dance and Folk Festival, Asheville
  New World Festival of the Arts, Manteo
  North Carolina Apple Festival, Hendersonville, through Labor Day
  Shrimp Festival, Sneads Ferry
September
  Broad River Festival, Cliffside

Clogging Festival, Chimney Rock
Coastal Carolina Folklife Festival, Wilmington
Indian Heritage Week, Raleigh
North Carolina State Championship Horse Show, Raleigh
Square-Up Fiddler's Grove Campground Dance Festival, Union Grove
Starving Artists Festival, Gastonia
Tryon Palace Colonial Living Day, New Bern
October
Autumn Leaves Festival, Mount Airy
Fall Festival, Cherokee
Fall Guild Fair of Southern Highland Handicraft Guild, Asheville
National Balloon Rally, Statesville
National 500 Week, Charlotte
North Carolina State Fair, Raleigh
Peanut Festival, Edenton
Swiss Bear Festival, New Bern
November
High Country Christmas Art and Craft Show, Asheville
North Carolina State Championship Walking Horse Show, Raleigh
Piedmont Crafts Fair, Winston-Salem
December
Christmas Floatilla of Decorated Sailboats, Swansboro
Ethnic Holiday Festival, Wilmington
First Flight Celebration, Kill Devil Hills
Religious Arts Festival, Washington
Salem Christmas in Old Salem, Winston-Salem

North Dakota

February
Winterfest, Minot
March
Country-Western Jamboree, Dickinson
Winter Show, Valley City
April
Country Show, Williston
May
Norwegian Independence Day, Fargo, May 17
Old Puncher's Reunion: Songs, Yarns, Fiddling, Poetry, Medora
June
Festival of Ethnic Musical Traditions in North Dakota, Grand Forks
International Festival of the Arts, Dunseith, through July
Red River Exhibition, Jamestown

Red River Valley Sugarbeet Festival, Grafton
July
    North Dakota State Fair, Minot
    Red River Valley Fair, West Fargo
    Roughrider Days, Dickinson
August
    Heritage Film Festival, Medora
    Pioneer Review Days, West Fargo
    Rodeo, Bottineau
    Summerthing Art Festival, Grand Forks
    Winter Wheat Show, Washburn
September
    Fall Festival, Grand Forks
    Oktoberfest, Bismarck
    United Tribes Pow Wow, Bismarck
October
    Arts and Crafts Fair, Devils Lake
    Northern Plains Ethnic Festival, Dickinson

Ohio

April
    International Film Festival, Athens
May
    Herb Fair, Bath
    International Chicken Flying Meet, Rio Grande
    International Festival, Toledo
    Springfest: Arts Festival, Cincinnati
    World Affair-International Festival, Dayton
June
    National Clay Week Festival, Uhrichsville
    Old Time Music Festival, Bath
    Swiss Cheese Festival, Littlefield
July
    Annie Oakley Days, Greenville
    Dayton International Airshow and Trade Exposition, Vandalia
    Ohio Hills Folk Festival, Quaker City
    Pottery Festival, Crooksville, Roseville
August
    All-American Soap Box Derby, Akron
    Bratwurst Festival, Bucyrus
    Guitar Festival, Kettering
    Ohio State Fair, Columbus

Shaker Festival, Kettering
September
  "Down by the Riverside" Regatta, Dayton
  Johnny Appleseed Festival, Lisbon
  Harvest Home Fair, Cheviot
  Ohio Honey Festival, Lebanon
October
  Applefest, Lebanon
  Circleville Pumpkin Show, Circleville
  Wonderful World of Ohio Mart, Akron
November
  International Folk Festival, Cincinnati
  Winterfest, Cincinnati
December
  Christmas in the Village: Sharon Woods Village, Cincinnati

Oklahoma

April
  Azalea Festival, Muskogee
  89er Celebration, Guthrie
  Festival of the Arts, Oklahoma City
  Sugarloaf Art–Dogwood Festival, Poteau
  Wichita Mountains Easter Sunrise Service, Lawton, or in March,
    movable date
May
  Italian Festival, McAlester
  Kolache (Sweet Roll) Festival, Prague
  Mayfest-Celebration of Spring, Tulsa
  Rooster Celebration, Broken Arrow
  Strawberry Festival, Stilwell
  Tri-State Music Festival, Enid
June
  Kiamichi Owa Chito Festival of the Forest, Broken Bow
  Love County Frontier Days, Marietta
  Oklahoma Heritage Days, Tulsa
  Santa Fe Trail Daze, Boise City
  Summer Arts Institute, Altus
July
  Belle Starr Festival, Wilburton
  Comanche Homecoming Pow Wow, Walters
  Huckleberry Festival, Jay
  International Brick and Rolling Pine Event, Stroud

    Old Santa Fe Days, Shawnee
    Pow Wow, Oklahoma City
    Pow Wow, Tulsa
August
    American Indian Exposition, Anadarko
    Inter-Tribal Pow Wow, Tulsa
    Peach Festival, Porter
    Watermelon Festival, Rush Springs
September
    Cattle Trails Festival and Celebration of the Arts, Elk City
    Cherokee National Holiday, Tahlequah
    Great Raft Race, Sand Springs, Tulsa
    Hot Air Balloon Festival, Chickasha
    Oklahoma State Prison Rodeo, McAlester
    State Fair of Oklahoma, Oklahoma City, through early October
    Tulsa State Fair, Tulsa, through early October
December
    National Finals Rodeo, Oklahoma City

Oregon

January
    All Breed Dog Show, Portland
    Oregon Mid-Winter Square and Round Dance Festival, Eugene
    Portland Day Trail Race, Mt. Hood
February
    Central Oregon Farm Fair, Madras
    Great American Choral Festival, Eugene
    Oregon Indoor Track Meet, Portland
    Oregon Shakespearean Festival, Ashland, through October
    Seafood and Wine Festival, Newport
March
    All-Northwest Barbershop Ballad Contest and Gay 90's Festival,
      Forest Grove
    Festival of Jazz, Portland
    Klamath Basin Home Fair, Klamath Falls
    Oregon Invitational Relays, Eugene
April
    Kite Festival, Rockaway
    Loyalty Days and Seafare Festival, Newport
    Pear Blossom Festival, Medford
    Spring Arts Festival, Albany
May

Azalea Festival, Brookings
Central Oregon Timber Carnival, Prineville
Fleet of Flowers Memorial Service, Depoe Bay, May 30
Gem and Mineral Show, Eugene
Rhododendron Festival, Florence
Willamette Valley Folk Festival, Eugene

June
Buckeroo Square and Round Dance Roundup, Roseburg
Portland Rose Festival, Portland
Rockhound Pow-Wow, Prineville
Scandinavian Midsummer Festival, Astoria
Strawberry Festival, Lebanon

July
Chief Joseph Days Rodeo, Joseph
Children's Festival, Jacksonville
Concours d'Elegance (Cars), Forest Grove
Eastern Oregon Air Fair, Ontario
Emerald Empire Roundup Rodeo, Eugene
Oregon Broiler Festival, Springfield
World Championship Timber Carnival, Albany

August
Astoria Regatta Inboard Hydroplane Boat Races, Astoria
Folklife Festival, Aurora
Oregon Skydiving Championships and Antique Aircraft Show, Sheridan
Oregon State Fair, Salem, through early September
Peter Britt Festival, Jacksonville

September
Harvest Fair Folk Festival, Eugene
Indian Style Salmon Bake, Depoe Bay
Labor Day Festival, Cave Junction
Onion Festival, Ontario
White Water Races, Grants Pass
Wine, Cheese and Seafood Festival, Reedsport

October
Christopher Columbus Days, Garibaldi
Pacific International Livestock Exposition, Portland

November
Kraut and Sausage Feed and Bazaar, Verboort
Wine Festival, Salem

December
Christmas Pageant, Rickreall
Far West Classic Basketball Tournament, Portland
Victorian Christmas and Historic Homes Tours, Astoria
Winter Solstice Wine Festival, Bellevue

Pennsylvania

January
   Mummers Parade, Philadelphia, January 1
   Pennsylvania Farm Show, Harrisburg
   Philadelphia Track Classic, Philadelphia
   World Championship Snow Shovel Riding Contest, Old Economy
February
   Groundhog Day, Punxsutawney, February 2
   Maple Sugar Festival, Lima
   Pocono Winter Carnival, Stroudsburg
   Washington's Birthday Weekend, Valley Forge
March
   Maple Syrup Festival, Fallston
   Philadelphia Flower and Garden Show, Philadelphia
   Spring Flower Show, Pittsburgh
April
   Cherry Blossom Festival, Wilkes-Barre
   Pennsylvania Crafts Fair Day, Chadds Ford
   Pennsylvania Maple Festival, Meyersdale
   Strawberry Festival, Lahaska
May
   Bach Music Festival, Bethlehem
   Devon Horse Show and Country Fair, Devon, through early June
   Fine Arts Festival, Hazleton
   Fine Arts Fiesta, Wilkes-Barre
   Folk Fest, Doylestown
   Pittsburgh Folk Festival, Pittsburgh
June
   Anniversary of the Battle of Gettysburg, Gettysburg, late June through
       mid-July
   Elfreth's Alley Fete Days, Philadelphia
   Pennsylvania State Laurel Festival, Wellsboro, Brookville
   Rittenhouse Square Fine Art Annual, Philadelphia
   Scottish Games and Country Fair, Devon
   Three Rivers Arts Festival, Pittsburgh
   Three Rivers Shakespeare Festival, Pittsburgh, through mid-August
July
   Bavarian Summer Festival, Barnesville
   Fort Armstrong Folk Festival, Kittanning
   Independence Day Celebration, Philadelphia, July 4
   Pennsylvania Dutch Kutztown Folk Festival, Kutztown
   Port Indian Regatta on the Schuylkill River, Norristown
August

All-American Amateur Baseball Tournament, Johnstown
Bluegrass Festival, Bedford
Italian Festival, Uniontown
Lithuanian Festival, Barnesville
Pennsylvania Guild of Craftsmen State Fair, Lancaster
Philadelphia Folk Festival, Schwenksville
Summerfest, Wilkes-Barre
September
Fairmount Park Fall Festival, Philadelphia
Grape Festival, Erie
Inter-State Fair, York
Lackawanna Arts Festival, Scranton
McClure Bean Soup Festival, McClure
Polish Festival, Doylestown
Traditional Irish Music and Dance Festival, Lansdale
Ukrainian-American Festival, Nanticoke
October
Autumn Leaf Festival, Clarion
Harvest Days, Lancaster
National Apple Harvest Festival, Biglerville
Pennsylvania Flaming Foliage Festival, Renovo
Super Sunday, Philadelphia
November
Craft Show, Philadelphia
Festival of the Trees, Erie
Gimbels Thanksgiving Day Parade, Philadelphia
December
Christmas Evening Conservatory Display and Christmas Tree Lane at
    Longwood Gardens, Kennett Square
19th Century Christmas at Old Economy Village, Ambridge
Re-enactment of Washington Crossing the Delaware, Washington Crossing
    State Park, December 25

Rhode Island

April
International Fair, Providence
International Spring Festival, Providence
May
Festival of Historic Houses, Providence
Gaspee Days, Cranston, Warwick, late May through mid-June
Heritage Month, statewide
June

Motor Car Festival, Newport
National Tennis Week Tournament, Woonsocket
Summer Surf Championships, Narragansett
July
Art Festival, Narragansett
Art Festival, Wickford
Blessing of the Fleet, Galilee
Bristol Fourth of July Celebration, Bristol
Newport Music Festival, Newport
Newport Outdoor Art Festival, Newport
August
American Indian Federation Pow-Wow, Kingstown
Arts and Crafts Festival, Tiverton
Newport Jazz Festival, Newport
Ocean Front Sculpture Contest, Narragansett
Rocky Hill "State" Fair, East Greenwich
September
Arts and Crafts Festival, Coventry
Florentine Faire, Lincoln
Harvest Fair, Bristol
International Jumping Derby, Portsmouth
October
Art Festival, Scituate
Autumnfest, Woonsocket
Jonnycake Festival, Usquepaugh (South Kingstown), Richmond
November
"Ocean State" Marathon Championship and Open Race, Newport
Thanksgiving Procession and Pilgrim Service, Pawtucket, fourth Thursday
December
Christmas in Newport, Newport
Roger Williams Park Annual Christmas Show, Providence

South Carolina

January
Coastal Carolina Camellia Show, Charleston
February
Camellia Show, Beaufort
Opening of Cypress Gardens, Charleston, through May 1
Polo Matches, Aiken, through April
March
Egg and Dairy Festival, Newberry
Festival of Houses, Charleston, through mid-April

Steeplechase and Hunt Meet, Aiken

April

Arts and Crafts Festival, Murrells Inlet

Clarendon County Striped Bass Festival, Manning

Come-See-Me-Festival, Rock Hill

Renaissance Festival, Lake City

Spring Arts and Crafts Festival, Cheraw

May

Hell Hole Swamp Festival, Jamestown

Iris Festival, Sumter

Mayfest, Columbia

Palmetto State Balloon Classic, Camden

Spoleto Festival USA, Charleston, through early June

June

Catfish Festival, Ware Shoals

Gateway Summer Folk Festival, Walhalla

Hampton County Watermelon Festival, Hampton

Sun Fun Festival, Myrtle Beach

July

Hillbilly Day, Mountain Rest

Summerthing Arts Festival, Sumter

Water Festival, Beaufort

August

Foothills Festival, Easley

Peanut Party, Pelion

Schuetzenfest: Hunter's Festival, Ehrhardt

September

Atalaya Arts Festival, Murrells Inlet

Raylrode Daze Festival, Branchville

Scottish Games and Highland Gathering, Charleston

South Carolina Apple Festival, Westminster, Long Creek

Southern 500 Race and Festival, Darlington

October

Fall Fiesta of the Arts, Sumter

House and Garden Candlelight Tours, Charleston

Jazz Festival, Lake City

Lancing Tournament, Charleston

Lee County Cotton Pickin' Festival, Bishopville

South Carolina State Fair, Columbia

November

Chitlin' Strut, Salley

Holiday Fiesta, Myrtle Beach, through December

Plantation Days, Charleston

Southeastern Hobby Fair, Jackson

December
    Christmas Celebration at Rose Hill Mansion, Union
    Memories of Christmas House Tour, Columbia

South Dakota

January
    American College Theatre Festival, Vermillion
    Snow Queen Festival, Aberdeen
    South Dakota Governor's Cup Cross Country Snowmobile Race, Aberdeen
February
    All Indian Basketball Tournament, Rapid City
    Black Hills Winter Carnival, Deadwood
    Winter Carnival, Custer
March
    Junior Music Festival, Vermillion
    Schmeckfest (Food Tastings), Freeman
    Town and Country Fair, De Smet, Huron
    University of South Dakota Coyotee Jazz Festival, Vermillion
April
    Christian Arts Festival at Blue Cloud Abbey, Marvin
    Jack Rabbit Stampede, Brookings
    Northern Plains Farm Expo, Aberdeen
    South Dakota Old Time Fiddlers Jamboree, Lake Norden
    Tribal Pow Wow, Sisseton
May
    Dakota Days Band Festival, Rapid City
    Maverick Stampede Rodeo, Rapid City
    River Rat Regatta, Springfield
June
    Antique Auto Show and Parade, Sisseton
    Arts Festival, Aberdeen
    Czech Days, Tabor
    Fort Sisseton Historical Festival, Sisseton
    Governor's Cup Walleye Tourney, Pierre
July
    Days of '83 Rodeo, Gettysburg
    Days of 1910 Rodeo and Celebration, Timber Lake
    Gold Discovery Days, Custer
    Sitting Bull Stampede, Mobridge
    South Dakota State Outdoor Racquetball Championships, Rapid City
    Summer Folk Arts Festival, Brookings
August

Annual Indian Fair and Pow Wow, Fort Thompson
Black Hills Motorcycle Classic, Sturgis
Days of '76, Deadwood
German Summerfest, Rapid City
Old Time Threshing Bee, Burke
Sioux Empire Fair, Sioux Falls
South Dakota State Fair, Huron, through Labor Day weekend
September
Cheyenne River Sioux Tribal Fair and Rodeo, Eagle Butte
Corn Palace Festival, Mitchell
Fall Festival, Custer
Harvest Festival Celebration, Dell Rapids
October
Buffalo Roundup, Custer State Park
Gypsy Days, Aberdeen
Oktoberfest, Yankton
November
Creative Crafts Show 'n Sell, Madison
Good Earth Christmas Art Sale, Brookings
December
Christmas in the Hills, Hot Springs
German Heritage Christmas Celebration, Madison
NCC Holiday Basketball Tournament, Sioux Falls

Tennessee

January
Reelfoot Eagle Watch Tours, Tiptonville, through March 15
February
"Heart of Country" Antique Show, Nashville
National Field Trial Championships, Grand Junction
March
Valleydale 500, Bristol
April
Dogwood Arts Festival, Knoxville
Old Time Fiddlers' Championships, Clarksville
Spring Wildflower Pilgrimage, Gatlinburg
World's Biggest Fish Fry, Paris
May
Cotton Carnival and MusicFest, Memphis, through mid-June
Great Smoky Mountains Highland Games, Gatlinburg
International Folkfest, Murfreesboro
Memphis in May International Festival, Memphis

Mountain Music Homecoming', Gatlinburg
Tennessee Crafts Fair, Nashville
West Tennessee Strawberry Festival, Humboldt
June
Covered Bridge Celebration, Elizabethton
International Country Music Fan Fair, Nashville
National Mountain Music Festival, Pigeon Forge
Rhododendron Festival, Roan Mountain
July
Craftsmen's Fair, Gatlinburg
Old Time Fiddlers Jamboree and Crafts Festival, Smithville
Rocky Mount Festival, Johnson City
Tennessee River Bluegrass Festival, Savannah
August
Appalachian Fair, Gray
Elvis International Tribute Week, Memphis
International Grand Championship Walking Horse Show, Murfreesboro
Riverbend Festival, Chattanooga
Tennessee Walking Horse National Celebration, Shelbyville
September
Folk Festival of the Smokies, Cosby
Memphis Music Heritage Festival, Memphis
Mid-South Fair, Memphis
Tennessee Forest Festival, Bolivar
October
Craftsmen's Fair, Gatlinburg
Fall Color Cruise and Folk Festival, Chattanooga
National Storytelling Festival, Jonesboro/Jonesborough
Reelfoot Lake Arts and Crafts Festival, Tiptonville
November
Mid-South Arts and Crafts Show/Sale, Memphis
December
Christmas in the City Celebration, Knoxville
Liberty Bowl Football Classic, Memphis

Texas

January
Cotton Bowl Parade and Football Classic, Dallas, January 1
Great Country River Festival, San Antonio
Southwestern Exposition Stock Show and Rodeo, Fort Worth, through
   early February
Texas Citrus Fiesta, Mission

February
   Rattlesnake Roundup, Sweetwater
   Southwestern Stock Show and Rodeo, El Paso
   Sugar Cane Festival, Weslaco
   Washington's Birthday Celebration, Laredo
March
   Craft Market, Dallas
   Dogwood Festival, Woodville
   Houston Festival: Visual and Performing Arts, Houston
   Oysterfest, Fulton
   Shakespeare Festival, Odessa
April
   Buccaneer Days, Corpus Christi
   Fiesta San Antonio, San Antonio
   Neches River Festival, Beaumont
   Prairie Dog Chili Cook-off and World Championship of Pickled Quail
      Eating, Grand Prairie
   Shrimp Festival, Galveston
May
   Artfest, Dallas
   Chisholm Trail Roundup, Lockhart
   Cinco de Mayo Celebration, Hondo
   Mayfest, Fort Worth
   Texas State Arts and Crafts Fair, Kerrville, through early June
June
   Fiesta Noche del Rio, San Antonio, through August
   International Festival-Institute, Round Top, through July
   Square and Round Dance Festival, Houston
   Texas Championship Billfish Tournament, Port Aransas
July
   Art Festival, Rockport
   Black-Eyed Pea Jamboree, Athens
   Borderfest, Laredo
   Gulf Coast Sports Aviation Fly-In, Port Lavaca
   Texas Cowboy Reunion and Rodeo, Stamford
August
   Aqua Festival, Austin
   Great Texas Mosquito Festival, Clute
   Texas Folklife Festival, San Antonio
September
   Bayfest, Corpus Christi
   Cityfest, Dallas, through October
   Fall Harvest Festival, Dallas
   Oatmeal Festival, Bertram

Old Market Square Art Show and Folk Festival, Houston
Pecan Valley Arts Festival, Brownwood
Spindletop Boom Days, Beaumont
October
 Festival of Arts and Crafts, Corpus Christi
 Seafair, Rockport
 Shrimporee, Aransas Pass
 State Fair of Texas, Dallas
 Texas Prison Rodeo, Huntsville
 Texas Renaissance Festival, Plantersville, through November
November
 Chili Cook-off, Terlingua
 Roping Fiesta, San Angelo
 Sun Bowl Carnival, El Paso, through January
December
 Dickens' Evening on the Strand, Galveston
 Fiesta Navidena in El Mercado, Fiesta de las Luminarias, Las Posadas,
  San Antonio

Utah

January
 Winter Sleigh Rides and Elk Feeding at Hardware Ranch, Hyrum, through
  February
 Winterskol: Winter Carnival, Snowbird
February
 Osmond United States Ski Team Celebrity Classic: Winter Carnival,
  Park City
March
 Snow Sculpture Contest, Park City
 Spring Carnival, Brianhead
April
 Arts Festival, St. George
 Ute Bear Dance, Ouray, Randlett, Whiterocks
May
 Dairy Days, Smithfield
 Pioneer Spring Days, Salt Lake City
 Scandinavian Jubilee, Ephraim
June
 Utah Arts Festival, Salt Lake City
 Utah Pageant of the Arts, American Fork
July
 Festival of the American West, Logan, through early August

Mormon Miracle Pageant, Manti
Pioneer Days of 1847, Salt Lake City
Utah Shakespearean Festival, Cedar City, through late August
August
Arts Festival, Park City
Chief Kanosh Pageant, Fillmore
September
Oktoberfest, Snowbird
Pioneer Harvest Days, Salt Lake City
Southern Utah Folklife Festival, Zion National Park
Utah State Fair, Salt Lake City
October
Marathon, St. George
December
Christmas Festival and Ski Torchlight Parade, Park City
Festival of the Trees, Salt Lake City
Winter Carnival, Parowan

Vermont

January
Killington Klassic Stunt Ballet and Aerial Skiing, Killington
Stowe Winter Carnival, Stowe
February
Vermont Cross-Country Marathon, Brandon
Winter Carnival, Middlebury
March
Green Mountain Country Music Contest, Barre
Maple Sugar Square Dance Festival, Burlington
Spring Thing Weekend, Bolton Valley
April
Mogul King and Queen Contest, Killington
Skull and Swords Parade at Norwich University, Northfield
Vermont Maple Festival, St. Albans
May
Music Festival, Burlington
Sheep and Wool Festival, East Burke
Vermont Morgan Horse Field Day, Weybridge
June
Festival of the Arts, Manchester, through October
Hot Air Balloon Festival, Quechee
Lake Champlain Discovery Festival, Burlington, through July 4
Vermont Dairy Festival, Enosburg Falls

July
   Champlain Shakespeare Festival, Burlington, through August
   Connecticut Valley Fair, Bradford
   Ethnic Festival, Barre
   Music Festival, Marlboro, through August
   Slavic Festival, Northfield
   Summer Festival, Swanton
   Vermont Mozart Festival, Burlington, through August
August
   Champlain Valley Exposition, Essex Junction
   Deerfield Valley Farmer's Day, Wilmington
   St. Mark's Antique Show and Sale, Burlington
September
   Apple Pie Festival, Dummerston Center
   Fall Foliage Festival of Round and Square Dancing, Montpelier
   Harvest Festival, Shelburne
   Northeast Kingdom Fall Foliage Festival, Walden, Cabot, Plainfield,
      Peacham, Barnet Center, Groton, through early October
   Stratton Arts Festival, Stratton Mountain, through mid-October
   Vermont State Fair, Rutland
   Vermont's World's Fair, Tunbridge
October
   Fall Festival of Art, Rutland
   Fall Festival of Vermont Crafts, Montpelier
   National Traditional Old-Time Fiddlers' Contest, Barre
November
   Vermont Handcrafters Annual Show, Burlington
   Wild Game Supper, Bradford
December
   Early American Christmas Ceremony, Guilford

Virginia

January
   Antiques Forum at Colonial Williamsburg, Williamsburg, through early
      February
   Lee's Birthday Celebration, Alexandria
February
   George Washington Birthday Celebration, Alexandria
   Point-to-Point Races, Warrenton
March
   Annual Needlework Exhibit at Woodlawn Plantation, Mount Vernon
   Kite Festival at Gunston Hall Plantation, Lorton

Maple Festival, Highland County
Mid-Atlantic Wildfowl Festival, Virginia Beach
April
Dogwood Festival, Charlottesville
Folklife Festival, Vinton
Historic Garden Week, statewide
International Azalea Festival, Norfolk
Poplar Lawn Art Festival, Petersburg
Spring Folklife Weekend, Cumberland Gap National Historical Park
Wildflower Pilgrimage, Roanoke
May
Festival-on-the-River, Roanoke
Jamestown Day Celebration, Jamestown Island
Knox Creek Mountain Festival, Hurley
Prelude to Independence, Williamsburg, through July 4
Re-enactment of Battle of New Market, New Market
Shenandoah Apple Blossom Festival, Winchester
Tidewater Scottish Festival and Clan Gathering, Virginia Beach
June
Gunston Hall Arts and Crafts Celebration, Lorton
Harborfest, Norfolk
National Hall of Fame Jousting Tournament, Mt. Solon
Page Valley's Fete Champetre—Summer Outdoor Concert and Theatre
    Series, Luray
July
Ash Lawn Summer Festival/Colonial Crafts Weekend, Charlottesville
Black Arts Festival, Fredericksburg
Chincoteague Pony Round-Up and Penning, Chincoteague
Farm Craft Days at Belle Grove Plantation, Middletown
Virginia Highlands Festival, Abingdon, through mid-August
Virginia Scottish Games, Alexandria
August
Boardwalk Art and Craft Show, Colonial Beach
Jousting Tournament, Mt. Solon
Quilt Festival, Cumberland Gap National Historical Park
Seawall Outing and Seafood Festival, Portsmouth
Virginia Wine Festival and Vineyard Tour, Middleburg
September
Chesapeake Bay Days, Hampton
Fall Festival, Norton
Greenwood Arts and Crafts Fair, Charlottesville
International Festival, Richmond
Neptune Festival, Virginia Beach, through early October
State Fair of Virginia, Richmond, through early October

Virginia Peanut Festival, Emporia
October
  Albemarle Harvest Wine Festival, Charlottesville
  Antique Show at Historic Castle Hill, Charlottesville, Cobham
  Festival of Leaves, Front Royal
  Fredericksburg Dog Mart, Fredericksburg
  Historic Appomattox Railroad Festival, Appomattox
  Nostalgiafest, Petersburg
  Oyster Festival, Chincoteague
  Yorktown Day Celebration, Yorktown, October 19.
November
  Craft Festival, Roanoke
  Virginia Thanksgiving Festival at Berkeley Plantation, Charles City County
  Waterfowl Week, Chincoteague
December
  Carols by Candlelight at Woodlawn Plantation, Mt. Vernon
  Grand Illumination at Colonial Williamsburg, Williamsburg
  Merrie Old England Christmas Festival, Charlottesville
  Scottish Christmas Walk, Alexandria
  Scottish New Year's Eve Celebration, Alexandria

Washington, D.C.

January
  Presidential Inauguration Ceremonies and Parade, once every four years
  Washington Antique Show
February
  Abraham Lincoln's Birthday Observance at the Lincoln Memorial,
    February 12
  Black History Month at Afro-American Museum
  Chinese New Year's Festival, movable date
  George Washington's Birthday Celebration at Washington Monument, Feb-
    ruary 22
  Winter Festival at the Ellipse
March
  Bach Marathon—Music Competition
  Cherry Blossom Festival, movable date, late March or early April
  Kite Festival, Washington Monument Grounds, late March
April
  American Classic Antique Show
  Georgetown House Tour, late April
  Imagination Celebration at Kennedy Center
  White House Spring Garden Tour

White House Easter Egg Roll, always Monday after Easter Sunday, movable date

William Shakespeare's Birthday at Folger Shakespeare Library, April 23

May

Asian Pacific American Heritage Festival at Sylvan Theater on grounds of the Washington Monument

Flower Mart at Washington Cathedral

Smithsonian Institution's Spring Celebration at Mall entrance of National Museum of American History

June

Kool Jazz Festival at Kennedy Center

July

Bastille Day Race at 20th and Pennsylvania Ave., N.W., July 14

Caribbean Summer Festival in Park on the Ellipse

Independence Day Celebration and Parade plus Fireworks over the Washington Monument, July 4

August

1821 Overture Concert at Sylvan Theatre, Washington Monument Grounds

Potomac Ramblin' Raft Race on the Potomac River

September

Croquet Tournament on 17th Street side of Ellipse

Folklore Society Mini Folk Festival

National Hispanic Heritage Week

Smithsonian's Frisbee Disc Festival on the Mall

October

New Music America Festival near Smithsonian Institution

9th Street Festival: Performing and Visual Arts at Lisner Auditorium and National Building Museum

December

Caribbean Christmas Festival

Pageant of Peace, through early January

Traditional Smithsonian Holiday Celebration at Museum of American History

White House Candlelight Tour

Washington

January

Ski Jumping Tournament, Leavenworth, last weekend, weather permitting

February

World Smelt Derby, La Conner, first Saturday

March

Old Time Music Festival, Tenino

Puyallup Valley Daffodil Festival, Puyallup, Tacoma, Sumner, Orting, Fife, through early April

April

Apple Blossom Festival, Wenatchee, through early May

May

Asian American Heritage Festival, Tacoma

Hot Air Balloon Stampede and Allied Arts Show, Walla Walla

Lilac Festival, Spokane

Rhododendron Festival, Port Townsend

Viking Fest Arts and Crafts Festival, Poulsbo

June

Art Festival, Edmonds

Festival of American Fiddle Tunes, Port Townsend

Loggerodeo, Sedro-Woolley, through July 4

July

Celebration of the Arts, Spokane

International Air Fair, Everett

Pacific Northwest Arts and Crafts Fair, Bellevue

Pacific Northwest Festival, Seattle, through early August

Seafair, Seattle, through early August

August

Omak Stampede and Suicide Race, Omak

Spokane Indian Day, Wellpinit

Washington Olde Time Fiddlers Festival, Tri-Cities

September

Bumbershoot: Arts Festival, Seattle, Labor Day weekend

Harbor Days Festival and Tug Boat Races, Olympia

International Folk Music/Dance Festival, Port Townsend

Interstate Fair, Spokane

October

Master Craftsman Fair, Tacoma

Octoberfest, Spokane

Salmon Days Festival, Issaquah

West Virginia

January

Alpine Winter Festival, Davis

Winter Film Festival, Charleston, through mid-February

March

Governor's Cup Race Weekend, Davis

Nordic Spring Festival, Davis

West Virginia Ski Pro Classic, Snowshoe

April
  Dogwood Arts and Crafts Festival, Huntington, through early May
  Heritage Days, Parkersburg
  West Virginia Dance Festival, Charleston
  West Virginia Jazz Festival, Charleston
May
  Back to Nature Weekend at Blackwater Falls State Park, Davis
  Coal River Canoe Marathon, Peytona
  Cranberry Mountain Spring Nature Tour, Richwood
  Three Rivers Coal Festival, Fairmont
  Wildflower Pilgrimage, Davis
June
  Mountain Heritage Arts and Crafts Festival, Harpers Ferry
  Rhododendron Arts and Crafts, Charleston
  Tri-State Fair and Regatta, Huntington, through mid-July
July
  Augusta Heritage Arts Workshop, Elkins, through mid-August
  Pioneer Days in Pocahontas County, Marlinton
August
  Cherry River Festival, Richwood
  Ohio River Festival, Ravenswood
  State Fair of West Virginia, Lewisburg
  Sternwheel Regatta Festival, Charleston, through early September
  West Virginia Water Festival, Hinton
September
  Country Roads Festival, Pennsboro
  Fall Mountain Heritage Arts and Crafts Festival, Charles Town
  Harvest Moon Festival, Parkersburg
  King Coal Festival, Williamson
  Octoberfest, Shepherdstown
  Preston County Buckwheat Festival, Kingwood
  West Virginia Italian Heritage Festival, Clarksburg
  West Virginia Molasses Festival, Arnoldsburg
  West Virginia Oil and Gas Festival, Sistersville
October
  Country Festival, Point Pleasant
  Mountain State Forest Festival, Elkins
  Old Fashioned Apple Harvest Festival, Burlington
  West Virginia Black Walnut Festival, Spencer
  West Virginia Honey Festival, Parkersburg
November
  Capital City Art and Craft Show, Charleston
  Thanksgiving Harvest in the Mountains, Berkeley Springs, fourth Thursday

December
   Christmas in the Country Tour, Martinsburg
   Old Tyme Christmas, Harpers Ferry

Wisconsin

January
   World Championship Snowmobile Derby, Eagle River
February
   Birkebeiner Cross-Country Ski Races, Cable, last Saturday
   Winter Festival, Cedarburg
March
   Ice Box Derby, Three Lakes
   Indian Head Country's Art Fair, Eau Claire
April
   Bye-Gosh Fest, Oshkosh
   Hopa Tree Art Festival, Wisconsin Rapids
May
   Balloon Rally, Lake Geneva, Fontana
   Conservation Festival, Alma
   Indian Pow-wow, Black River Falls
   Syttende Mai: Norwegian Independence Day Celebration,
      Stoughton, May 17
June
   Great Wisconsin Dells Balloon Rally, Wisconsin Dells
   Heidi Festival, New Glarus
   Lakefront Festival of Arts, Milwaukee
   Summerfest, Milwaukee, through early July
   Walleye Weekend, Fond du Lac
July
   Art Fair on the Square, Madison
   EAA Fly-In, Oshkosh, through early August
   Fiesta Italiana, Milwaukee
   Holland Festival, Cedar Grove
   Lumberjack World Championships, Hayward, through early August
August
   Fiesta Mexicana, Milwaukee
   German Fest, Milwaukee
   International Aerobatic Championships, Fond du Lac
   Irish Fest, Milwaukee
   Peninsula Music Festival, Fish Creek
   Sweet Corn Festival, Sun Prairie
   Wisconsin State Fair, Milwaukee

September
    Colorama, Vilas County
    Cranberry Festival, Warrens
    Great River Music and Crafts Festival, La Crosse
    Octoberfest, Milwaukee
    Wilhelm Tell Festival, New Glarus
    World Dairy Expo, Madison
October
    Apple Festival, Bayfield
November
    Holiday Folk Fair, Milwaukee

Wyoming

January
    Wyoming State Winter Fair, Lander
February
    Cutter Races, Jackson
    "Snowsation" Winter Carnival, Saratoga
    Winter Carnival, Dubois
    Winter Festival, Pinedale
March
    State Championship Chariot Race, Pinedale
April
    Pole, Peddal and Paddle Race, Teton Village
May
    Old Time Fiddle Contest, Shoshoni
June
    Woodchoppers Jamboree, Encampment
July
    Cheyenne Frontier Days, Cheyenne
    Green River Rendezvous, Pinedale
    Indian Tribal Pow-Wows and Sun Dances, Fort Washakie
August
    Gift of the Waters Pageant, Thermopolis
    Wyoming State Fair, Douglas
September
    Cowboy Days, Evanston
    Mountain Man Rendezvous and Black Powder Shoots, Fort Bridger
    Oktoberfest, Worland

American Samoa

January
    Cricket Season, Pago Pago, through mid-April
April
    Flag Day, Pago Pago, April 17
August
    American Samoa International Open, Pago Pago, second week
October
    Swarm of the Palolo, through November
    Whit Sunday, Pago Pago, second Sunday

Puerto Rico

January
    De Hostos Birthday, islandwide, January 11
    International Folkloric Festival, San Juan
    Puppet Theater Festival, San Juan
    Three Kings Day or Epiphany, islandwide, January 6
February
    Crafts and Agricultural Festival, Camuy
    Cultural Festival, Vieques
    San Blas Marathon, Coamo
March
    Coffee Harvest Festival, Yauco
    Crafts Fair, Ponce
    Emancipation Day, islandwide, March 22
    Festival of the Fish, Puerto Real
    Puerto Rican Theater Festival, San Juan
    Sugarcane Harvest Festival, Guanica
April
    De Diego Day, islandwide, April 16
    Jayuya Indian Festival, Utuado
    Spring Festival, Comerio
May
    Festival of the Cross, San Juan
    Puerto Rican Music Festival, Old San Juan
    Weaving Fair, Isabela
June
    Casals Festival/Festival Casals, San Juan
    Flower Festival, Aibonito
    San Juan Fiesta, San Juan, June 24
July
    Barbosa Birthday, islandwide, July 27
    Constitution Day, islandwide, July 25

Crafts Fair, Arecibo
Crafts Fair, Barranquitas
Munoz Rivera Birthday, islandwide, July 17
San Salvador Folk Festival, Caguas
August
Ceramic Festival, San Juan
Summer Arts Festival at El Morro Fortress, Old San Juan
September
Black Virgin of Monserrate Festival, Hormigueros
Children's Cultural Festival, San Juan
Folk Festival, Rincon
Orchid Festival, Aibonito
October
Columbus Day, islandwide, now a movable date
Fine Arts Festival, Anasco
International Theater Festival, San Juan, Mayaguez, Ponce
Sports Fishing Tournament, San Juan
November
Festival of St. Cecilia, Humacao, November 22
Fisherman Festival, Fajardo
Jayuya Festival of Indian Lure, Jayuya
Veterans Day, islandwide, November 11
December
Crafts Fair, Catanto
Festival of Masks, Hatillo
Folk Festival, Arceibo
Navidades: Christmas Season, islandwide, December 15–January 6
Typical Cuisine Festival, Luquillo

U.S. Virgin Islands

January
Three Kings Day, all three islands, January 6
February
Abraham Lincoln's Birthday, all three islands,
February 12
George Washington's Birthday, all three islands, movable date
March
Transfer Day, all three islands
April
Virgin Islands Carnival, Charlotte Amalie, St. Thomas
May
Memorial Day Yacht Races, St. Croix, last Monday

June

    Organic Act Day, all three islands, June 20

July

    Danish West Indies Emancipation Day, Frederiksted,
      St. Croix, July 3

    Hurricane Supplication Day, all three islands, July 25

    St. John Fourth of July Celebration, St. John, late June through July 4

September

    Labor Day Parade, Picnics and Boating, Coral Bay,
      St. John, first Monday

October

    Columbus Day and Puerto Rico/Virgin Islands Friendship Day, all three
      islands

    Hurricane Thanksgiving Day, all three islands, third Monday

November

    Liberty Day, all three islands, November 1

    Veteran's Day, all three islands, November 11

December

    Crucian Christmas Fiesta, St. Croix, through January 6

APPENDIX: Types of Festivals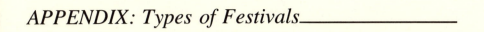

Agriculture

Alabama
National Peanut Festival, Dothan

California
National Date Festival, Indio

Colorado
Colorado State Fair, Pueblo
National Western Stock Show, Denver

Indiana
Persimmon Festival, Mitchell

Iowa
Iowa State Fair, Des Moines

Kentucky
Kentucky Apple Festival of Johnson County, Paintsville

Louisiana
Louisiana State Fair, Shreveport

Massachusetts
Big "E"/Eastern States Exposition, West Springfield
Marshfield Fair, Marshfield
Massachusetts Cranberry Festival, South Carver

Michigan
National Cherry Festival, Traverse City

Missouri
Missouri State Fair, Sedalia

Nebraska
AK-SAR-BEN Livestock Exposition and Rodeo, Omaha

New Jersey
Flemington Fair, Flemington

New York
> Dutchess County Fair, Rhinebeck
> I Love New York State Fair/The Great New York State Fair, Syracuse

Ohio
> Circleville Pumpkin Show, Circleville
> Johnny Appleseed Festival, Lisbon

Oklahoma
> State Fair of Oklahoma, Oklahoma City

Oregon
> Oregon State Fair, Salem

Pennsylvania
> National Apple Harvest Festival, Biglerville

Texas
> State Fair of Texas, Dallas

Utah
> Utah State Fair, Salt Lake City

Vermont
> Vermont Dairy Festival, Enosburg Falls
> Vermont's World's Fair, Tunbridge

Virginia
> Shenandoah Apple Blossom Festival, Winchester

Architecture, House Tours

Delaware
> A Day in Old New Castle, New Castle

Florida
> Old Island Days, Key West

Louisiana
> Spring Fiesta, New Orleans

Mississippi
> Natchez Pilgrimage, Natchez

Pennsylvania
> Elfreth's Alley Fete Days, Philadelphia
> Fairmount Fall Festival, Philadelphia

Rhode Island
> Heritage Month, statewide

South Carolina
> Festival of Houses, Charleston

Tennessee
Dogwood Arts Festival, Knoxville

Virginia
Historic Garden Week, statewide

Art, Arts and Crafts

California
Festival of Arts and Pageant of the Masters, Laguna Beach

Georgia
Arts Festival of Atlanta, Atlanta

Hawaii
Aloha Week Festival, all islands
Cherry Blossom Festival, Honolulu

Illinois
Gold Coast Art Fair, Chicago
Ravinia Festival, Chicago

Indiana
Three Rivers Festival, Fort Wayne

Kentucky
Capital Expo, Frankfort
Kentucky Derby Festival, Louisville
Kentucky Guild of Artists and Craftsmen's Spring Fair, Berea
Shaker Festival, South Union

Louisiana
Holiday in Dixie, Shreveport

Minnesota
Festival of Nations, St. Paul

Mississippi
Choctaw Indian Fair, Philadelphia
Gum Tree Festival, Tupelo

Montana
Crowe Fair Celebration and Powwow, Crow Agency

New Hampshire
Craftsmen's Fair, Newbury

New Mexico
Indian Market, Santa Fe

New York
52nd Street Festival, New York City

North Carolina
    Piedmont Crafts Fair, Winston-Salem

North Dakota
    Pioneer Review Days, West Fargo
    International Festival of the Arts, Dunseith

Ohio
    Circleville Pumpkin Show, Circleville
    International Festival, Toledo
    National Clay Week Festival, Uhrichsville
    Pottery Festival, Crooksville, Roseville
    Wonderful World of Ohio Mart, Akron

Oklahoma
    Festival of the Arts, Oklahoma City
    Kiamichi Owa Chito Festival of the Forest, Broken Bow

Pennsylvania
    Pennsylvania Dutch Kutztown Folk Festival, Kutztown
    Pittsburgh Folk Festival, Pittsburgh
    Three Rivers Arts Festival, Pittsburgh

Tennessee
    Dogwood Arts Festival, Knoxville
    Memphis in May International Festival, Memphis
    Old Time Fiddlers Jamboree and Crafts Festival, Smithville

Texas
    Black-Eyed Pea Jamboree, Athens
    Texas Folklife Festival, San Antonio
    Texas State Arts and Crafts Fair, Kerrville

Utah
    Festival of the American West, Logan
    Utah Arts Festival, Salt Lake City

Vermont
    Festival of the Arts, Manchester
    Vermont Dairy Festival, Enosburg Falls

Virginia
    Shenandoah Apple Blossom Festival, Winchester

West Virginia
    Alpine Winter Festival, Davis
    Mountain State Forest Festival, Elkins
    West Virginia Oil and Gas Festival, Sistersville

Wisconsin
    Lakefront Festival of Arts, Milwaukee
    Summerfest, Milwaukee

Puerto Rico
    Crafts Fair, Barranquitas

Aviation

Nevada
    National Championship Air Races, Reno

Wisconsin
    EAA Fly-In, Oshkosh

Ballet, Modern Dance, Other Dance

Alabama
    Birmingham Festival of Arts, Birmingham

Arkansas
    Arkansas Folk Festival, Mountain View

Georgia
    Arts Festival of Atlanta, Atlanta

Illinois
    Ravinia Festival, Chicago

Indiana
    Romantic Festival, Indianapolis

Massachusetts
    Jacob's Pillow Dance Festival, Becket

Mississippi
    Blessing of the Fishing Fleet and Biloxi Shrimp Festival and Fais Do Do, Biloxi
    Choctaw Indian Fair, Philadelphia

Montana
    Crowe Fair Celebration and Powwow, Crow Agency

New York
    International Polka Festival, Hunter
    Lincoln Center Out-of-Doors Festival, New York City
    Saratoga Festival/Saratoga Performing Arts Center, Saratoga Springs

North Dakota
    International Festival of the Arts, Dunseith

Ohio
    International Festival, Toledo

Pennsylvania
    Pittsburgh Folk Festival, Pittsburgh
    Three Rivers Arts Festival, Pittsburgh

South Carolina
   Spoleto Festival USA, Charleston

Tennessee
   Memphis in May International Festival, Memphis

Utah
   Ute Bear Dance, Ouray, Randlett, Whiterocks

Boats. See Ships

Canoes. See Ships

Carnivals, Mardi Gras Celebrations

Alabama
   Mardi Gras Celebration, Mobile

Arkansas
   White River Water Carnival, Batesville

Louisiana
   Mardi Gras, New Orleans

Minnesota
   St. Paul Winter Carnival, St. Paul

North Dakota
   Winterfest, Minot

Oregon
   World Championship Timber Carnival, Albany

Tennessee
   Cotton Carnival and MusicFest, Memphis

Texas
   Sun Bowl Carnival, El Paso

Vermont
   Stowe Winter Carnival, Stowe

U.S. Virgin Islands
   Virgin Islands Carnival, Charlotte Amalie, St. Thomas

Charitable

Connecticut
   Children Services Horse Show and County Fair, Farmington

Christmas Celebrations

Illinois
Christmas Around the World, Chicago

Rhode Island
Christmas in Newport, Newport

Washington, D.C.
Pageant of Peace

Circus

Connecticut
Barnum Festival, Bridgeport

Indiana
Circus City Festival, Peru

Commemorative

Alaska
Fur Rendezvous, Anchorage

Florida
Edison Pageant of Light, Fort Myers

Indiana
James Whitcomb Riley Festival, Greenfield

Missouri
Kewpiesta, Branson

Nevada
Jim Butler Days, Tonopah

Pennsylvania
McClure Bean Soup Festival, McClure

Virginia
George Washington Birthday Celebration, Alexandria

Wyoming
Green River Rendezvous, Pinedale

Competitions, Contests

Connecticut
Yale-Harvard Regatta, New London

Florida
    Junior Orange Bowl Festival, Coral Gables
    Sebring 12 Hours/Automobile Hall of Fame Week, Sebring

Georgia
    The Annual Masters Water Ski Tournament, Pine Mountain

Idaho
    National Old-Time Fiddlers' Contest, Weiser

Iowa
    Drake Relays, Des Moines
    U.S. National Hot Air Balloon Races, Indianola

Kansas
    Kansas Relays, Lawrence

Louisiana
    Holiday in Dixie, Shreveport

Maryland
    Labor Day Skipjack Races, Deal Island
    Maryland Kite Festival, Baltimore
    St. Mary's County Maryland Oyster Festival, Leonardtown

Minnesota
    All American Championships Sled Dog Races, Ely

Nevada
    National Championship Air Races, Reno

New Jersey
    Benihana Grand Prix Power Boat Regatta/N.J. Offshore Grand Prix, Point Pleasant
      Beach

New York
    General Clinton Canoe Race, Bainbridge
    National Polka Festival, Hunter

North Carolina
    National Hollerin' Contest, Spivey's Corner

North Dakota
    Winterfest, Minot

Ohio
    All-American Soap Box Derby, Akron

Oklahoma
    Great Raft Race, Sand Springs, Tulsa
    National Finals Rodeo, Oklahoma City

Oregon
    World Championship Timber Carnival, Albany

Pennsylvania
  Devon Horse Show and Country Fair, Devon

Tennessee
  International Country Music Fan Fair, Nashville
  Old Time Fiddlers Jamboree and Crafts Festival, Smithville
  Tennessee Walking Horse National Celebration, Shelbyville

Texas
  Black-Eyed Pea Jamboree, Athens
  Sun Bowl Carnival, El Paso
  Texas Prison Rodeo, Huntsville

U.S. Virgin Islands
  Virgin Islands Carnival, Charlotte Amalie, St. Thomas

Vermont
  Stowe Winter Carnival, Stowe

Virginia
  Fredericksburg Dog Mart, Fredericksburg

West Virginia
  Alpine Winter Festival, Davis

Wisconsin
  Birkebeiner Cross-Country Ski Races, Cable
  Lumberjack World Championships, Hayward

Wyoming
  Cheyenne Frontier Days, Cheyenne

Conservation, Ecology, Environmental, Restoration

California
  Mule Days Celebration, Bishop

Georgia
  Yellow Daisy Festival, Stone Mountain

Iowa
  Tulip Time, Pella

Maine
  National Dump Week, Kennebunkport

Maryland
  Catoctin Colorfest, Thurmont

Nebraska
  Arbor Day Celebration/Arts Festival, Nebraska City

Oklahoma
  Azalea Festival, Muskogee

Pennsylvania
>   Elfreth's Alley Fete Days, Philadelphia

South Carolina
>   Festival of Houses, Charleston

Vermont
>   Festival of the Arts, Manchester

Virginia
>   Chincoteague Pony Round-Up and Penning, Chincoteague
>   Historic Garden Week, statewide

West Virginia
>   Mountain State Forest Festival, Elkins

Contests. See Competitions

Crafts. See Art, Arts

Culture

Alabama
>   Birmingham Festival of Arts, Birmingham

Arizona
>   Heard Museum Guild Indian Fair, Phoenix
>   Poetry Festival, Bisbee
>   Tucson Festival, Tucson

Arkansas
>   Arkansas Folk Festival, Mountain View

California
>   Festival of Arts and Pageant of the Masters, Laguna Beach
>   Monterey Jazz Festival, Monterey

Colorado
>   Aspen Music Festival, Aspen
>   Central City Festival, Central City
>   International Film Festival, Telluride

Florida
>   Old Island Days, Key West

Georgia
>   Arts Festival of Atlanta, Atlanta

Hawaii
>   Aloha Week Festival, all islands
>   Cherry Blossom Festival, Honolulu

Idaho
National Old-Time Fiddlers' Contest, Weiser

Illinois
Chicagofest, Chicago
Christmas Around the World, Chicago
Gold Coast Air Fair, Chicago
Ravinia Festival, Chicago

Indiana
James Whitcomb Riley Festival, Greenfield
Romantic Festival, Indianapolis
Three Rivers Festival, Fort Wayne

Kentucky
Kentucky Derby Festival, Louisville

Louisiana
Holiday in Dixie, Shreveport
New Orleans Jazz and Heritage Festival, New Orleans
Spring Fiesta, New Orleans

Maryland
Preakness Festival, Baltimore

Massachusetts
Berkshire Music Festival at Tanglewood, Lenox
Jacob's Pillow Dance Festival, Becket

Minnesota
Festival of Nations, St. Paul
Minneapolis Aquatennial, Minneapolis

Mississippi
Gum Tree Festival, Tupelo

Missouri
Kewpiesta, Branson

New Mexico
Indian Market, Santa Fe
Santa Fe Chamber Music Festival, Santa Fe
Santa Fe Opera Festival, Santa Fe

New York
Lincoln Center Out-of-Doors Festival, New York City
Saratoga Festival/Saratoga Performing Arts Center, Saratoga Springs

North Carolina
Singing on the Mountain, Linville

North Dakota
International Festival of the Arts, Dunseith

Ohio
    International Festival, Toledo

Oklahoma
    Festival of the Arts, Oklahoma City

Oregon
    Oregon Shakespearean Festival, Ashland
    Peter Britt Festival, Jacksonville

Pennsylvania
    Bach Music Festival, Bethlehem
    Fairmount Fall Festival, Philadelphia
    Super Sunday, Philadelphia
    Three Rivers Arts Festival, Pittsburgh

Rhode Island
    Newport Music Festival, Newport

South Carolina
    Festival of Houses, Charleston
    Spoleto Festival USA, Charleston

Tennessee
    Cotton Carnival and MusicFest, Memphis
    Dogwood Arts Festival, Knoxville
    International Country Music Fan Fair, Nashville
    Memphis in May International Festival, Memphis
    National Storytelling Festival, Jonesboro
    Old Time Fiddlers' Jamboree and Crafts Festival, Smithville

Texas
    Fiesta San Antonio, San Antonio
    International Festival-Institute, Round Top

Utah
    Festival of the American West, Logan
    Utah Arts Festival, Salt Lake City
    Ute Bear Dance, Ouray, Randlett, Whiterocks

Vermont
    Festival of the Arts, Manchester

Virginia
    International Azalea Festival, Norfolk

Washington
    Pacific Northwest Festival, Seattle

Wisconsin
    Lakefront Festival of Arts, Milwaukee
    Peninsula Music Festival, Fish Creek
    Summerfest, Milwaukee

Puerto Rico
    Casals Festival/Festival Casals, San Juan
    Jayuya Festival of Indian Lore/Jayuya Indian Festival, Jayuya

U.S. Virgin Islands
    Virgin Islands Carnival, Charlotte Amalie, St. Thomas

Dog and Horse Shows, Races

Connecticut
    Children Services Horse Show and Country Fair, Farmington

Kentucky
    Kentucky Derby Festival, Louisville

Maryland
    Preakness Festival, Baltimore

Minnesota
    All American Championships Sled Dog Races, Ely

Pennsylvania
    Devon Horse Show and Country Fair, Devon

Tennessee
    Tennessee Walking Horse National Celebration, Shelbyville

Virginia
    Chincoteague Pony Round-Up and Penning, Chincoteague
    Fredericksburg Dog Mart, Fredericksburg

Drama

Alabama
    Birmingham Festival of Arts, Birmingham

Georgia
    Arts Festival of Atlanta, Atlanta

Illinois
    Ravinia Festival, Chicago

Kentucky
    Kentucky Derby Festival, Louisville

New York
    Lincoln Center Out-of-Doors Festival, New York City
    Saratoga Festival/Saratoga Performing Arts Center, Saratoga Springs

North Dakota
    International Festival of the Arts, Dunseith

Oregon
        Oregon Shakespearean Festival, Ashland

Pennsylvania
        Three Rivers Arts Festival, Pittsburgh

South Carolina
        Spoleto Festival USA, Charleston

Utah
        Festival of the American West, Logan
        Utah Arts Festival, Salt Lake City

Easter Celebration

Oklahoma
        Wichita Mountains Easter Sunrise Service, Lawton

Ecology. See Conservation

Economic

Alabama
        Birmingham Festival of Arts, Birmingham
        National Peanut Festival, Dothan

Alaska
        Fur Rendezvous, Anchorage
        Ice Worm Festival, Cordova

Arizona
        Heard Museum Guild Indian Fair, Phoenix
        London Bridge Days, Lake Havasu City

Arkansas
        Arkansas Folk Festival, Mountain View
        White River Water Carnival, Batesville

California
        Long Beach International Sea and Sports Festival, Long Beach
        Mother Goose Parade, El Cajon
        Mule Days Celebration, Bishop
        National Date Festival, Indio

Colorado
        Colorado State Fair, Pueblo
        National Western Stock Show, Denver
        Navajo Trails Fiesta, Durango

Connecticut
  Barnum Festival, Bridgeport
  Oyster Festival, Norwalk

Florida
  Gasparilla Pirate Invasion and Parade, Tampa
  Old Island Days, Key West

Georgia
  Rose Festival, Thomasville
  Yellow Daisy Festival, Stone Mountain

Hawaii
  Aloha Week Festival, all islands

Illinois
  Chicagofest, Chicago
  Gold Coast Art Fair, Chicago

Indiana
  Circus City Festival, Peru
  Persimmon Festival, Mitchell
  Three Rivers Festival, Fort Wayne

Iowa
  Iowa State Fair, Des Moines
  Tulip Time, Pella

Kansas
  Dodge City Days, Dodge City

Kentucky
  Kentucky Apple Festival of Johnson County, Paintsville
  Kentucky Derby Festival, Louisville
  Kentucky Guild of Arts and Craftsmen's Spring Fair, Berea

Louisiana
  Crawfish Festival, Breaux Bridge
  Holiday in Dixie, Shreveport
  Louisiana Shrimp and Petroleum Festival, Morgan City
  Louisiana State Fair, Shreveport
  Mardi Gras, New Orleans
  New Orleans Food Festival, New Orleans

Maine
  Central Maine Egg Festival, Pittsfield
  Maine Seafoods Festival, Rockland

Maryland
  Catoctin Colorfest, Thurmont
  St. Mary's County Maryland Oyster Festival, Leonardtown

Massachusetts
> Big "E"/Eastern States Exposition, West Springfield
> Marshfield Fair, Marshfield
> Massachusetts Cranberry Festival, South Carver

Michigan
> Blossomtime Festival, St. Joseph, Benton Harbor
> National Cherry Festival, Traverse City
> Tulip Time Festival, Holland

Minnesota
> Minneapolis Aquatennial, Minneapolis
> St. Paul Winter Carnival, St. Paul

Mississippi
> Blessing of the Fishing Fleet and Biloxi Shrimp Festival and Fais Do Do, Biloxi
> Choctaw Indian Fair, Philadelphia
> Natchez Pilgrimage, Natchez

Missouri
> Missouri State Fair, Sedalia

Nebraska
> AK-SAR-BEN Livestock Exposition and Rodeo, Omaha

Nevada
> Jim Butler Days, Tonopah
> National Championship Air Races, Reno

New Hampshire
> Craftsmen's Fair, Newbury

New Jersey
> Baby Parade, Ocean City
> Flemington Fair, Flemington

New Mexico
> Indian Market, Santa Fe

New York
> Dutchess County Fair, Rhinebeck
> 52nd Street Festival, New York City
> German Alps Festival, Hunter
> I Love New York State Fair/The Great New York State Fair, Syracuse
> International Polka Festival, Hunter
> Maple Festival, Franklinville
> Ninth Avenue International Festival, New York City

North Carolina
> North Carolina Azalea Festival, Wilmington
> Piedmont Crafts Fair, Winston-Salem

North Dakota
  Pioneer Review Days, West Fargo
  Winterfest, Minot

Ohio
  Circleville Pumpkin Show, Circlevile
  Johnny Appleseed Festival, Lisbon
  National Clay Week Festival, Uhrichsville
  Ohio Honey Festival, Lebanon
  Pottery Festival, Crooksville, Roseville
  Wonderful World of Ohio Mart, Akron

Oklahoma
  Azalea Festival, Muskogee
  State Fair of Oklahoma, Oklahoma City

Oregon
  Oregon State Fair, Salem
  Portland Rose Festival, Portland
  World Championship Timber Carnival, Albany

Pennsylvania
  Bavarian Summer Festival, Barnesville
  Devon Horse Show and County Fair, Devon
  National Apple Harvest Festival, Biglerville
  Philadelphia Flower and Garden Show, Philadelphia
  Super Sunday, Philadelphia

South Carolina
  Chitlin' Strut, Salley
  Festival of Houses, Charleston
  Hell Hole Swamp Festival, Jamestown
  Sun Fun Festival, Myrtle Beach

South Dakota
  Corn Palace Festival, Mitchell

Tennessee
  Cotton Carnival and MusicFest, Memphis
  Dogwood Arts Festival, Knoxville
  International Country Music Fan Fair, Nashville
  Memphis in May International Festival, Memphis
  Old Time Fiddlers Jamboree and Crafts Festival, Smithville
  World's Biggest Fish Fry, Paris

Texas
  Black-Eyed Pea Jamboree, Athens
  State Fair of Texas, Dallas
  Sun Bowl Carnival, El Paso
  Texas State Arts and Crafts Fair, Kerrville

Utah
  Festival of the American West, Logan
  Utah State Fair, Salt Lake City

Vermont
  Stowe Winter Carnival, Stowe
  Vermont Dairy Festival, Enosburg Falls
  Vermont Maple Festival, St. Albans
  Vermont's World's Fair, Tunbridge

Virginia
  Chincoteague Pony Round-Up and Penning, Chincoteague
  Fredericksburg Dog Mart, Fredericksburg
  George Washington Birthday Celebration, Alexandria
  Harborfest, Norfolk
  International Azalea Festival, Norfolk
  Shenandoah Apple Blossom Festival, Winchester

Washington, D.C.
  Cherry Blossom Festival

Washington
  Puyallup Valley Daffodil Festival, Puyallup, Tacoma, Sumner, Orting, Fife
  Seafair, Seattle

West Virginia
  Alpine Winter Festival, Davis
  Mountain State Forest Festival, Elkins
  West Virginia Oil and Gas Festival, Sistersville

Wisconsin
  Lakefront Festival of Arts, Milwaukee
  Lumberjack World Championships, Hayward
  Summerfest, Milwaukee

Puerto Rico
  Crafts Fair, Barranquitas

U.S. Virgin Islands
  Virgin Island Carnival, Charlotte Amalie, St. Thomas

Educational

Massachusetts
  Berkshire Music Festival at Tanglewood, Lenox
  Jacob's Pillow Dance Festival, Becket

New York
  Saratoga Festival/Saratoga Performing Arts Center, Saratoga Springs

Ohio
  National Clay Week Festival, Uhrichsville
  Pottery Festival, Crooksville, Roseville

Texas
>	International Festival-Institute, Round Top
>	Texas State Arts and Crafts Fair, Kerrville

Vermont
>	Festival of the Arts, Manchester

Virginia
>	Historic Garden Week, statewide
>	Prelude to Independence, Williamsburg

Environmental. See Conservation

Ethnic

Alabama
>	Mardi Gras Celebration, Mobile

Alaska
>	World Eskimo Indian Olympics, Fairbanks

Arizona
>	Heard Museum Guild Indian Fair, Phoenix
>	Tucson Festival, Tucson

California
>	Cherry Blossom Festival, San Francisco
>	Fiesta de la Primavera, San Diego
>	Pan American Festival Week, Lakewood

Colorado
>	Navajo Trails Fiesta, Durango

Florida
>	Old Island Days, Key West

Hawaii
>	Aloha Week Festival, all islands
>	Cherry Blossom Festival, Honolulu
>	Chinese Narcissus Festival, Honolulu

Ilinois
>	Christmas Around the World, Chicago

Indiana
>	Feast of the Hunters' Moon, Lafayette
>	Three Rivers Festival, Fort Wayne

Iowa
>	Nordic Fest, Decorah
>	Tulip Time, Pella

Kansas
    Swedish Homage Festival, Lindsborg

Kentucky
    Capitol Expo, Frankfort

Louisiana
    St. Joseph's Feast, New Orleans

Massachusetts
    Festival of the Blessed Sacrament, New Bedford
    Festival of the Holy Ghost, Plymouth

Michigan
    Highland Festival and Games, Alma
    Tulip Time Festival, Holland

Minnesota
    Festival of Nations, St. Paul
    Svenskarnas Dag, Minneapolis

Mississippi
    Choctaw Indian Fair, Philadelphia

Missouri
    Jour de Fete a Sainte Genevieve Days of Celebration, Ste. Genevieve
    Maifest, Hermann

Montana
    Crowe Fair Celebration and Powwow, Crow Agency
    Festival of Nations, Red Lodge

Nebraska
    Czech Festival, Wilber
    Nebraska Danish Days/Danish Ethnic Festival, Minden

Nevada
    All Indian Rodeo and Stampede, Fallon
    National Basque Festival, Elko

New Mexico
    Indian Market, Santa Fe

New York
    Feast of San Gennaro, New York City
    French Festival/French Day, Cape Vincent
    German Alps Festival, Hunter
    International Polka Festival, Hunter
    Ninth Avenue International Festival, New York City

Ohio
    International Festival, Toledo

Oklahoma
    Kiamichi Owa Chito Festival of the Forest, Broken Bow

Pennsylvania
  Bavarian Summer Festival, Barnesville
  Pennsylvania Dutch Kutztown Folk Festival, Kutztown
  Pittsburgh Folk Festival, Pittsburgh
  Polish Festival, Doylestown
  Super Sunday, Philadelphia

Tennessee
  Memphis in May International Festival, Memphis

Texas
  Texas Folklife Festival, San Antonio

Utah
  Ute Bear Dance, Ouray, Randlett, Whiterocks

Wisconsin
  Birkebeiner Cross-Country Ski Races, Cable
  Holiday Folk Fair, Milwaukee
  Summerfest, Milwaukee

Puerto Rico
  Jayuya Festival of Indian Lore/Jayuya Indian Festival, Jayuya

Fairs, Markets

Arizona
  Heard Museum Guild Indian Fair, Phoenix

Colorado
  Colorado State Fair, Pueblo
  National Western Stock Show, Denver

Connecticut
  Children Services Horse Show and Country Fair, Farmington

Illinois
  Gold Coast Art Fair, Chicago

Iowa
  Iowa State Fair, Des Moines

Kentucky
  Kentucky Guild of Artists and Craftsmen's Spring Fair, Berea

Louisiana
  Louisiana State Fair, Shreveport

Massachusetts
  Big "E"/Eastern States Exposition, West Springfield
  Marshfield Fair, Marshfield

Michigan
  Blossomtime Festival, St. Joseph, Benton Harbor

Mississippi
   Choctaw Indian Fair, Philadelphia

Missouri
   Missouri State Fair, Sedalia

Montana
   Crowe Fair Celebration and Powwow, Crow Agency

Nebraska
   AK-SAR-BEN Livestock Exposition and Rodeo, Omaha

New Hampshire
   Craftsmen's Fair, Newbury

New Jersey
   Flemington Fair, Flemington

New Mexico
   Indian Market, Santa Fe

New York
   Dutchess County Fair, Rhinebeck
   52nd Street Festival, New York City
   I Love New York State Fair/The Great New York State Fair, Syracuse

North Carolina
   Piedmont Crafts Fair, Winston-Salem

Ohio
   Wonderful World of Ohio Mart, Akron

Oklahoma
   State Fair of Oklahoma, Oklahoma City

Oregon
   Oregon State Fair, Salem

Pennsylvania
   Devon Horse Show and Country Fair, Devon

Tennessee
   International Country Music Fan Fair, Nashville

Texas
   State Fair of Texas, Dallas
   Texas State Arts and Crafts Fair, Kerrville

Utah
   Utah State Fair, Salt Lake City

Vermont
   Vermont's World's Fair, Tunbridge

Virginia
   Fredericksburg Dog Mart, Fredericksburg

Washington
    Seafair, Seattle

Wisconsin
    Holiday Folk Fair, Milwaukee

Puerto Rico
    Crafts Fair, Barranquitas

Film Festivals

Colorado
    International Film Festival, Telluride

Georgia
    Arts Festival of Atlanta, Atlanta

Utah
    Utah Arts Festival, Salt Lake City

Vermont
    Festival of the Arts, Manchester

Fish Festivals

Connecticut
    Oyster Festival, Norwalk

Louisiana
    Crawfish Festival, Breaux Bridge
    Louisiana Shrimp and Petroleum Festival, Morgan City

Maine
    Maine Seafoods Festival, Rockland

Maryland
    St. Mary's County Maryland Oyster Festival, Leonardtown

Mississippi
    Blessing of the Fishing Fleet and Biloxi Shrimp Festival and Fais Do Do, Biloxi

Tennesse
    World's Biggest Fish Fry, Paris

Floral, Flowers

Georgia
    Rose Festival, Thomasville
    Yellow Daisy Festival, Stone Mountain

Hawaii
    Aloha Week Festival, all islands

Iowa
    Tulip Time, Pella

Kentucky
    Kentucky Mountain Laurel Festival, Pineville

Michigan
    Blossomtime Festival, St. Joseph, Benton Harbor
    Tulip Time Festival, Holland

North Carolina
    North Carolina Azalea Festival, Wilmington

Oklahoma
    Azalea Festival, Muskogee

Oregon
    Portland Rose Festival, Portland

Pennsylvania
    Philadelphia Flower and Garden Show, Philadelphia

Tennessee
    Dogwood Arts Festival, Knoxville

Virginia
    Historic Garden Week, statewide
    International Azalea Festival, Norfolk
    Shenandoah Apple Blossom Festival, Winchester

Washington, D.C.
    Cherry Blossom Festival

Washington
    Puyallup Valley Daffodil Festival, Puyallup, Tacoma, Sumner, Orting, Fife

Flowers. See Floral

Folklore

Arkansas
    Arkansas Folk Festival, Mountain View

Idaho
    National Old-Time Fiddlers' Contest, Weiser

Illinois
    Wedding of the Wine and Cheese Pageant/Grape Festival, Nauvoo

Kentucky
    Capital Expo, Frankfort

North Carolina
>   National Hollerin' Contest, Spivey's Corner

Ohio
>   Johnny Appleseed Festival, Lisbon

Pennsylvania
>   Pennsylvania Dutch Kutztown Folk Festival, Kutztown
>   Pittsburgh Folk Festival, Pittsburgh

Tennessee
>   National Storytelling Festival, Jonesboro

Texas
>   Fiesta San Antonio, San Antonio
>   Texas Folklife Festival, San Antonio

Wisconsin
>   Holiday Folk Fair, Milwaukee

Food Festivals

Louisiana
>   Crawfish Festival, Breaux Bridge
>   Louisiana Shrimp and Petroleum Festival, Morgan City
>   New Orleans Food Festival, New Orleans
>   New Orleans Jazz and Heritage Festival, New Orleans
>   St. Joseph's Feast Day, New Orleans

Maine
>   Central Maine Egg Festival, Pittsfield
>   Maine Seafoods Festival, Rockland

Maryland
>   St. Mary's County Maryland Oyster Festival, Leonardtown

Massachusetts
>   Massachusetts Cranberry Festival, South Carver

Mississippi
>   Gum Tree Festival, Tupelo

New York
>   Feast of San Gennaro, New York City
>   Ninth Avenue International Festival, New York City

North Dakota
>   Winterfest, Minot

Ohio
>   Circleville Pumpkin Show, Circleville
>   International Festival, Toledo

Pennsylvania
>   McClure Bean Soup Festival, McClure
>   National Apple Harvest Festival, Biglerville
>   Pennsylvania Dutch Kutztown Folk Festival, Kutztown
>   Pittsburgh Folk Festival, Pittsburgh

Rhode Island
>   Jonnycake Festival, Usquepaugh, South Kingstown, Richmond

South Carolina
>   Chitlin' Strut, Salley

Tennessee
>   Memphis in May International Festival, Memphis
>   World's Biggest Fish Fry, Paris

Texas
>   Black-Eyed Pea Jamboree, Athens
>   Texas Folklife Festival, San Antonio

Vermont
>   Vermont Dairy Festival, Enosburg Falls
>   Vermont Maple Festival, St. Albans

Virginia
>   Shenandoah Apple Blossom Festival, Winchester

Harvest

Alabama
>   National Peanut Festival, Dothan

California
>   National Date Festival, Indio

Indiana
>   Persimmon Festival, Mitchell

Kentucky
>   Kentucky Apple Festival of Johnson County, Paintsville

Maryland
>   Catoctin Colorfest, Thurmont

Massachusetts
>   Massachusetts Cranberry Festival, South Carver

Michigan
>   National Cherry Festival, Traverse City

Ohio
>   Circleville Pumpkin Show, Circleville
>   Johnny Appleseed Festival, Lisbon

Pennsylvania
    National Apple Harvest Festival, Biglerville

South Dakota
    Corn Palace Festival, Mitchell

Heritage

Alabama
    Mardi Gras Celebration, Mobile

California
    Fiesta de la Primavera, San Diego

Connecticut
    Oyster Festival, Norwalk

Kansas
    Swedish Homage Festival, Lindsborg

Kentucky
    Capital Expo, Frankfort
    Kentucky Mountain Laurel Festival, Pineville
    Shaker Festival, South Union

Louisiana
    New Orleans Jazz and Heritage Festival, New Orleans
    Spring Fiesta, New Orleans

Maine
    Windjammer Days, Boothbay Harbor

Maryland
    Chesapeake Appreciation Days, Annapolis
    Labor Day Skipjack Races, Deal Island

Michigan
    Tulip Time Festival, Holland

Oklahoma
    Kiamichi Owa Chito Festival of the Forest, Broken Bow

Rhode Island
    Heritage Month, statewide

Tennessee
    Memphis in May International Festival, Memphis

Utah
    Festival of the American West, Logan
    Ute Bear Dance, Ouray, Randlett, Whiterocks

Virginia
    Harborfest, Norfolk

Puerto Rico
Jayuya Festival of Indian Lore/Jayuya Indian Festival, Jayuya

Historic

Alabama
Mardi Gras Celebration, Mobile

Alaska
Fur Rendezvous, Anchorage

Arizona
Tucson Festival, Tucson

California
Fiesta de la Primavera, San Diego

Delaware
A Day in Old New Castle, New Castle

Florida
De Soto Celebration, Bradenton

Georgia
Georgia Week Celebration, Savannah

Hawaii
King Kamehameha Celebration, Honolulu

Kansas
Dodge City Days, Dodge City

Massachusetts
Pilgrim Progress Pageant, Plymouth
Thanksgiving Day Celebration, Plymouth

Nevada
Jim Butler Days, Tonopah

New York
General Clinton Canoe Regatta, Bainbridge

North Dakota
Pioneer Review Days, West Fargo

Pennsylvania
Elfreth's Alley Fete Days, Philadelphia

Rhode Island
Gaspee Days, Cranston, Warwick
Heritage Month, statewide

South Carolina
Hell Hole Swamp Festival, Jamestown

South Dakota
>Days of '76, Deadwood

Texas
>Fiesta San Antonio, San Antonio

Virginia
>George Washington Birthday Celebration, Alexandria
>Prelude to Independence, Williamsburg

Washington, D.C.
>Cherry Blossom Festival

Wyoming
>Gift of the Waters Pageant, Thermopolis

>Green River Rendezvous, Pinedale

Honey Festivals. See Maple, Honey Festivals

Horticultural

Pennsylvania
>Philadelphia Flower and Garden Show, Philadelphia

Virginia
>Historic Garden Week, statewide

Washington
>Puyallup Valley Daffodil Festival, Puyallup, Tacoma, Sumner, Orting, Fife

House Tours. See Architecture

Legendary

Alaska
>Ice Worm Festival, Cordova

California
>Jumping Frog Jamboree, Del Mar

Connecticut
>Barnum Festival, Bridgeport

Illinois
>Wedding of the Wine and Cheese Pageant/Grape Festival, Nauvoo

Ohio
>Johnny Appleseed Festival, Lisbon

South Dakota
>   Days of '76, Deadwood

Utah
>   Festival of the American West, Logan
>   Ute Bear Dance, Ouray, Randlett, Whiterocks

Literature, Poetry, Prose

Arizona
>   Poetry Festival, Bisbee

Indiana
>   James Whitcomb Riley Festival, Greenfield

Tennessee
>   National Storytelling Festival, Jonesboro

Utah
>   Utah Arts Festival, Salt Lake City

Maple, Honey Festivals

New York
>   Maple Festival, Franklinville

Ohio
>   Ohio Honey Festival, Lebanon

Vermont
>   Vermont Maple Festival, St. Albans

Mardi Gras. See Carnivals

Markets, Marts. See Fairs

Modern Dance, Other Dances. See Ballet

Music

Alabama
>   Birmingham Festival of Arts, Birmingham

California
>   Monterey Jazz Festival, Monterey

Colorado
    Aspen Music Festival, Aspen
    Central City Festival, Central City

Georgia
    Arts Festival of Atlanta, Atlanta

Hawaii
    Aloha Week Festival, all islands
    Cherry Blossom Festival, Honolulu

Idaho
    National Old-Time Fiddlers' Contest, Weiser

Illinois
    Chicagofest, Chicago
    Ravinia Festival, Chicago

Indiana
    Romantic Festival, Indianapolis
    Three Rivers Festival, Fort Wayne

Kentucky
    Capital Expo, Frankfort

Louisiana
    Holiday in Dixie, Shreveport
    New Orleans Jazz and Heritage Festival, New Orleans

Maryland
    Preakness Festival, Baltimore

Massachusetts
    Berkshire Music Festival at Tanglewood, Lenox

Minnesota
    Festival of Nations, St. Paul

New Mexico
    Santa Fe Chamber Music Festival, Santa Fe
    Santa Fe Opera Festival, Santa Fe

New York
    52nd Street Festival, New York City
    Lincoln Center Out-of-Doors Festival, New York City
    Saratoga Festival/Saratoga Performing Arts Center, Saratoga Springs

North Carolina
    Singing on the Mountain, Linville

North Dakota
    International Festival of the Arts, Dunseith

Ohio
    International Festival, Toledo

Oregon
    Peter Britt Festival, Jacksonville

Pennsylvania
    Bach Music Festival, Bethlehem
    Pittsburgh Folk Festival, Pittsburgh

Rhode Island
    Newport Music Festival, Newport

South Carolina
    Chitlin' Strut, Salley
    Festival of Houses, Charleston
    Spoleto Festival USA, Charleston

Tennessee
    Cotton Carnival and MusicFest, Memphis
    International Country Music Fan Fair, Nashville
    Memphis in May International Festival, Memphis
    Old Time Fiddlers Jamboree and Crafts Festival, Smithville

Texas
    Fiesta San Antonio, San Antonio
    International Festival-Institute, Round Top
    Texas Folklife Festival, San Antonio

Utah
    Festival of the American West, Logan
    Utah Arts Festival, Salt Lake City

Vermont
    Festival of the Arts, Manchester

Virginia
    International Azalea Festival, Norfolk
    Shenandoah Apple Blossom Festival, Winchester

Washington
    Pacific Northwest Festival, Seattle

Wisconsin
    Peninsula Music Festival, Fish Creek
    Summerfest, Milwaukee

Puerto Rico
    Casals Festival/Festival Casals, San Juan

U.S. Virgin Islands
    Virgin Islands Carnival, Charlotte Amalie, St. Thomas

Musicals. See Opera

New Year Celebration

Hawaii
    Chinese Narcissus Festival, Honolulu

Opera, Operettas, Musicals

Colorado
    Aspen Music Festival, Aspen
    Central City Festival, Central City

Illinois
    Ravinia Festival, Chicago

New Mexico
    Santa Fe Opera Festival, Santa Fe

South Carolina
    Spoleto Festival USA, Charleston

Tennessee
    Memphis in May International Festival, Memphis

Utah
    Utah Arts Festival, Salt Lake City

Washington
    Pacific Northwest Festival, Seattle

Pageantry

Florida
    De Soto Celebration, Bradenton
    Edison Pageant of Light, Fort Myers
    Gasparilla Pirate Invasion and Parade, Tampa

Hawaii
    King Kamehameha Celebration, Honolulu

Illinois
    Wedding of the Wine and Cheese Pageant/Grape Festival, Nauvoo

Indiana
    Feast of the Hunters' Moon, Lafayette

Kansas
    Dodge City Days, Dodge City

Massachusetts
    Pilgrim Progress Pageant, Plymouth

Minnesota
   St. Paul Winter Carnival, St. Paul

Mississippi
   Choctaw Indian Fair, Philadelphia

New York
   Hill Cumorah Pageant, Palmyra

Rhode Island
   Christmas in Newport, Newport

Tennessee
   Cotton Carnival and MusicFest, Memphis

Texas
   Sun Bowl Carnival, El Paso

Virginia
   George Washington Birthday Celebration, Alexandria
   International Azalea Festival, Norfolk

Washington, D.C.
   Pageant of Peace

Wyoming
   Gift of the Waters Pageant, Thermopolis
   Green River Rendezvous, Pinedale

Parades

California
   Mother Goose Parade, El Cajon

Florida
   Gasparilla Pirate Invasion and Parade, Tampa

New Jersey
   Baby Parade, Ocean City

Patriotic

Massachusetts
   Thanksgiving Day Celebration, Plymouth

New York
   Harbor Festival, New York City

Rhode Island
   Fourth of July Celebration, Bristol

Texas
   Fiesta San Antonio, San Antonio

Virginia
 George Washington Birthday Celebration, Alexandria
 Prelude to Independence, Williamsburg

American Samoa
 Flag Day, Pago Pago

U.S. Virgin Islands
 Fourth of July Celebration, St. John

Political

Virginia
 International Azalea Festival, Norfolk

Preservation

Pennsylvania
 Elfreth's Alley Fete Days, Philadelphia

South Carolina
 Festival of Houses, Charleston

Virginia
 Historic Garden Week, statewide

Rehabilitation

Texas
 Texas Prison Rodeo, Huntsville

Religious

Alabama
 Mardi Gras Celebration, Mobile

Arizona
 Tucson Festival, Tucson

Illinois
 Christmas Around the World, Chicago

Louisiana
 Mardi Gras, New Orleans
 St. Joseph's Feast Day, New Orleans

Massachusetts
 Festival of the Blessed Sacrament, New Bedford
 Festival of the Holy Ghost, Plymouth
 Pilgrim Progress Pageant, Plymouth

Mississippi
    Blessing of the Fishing Fleet and Biloxi Shrimp Festival and Fais Do Do, Biloxi

New York
    Feast of San Gennaro, New York City
    Hill Cumorah Pageant, Palmyra

North Carolina
    Singing on the Mountain, Linville

Oklahoma
    Wichita Mountains Easter Sunrise Service, Lawton

Rhode Island
    Christmas in Newport, Newport

Washington, D.C.
    Pageant of Peace

Restoration. See Conservation

Rodeos

Colorado
    National Western Stock Show, Denver

Nebraska
    AK-SAR-BEN Livestock Exposition and Rodeo, Omaha

Nevada
    All Indian Rodeo and Stampede, Fallon

Oklahoma
    National Finals Rodeo, Oklahoma City

South Dakota
    Days of '76, Deadwood

Texas
    Texas Prison Rodeo, Huntsville

Wyoming
    Cheyenne Frontier Days, Cheyenne

Satiric

Maine
    National Dump Week, Kennebunkport

Ships, Boats, Canoes

Arkansas
  White River Water Carnival, Batesville

Connecticut
  Yale-Harvard Regatta, New London

Maine
  Windjammer Days, Boothbay Harbor

Maryland
  Chesapeake Appreciation Days, Annapolis
  Labor Day Skipjack Races, Deal Island

Mississippi
  Blessing of the Fishing Fleet and Biloxi Shrimp Festival and Fais Do Do, Biloxi

New Jersey
  Benihana Grand Prix Power Boat Regatta/N.J. Offshore Grand Prix, Point Pleasant
    Beach

New York
  General Clinton Canoe Regatta, Bainbridge
  Harbor Festival, New York City

Virginia
  Harborfest, Norfolk

Washington
  Seafair, Seattle

Sports

Alaska
  World Eskimo Indian Olympics, Fairbanks

Arkansas
  White River Water Carnival, Batesville

California
  Long Beach International Sea and Sports Festival, Long Beach

Connecticut
  Children Services Horse Show and Country Fair, Farmington
  Yale-Harvard Regatta, New London

Florida
  Junior Orange Bowl Festival, Coral Gables
  Sebring 12 Hours/Automobile Hall of Fame Week, Sebring

Georgia
  Annual Masters Water Ski Tournament, Pine Mountain

Hawaii
  Aloha Week Festival, all islands

Indiana
>   "500" Festival, Indianapolis

Iowa
>   Drake Relays, Des Moines
>   U.S. National Hot Air Balloon Races, Indianola

Kansas
>   Kansas Relays, Lawrence

Louisiana
>   Holiday in Dixie, Shreveport
>   Louisiana Shrimp and Petroleum Festival, Morgan City
>   Sugar Bowl Classic, New Orleans

Maine
>   Windjammer Days, Boothbay Harbor

Maryland
>   Chesapeake Appreciation Days, Annapolis
>   Labor Day Skipjack Races, Deal Island
>   Maryland Kite Festival, Baltimore
>   Preakness Festival, Baltimore

Massachusetts
>   Massachusetts Cranberry Festival, South Carver

Minnesota
>   All American Championships Sled Dog Races, Ely
>   Minneapolis Aquatennial Minneapolis
>   St. Paul Winter Carnival, St. Paul

Mississippi
>   Choctaw Indian Fair, Philadelphia

Montana
>   Crowe Fair Celebration and Powwow, Crow Agency

Nevada
>   National Championship Air Races, Reno

New Jersey
>   Benihana Grand Prix Power Boat Regatta/N.J. Offshore Grand Prix, Point Pleasant
>   Beach

New York
>   General Clinton Canoe Regatta, Bainbridge

North Dakota
>   Winterfest, Minot

Ohio
>   All-American Soap Box Derby, Akron

Oklahoma
>   Great Raft Race, Sand Springs, Tulsa
>   Kiamichi Owa Chito Festival of the Forest, Broken Bow
>   National Finals Rodeo, Oklahoma City

Pennsylvania
>   Devon Horse Show and Country Fair, Devon
>   Fairmount Fall Festival, Philadelphia

South Carolina
>   Sun Fun Festival, Myrtle Beach

Tennessee
>   Tennessee Walking Horse National Celebration, Shelbyville

Texas
>   Sun Bowl Carnival, El Paso
>   Texas Prison Rodeo, Huntsville

Vermont
>   Stowe Winter Carnival, Stowe

Virginia
>   Harborfest, Norfolk
>   International Azalea Festival, Norfolk

Washington, D.C.
>   Frisbee Festival

Washington
>   Seafair, Seattle

West Virginia
>   Alpine Winter Festival, Davis

Wisconsin
>   Birkebeiner Cross-Country Ski Races, Cable
>   Lumberjack World Championships, Hayward

Wyoming
>   Cheyenne Frontier Days, Cheyenne

Touristic

Arizona
>   London Bridge Days, Lake Havasu City

New Jersey
>   Baby Parade, Ocean City

New York
>   52nd Street Festival, New York City

South Carolina
    Sun Fun Festival, Myrtle Beach

Washington
    Seafair, Seattle

INDEX

The following entries offer full descriptions of events. For names of additional events, arranged by state, refer to pages 289-330.

About the Author

FRANCES SHEMANSKI is a freelance travel writer and a contributing editor for *The Travel Agent Magazine*. She is president of the New York Travel Writers Association, and an active member of the Society of American Travel Writers, the New York Press Club, and The Newswomen's Club of New York. Her articles on travel and calendars of events regularly appear in *The Los Angeles Times, The New York Times, The Boston Globe, Chicago Tribune, Newsday, New York Daily News, The Star Ledger, The Denver Post, Food & Wine Magazine, Family Circle, Ladies Home Journal*, and many others.